Advising British Expats

Tax and Financial Planning

1st Edition

Jon Golding and Juliet Connolly

Advising British Expats

Tax and Financial Planning

1st Edition

Jon Golding and Juliet Connolly

Published by:

Claritax Books Ltd
6 Grosvenor Park Road
Chester, CH1 1QQ

www.claritaxbooks.com

ISBN: 978-1-908545-98-5

Other titles from Claritax Books

Other titles from Claritax Books include:

- A-Z of Plant & Machinery
- Capital Allowances
- Construction Industry Scheme
- Discovery Assessments
- Employee Benefits & Expenses
- Employment Status
- Enterprise Investment Scheme
- Entrepreneurs' Relief
- Financial Planning with Trusts
- Furnished Holiday Lettings
- Main Residence Relief
- Pension Tax Guide
- Research & Development
- Residence: The Definition in Practice
- Stamp Duty Land Tax
- Tax Chamber Hearings
- Tax Losses
- VAT Registration

See www.claritaxbooks.com for details of further titles due for publication in the coming months.

About the authors

Jon Golding ATT (Fellow), TEP brings 40 years of professional experience to this book. An author and speaker in the field of taxation he has worked for H M Revenue & Customs, PwC, KPMG, EY and LexisNexis, and now works in the Far East advising expatriates on tax and financial strategies. Jon's full contact details are available on the relevant Author page of the Claritax Books website.

Juliet Connolly BA (Hons), ACA, CTA is also an expat herself, having lived in Melbourne, Australia for over 10 years. Juliet has worked in the accounting profession for over 30 years. She trained with small firms and then for a number of years worked at a Big 4 firm, where in 1996 she started advising on expatriate taxation. Juliet left in 2002 to set up her own business, UK Expat, advising and assisting expatriates – from all walks of life and located all over the world – on their UK tax affairs.

Juliet can be contacted by email at jgc@ukexpat.net or by phone on +44 (0)20 3239 4140 (UK) or +61 (0)3 9017 0179 (Australia). Visit www.ukexpat.net or follow Juliet on LinkedIn or UK Expat Taxation on Twitter or Facebook.

About the publisher

Claritax Books publishes specialist tax titles, complementing what is on offer from the larger tax publishers. Typically, our books cover niche topics in greater depth or take a more practical approach to particular tax issues. Our titles are written for accountants (both in-house and in practice), tax advisers, employers, lawyers and other professionals. Our authors include barristers, solicitors, accountants and other experienced tax specialists.

Claritax Books titles cover (among other topics) tax appeals, capital allowances, the statutory residence rules, CGT reliefs, the CIS scheme, pensions and trusts, stamp duty land tax, VAT, employment taxes and furnished holiday lettings. Visit www.claritaxbooks.com for details of all our books.

Claritax Books is a trading name of Claritax Books Ltd (company number 07658388, VAT number 114 9371 20). The company is based in Chester, England.

Abbreviations

A&M	Accumulation and maintenance
ADR	Alternative dispute resolution
ANZSCO	Australia and New Zealand Standard Classification of Occupations
APR	Agricultural property relief
APT	Asset protection trust
ARLA	Association of Residential Letting Agents
ATED	Annual tax on enveloped dwellings
ATI	Adjusted total income
ATO	Australian Tax Office
B2C	Business to customer
BALPA	British Airline Pilots' Association
BAR	British Association of Removers
BCE	Benefit crystallisation event
BIM	Business Income Manual
BPR	Business property relief
BVI	British Virgin Islands
CA	Capital Allowances Manual
CAA 2001	Capital Allowances Act 2001
CETV	Cash equivalent transfer value
CG	Capital Gains Manual
CGT	Capital gains tax
Ch	Chapter
Ch D	Chancery Division
CII	Chartered Insurance Institute
CLT	Chargeable lifetime transfer
CPA	Certified public accountant
CPA 2004	Civil Partnership Act 2004
CPI	Consumer prices index
CRS	Common reporting standard
CTA	Corporation Tax Act
CTM	Company Tax Manual
DIFC	Dubai International Financial Centre
DOTAS	Disclosure of tax avoidance schemes
DOV	Deed of variation
DT	Double Taxation Relief Manual

DVA	Drive and Vehicle Agency
DVLA	Driver and Vehicle Licensing Agency
EEA	European Economic Area
EFRBS	Employer-financed retirement benefits scheme
EHIC	European health insurance card
EIM	Employment Income Manual
EIS	Enterprise investment scheme
EMI	Enterprise management incentive
EP	Employment Procedures Manual
ESC	Extra statutory concession
ESOS	Employee share option scheme
ESS	Employee share scheme
EU	European Union
EWHC	England and Wales High Court
FA	Finance Act
FAD	Flexi-access drawdown
FATCA	Foreign Account Tax Compliance Act
FCO	Foreign and Commonwealth Office
FDR	Formerly domiciled resident
FHL	Furnished Holiday Letting
FI	Foreign Institution
FRCGW	Foreign residential capital gains withholding
FREA	Fixed rate expense allowance
FSCS	Financial services compensation scheme
FSMA 2000	Financial Services and Markets Act 2000
FSR	Foreign service relief
FTC	Failure to correct
FTT	First-tier Tribunal
FURBS	Funded unapproved retirement benefits scheme
GAAP	Generally accepted accounting principles
GAAR	General anti-abuse rule
GROB	Gift(s) with reservation of benefit
GDPR	General data protection regulations
GROB	Gift with reservation of benefit
GST	Goods and services tax
HKEC	Hong Kong Electronic Citation
HMO	House of Multiple Occupation
HMRC	Her Majesty's Revenue & Customs
HNWI	High net worth individual
ICTA 1988	Income and Corporation Taxes Act 1988

IHT	Inheritance tax
IHTA 1984	Inheritance Tax Act 1984
IHTM	Inheritance Tax Manual
IIP	Interest in possession
IME	Internationally mobile employee
INTM	International Manual
IOV	Instrument of variation
IPDI	Immediate post-death interest
IPO	Income payments order
IPTM	Insurance Policyholder Taxation Manual
IRBM	Inland Revenue Board of Malaysia
IRS	(US) Internal Revenue Service
ISA	Individual savings account
ITA 2007	Income Tax Act 2007
ITEPA 2003	Income Tax (Earnings & Pensions) Act 2003
ITIN	Individual taxpayer identification number
ITTOIA 2005	Income Tax (Trading and Other Income) Act 2005
KRE	Kidnap, ransom and extortion
LEL	Lower earnings limit
LTA	Lifetime allowance
LTIP	Long term incentive plan
MARD	(EU) Mutual Assistance Recovery Directive
MM2H	Malaysia My Second Home
MOSS	(VAT) Mini One Stop Shop
MPF	Mandatory pension fund
MS	Member State (of EU)
NARIC	National Academic Recognition Information Centre
NASBA	National Association of State Boards of Accountancy
NCND	Non-US citizens not domiciled
NEST	National Employment Savings Trust
NETP	Non-established taxable person
NFFE	Non-financial foreign entities
NHS	(UK) National Health Service
NIC	National Insurance contributions
NIM	National Insurance Manual
NISA	New individual savings account
NRB	Nil rate band
NRCGT	Non resident capital gains tax
NRLS	Non resident landlord scheme
NT	No tax (PAYE code)

OECD	Organisation for Economic Cooperation and Development
OIG	Offshore income gains
ORSO	Occupational retirement schemes ordinance
OWD	Overseas work days relief
PAYE	Pay as you earn
PCLS	Pension commencement lump sum
PE	Permanent establishment
PENP	Post employment notice pay
PEP	Politically exposed person
PEP(2)	Personal equity plan
PES	Personal export scheme
PET	Potentially exempt transfer
PIM	Property Income Manual
PoA	Payment on Account
POA(T)	Pre-owned assets (tax)
PPB	Personal portfolio bonds
PPI	Payment protection insurance
PPLI	Private placement life insurance
PRR	Private residence relief
PSA (1)	PAYE settlement agreement
PSA (2)	Personal savings allowance
Pt.	Part
PTM	Pensions Tax Manual
QDOT	(US) qualified domestic trust
QROPS	Qualifying recognised overseas pension scheme
QTIP	(US) qualified terminable interest property
RBC	Remittance basis charge
RCA	Readily convertible asset
RDR	(HMRC) guidance notes for residence, domicile and the remittance basis
RDRM	Residence, Domicile and Remittance Basis Manual
RNRB	Residence nil rate band
RoW	Rest of the world
RPGT	Real property gains tax (Malaysia)
ROPS	Recognised overseas pension scheme
RRQP	Restricted relief qualifying policy
RTA	Relevant termination award
RTC	Requirement to correct
RSU	Restricted share unit

S.	Section
SACM	Self Assessment Claims Manual
SAIM	Savings and Investment Manual
SAYE	Save as you earn
Sch.	Schedule
SDLT	Stamp duty land tax
SEIS	Seed enterprise investment scheme
SI	Statutory instrument
SIP	Share incentive plan
SIPP	Self-invested personal pension
SIR	Social investment relief
SMC	Skilled migrant category
SNRB	Settlement nil rate band
SRT	Statutory residence test
STTG	Scottish Taxpayer Technical Guidance manual
SWT	Special withholding tax
TA	Trustee Act
TC	Tax cases
TCGA 1992	Taxation of Chargeable Gains Act 1992
TFN	(Australia) Tax file number
TIOPA 2010	Taxation (International and Other Provisions) Act 2010
TMA 1970	Taxes Management Act 1970
TNR	Treaty non-resident
TNRB	Transferable nil rate band
TOPA 2014	Taxation of Pensions Act 2014
TRS	Trust registration service
TSEM	Trusts, Settlements and Estates Manual
UAE	United Arab Emirates
UKSC	United Kingdom Supreme Court
UTR	Unique taxpayer reference
VAT	Value added tax
WDF	Worldwide disclosure facility

Preface

The world of commerce is changing so fast that when the authors started work on this book Brexit, President Trump, China's economic expansion were very different than today as we go to print on our first edition. These fast moving events give opportunities for companies to take advantage of new openings and commercial opportunities. Most countries with projects abroad will need to send staff to foreign climes, or employ staff specifically, to administer these projects and the UK will hopefully be in the forefront. This means that their staff who move from their home countries to service these projects need advice on all manner of tax and financial planning, not to mention the cultural challenges many of these employees, and in particular their spouses and families, will face. We, the authors, hope we have helped to provide such advice, for the individuals concerned but also for their employers and professional advisers. The book takes the adviser from the initial preparation to leaving UK, arriving abroad and then returning or staying permanently abroad.

The authors are based overseas (Malaysia and Australia) and have been advising British expats, and expatriates of other nationalities, on tax mitigation and financial planning for many years. The book covers many true to life anonymised examples to assist the adviser. Such examples would be the expat who is lost in the jungle on a Hash (running club) run and whose body is never found – what would an adviser when contacted by the family do? The removal from UK to another country of furniture and possessions where the customs officials of the arrival country refuse entry of many items of everyday use that are banned. The penalties for not paying foreign 'exit' taxes when departing some countries after a concluding period of work in that country which can in some cases result in the expat being held in immigration 'lock up' until taxes are paid! The mitigation of property taxes and penalties when buying and selling UK property and adherence to the statutory residence rules which can, if not monitored, result in unnecessary tax imposition by H M Revenue & Customs. The tax advantages of offshore investment bonds/portfolio bonds and the potential tax disadvantages of returning to the UK without having taken certain actions before leaving the foreign jurisdiction. These many and varied examples guide the adviser by pointing out implications of taking certain actions and where no action is taken resulting in consequences for the client and adviser.

As the book has been written, the contents have expanded from what was envisaged at the outset, partly to reflect the practical experience of the two authors in dealing with the implications of the global changes referred to above. There is always more that can be said, of course, and the authors will be pleased to hear from any readers with suggestions of topics that should be added or expanded in future editions.

Jon Golding would like to acknowledge the valuable support shown by Absolute Financial Solutions Ltd in Kuala Lumpur during the writing of the book. Also, a number of examples in the book have been inspired by Bill Knight, Mike Green and Frank Twynam who have recounted foreign incidents which they experienced in their work around the world. Juliet Connolly would also like to thank Jim, her husband, for his unwavering support and belief in her, and all her clients, both past and present, whose many and varied situations have provided her with the knowledge and experience to write this book.

In this book we, the authors, have attempted to provide comprehensive explanations of the relevant law and outcomes based on our experience in practice, as well as our professional interpretation of the provisions.

Despite its title, many of the areas covered in this book may equally apply to non-residents of other nationalities who have left the UK, perhaps having worked there for a period of time, and who have retained an interest (such as a rental property) in the UK.

Tax advisers, accountants, solicitors and HR personnel, for whom the book will be useful, should of course refrain from advising on specific investments – i.e. making recommendations as to which shares to invest in. Independent financial advisers require FCA authorisation, so other professional advisers need to have at least one financial adviser, familiar with the schemes, among their professional contacts, to whom clients can potentially be referred.

This first edition contains the changes made by *Finance Act* 2017 and *Finance (No. 2) Act* 2017, and also takes into account the autumn Budget statement and uprated allowances for 2018-19. Reference within the book is made to the United Kingdom but in some cases it is necessary for the adviser to refer to separate rules regarding Scotland, Northern Ireland and Wales, which may differ from those applying in England (e.g. income tax rates, stamp duty, etc.).

The law is stated as at 2 April 2018.

Jon Golding
Juliet Connolly
April 2018

Table of contents

1. Outbound

1.1 Introduction

All British expats intending to retire or work abroad have a myriad of different matters to consider before they leave the UK. Once abroad it may be too late to rectify omissions and oversights. The financial consequences of doing the wrong thing can be dire. One important factor of the financial implications of working and retiring abroad is, if overlooked, costly in terms of excessive taxes paid, reduced pension entitlement, lack of insurance protection and so on.

For the retiree, the internationally mobile employee and the assigning company the first point of call for answers is their accountant, tax adviser, financial adviser, company personnel department or solicitor. However, expat taxation and financial advice is a complex specialist area and the adviser may only be familiar with certain areas, e.g. pensions.

In this book the authors seek to offer guidance in all areas to others, gained from direct experience of living abroad and advising on such matters. The book does not attempt to be, nor should it be viewed as, a substitute for actual specialist professional advice in all the areas mentioned. The book takes a step by step approach starting with "Outbound", this first chapter, and completing with ("Back Home" (**Chapter 9**).

1.2 Preparing to live abroad

1.2.1 Local working conditions

Although the contract of employment may be straightforward and bear a resemblance to the contracts of employment previously signed in the UK, working practices and employment laws abroad can be *very* different.

In Europe workers receive a degree of protection not matched in other non-European countries. Health and safety in some Middle East and Far East countries is very lax depending on the type of assignee's employment. What happens if the assignee accepts a job in Qatar and on arrival finds that the office is in fact a metal Portakabin with no air conditioning and that temperatures reach 110° during the day in the summer? What if the individual were to travel all the way to Australia to commence those new duties and after six weeks the firm can no longer avail itself of the individual's services due to the worldwide recession? – is redundancy offered for such a short time period? If so, does the company have a statutory duty to report the redundancy or make adequate recompense in line with the UK's *Employment Rights Act* 1996?

There are likely to be statutory benefits provided by employers, such as local social security payments, injury compensation payments and so on. But perhaps more importantly and not so easily revealed is *information* on statutory benefits.

For a prospective assignee who is leaving the UK to work for a company abroad, or for a UK subsidiary, the contract may be UK generated. This has both advantages and disadvantages. Accepting a job abroad may be an inference that the assignee is on the fast track to promotion; yet this very fact may reduce the benefits to which the assignee should be entitled. Also, there may be other non-work related financial disadvantages of accepting the assignment as shown in the Ivor example at **1.3.7** below.

It is therefore important for the assignee to determine what the norm is and, notwithstanding the implied prospects of promotion after the assignment, the individual should be entitled to that norm, i.e. a comprehensive expatriate employment package. Many employers are now promoting foreign assignments as an attractive "lifestyle" choice for younger assignees with family and, with that in mind, are offering less attractive foreign assignment packages.

1.2.2 Schooling

Expats who move abroad for work may be able to obtain help from their assigning employer for educating their children. Whilst this has been a standard financial support in the past it is not nowadays a certainty. Normally it would not be unreasonable in these circumstances to expect company financial assistance when being asked to move to a less developed country where the child's educational progress may be impaired.

Some may choose to send their child to a local school, mainly for the additional advantage of learning a new language. However, in certain countries there have been cases of demands for "ad hoc" payments ("tea money") to secure the child's place at a school (see Bangkok Post, 8 June 2011).

Many foreign countries have international schools with an education system which is designed for the children of expats who want them to follow a UK curriculum or one that is similar. These international schools comprise French, British, American and Japanese schools which are usually available in the more developed countries' capital cities. Elsewhere it may be a case of relying on tutoring, home schooling, local schools or UK boarding schools.

Boarding schools

Fees for boarding school (as opposed to day schooling) are expensive. In addition, there are supplementary costs such as registration fee, purchase of a uniform, insurance, activity fees and transport to and from the foreign jurisdiction. If a UK boarding school is chosen then does it offer seven-day boarding (as some schools expect their students to go home or be cared for by relatives at weekends)? Many UK boarding schools are used to catering for expat children and foreign students but it is important to know which schools have that expertise.

International schools

Many international schools have waiting lists. It is best to enrol the child as soon as possible when arriving in the jurisdiction, or ideally before if possible. This may require examination to assess the child's competences in education and language.

Many well known British private schools are opening affiliated branches abroad offering private education in different locations across the world to cater for the expatriate demand. They offer boarding and day school options and are ideal for those families who would normally continue to educate their children at a boarding school in the UK, e.g. Harrow school in Hong Kong and also in Bangkok and Beijing. Sherborne School has a branch in Qatar, Dulwich College has several schools already established in China and several others have branches in the Middle East and Far East.

Bear in mind that international schools, especially in Asia, actually have a high percentage of local students enrolled and some employ a number of local teachers and teaching assistants but invariably the emphasis is to employ UK trained teachers where the need is on English language and teaching methods. Most international schools are privately run, and are often administered either by an appointed individual or by a board of management elected from the parent UK body.

Local schools

For those with a permanent or long-term assignment abroad it sometimes makes sense to educate through the local school system if there are no foreigner enrolment restrictions. In some countries where local education is free there are restrictions on expat children enrolling and the only alternatives are UK boarding schools or international schools, which are expensive. An important point to bear in mind is that local schools in many countries adhere strictly to a religious curriculum, e.g. Islamic, Jewish, Roman Catholic faiths as part of the curriculum, and this may differ from the parents' wish for their child.

Finance

It is difficult to make financial plans in advance without a firm idea of which school the expatriate's child will be attending. Tuition fees vary in different regions of the world, though most private schools will charge the equivalent of many thousands of pounds each year. However, there can be an exchange rate benefit in some countries where the pound is strong against the local currency in which the fees are paid. So, when compared with the cost of similar private education in the UK there may be an exchange rate "discount" on the fees. Clearly if the salary is being paid wholly in local currency then this is not in point. Typical country fee comparisons for junior school might be:

Country	Average fee p.a. £
Australia	28,640
Canada	20,288
Hong Kong	21,750
Japan	15,640
Korea	26,843
Singapore	26,844
Switzerland	15,958
UAE	19,903
UK	22,050
USA	24,770

Some private schools (both in the UK and abroad) make a small number of bursaries and scholarships available but these are typically reserved for children who achieve excellent grades or who excel in one particular subject area. The child will have to take examinations to enrol and parents should be aware that not all of the costs of tuition and extra items will be covered.

The school may also have funds to help those who would otherwise find it difficult to meet the fees, although parents may find that these funds only cover part of the fees and the bulk of the money still has to be provided.

Negotiation of reduced fees may be possible when more than one child from the same family attends the same school, although this is not always the case. In certain oil producing nations there has been a downturn and layoffs of workers have meant that school places are not as well subscribed and the UK expat parent may secure a variable discount on fees, especially if these are paid up front.

1.2.3 University

The cost of children attending university is a further added expense and will rarely be covered by the assigning company. In some foreign countries, university degree costs can be extremely expensive if they are being funded out of net income. Here the parent has to think carefully about finance planning options (see the example at **7.2.4**).

For graduates, MIT Sloan Schools of Management in Asia in collaboration with Massachusetts Institute of Technology (MIT) in Cambridge (USA), provide collaborative courses in Bangkok and elsewhere worldwide to cater for those in the region at an estimated 20 month course cost of US$102,000.

Guidance: Gabbitas Education, UK; Bangkok Post

1.2.4   Living costs

When offered an expat package the individual will need to take many things into account in respect of the cost of living in the new jurisdiction. A comparison can be made between, say, London and expensive Tokyo or the much cheaper New Delhi as shown below. What may look like being a good package compared to London prices when offered a job in Japan turns out to be an expensive posting leaving little over for savings. However, the package that appears to be a low salary in the home country may turn out to be much higher in India which has a low cost of living in comparison to the UK.

Other matters have to be taken into account such as car transport where, in some low cost of living countries, foreign car purchase is hit with premium import duty rates. Also some countries such as the Middle East impose little or no income tax, which gives the expat more disposable income for savings but the cost of living may be higher.

Many expats purchase familiar home imported groceries catered for by the international supermarket chains which are more expensive than local goods. Restaurant prices can vary enormously, such as in Singapore where a visit to a high end restaurant will be just as much as a London restaurant but expats tend to entertain colleagues and friends by eating out far more regularly than in the UK. Yet in Singapore eating at a food court can be very inexpensive.

However, the higher cost of some items, such as imported alcohol in parts of Asia, is often offset by savings in other areas, such as cheaper power and water costs. Employment of domestic maids by expats is almost a given in Asia and the Middle East and it is uncommon to see a household without a domestic maid, especially where there are children in the family. The cost of such help would be about one tenth of the cost of a "live in" domestic or carer in the UK.

Cost of living indexes are easily available for many countries and a comparison can be made between the UK current location and the intended destination. For instance, in the comparisons below, mid 2017 living costs comparisons between London and Tokyo, Japan (table 1 of higher costs) and New Delhi, India (table 2 of lower costs) are as follows:

Table 1 – Tokyo	
Prices overall are higher but restaurant prices are lower	
Local purchasing power is	1.18% higher
Grocery prices are	61.51% higher
Consumer prices including rent are	9.98% higher
Consumer prices in Japan are	22.64% higher

Table 2 – New Delhi	
Cost of living prices are all lower than prices in London	
Consumer prices including rent are	73.11% lower
Consumer prices are	62.59% lower
Rent prices are	86.42% lower
Restaurant prices are	72.74% lower

Guidance: Numbeo cost of living indexes

1.2.5   Accommodation

Rental accommodation costs, as can be seen above, vary enormously worldwide. It is standard practice in some countries, such as Dubai, to pay as much as six or twelve months' rent in advance when entering into a rental agreement. It may be appropriate to ensure that an "expat clause" is inserted into a rental agreement stating that should the expat have to leave the country for certain reasons (such as losing his or her job, war / civil unrest, etc.) then the rental contract can terminate within two months of such an event being notified to the landlord.

Where accommodation is not furnished the expat will need to purchase new furniture and appliances, which can be expensive when these are imported. An alternative is shipping the expat's items from the UK home and this is covered in **section 3.3** (Furniture and possessions). The less costly option is to purchase furniture and appliances from departing expats who advertise on expat social media sites such as Facebook and others.

Ideally accommodation is close to the workplace to save on transport costs where taxis are too expensive, unreliable or just plain dangerous. Otherwise costing in transport needs to be factored in to the budget.

As stated at **3.3.3** (Motor vehicles), if importing a car from the UK is not an option because of import duty then a locally purchased vehicle may be an option subject to paying duty. It will be necessary to take account of local restrictions and laws. For instance, guidelines for importing a car to Singapore state that the car must be less than three years old and that it must meet a wide range of specified safety criteria. There is also a substantial surcharge for used cars imported and registered in Singapore.

1.2.6   *Relocation expenses*

For those going to work abroad, whether self-employed or as an employee, travel and subsistence expenses are allowable deductions if "wholly and exclusively" incurred by the former and "wholly, exclusively and necessarily" incurred by the latter. If the individual *self employed person* (or individual in partnership) carries on a trade wholly outside the UK, expenses on travel, board and lodging which are incurred in connection with the trade are allowable as a deduction against profits. Such expenses can be those incurred by way of:

1. Travel between the UK office and the location of the foreign entity.
2. Board and lodging at the foreign entity. Living expenses are regarded as including the cost of accommodation, food and drink attributable to the individual. If he is accompanied by his family or other dependants, the costs attributable to them will not be allowed.

3. Travel between the foreign entity location and another non-UK location of any other trade carried on by the entity in another non-UK jurisdiction.

4. The cost of journeys by a spouse / civil partner / child where the individual's UK absence exceeds 60 days. However, this also applies at the beginning of the period abroad or for visits after the individual departs for the foreign jurisdiction, but is limited to two outward and return journeys per person for each tax year. The child must be under 18 years old.

It should be noted that where there is more than one foreign trading entity the expenses in 1, 2 and 4 are allocated to the trades on a "just and reasonable basis". In respect of 3 above, the travel expense is allocated to the trading entity at the destination of travel. Failing this the expense is allocated to the trading entity at the place of departure. Private expenditure, for example on holidays taken in the course of a business trip, is not allowed as a cost deduction.

HMRC allow the cost of the employee's accommodation or subsistence outside the UK where all conditions are satisfied. If the accommodation or subsistence is wholly for the purpose of enabling the employee to perform the duties of the employment, then the deduction will be equal to the amount included in earnings.

For UK based employees HMRC have a complex set of rules which determine the tax treatment of entertainment costs, foreign travel and hospitality. The UK company has to prove that there is a business benefit to reclaiming such expenses. The following can usually be regarded as reasonable and genuine business occasions:

- genuine product launches;
- lunches, etc. for customers or potential customers at which business is discussed;
- reasonable entertaining at exhibitions, etc. at which products are on display for customers.

Also, the expenses incurred by an employee in relation to an overseas conference/seminar or tour will typically include travel, accommodation and subsistence costs. These costs are not deductible unless they are *necessarily* incurred in the performance of the duties of the employment.

Example

Following an invitation by the British Malaysian Chamber of Commerce to the Kuala Lumpur import/export event the sales director of a UK company that is hoping to have substantial business connections with Malaysia is required to attend the sales event. Attendance is part of his duties. His wife accompanies him to attend the social functions that are part of the conference programme.

The trip takes five days and the costs incurred are £3,600 for two Malaysia Airlines business class return air fares, £800 for four nights of hotel accommodation and £600 for meals. The hotel room is no different from the hotel room that he would have taken if he had been travelling by himself. The conference organisers have arranged some outside Malaysian entertainment for the delegates and also promotional prizes/gifts worth less than £250 each provided by third party organisations to promote future tourism here.

While the UK director's expenses are deductible, his wife's are not. So on the face of it £1,800 for the air fare and £300 for food will be disallowed but £2,900 for the sales director will be a claimable expense by the UK company. The hotel room for himself and his wife involved no extra cost as it was a twin room.

To obtain a deduction for his wife's expenses the employee must show that the expense of taking his spouse was necessarily incurred in the performance of the employee's duties, for example as a secretary, interpreter or social host.

The entertainment will not be taxable for the sales director and any prizes/gifts worth less than £250 will also not be taxable for him or his UK employer. This is because an employee or office holder is exempt from tax on certain goodwill entertainment, provided by third parties, for him or her or for a member of his or her family or household.

The exemption applies when all the following conditions are satisfied:

- the person providing the non-cash voucher, the credit-token or the benefit is neither the employee's employer nor a person connected with his employer;
- neither the individual's employer nor a person connected with the employer has directly or indirectly procured the provision of the entertainment.

Law: ITTOIA 2005, s. 34
Guidance: BIM 37000*ff.*

1.3 Employment contracts

1.3.1 Introduction

It is important to remember that the UK's comprehensive employment protection laws do not extend abroad. If, therefore, a problem arises once the contract for duties abroad has been signed, there may be no recourse open to the assignee. It is also important to avoid complications and to ensure that the written contract, of which the individual should have a copy (in English), is correct and that it covers all eventualities from the assignee's point of view.

For instance, what if the assignee signed the contract prior to going to Venezuela without a stipulation that, if duties there were to cease, repatriation costs would be paid in the event of war/riots/acts of God (force majeure)? In this case the employer should assess what is the business interruption (BI) ratio of the country to which the assignee is being posted (*Allianz Risk Barometer* 2017).

1.3.2 Contracts overview

Other matters that are of importance in the contract will be whether accommodation is paid for or provided by the foreign employer. Also, will family visits be paid for and (if so) how many in a year? Will the company bear the cost of hotels? Will school fees be covered for the assignee's children? On receiving the contract these further questions should also be clarified by the assignee:

- To whom will he/she be reporting?
- What hours of work will he/she be required to do?

- If he/she is sick, will sick pay be paid?
- What happens he/she does not settle in the country?
- Will he/she be entitled to paid holidays, and when?
- Can he/she get his/her salary (or part) paid outside the country?
- Is he/she entitled to relocation or removal expenses?
- Is tax equalisation or tax protection to be operated (see below)?
- Is there a termination payment/end of service gratuity made and when?
- How is the individual's National Insurance/social security position affected?

If the assignee is working for a foreign subsidiary of the UK company it may be easier to secure changes to the contract of employment. Even in this case the individual assignee should ensure that there is plenty of time to enable changes to be made to the contract before the duties abroad have commenced.

1.3.3 Home v host country based systems

A company may choose a "home country" (also called a balance sheet approach) to apply for a foreign assignment employee or a "host country" based system. Others may look at a mixture of both of these.

Home country system

The home country system uses the UK salary and then adjusts it upwards or downwards to account for the foreign location differences in pay, taxes, housing, services, living costs, etc. The end result should be that the assignee is no better or worse off by taking the assignment, but other financial problems may arise for the assignee (see "Taking independent advice" below). However, in order to prevent situations of assignee ill will for the disruption, a premium is often paid on top (see Example below). "Hardship" locations may also attract a further premium due to crime incidence, lack of amenities, etc.

Example

Jon works for an offshore oil structure maintenance company and is assigned to Nigeria for a year. His base salary is £78,000 a year but Nigeria attracts a foreign allowance premium of 35% which equates to an amount of £27,300 on top of his salary. He will be working offshore so accommodation is not in point and a crime premium is not applicable. His few onshore days in Port Harcourt are spent at an International Hotel with armed security paid for by the company. Had this not been the case the premium may have been higher if an assignee was posted to, say, South Sudan.

Host country system

The host country system is to treat the assignee as if he or she were a locally recruited employee but with a premium to cover the fact that the assignee is not familiar with the country and will therefore incur additional costs to the local employee because of unfamiliarity. Also, there will be a supplement for assistance with housing, education fees, continuing retirement contributions, etc.

The different foreign postings will necessarily require different calculations as local salaries and premiums will vary substantially. It may also, in some locations, prove disruptive for the company where their assignees receive a substantially greater salary than an equivalent locally based employee. For these reasons many companies prefer the home country system.

Other systems

Other systems can be employed for assignees. For example:

- Home and host based systems comparisons are made, with the company choosing the most appropriate to stop unfavourable comparisons being made locally.
- Split package system which pays part salary in the host country and the balance is paid in the home country. This gives a number of advantages, such as limiting foreign exchange fluctuations and avoiding unfavourable local comparisons.
- Artificial base systems, where there is a common approach to salary relevant to, say, UK head office in London. This would be advantageous for multinational countries

13

wanting to have all employees on an even footing worldwide but in certain locations, e.g. with Japan's high cost of living, it may prove difficult to fill an assignment place.

1.3.4   Tax protection

Tax protection is a process that reimburses assignees the excess taxes they incur while on an international assignment. The assignee is generally responsible for the payment of all actual home and host country taxes. The annual tax protection calculation then compares the home hypothetical tax to the actual worldwide taxes paid by the employee. If the actual worldwide taxes exceed the home tax amount (as determined under the company's policy) the company reimburses the excess to the employee. If the actual worldwide taxes are less than the home tax, the employee retains the tax benefit. Tax protection generally puts the burden of filing and paying home and host country taxes on the assignee.

The assignee's income flow may be seriously impaired under tax protection in a high tax rate country such as the Scandinavian countries. Normally, the assignee must first pay both his actual home and host country taxes, then request a home tax calculation, and finally be reimbursed for excess taxes.

Assignee compliance with the host and home country tax laws is sometimes ignored or "forgotten" since the assignee is solely responsible for filing and paying his home and host country taxes. If the assignee fails to comply with the country tax reporting rules and the failure is exposed, the company/assignee may be prevented from leaving the country and unexpected/unfavourable publicity ensues (see "Sailing permits" at **8.6.1**). The assignee has a personal financial incentive to minimise the actual tax paid and this may exacerbate the problem. High tax country postings tend to restrict assignees' cash flow and low tax countries tend to make the assignee sanguine to future tax liabilities, which are often strictly enforced!

In general, though, when tax protection is utilised, the assignee may reap a significant financial benefit if his or her assignment location country has no tax or a very low tax such as the Middle East where there is little or no direct taxation.

1.3.5   Tax equalisation

Tax equalisation is a process that ensures that the tax costs (including NICs) incurred by an assignee on an international assignment approximate to what the tax costs would have been had he or she remained at home (i.e. had not gone on international assignment or received any assignment-related allowances or compensation items). The intent of tax equalisation is that the assignee neither suffers significant financial hardship nor obtains a financial benefit from the tax consequences of an international assignment.

When tax equalisation is utilised, the employer generally bears the responsibility for paying the assignee's actual home and host country tax costs. In exchange, the assignee pays to the employer a hypothetical tax as determined under the company's tax equalisation policy, which in many large organisations is usually controlled by large international accountancy practices or specialised in-house payroll staff. The estimated home country hypothetical tax should be collected from the employee each pay period (i.e. through a modified payroll deduction scheme – see HMRC's *Employment Procedures* (EP) Appendix 4, 5, 6, 7a, 7b) and there should be an end of year tax balancing calculation to reconcile the estimate withholding amount to the final hypothetical tax liability for the year. As a result of this final tax balancing, the employee may owe the company additional tax, or the company may need to return part of the home tax deduction to the employee.

Example 1

Ivor (see also **Example 2** below) is provided a balance sheet calculation which includes a hypothetical tax calculation by his company in advance of his assignment to Jeddah, Saudi Arabia as follows:

	£
UK salary	75,000
UK tax and NICS	25,600
	49,400
Add foreign service premium: 15% of benchmark	11,250
Cost of living allowance: 12% x (50%of gross)	4,500
Ideal	65,150
Add foreign tax liability Saudi Arabia	NIL
Gross remuneration	65,150

Net home based salary.	Add standard cost of living allowance for the location.	Add foreign service premium, accommodation allowance, schooling fees, etc.	This is the net assignment salary for the assignee to make them no better or worse.

Note: The foreign service premium is based on an international benchmark that can be altered and the cost of living allowance depends on which city in Saudi Arabia the assignee is posted to. The cost of living premium is based on a proportion of the individual's gross salary as it forms only part of the assignee's additional expense. His tax code would be NT and his Class 1 primary and secondary contributions would be through the monthly modified payroll under Appendix 7b.

Law: ITEPA 2003, Pt. 5, Ch. 4, 5
Guidance: PAYE 82000-82004; EP Appendix 7b; TMF Group (Worldwide accounting, tax, payroll services)

1.3.6   Taking independent advice

The prospective assignee, once offered an expat package, should obtain independent advice before committing to or signing a contract. One option will be to take independent advice from one of the many providers although some large employers already subscribe to these organisations to ensure fairness to their employees. Independent research shows that the value of a typical expat package for middle managers in Singapore now stands at US$316,600 per annum.

An expat package normally comprises the base cash salary, tax and benefits such as accommodation, international schools, utilities or cars. In Japan, on average, a package for middle managers posted there is worth US$493,900. Japan is followed by China and India. Malaysia, in the region, continues to offer the cheapest expat package at just under US$225,900, behind both Pakistan and Sri Lanka. Malaysia's package has fallen by 13 per cent since 2012 in US dollar terms.

Example 2

Ivor (see also **Example 1** above), who is a construction engineer, has been offered an assignment by his company in Saudi Arabia to build an international hotel over a period of three years.

Because there is no income tax in Saudi Arabia his company will be paying his UK salary under the balance sheet method above with half his salary being paid through the subsidiary company in Jeddah. His total gross salary will be £75,000.

His wife Melinda, who works part time in Croydon on a yearly salary of £14,000 per annum, will join him but as an expatriate wife she is not allowed to work in Saudi Arabia.

Ivor contributes the maximum amount each year for himself and his wife into ISAs to supplement their pension planning. Ivor also received an asset two years ago on which a gain of £6,150 was held over for capital gains tax under TCGA 1992 section 260.

The independent adviser he approaches says his increase in income of £19,000 is counter-acted by a number of factors, including the loss of ISA contributions of £20,000 each year for both of them as they are non-resident and therefore not allowed. Also, the clawback on the held over gain on non-residence is £6,150 (under TCGA 1992, s 261(1), but note that if the asset had been a business asset the clawback would not have applied). There is also the loss of his wife's yearly salary of £14,000. Finally, Ivor plans to invest in an Enterprise Investment Scheme (EIS) in the current tax year to reduce his income tax for 2018-19. Whilst this investment will be allowable whilst UK resident, if his job abroad exceeds three years there will be a potential clawback of income tax relief.

So Ivor may have to reconsider his contract terms or pass up the opportunity to go to Saudi Arabia and maybe jeopardise future promotion prospects.

Ivor is told by the independent adviser that he could rent out his property in the UK whilst he is in Saudi Arabia but he will come under the non-resident landlord scheme. Also, he will have to put his furnishings in store as long term tenants generally prefer to have a property unfurnished for their own belongings. The property would not be available to visit by Ivor and his wife during the letting period.

Ivor must weigh up all these additional factors before committing to the foreign assignment.

Law: TCGA 1992, s. 168(5), 260(3), 261(1); ITA 2007, s. 234

Guidance: ECA International's *MyExpatriate Market Pay* survey report

1.4 Familiarisation

1.4.1 Significance

A move abroad, either for retirement or work, is a stressful time and not helped where couples have differing expectations on the jurisdiction they are moving to. One party to the marriage may be comfortable with the move but the other may not. It is important to consider the various foreign "familiarisation" courses in the UK that are offered to intending expats.

1.4.2 Course providers

Farnham Castle Intercultural Training (see **Appendix 1**) is one of a number of companies that supply familiarisation services for intending British expats and their employers. For instance, it is important that companies planning a footprint in a new area of opportunity have the correct business etiquette when meeting prospective clients and suppliers. For example:

- In Asia business cards are always exchanged at the beginning of a meeting and these should be proffered by holding the card with thumb and index finger of *both* hands. Receiving a business card is accepted the same way with both hands and then placed on the table in front as a sign of respect for the prospective client.

- Also in Asia, when pointing at, say, a clause in a business contract the individual should wrap the index finger around the thumb as pointing in the Western manner is considered a rude gesture.

- In Islamic countries there may be a woman with the hijab or abaya in attendance, and shaking hands would be frowned upon unless that woman makes the first offer of a hand shake.

- It should be appreciated that many Chinese will want to consult with the stars or wait for a lucky day before they make an important business decision which might cause a delay in negotiations.

1.4.3   Local customs

Unless they have been on a specific country familiarisation course, many expats will unknowingly break some cultural norms when they first go to live in a different country. Often the country's locals will break UK cultural norms, e.g. in Asia one of the first things locals may ask is "how much do you earn?" whereas this is uncommon in the UK.

In certain parts of the US locals do not like to reveal the cost of their home whereas this is a common area for mutual discussion in the UK. In some countries, however, especially those where there are strong religious or cultural taboos, it may be easy to cause offence or upset a local without meaning to because of a careless word mispronounced or misunderstood.

In Thailand the word "why?" can be misunderstood for a similar sounding word for water buffalo which is an extreme insult in that country. Similarly there, to make an insensitive remark about the Royal Family in that country can have very serious implications. Comments about local politics or heads of state are best avoided, however frustrating; the UK tends to be very relaxed about derogatory comments directed towards politicians but elsewhere it is not the same.

1.4.4   Do's and do nots

Criticism

"Loss of face" in Asia is a difficult concept for British expats to overcome. In the UK acceptance of criticism is a normal course of everyday dealings, both socially and in business. However, it is a source of shame in many Asian societies so it is very important that no offence is caused, by being particularly careful in criticism to local colleagues. In Asia, individuals will often respond by laughing to cover their deep embarrassment of criticism which only further angers the expat. Better to respond by encouragement but then suggesting another way of looking at the problem/mistake.

Dress code

In Islamic societies, particularly those of the Middle East, it is very important to observe religious customs and sensitivities about dress. Depending on the country concerned, women may be required to cover up their bodies, while men should also dress modestly. In particularly strict Islamic countries, such as Saudi Arabia, women are expected to wear a black abaya and to cover their hair when in public. They may also not be allowed to drive or travel alone.

Guidance: Farnham Castle Intercultural Training; ExpatFocus guides

2. UK taxation

2.1 Domicile

2.1.1 *Significance*

The concept of UK "domicile" can be traced back to Roman times, referring to a place of habitual residence in a diocese in Roman canon law: even in Roman times a person had to pay his taxes somewhere so there had to be a place where he had his *origo* (origin). This concept was then adopted into English canon law.

As more and more individuals leave the UK to work and then live abroad, the significance of domicile will become more pertinent. The UK, in contrast to many other countries where country ties relate to citizenship, permanent residence and nationality (see Passports at **5.1.1**), the emphasis is on domicile. This is determined as a person's domicile of *origin*, *choice* or *dependency*. The term *deemed* domicile is a tax generated term which depends on a person's UK residence under the statutory residence test and on where the individual was born – see Residence at **2.2**).

A person may have only one place of domicile at any given time but he can replace that with a domicile of choice. If the latter is given up, his domicile of origin is reinstated. HMRC look at an individual's domicile when taking into account the imposition of IHT, focusing on country attachment and now residence under the statutory residence test (SRT).

Previously a determination of domicile could be sought from HMRC on form DOM1 (now no longer issued) but currently HMRC will only look at this question when there is a chargeable transfer for IHT purposes. The perceived answer to this withdrawal of DOM1 was to use the discretionary trust chargeable transfer route (see Trusts at **7.2.5**). However, following the *Gulliver* case this is probably not now a feasible option as in that case the original confirmed non-domicile ruling was later ignored. Those returning to the UK were required to fill in form P86, which included a section on domicile, but this form has now been withdrawn too. However, the self-assessment residence pages in form SA109 do ask for a person's domicile.

Trying to change domicile of birth to a domicile of choice in another country where estate duty does not apply is difficult. In the well known case of Sir Richard Burton – the actor who lived in Switzerland for the last 26 years of his life and was buried there – his request to be buried in a red suit with a copy of Dylan Thomas' poems in his coffin, added to the fact that the coffin was draped with the Welsh flag, attracted the attention of HMRC. Burton's continuing "attachment" to Wales, as part of the UK, resulted in UK estate duty taxes.

Non-UK domiciles who have been resident in the UK for 15 out of the last 20 tax years, and then leave, will now still have a trailing UK "deemed" domicile status which applies for four complete tax years after they leave the UK (see **2.1.2** below). In another historical case, the late British financier Sir Charles Clore had retired to Monaco for tax reasons. HMRC investigated in great detail his personal circumstances when he died. It was clear from his friends and acquaintances that Sir Charles was not happy in Monaco and spent much of his time in Paris. He also mentioned to close friends that he longed to return to England. On his death HMRC went to the trouble of calling witnesses to Court to testify that Sir Charles had not been happy in Monaco and longed to return to the UK.

Law: IHTA 1984, s. 267 (as amended by F(No.2)A 2017, s. 30)

Cases: *Re Clore (Deceased)(No 2), Official Solicitor v Clore and Others,* ChD [1984] STC 609; *Gulliver v HMRC* [2017] UKFTT 222 (TC)

Guidance: RDR1, para. 5.10-5.20, 5.21-5.22; RDRM 22010

2.1.2 Determining domicile

One aspect which is often focused on by HMRC when assessing domicile at death is where one is buried, or whether a grave plot in the new country of choice has been purchased. Following the case of *Agulian* – which involved a claim under the *Inheritance (Provision for Family and Dependants Act)* 1975 (see UK Wills at **2.6.4**) – the importance of a burial plot in the chosen foreign country is not such a determining factor, taken together with or in isolation from other factors. Many further investigative questions are undertaken by HMRC and another important factor is whether there an "adhesive quality" to one's domicile of origin/birth. This was the factor that attracted HMRC's attention to Sir Richard Burton's estate and was a vital factor in the imposition of a tax charge.

Any UK domiciliary can try to alter his or her UK domicile of origin/choice to a new domicile of choice but this is difficult, as many court cases have proved. It is possible, if the individual follows a checklist of actions and sticks to them, to ensure a favourable non-UK domicile determination. There is no point in then settling in a country that also has estate duty – better to choose countries where there are no estate duty taxes, e.g. Australia, New Zealand or most Middle East countries. Also, there are some countries which have double tax agreements with the UK, e.g. India and Pakistan, which can prove very tax advantageous. See **2.1.7** below.

Law: *Inheritance (Provision for Family and Dependants) Act* 1975
Cases: *Agulian v Cyganik* [2006] EWCA 129 (Civ); *R (Gaines-Cooper) v The Commissioners for HMRC* [2011] UKSC 47
Guidance: RDRM 23080

2.1.3   Legislation

New legislation on the rules for determining deemed domicile was introduced belatedly in the *Finance (No. 2) Act* 2017 to apply from 6 April 2017 onwards. The legislation affects those individuals resident in the UK for 15 out of the last 20 tax years and relates to foreign born domiciliaries living in the UK for long periods. Additionally, those UK born and bred individuals who moved abroad, but return to the UK having already chosen a foreign domicile, will have their UK domicile revert immediately where they are resident in the UK for the tax year and at least one of the two immediately preceding tax years. In this latter case individuals are referred to as "formerly domiciled resident" (FDR). A saving grace is if the individual leaves the UK again and his domicile of choice is resurrected elsewhere it would apply from the tax year following departure.

Those UK individuals who are born abroad to UK domiciled parents do not fit into category (b) below and are treated slightly differently (see the Jacqueline example below). Also, minors who were born abroad are treated differently (see the Sven example at **2.1.6** below) and come within the 15/20 years rule below.

The new legislation from 6 April 2017 regarding those treated as domiciled in UK refers to:

23

(a) an individual who has been resident in the UK for at least 15 of the 20 tax years immediately preceding the tax year in question; and

(b) an individual originally born in the UK with a UK domicile of origin, who has acquired a domicile of choice elsewhere, who will be treated as domiciled for IHT purposes if at any time he/she is resident in the UK and has been resident in the UK in at least one out of the two previous tax years.

The legislation in the latter case (b) is detailed in IHTA 1984, s. 267 (1)(aa) as so:

(aa) he is a formerly domiciled resident for the tax year in which the relevant time falls ("the relevant tax year").

A formerly domiciled resident (FDR) individual is then described as follows:

(a) he was born in the UK;

(b) his domicile of origin was in the UK;

(c) he was resident in the UK for that tax year; and

(d) he was resident in the UK for at least one of the two tax years immediately preceding that tax year.

If the FDR then departs the UK to live abroad and also become non-resident the rule above is not completely met because, after two tax years abroad, condition (d) is not met and the individual's domicile of choice can revert. It should be remembered that split tax years for residence purposes can count as a whole year even though residence in the UK may only be for a short period. Generally it is recommended that non-domiciles leave within the 14 years' residence in the UK to avoid deemed domicile applying by default.

Example 1

Jacqueline is born in Bermuda in 1960 to UK born and previously UK resident parents who were working at an international hotel on the island. She was educated at boarding school in the UK from the age of 13 years whilst her parents were in Bermuda on hotel management assignment.

Jacqueline subsequently moves after University to Bermuda to live and work, as she has Bermuda Status granted (section 20A) by the Bermudian Minister of Status because of her birth there (i.e. she is a "belonger"). Over many years there she builds up a portfolio of Bermudian holiday let properties which she places into a Bermuda trust (see **7.2.8** – Excluded property trusts).

Subsequently she relocates to the UK in 2018 and she dies in the UK 13 years later. Although her own UK estate will be taxable, the trust property remains excluded property because she was born abroad and cannot therefore be a formally domiciled resident (FDR).

The rule is therefore that if she has a UK domicile of origin but is not born in the UK (but, in this case, in Bermuda) and if she claims a domicile of choice elsewhere (in this case, supported by Bermuda birth and status approval) then she is not a UK FDR. In this case, therefore, the 15-year rule which would normally apply does not because she has set up a trust while foreign domiciled and it only loses IHT protection from year 15 of UK residence.

If Jacqueline had been an FDR she would have lost protection for the trust from the second year of residence in the UK and, on her death, it would have formed part of her taxable estate. Note: Bermudian status application under section 20A had to be made prior to 31 July 2008. (*Bermuda Immigration and Protection Amendment Act* 1980; *British Nationality Act* 1948, s. 5(1)(b) amended by *Nationality, Immigration and Asylum Act* 2002, s. 13).

In the case of (a) above the rule is stricter for non-domiciles from 6 April 2017 who acquire UK domicile status by being in the UK for 15 out of the last 20 tax years as they would have to wait to be non-UK resident for six tax years after leaving the UK before they could reacquire non-domicile status. This rule applies for income tax and capital gains tax purposes (see **2.3** and **2.4** below).

For IHT purposes the individual with deemed domicile would have to be non-resident for four full consecutive tax years, with the proviso that there is no return to the UK within six years (if he or she intends to return). So, a deemed domiciliary leaving the UK permanently in 2018-19, and who was non-resident in that year, would lose that deemed status from 6 April 2022, but see the Gio example below.

The legislation states:

"(b) he was resident in the United Kingdom—

(i) for at least fifteen of the twenty tax years immediately preceding the relevant tax year, and

(ii) for at least one of the four tax years ending with the relevant tax year."

The previous legislation's words "year of assessment" now mean tax years (i.e. 6 April to the following 5 April). Also, the word "resident" means resident for income tax purposes from that date under split-year SRT treatment (i.e. 2018-19 tax year in the above case even though the individual may have been abroad for some of that tax year).

Example 2

Canadian born Gio has been resident in the UK after arriving from Canada in 2002-03 so in 2017-18 he has been resident in the UK for 16 tax years. Gio had intended to return to Canada prior to 5 April 2018 to reaffirm his non-UK domicile prior to the expiry of the 17-year period under the previous rules. However, he now has deemed UK domicile under the rules applying from 6 April 2017 and in order to avoid his substantial Canadian assets becoming subject to IHT he will have to be non-UK resident for the next four consecutive tax years and then must continue to be non-resident for the following two years if he has an intention of returning to the UK to start his next 15-year period. This would, if not adhered to, throw Gio into the five-year UK trailing residence period in the last 20 years.

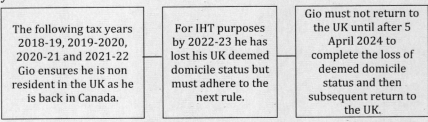

| The following tax years 2018-19, 2019-2020, 2020-21 and 2021-22 Gio ensures he is non resident in the UK as he is back in Canada. | For IHT purposes by 2022-23 he has lost his UK deemed domicile status but must adhere to the next rule. | Gio must not return to the UK until after 5 April 2024 to complete the loss of deemed domicile status and then subsequent return to the UK. |

Note: should Gio return before the six years have elapsed, the 15/20 years rule then applies for UK taxes from return to the UK.

Therefore the income tax residence treatment also potentially affects inheritance tax domicile: see point 3 in the Introduction to the Statutory Residency Test (SRT) guidance notes. So for an individual classed as having a "deemed domicile" in the UK, within the IHT legislation above, it states 15 out of the last 20 tax years of assessment, but this may not be actual whole years spent in the UK; because of the mechanics of the SRT it may well be less in terms of days. See Residence at **2.2.1** below.

Law: IHTA 1984, s. 267(1)(b), 267(8)(b); F(No.2)A 2017, s. 30
Guidance: RDR1 and 3

2.1.4 Married women

Newly married women now retain their domicile but up until 1 January 1974 a woman automatically took her husband's domicile and this would subsist throughout their marriage. If the husband changed his domicile then his wife's domicile would change as well, as a domicile of dependency, unless she changes it by choice. On the husband's death her domicile will still be her late husband's until it is changed by acquisition or revival of another domicile on or after 1 January 1974. This can be overlooked when calculating the incidence of IHT on death, and Form 401 at box 14 asks this specific question.

However, for a US woman national married, prior to 1 January 1974, to a man domiciled within the UK, then for the purposes of determining her domicile for UK tax purposes the marriage is deemed to have taken place on 1 January 1974. See *UK/USA Double Taxation Convention* 2002, art. 4(6).

Where, immediately before this section came into force, a woman was married and then had her husband's domicile by dependence, she is to be treated as retaining that domicile (as a domicile of choice, if it is not also her domicile of origin) unless and until it is changed by acquisition or revival of another domicile, either on or after the coming into force of this section.

Example

Anne is born in Wales to a farming family and attends Aberystwyth University, undertaking the livestock science course in 1970. She meets Jim who is a New Zealand national also studying there. They are married in June 1973 and leave the UK to run a sheep farm in New Zealand and only return to the UK periodically to visit family and friends. Jim dies in New Zealand in 1989 and Anne continues to run the farm there, now with her two sons.

Anne inherits her parents' Welsh farm, which is run by a manager, and she continues to manage her assets in New Zealand, not choosing to return to the UK. As Anne has retained her New Zealand domicile by marriage, and spends few days in the UK, the IHT position will be such that only her UK assets, the inherited Welsh farm, will be subject to IHT on her death, and New Zealand property will be excluded property.

If Anne visits the UK and becomes resident as a "formerly domiciled resident" her worldwide assets would be subject to IHT. However, then the Welsh farm would be within the agricultural property relief exemption but the New Zealand farm and assets would be subject to tax by reason of not being in the UK or EEA. By retaining her pre 1 January 1974 domicile of dependency by marriage, of New Zealand domicile, no tax arises in either country on her demise.

Law: *Domicile and Matrimonial Proceedings Act* 1973, s. 1, 17(5); IHTA 1984, s. 6(1), 115(5), 116; *Estate Duty Abolition Act* 1993, s. 3; UK/USA Double Taxation Convention 2002, Art 4(6);

Guidance: RDRM 20000

2.1.5   Minors

A child/minor is able to change his domicile from the age of 16 years (14 for boys and 12 for girls in Scotland) or if he or she marries under that age. Prior to that the child/minor takes the domicile of the adult on whom he/she is dependent. This will usually be the father but if the husband and wife are living apart it will be the mother's domicile if the child/minor is living with her.

The new 15 out of 20 years rule applies to children/minors born in the UK to non-domiciled parents so that from 16 years they become deemed UK domiciled if they have been continuously resident.

HMRC provided a number of flowcharts in RDR1 to determine domicile but with the proviso that HMRC's warning is heeded:

> "If, when using the flowcharts, you arrive at the conclusion you are 'domiciled in the UK' or 'probably domiciled in the UK'

you may simply accept that conclusion. If you do, you should not tick the 'non-domiciled' box on form SA 109 (Residence, remittance basis etc. Self Assessment supplementary page). You will then be taxed on the arising basis."

In the recent *Henderson* case it was decided that the appellants, father and son, were UK domiciled from birth. This was because their father and grandfather had not established a domicile of choice in Brazil, when moving there, with the result that both son and grandson had UK domicile of origin each inherited from their respective fathers. See also RDR1 para. 5.23 note 5.

Example

Sven was born and raised in Sweden by his parents. At the age of 11 years, in July 2000, he moves to England because of his father's work requirements. Sven is educated in England at boarding school and then Oxford University until 2014. After University he takes a job with a UK company and is posted three years later, in June 2017, to Sweden because of his language capabilities. He still has a grandfather and grandmother in Sweden whom he visits periodically.

At birth he has Swedish domicile because of his dependency on his father's domicile of origin. His domicile of dependency with that of his father was only until he is 16. Sven can then choose the UK as his domicile of choice but does not do so. In looking at the flowcharts 3 and 4 in RDR1 there may be a disparity in the advice offered as to determination of domicile. See above.

However, the deemed domicile rules from April 2017 mean that Sven was in the UK for more than 15 out of the last 20 tax years by the time of his departure. He is therefore deemed to have a UK domicile as the rules had changed by 2017-18, whereas under the old rules he would not have been in the UK for 17 years to result in him having a deemed domicile status. He will now have to be non-resident for four tax years following departure to shake off the trailing IHT worldwide tax implications.

Law: *British Nationality Act* 1948, s. 5(1)(b); *Domicile and Matrimonial Proceedings Act* 1973, s. 3; IHTA 1984, s. 267(1)

Case: *Henderson & Others* [2017] UKFTT 556 (TC)

Guidance: RDR1

2.1.6   *Historical treaties*

"Deemed domicile" in the UK for inheritance tax purposes can apply inheritance tax to anyone's worldwide assets if they are resident in the UK for 15 out of the last 20 *tax years*. Leaving and entering the UK in the tax year may mean that UK residence applies under split-year treatment (see Residence at **2.2**) at the date of departure.

The UK's *deemed* domicile rule is sometimes ignored where there is an overriding double tax treaty relevant to estate taxes. So in relation to subsection IHTA 1984, s. 267(2) the wording states that the deemed domicile rules "shall not affect the interpretation of any such provision as is mentioned in section 158(6) above" [vis double tax conventions] on the effect of historical treaties affecting deemed domicile.

These treaties are few but must be taken into account as they can affect the tax position quite markedly. This would preclude UK estate duty/inheritance tax being applied on overseas assets at the time of death as long as the person is domiciled under common law in a country that has such an agreement, such as India (see the example below). There are also different historical estate duty treaties with Italy (SI 1968/304), Pakistan (SI 1957/1522), Ireland (SI 1978/1107), the USA (SI 1979/998) and France (SI 1963/1319), each of which imposes varying treatment for individuals from those countries.

Example

Raj (in the Residence section at **2.2** below at Example 7) looks at the three "automatic UK tests". As he is conclusively UK resident due to the SRT automatic UK tests, the sufficient ties test does not need to be applied.

However, the split-year treatment (see **2.2.6** onwards) should be considered for 2017-18. In subsequent years he is clearly UK resident. However, for domicile purposes he is resident in 2017-18 and after 15 years he will be deemed to be domiciled in the UK.

His other assets are situated in India on the Indian stock exchange so would be Indian *situs* assets. Raj would therefore normally be subject potentially to IHT on his worldwide assets. Yet IHTA 1984, s. 267(2) below excludes the *deemed* domicile rules from applying in these circumstances, as the previous rules "remain in force and have effect as if any provision made by those arrangements in relation to estate duty extended to inheritance tax".

"(2) Subsection (1) above shall not apply for the purposes of section 6(2) or (3) or 48(4) above and shall not affect the interpretation of any such provision as is mentioned in section 158(6) above."

In the UK/India 1956 treaty, Art. III para. 3 says:

"Duty shall not be imposed in Great Britain on the death of a person who was not domiciled at the time of his death in any part of Great Britain but was domiciled in some part of India on any property situate outside Great Britain ... ."

So although India abolished estate duty in 1985 the treaty still stands good and no assets would be subject to estate taxes in India on Raj's death under Indian common law. If he were to be domiciled in India by choice/origin this does not matter because of the application of section 267(2). However, Raj has emigrated to the UK and this would mean his worldwide assets would be subject to IHT. See example 2 at **2.2.3** below.

The deemed domicile rule should be looked at in conjunction with the above estate duty/death duty (i.e. now inheritance tax) treaties for individuals from these jurisdictions.

Law: IHTA 1984, s. 158(6), 267 (1)(b), (2); UK/India 1956, SI 1956/ 998
Guidance: RDR3, para. 5.21

2.2   Residence

2.2.1   *Introduction – statutory residence test*

A person's tax residence status is fundamental as to how he or she will be taxed in the UK. Resident taxpayers are taxed in the UK on their worldwide income, whereas non-residents are taxed on just their UK sourced income such as:

- interest from UK bank accounts;
- dividends from UK companies;
- UK pensions;

31

- rental income from UK properties;
- earnings from work physically performed in the UK while overseas; and
- earnings from a time when still resident and working in the UK, e.g. deferred bonuses, exercise of share options and other employee share awards.

Prior to 6 April 2013, the "old rules" for residence applied. These were largely based on case law and whether a "distinct break" from the UK had occurred and were difficult to interpret in some cases. There was also the concept of "ordinary residence", which was a more permanent type of residence status. However, ordinary residence was abolished from 6 April 2013. See HMRC's past publications IR20 and HMRC6 (potentially via the National Archives website).

These rules were replaced by the new statutory residence test (SRT) rules which were eventually supported by HMRC's explanatory leaflets RDR1 and RDR3.

The legislation sets out a basic rule under the SRT which is as follows:

> "An individual ("P") is resident in the UK for a tax year ("year X") if—
>
> (a) the automatic residence test is met for that year, or
>
> (b) the sufficient ties test is met for that year."

It then goes on to state:

> "The automatic residence test is met for year X if P meets—
>
> (a) at least one of the automatic UK tests, and
>
> (b) none of the automatic overseas tests."

In practice, therefore, the SRT rules consider a person's residence in a set order of tests; firstly, the automatic overseas tests (see **2.2.2** below); secondly, the automatic UK tests (see **2.2.3**); and if neither of these gives a decision then the sufficient ties tests (see **2.2.4**) are applied.

When referring to days in the UK, this means days when the individual is present in the UK at midnight unless otherwise stated.

Reference is often made to "arrivers" and "leavers", the former being where an individual has been non-resident for all three of the previous tax years to a tax year and the latter where he or she was resident in one or more of the three previous tax years. These terms arose from HMRC's consultation on the SRT, but have not subsequently been referred to in the legislation.

Law: FA 2013, Sch. 45

Guidance: HMRC's RDR3 – Guidance note: Statutory Residence Test (SRT) (published August 2016); See also *Residence: The Definition in Practice,* from Claritax Books

2.2.2   *The automatic overseas tests*

For an individual to be definitively non-UK resident in a tax year the individual must meet one of the following conditions:

1. Be present in the UK for fewer than 16 days in the current tax year, where that individual has been UK resident in one or more of the previous three tax years (see Example 1 below).

2. Be present in the UK for fewer than 46 days, where the individual has *not* been resident in the UK in any of the three previous tax years (see Example 2 below).

3.   (i)   Work sufficient hours overseas (on average 35 or more hours per week);

    (ii)   with no significant breaks in this (this being a break of more than 30 consecutive days where the individual has not worked more than three hours per day overseas or was not working on a day when he or she would normally be working more than three hours and this was not due to being on annual, sick or parental leave, so is in respect of exceptional breaks such as compassionate leave);

    (iii)   he or she is present in the UK (for whatever reason) for fewer than 91 days in the tax year; *and*

    (iv)   spends fewer than 31 working days (only days where more than three hours' work has been performed) in the UK in the tax year.

33

The legislation sets out a specific way of establishing whether or not an individual works sufficient hours overseas (see FA 2013, Sch. 45, para. 14(3) and see also **Appendix 5** of this book). This test is often referred to as simply "the third automatic overseas test" and indeed the residence, remittance basis etc. supplementary pages of the self-assessment tax return (SA109) specifically refer to this. See RDR3, para. 1.7 to 1.21 and Example 3 below.

Certain transport workers are excluded from this test (FA 2013, Sch. 45, para. 14(4) and 30).

1. Die in the tax year in which the individual spends fewer than 46 days in the UK and (i) he was not resident in the UK for the two previous tax years or (ii) he was not resident for the preceding tax year and Cases 1 to 3 split-year treatment (see **2.2.7**) applied for the tax year prior to this preceding year (see Example 4 below).

2. Die in the tax year with full-time work overseas (as shown above under 3), but this is only considered for the period from the start of the tax year to the day before death. As for (4) above, it is necessary that (i) the individual was not resident in the UK for the two preceding tax years, but as a result of meeting the third automatic overseas test above OR (ii) he was not resident in the UK in the preceding tax year, again because he or she met the third automatic overseas test for that year and the tax year before that was a split year under Case 1 (see **2.2.7**). The sufficient hours worked overseas calculation, for the year of death, must be modified by applying it to this shorter period and there must also be no significant break during this work period (see Example 5 below).

Law: FA 2013, Sch. 45, para. 11 to 16
Guidance: HMRC's RDR3, Chapter 1 pages 9 to 17, para. 1.4 to 1.21

The Automatic Overseas Tests		
Present in the UK for fewer than 16 days in the tax year? **No – go below**	YES →	
Present in the UK for fewer than 46 days AND not resident in all of the 3 previous tax years? **No – go below**	YES →	
Leave UK for full-time work overseas as defined above; present in the UK for fewer than 91 days and work in the UK for fewer than 31 days? **No – go below**	YES →	
Die in the tax year but spends fewer than 46 days in the UK and not resident in the UK for the two previous tax years or the previous year and the preceding year to this was a split year under any Case 1 to 3? **No – go below**	YES →	NOT resident in the UK
Die in a tax year of full-time work overseas (consider only the period from the start of the tax year to the day before death in this respect). Also, not resident in the UK for the two preceding tax years OR not resident in the UK in the preceding tax year because the third automatic overseas test is met for these tax years and the tax year before the previous year was a split year under Case 1? **NO – go to Automatic UK tests below**	YES →	

Example 1

Alex and his wife Maureen have sold their small business having won the Euro millions lottery. They purchase a super yacht and decide they will tour the world seeing places they never were able to whilst working. They rent out their jointly owned UK property in Cheshire and their letting agent assists them in completing the non-resident landlord scheme form NRL1 and, depending on the rental amounts, they may not pay tax on the rents received (see **3.1**). They leave Liverpool in their super yacht on 1 March 2017 and intend to return for Christmas 2018, where they will moor the boat for two weeks in Liverpool before departing again.

They will be resident for 2016-17, but split-year treatment (see **2.2.7**) will not apply under Case 3, as they have not moved to just one country and so there will be no sufficient link with a country (they are not working so Cases 1 and 2 do not apply). For 2017-18 they will be non-resident as they will not have spent any days in the UK and will, therefore, come within 1 above.

It is established that their travels will not make them resident in any country, as they will never spend more than the requisite period in any country to become resident before moving on. There is no requirement that they have to be resident in any country to be non-UK resident.

On return to Liverpool for the Christmas period during 2018-19 they will not become resident in the UK provided they do not stay beyond 15 days.

In other circumstances concerning connecting factors under the sufficient ties test (see **2.2.4**), the yacht might be treated as available accommodation in the UK (as per RDR3 paragraph A30 page 92) and they will also have the 90 day tie. However, it is important to realise that if either the automatic overseas or UK tests apply, the sufficient ties test does not need to be considered. This means that as long as Alex and Maureen spend fewer than 16 midnights in the UK during 2018-19, then there will be no need to consider ties they have with the UK and the sufficient ties test. It would only be if they did not satisfy the overseas or UK tests that they would then need to consider the sufficient ties test to establish their UK tax residence.

Example 2

Brian is resident in Gibraltar and works for an online betting company resident there, but with no establishment in the UK. Brian has not been UK resident since he left four years ago. He is to visit London at the beginning of May 2018 to arrange an international poker tournament at the Excel Centre for the end of June. He estimates that it will take nearly 50 days to organise the five day tournament.

Brian should try to limit his time in the UK to fewer than 46 days for 2018-19 to come within (2) above. If Brian can split his time between two tax years he could come within the 46 days limit for each tax year and be non-resident under (2) above, but this will depend on his and his employer's organisational flexibility to begin, say, on 1 April 2018, assuming he has not visited the UK prior to this during 2017-18.

If this split of his days is not possible, then as Brian will be working in the UK, he will not meet the third automatic overseas test above – as he will spend more than 30 days in 2018-19 working in the UK (see Sch. 45, para. 14(1)(c)) – and so he would then need to see if any of the automatic UK tests (see **2.2.3** below) are satisfied. If not, he will then need to progress to the sufficient ties test shown under **2.2.4** to establish whether or not he is resident in the UK.

Even if Brian is non-resident, the earnings from his UK work are taxable in the UK (see **2.3.9**). As there is no double tax treaty between the UK and Gibraltar, he will not be able to claim exemption from UK tax under a double tax treaty, unless he (say) lived in Spain and was resident there and commuted to his work in Gibraltar. In this scenario, he may then be able to claim exemption from UK tax on his UK earnings under the double tax treaty between the UK and Spain, even though his employer is resident in Gibraltar and not in Spain, as the treaty does not state that the employer needs to be resident in Spain (see **2.3.3**).

Brian and his employer would also need to consider any PAYE and NIC obligations that may arise by virtue of him working in the UK (see **2.3.19** and **2.7**).

Example 3

Sally goes to work in Malta for an international tour company at the end of March 2017 working 9am to 7pm five days a week with two and a half hours for siesta in the afternoon, so 7½ hours per day. She leaves her job on 2 June and on 26 June goes to work for a competitor company in Valletta with the same working conditions. On 25 November to 1 December she returns to the UK on compassionate leave to sort out her mother's funeral arrangements.

From 23 December to 1 January 2018 she takes a holiday in Tanzania, returning to work on the next day. On 17 February to 18 March 2018 she takes sick leave with malaria contracted in Tanzania and during this time spends two weeks recuperating in the UK, returning to work on 19 March 2018 until the end of the UK tax year 5 April 2018. The number of net overseas hours worked, after taking into account 11 religious public holidays within those work days, has been 1,447.50 (193 days x 7.5 hours per day).

For 2017-18, Sally does not satisfy the first automatic overseas test above, as she has been present in the UK for more than 15 days. The second automatic test is not applicable as she was resident up to and including 2016-17. Sally therefore needs to see if she has satisfied the third automatic overseas test and working sufficient hours overseas. In this respect, she needs to calculate her days in the UK, which are fewer than 91, so she passes that test, and she has not spent any days working in the UK, passing that test as well.

Sally also has to look at whether she has satisfied the "sufficient hours worked overseas" test (see **Appendix 5**) and also see whether there is a significant break in her overseas work during the 2017-18 tax year. For the former, Sally needs to establish how many days there are in the reference period. The starting point in this respect is 365 days, being the number of days in the 2017-18 tax year. From this she can deduct certain days as follows.

The change of work period is 23 consecutive days, so there is no significant break being less than 31 days. However, it does exceed the maximum 15 days that can be deducted when looking at the reference period for the sufficient hours worked overseas test, so only the maximum of 15 days can be deducted from the total number of days during 2017-18 of 365 days. The UK funeral arrangements of five work days were compassionate leave which cannot be deducted. However, Sally's three days of holiday in Tanzania can be (work days excluding weekends and public holidays over Christmas and new year period). Her sick period was 28 days, which again can be deducted, but only up to 20 days which are the days she should have been working on, but was off sick.

Sally can also deduct six embedded days. These are days upon which Sally would not normally be expected to work and does not actually work on, such as weekends and public holidays, and which are embedded in a period of annual, sick or parenting leave. To be embedded the day must both be preceded and followed by three consecutive days of leave. In Sally's case she can deduct six days which were embedded in her block of sick leave. There were no embedded days in her holiday to Tanzania.

The reference period is, therefore, as follows:

	Days
Total number of days in 2017-18	365
Less:	
Days on annual leave	(3)
Days on sick leave	(20)
Gap between employments – maximum	(15)
Embedded days	(6)
Days in reference period	321

The above 321 days is then divided by 7 to give 45.86 which is round down to 45. The overseas hours of 1,447.50 is rounded up to 1,448 (as it is .5 and above) and is divided by 45 to give 32.17 hours per week on average, which is less than the required figure of 35 hours per week as per Step 5 of HMRC's RDR3 calculation at paragraph 1.10. Sally has not, therefore, met the "sufficient hours worked overseas" test and now needs to consider the automatic UK tests below.

As an aside, if Sally had performed some work in the UK during 2017-18, then these UK work days would be treated as disregarded days and deducted from the 365 days above, when looking at the number of days in the reference period.

Example 4

John moved to Malaysia from the UK for work in the middle of the 2014-15 tax year (see also split-year treatment (Case 1) below at **2.2.7**) having been resident in the UK for previous years. During a weekend running in the jungle with the Hash House Harriers, he is lost on Saturday 27 May 2017 and his body is never found. He is presumed to have died somewhere in the jungle (see also Wills at sections **2.6.4** and **6.7**). As John had not been present in the UK in the current tax year for more than 45 days, *and* had been non-resident for the two previous tax years 2016-17 and 2015-16 (having left for full-time work abroad), he would be deemed non-resident for 2017-18.

If his parents did not apply for an order in the UK under s. 1 of the *Presumption of Death Act* 2013, then it would not be possible to wind up the estate. After seven years, under common law, a missing person might be presumed to be dead, although in many cases it is far longer than seven years before the death certificate is issued. In Malaysia there is no presumption of death legislation so reliance is instead placed on s. 108 of the Malaysian *Evidence Act* 1950. On the court making an order, John's death for tax purposes would not be 2017-18 (when he went missing) but when the order is made. In essence he would not have therefore come within the fourth automatic overseas test in these particular circumstances even if he had left for Malaysia in 2016-17 because seven years missing is the rule there before an application can be made.

Example 5

Ben moved to Malta from the UK in March 2014 but dies there on 18 June 2017 in a scuba diving accident. He had worked there for the same company until he died, with no breaks at all except for three bank holidays between 6 April and 17 June 2017. Under the conditions in (5) above he was not resident in the UK for the two preceding tax years as a result of the third automatic overseas test.

He did not need to meet the second requirement, which is that he was not resident in the UK in the preceding tax year, because he met the third automatic overseas test for that year and the tax year before that was a split year under Case 1 (see split-year treatment (Case 1) at **2.2.7** below).

The sufficient hours worked overseas calculation (see **Appendix 5**) for the year of death, must be modified by applying it to this shorter period of work from 6 April 2017 to 17 June 2017 and there must be no significant break during this period. This calculation is as follows:

Step 1 is identify any disregarded days: these are any days, from the start of the 2017-18 tax year to the day before his death, on which he worked for more than three hours in the UK, including those days when he also did some work overseas on the same day. This is none.

Step 2 is to calculate the net overseas hours: the total number of hours that Ben worked overseas, from the start of the 2017-18 tax year to the day before his death, 17 June 2017. The result is 382.5 (51 x 7.5 hours). Hours that Ben worked overseas on disregarded days (days performing work in the UK including part days worked in the UK) are not included.

Step 3 is to calculate the number of days in the reference period, which considers only the days from the start of 2017-18 up to and including 17 June 2017 (the day before the date of death) which equals 73. From this deduct reducing days such as the above disregarded days, days on annual and sick leave, which is none.

Step 4 is to divide the number of days at Step 3 by 7. This amounts to 10.

Step 5 is divide the number at Step 2 by the number resulting from Step 4. This amounts to 38. As this is more than 35 hours, Ben had worked sufficient hours overseas during the period 6 April to 17 June 2017 and hence is non-resident for 2017-18 under (5) above.

2.2.3   The automatic UK tests

If an individual does not meet any of the automatic overseas tests, he or she then needs to look at the automatic UK tests. To be definitively UK resident in a tax year the individual must meet at least one of the following conditions:

1. He or she spends 183 days or more in the UK in the tax year (see Example 1 below).

2. He has his home (see below) in the UK for all or part of the tax year, spends at least 30 days in that home during the relevant tax year, and has a period of at least 91 consecutive days (where at least 30 days must be in the tax year concerned) throughout which *either* he had no home overseas *or* (if he did have one or more homes overseas) he spent fewer than 30 days in each of these homes during the relevant tax year. A day of presence at a home is any time at all spent during a day in the home.

   See Example 2 below, HMRC's RDR3 Annex A and flowchart at 1.31 on page 22 and FA 2013, Sch. 45, para. 25.

3. He works *full-time* in the UK for any period of 365 days, with no significant break from UK work. This has a similar definition to full-time work overseas and the third automatic overseas test (see **2.2.2** above), only with regards to work performed in the UK rather than overseas and with the starting point for the reference period when calculating whether sufficient hours are worked in the UK (see Appendix 5), being over any 365-day period, all or part of which falls in the tax year concerned and with at least one day where more than three hours' work are performed in that tax year. In addition, fewer than 25% of days worked (more than three hours' work per day) must be performed overseas. See Example 3 below and FA 2013, Sch. 45, para. 9(2) to calculate sufficient hours worked in the UK.

4. He dies and was resident in each of the three previous tax years by satisfying the automatic residence test (see **2.2.1**), with the preceding tax year not being a split year if he was non-resident for the tax year of death. When the individual died, his home must have been in the UK (or if he had more than one home, at least one of them must have been in the UK). If during the year of death the individual had a home overseas, then he or she must not have spent "a sufficient amount of time" there. He will have spent a sufficient amount of time there if (i) he spent at least 30 days there (any part of the day, and the days do not need to be consecutive) or (ii) he was there for any part of the day on

every day from the beginning of the tax year of death up to and including the day of his or her death.

Home

In respect of the second test above, "home" is not particularly well defined in the legislation, so is open to different interpretations by HMRC and individuals and is considered to be one of the main areas of the SRT where disagreements between individuals and HMRC may arise.

Basically, for the purposes of the automatic residence test, a person's home will be determined by the facts of his or her situation and circumstances, with "home" taking on its normal everyday meaning. It is somewhere that someone stays with a reasonable degree of stability and permanence. It can be a building, vessel, vehicle or some other structure used by an individual as a home and can still be a home even if it is temporarily unavailable, e.g. it is being renovated. Residential accommodation is not treated as an individual's home if that accommodation is being commercially let and the individual has no right to live there. It is not a person's home if the property is advertised for sale or let and the individual lives in another residence. A holiday home will also not be regarded as a home if it is used only periodically for short breaks.

A property does not need to be owned by the individual in order for it to be regarded as his or her home, so rented accommodation – or living with a family member, relative or friend – would also count as a home, as would employer-provided accommodation.

A home in which a person spends fewer than 30 days during the tax year will be disregarded for the above test.

Law: FA 2013, Sch. 45, para. 6 to 10

Guidance: HMRC's RDR3 para. 1.22 to 1.41 (pages 17 to 28) and para. 4.6 to 4.9 (pages 47 to 49)

The Automatic UK Tests		
Spend 183 days or more in the UK in the tax year?	YES $\rightarrow$	
Have or had a home only in the UK during all or part of the tax year?	YES $\rightarrow$	Resident in the UK
Work full-time in the UK for any period of 365 days, with no significant break from UK work?	YES $\rightarrow$	
	NO $\rightarrow$	Go to sufficient ties tests below

Example 1

Bertie arrives in the UK on 16 April 2017, having been removed from his foreign country of employment due to corruption investigations and money laundering (see *Bribery Act* 2010 at **section 6.8**). He is under ongoing corruption investigations by the Fraud Office in London and has had his passport withheld as he is a flight risk. He will be resident in the UK from 6 April 2017 as it is clear that he will be in the UK for some period of time exceeding 182 days, although split-year treatment may apply (see **2.2.8**). Also see *Proceeds of Crime Act* 2002, s. 362E (inserted by the *Criminal Finances Act* 2017, s 1).

Example 2

Raj has lived in India all his life. In June 2017 he visits family in London and he decides to emigrate to the UK. He spends the next few months preparing for the move. He ceases his employment in India on 30 November 2017 and sells his Mumbai house (his only home) on 10 January 2018, arriving in the UK on 25 January 2018. He finds a flat in London and moves in on 1 February 2018. The London flat is now his only home and he lives there for a year. He does not find employment in the UK until after 5 April 2018 (so during the 2018-19 tax year).

During the tax year 2017-18 Raj is present in his Mumbai home on 250 days, and he is present in his London flat on 55 days. In 2017-18 Raj has a home in the UK from 1 February 2018 and is present in it on at least 30 days during the tax year. Also from 1 February 2018 there is a period of at least 91 consecutive days, of which at least 30 fell in 2017-18, when Raj has a UK home and no overseas home.

As Raj does not meet any of the automatic overseas tests, he is resident in the UK under this second automatic UK test from 6 April 2017 and so taxable on his worldwide income from this date, unless one of the Cases of split-year treatment (see **2.2.8**) applies. See RDR3 1.31 (page 22) for a flowchart and the second automatic UK test (only home in the UK test). See also Domicile at **2.1** for the position on death if Raj had kept assets in India.

Example 3

Jack is a British citizen who has been living in France for many years and so has been resident in France and not the UK for tax purposes. His French employer has seconded him to the UK for a year and he travels to the UK on 1 July 2017 to start work on the following day. His posting finishes on 1 July 2018 and he leaves the UK on 6 August 2018, just over 400 days after he arrived in the UK.

Over the 365-day period to 30 June 2018 Jack calculates that he worked full-time in the UK (in accordance with **Appendix 5**) and has not taken a significant break from his UK work during this period. The period falls within two tax years (i.e. the period of 365 days falls within the tax years 2017-18 and 2018-19).

Over the period of 365 days ending 30 June 2018 Jack works for over three hours on 240 days, 196 (82%) of which are days when Jack worked for more than three hours in the UK.

At least one day when Jack does more than three hours' work per day in the UK falls within the tax year 2017-18. Therefore, Jack is resident in the UK under the third automatic UK test for the tax year 2017-18 and so from 6 April 2017. There is also at least one day when Jack does more than three hours' work in the UK within the tax year 2018-19, so Jack also meets the third automatic UK test for that year and is resident until 5 April 2019, meaning he is potentially taxable in the UK on his worldwide income from 6 April 2017 to 5 April 2019.

Satisfying the conditions for split-year treatment will, therefore, be important for Jack for both 2017-18, the year of his arrival (most likely case 5, see **2.2.8**) and for 2018-19, the year of his departure (see **2.2.7**) if he is to avoid double tax (i.e. being taxed for a time in both the UK and France on the same income). If split-year treatment does not apply, then he will need to look at the double tax treaty between the UK and France to see if exemption or relief from double tax is available (see **2.3.3**).

In determining whether the third automatic UK test applied, the following was considered:

1. all or part of the 365-day period falls within the tax year concerned;
2. more than 75% of the total number of days in the 365-day period when Jack does more than three hours of work per day, are days when he did more than three hours work in the UK; and
3. at least one day which is both in the 365-day period and in the relevant tax year, is a day on which he does more than three hours of work in the UK.

2.2.4   Sufficient ties test

If the automatic overseas tests and the automatic UK tests do not apply, then an individual needs to look at the sufficient ties test to determine his or her UK tax residence. It is important to highlight to individuals that the sufficient ties test is only considered if they do not satisfy any of the automatic overseas or UK tests, i.e. if they do not meet the automatic residence test (see **2.2.1**). It is common for individuals to think it is necessary to look at the sufficient ties test, even though one of the overseas or UK tests has been satisfied, which can often lead to confusion.

Under the sufficient ties test, consideration is given to UK "ties" as set out in the legislation. The number of ties is determined depending on whether the individual is an arriver or leaver (see **2.2.1**) and is then taken together with the number of days spent in the UK to establish a person's residence status (see tables A and B in HMRC's RDR3 para. 1.45 on page 29). The ties are as follows:

1. a family tie;
2. an accommodation tie;
3. a work tie;
4. a 90-day tie, and – for "leavers" –
5. a country tie (see below).

Was the individual in the UK in any of the previous three tax years?	
YES = "Leaver" status	**NO = "Arriver" status**
1. Family: spouse/civil partner/ minor child(ren) in the UK?	Family?
2. Accommodation in the UK?	Accommodation?
3. Work in the UK equal to or greater than 40 days?	Work?
4. 90 days or more spent in UK in either of the two previous tax years?	90 days?
5. Country: spends more days in the UK than any other country in the tax year?	
Possible maximum of five ties for a "leaver"	Possible maximum of four ties for an "arriver"
Go to Leaver below	Go to Arriver below

Leavers' days in the UK up to a maximum of five ties	Arrivers' days in the UK up to a maximum of four ties
Fewer than 16 UK days = *not* resident	Fewer than 46 UK days = *not* resident
16-45 UK days = resident if 4 ties	
46-90 UK days = resident if 3 ties	46-90 UK days = resident if 4 ties
91-120 UK days = resident if 2 ties	91-120 UK days = resident if 3 ties
121-182 UK days = resident if 1 tie	121-182 UK days = resident if 2 ties
183 or more days in UK = resident	183 or more days in UK = resident

Law: FA 2013, Sch. 45, para. 17 to 20

Guidance: HMRC's RDR3 1.42 to 1.46 (pages 28 to 29)

2.2.5   Sufficient ties and SRT glossary

Family tie

There will be a family tie if there is a person, resident in the UK for tax purposes, who is a:

- spouse or civil partner living with the individual (i.e. not separated);
- partner of the individual (i.e. living together as husband and wife / civil partners); or
- child (including an adopted child) under 18 (but see below).

For a child who is under the age of 18, if the individual spends time with that child in the UK on fewer than 61 days (in total) in the relevant tax year, it is not a family tie. If the child turns 18 during that tax year and the parent sees that child in the UK on fewer than 61 days in the part of the tax year before the 18th birthday, then it is not a family tie in respect of that child. Seeing a child in person in the UK for all or part of a day counts as a day towards the 61 day total, so days spent with a child outside the UK will not count.

If a child under 18 is in full-time education, such as boarding school, he will not be regarded as resident (and so not a tie) if he is in the UK for fewer than 21 days outside term time during the tax year (half term breaks are considered term time) (see HMRC's RDR3 Annex C).

Accommodation tie

There is an accommodation tie if there is a place to live in the UK which is available to the individual for a continuous period of 91 days or more during the tax year and he or she spends one or more nights there during that year. It does not matter whether or not the accommodation is owned by the individual, so this can include rented and employer-provided accommodation.

A place to live in the UK can be a home, holiday home, temporary retreat in the UK, houseboat, or vessel or structure of any kind which is available to live in as accommodation in the UK.

Where, in the tax year, there is a gap of fewer than 16 days between periods that a particular place is available, that accommodation will continue to be regarded as being available to the individual during the gap.

If it is at the home of a close relative (see below), then it is regarded as an accommodation tie if 16 or more nights are spent there during the tax year and it is available to the individual for a continuous period of at least 91 days.

A close relative for the accommodation tie is a parent or grandparent, brother or sister, child or grandchild aged 18 or over. Also counted are blood or half-blood relatives or someone related through marriage or civil partnership. Adopted children are also counted as children for these purposes.

Care needs to be taken if staying with non-relatives. If a person were to stay with (say) a good friend, then if that friend was prepared to put the individual up for at least 91 days (or the Revenue could show this), an accommodation tie would occur even if he or she only spent one night there. It is therefore advisable, in these situations, that the individual is able to show that the accommodation was not available to him or her for 91 days.

Short stays in hotels or guesthouses will be excluded, provided the individual has not booked a room for at least 91 days continuously in a tax year, subject to the 16-day rule mentioned above. Also accommodation let out commercially is excluded.

An accommodation tie has less permanence and degree of stability than a "home" has for the purposes of the automatic UK test (see **2.2.3**). For example, a holiday home does not count for the home automatic UK test, but does for the accommodation tie test.

With regards to the accommodation tie, HMRC have indicated that, if needs be, they will enquire into whether an individual has an accommodation tie. Therefore, it is advisable to make sure the facts surrounding a place an individual stays at while in the UK are clear and everything is well documented, e.g. visits to the accommodation etc. (See HMRC's RDR3 Annex A.)

Work tie

A work tie for a tax year occurs if more than three hours of work a day are performed in the UK on at least 40 days in that year (whether continuously or intermittently). However, there are special rules about what constitutes three hours of UK work for people working on board a vehicle, aircraft or ship which is performing cross border travel (see **2.3.17**).

90 days tie

A 90-day tie for a tax year is where the individual has spent more than 90 days in the UK *in either or both of the two previous tax years.* (Individuals often misunderstand this tie to being 90 days spent in the tax year being looked at and not the two previous tax years.)

The deeming rule below does not apply when looking at this tie.

Country tie

A country tie for a tax year is if the UK is the country in which the individual is present at midnight for the greatest number of days in that tax year. If presence in a country at midnight is the same for two or more other countries in a tax year, and one of those countries is the UK, then it is a country tie for that tax year if that is the greatest number of days spent in any countries in that tax year.

Example – counting ties

Bruce has always lived in the UK.

He left the UK on 15 April 2018 to commence a work assignment in Dubai for five years for his UK employer and he moved into employer-provided accommodation when he arrived in Dubai on 16 April 2018.

His wife Sheila and their children Kylie, who is 4, and Jason, who is 6, remained living in the family home in Oxfordshire. Part of Bruce's work involves travelling to the UK to visit customers and suppliers and to report back to his UK employer and attend meetings there. During 2018-19 he spent 60 days working in the UK and his total number of midnights in the UK during the tax year was 82.

Bruce does not meet any of the automatic overseas and UK tests. He therefore needs to look at the sufficient ties test to establish his UK tax residence for 2018-19.

He has four ties with the UK during 2018-19:

- family;
- accommodation;
- work; and
- 90 days

As Bruce has four ties and is a leaver, this means that to be non-resident for 2018-19 he can only spend up to 15 midnights in the UK. This is not the case and so he will remain a resident for 2018-19 and will remain taxable in the UK on his worldwide income. This will be a hardship for him, as his gross salary was reduced by his UK employer to reflect the fact that the UAE does not tax salaries and so, as a non-resident, he would not be taxed on his earnings.

To be non-resident, Bruce would need to consider reducing the number of days he spends working in the UK to below 40 days, but even then he would still only be able to visit the UK for fewer than 46 midnights if he had three ties and worked more than 30 days in the UK (when he would still not satisfy the third automatic overseas test).

Assuming his family did not want to move to Dubai, or cannot move there because of the children's education, he would need to consider either reducing the number of days he spends in the UK generally to below 46 (perhaps by meeting up with his family outside the UK) or reducing the number of days he works in the UK to below 31 (so that he can satisfy the third automatic overseas test and working full-time overseas).

Law: FA 2013, Sch. 45 para. 17 to 20

Guidance: HMRC's RDR3 2.1 to 2.18 (pages 30 to 32)

Deeming rule

An anti-avoidance rule, known as the deeming rule, applies (since 2013-14) for those individuals who spend a large number of days in the UK, without being present at midnight.

This deeming rule will apply to individuals who:

- have been resident in the UK for one or more of the three previous tax years, i.e. a leaver;
- have at least three of the ties under the sufficient ties test (see **2.2.4**) for a tax year; and
- are present in the UK on more than 30 days at some point, but not at midnight, during the tax year concerned.

If an individual meets all of the above, then any days in excess of 30 days where he is present in the UK at any point but not at midnight, will be a day of presence and so will be included when establishing the number of days he has spent in the UK during a tax year.

Exceptional circumstances

For certain aspects of the SRT, days spent in the UK due to exceptional circumstances which are beyond the individual's control and which were unforeseen, such as national or local emergencies (e.g. natural disasters, civil unrest or war) or sudden or life threatening illness or injury, may be disregarded when day counting, although the number of days which can be disregarded due to exceptional circumstances will be restricted to 60 days in any tax year. The individual must have an intention after the exceptional circumstances have ended to leave the UK. HMRC have indicated that if someone actually does leave after the exceptional circumstances have ceased, then this is evidence that that person had this intention. Travel problems such as traffic congestion, delayed/cancelled trains which (say) cause a flight to be missed, will not be regarded as exceptional circumstances.

Disputes may arise with HMRC as to what exactly can count as an exceptional circumstance.

Transit days

In addition, if an individual is present in the UK at midnight but is just in transit as a passenger (e.g. travelling between two countries outside the UK), then that day will not be regarded as a day of presence providing certain conditions are satisfied. The person must not carry out anything in the UK that is unrelated to his or her passage through the UK, for example attending a business meeting, visiting family or friends, going to the theatre or cinema, and so on. The individual must also leave the UK the next day.

Minor activities performed in the UK while in transit, such as catching up on work emails, could potentially cause this exemption not to apply.

Law: FA 2013, Sch. 45, para. 22 and 23
Guidance: HMRC's RDR3 para. 3.1 to 3.9 (pages 31 to 38, Annex B)

2.2.6   Split-year treatment – introduction

If it is established under the SRT that a person is resident in the UK for a tax year, this will be for the whole tax year, so from 6 April to the following 5 April, regardless of when the person may have departed from or arrived in the UK. This will mean that the individual will remain taxable in the UK on his or her worldwide income and gains for all of the tax year, potentially resulting in double tax or – if the individual has moved to a country that does not impose tax, such as some Middle Eastern countries – in income and gains becoming taxed, which otherwise would not have been had he or she broken UK tax residence.

However, split-year treatment may apply to split a tax year between (i) a UK part when the individual is taxed as a resident and (ii) an overseas part, when he or she is taxed as if non-resident, even though technically the individual remains resident for all of the tax year. Prior to 6 April 2013, split-year treatment was not included in the tax legislation as it is now and was covered only in Revenue concessions ESC A11 (for income) and ESC D2 (for capital gains).

Under the current tax legislation, there are various "Cases" (situations) depending on whether an individual is arriving in or leaving the UK. If a person satisfies one of these Cases, then split-year treatment will apply – there is no choice in the matter if this happens, i.e. an individual cannot choose whether or not split-year treatment applies if the conditions for a Case are satisfied. For all Cases the individual must be resident for the tax year of departure from, or arrival to, the UK, so if an individual is not resident for the tax year of departure or arrival, then he or she does not need to consider split-year treatment.

Law: FA 2013, Sch. 45, Pt. 3
Guidance: HMRC's RDR3, chapter 5 (pages 52-70)

2.2.7   *Relevant Cases for those leaving the UK*

Case 1 – an individual commences working full-time overseas

The individual must:

- have been resident in the previous tax year;
- satisfy the third automatic overseas test – i.e. the test for working sufficient hours overseas (see **2.2.2 (3)**) – for the following tax year after the tax year of departure from the UK;
- satisfy the following overseas criteria for the period from the day the individual starts working overseas for more than three hours per day to the following 5 April:
  - o he works sufficient hours overseas over the above period. (This will be calculated in accordance with the sufficient hours worked overseas calculation shown in **Appendix 5** and any gaps between overseas employments will be restricted in accordance to HMRC's table below.);
  - o during this period of overseas work there are no significant breaks in his work (see **2.2.2(3)**);
  - o the number of days in the above period upon which the individual does more than three hours' work per day in the UK must not exceed the permitted limit set out in the HMRC table shown below; and
  - o the number of days spent in the UK generally during the above period, cannot exceed the permitted limit set by the HMRC table shown below.

HMRC Table in respect of permitted limits for Cases 1 and 2 (see below)

Overseas part of year starts on						
	6 to 30 Apr	1 to 31 May	1 to 30 June	1 to 31 July	1 to 31 Aug	1 to 30 Sept
Permitted limit for (i) days in the UK where more than 3 hours work are performed per day and (ii) the maximum number of days that can be subtracted for gaps between employments for the purposes of the sufficient hours worked overseas test [See **Appendix 5**]	30	27	25	22	20	17
Permitted limit on days spent generally in the UK	90	82	75	67	60	52

Overseas part of year starts on							
	1 to 31 Oct	1 to 30 Nov	1 to 31 Dec	1 to 31 Jan	1 to 29 Feb	1 to 31 Mar	1 to 5 Apr
Permitted limit for (i) days in the UK where more than 3 hours work are performed per day and (ii) the maximum number of days that can be subtracted for gaps between employments for the purposes of the sufficient hours worked overseas test [See **Appendix 5**]	15	12	10	7	5	2	0
Permitted limit on days spent generally in the UK	45	37	30	22	15	7	0

The overseas part will be from when the employee commences working more than three hours per day overseas until 5 April, the UK part being from 6 April until the day before this.

Example 1

Frank, an employee, leaves the UK on 10 October 2018 and starts working overseas on 15 October 2018 for more than three hours per day and is resident for all of 2018-19 under the SRT. In order for Case 1 split-year treatment to apply for this tax year, Frank must not perform more than 15 days of work in the UK (days of more than three hours' work) from 15 October 2018 to 5 April 2019 and must also not visit the UK for any reason for more than 45 midnights during this period.

Assuming Frank satisfies all the other conditions for Case 1 to apply, the overseas part of 2018-19 will be from 15 October 2018 to 5 April 2019, the UK part being from 6 April to 14 October 2018.

An important point to highlight is that the individual must be non-resident for the tax year following the tax year of departure, as a result of satisfying the sufficient hours worked overseas test at **2.2.2(3)**. It does not matter if the individual is non-resident under another test: if he or she does not satisfy this test then Case 1 split-year treatment will not apply. It is important, therefore, that this point is highlighted to individuals when they leave the UK and are relying on Case 1 to split the tax year. This is particularly true if they are moving to a country where their earnings and income will not be taxed and potentially there is no double tax treaty with the UK (e.g. some Middle Eastern countries when very often an individual's spouse and children remain in the UK) and so he or she cannot rely on Case 3 to split the tax year of departure from the UK.

If an individual were (say) to be made redundant, or cease overseas employment for some other reason during the tax year following the departure tax year, then there is a very real chance that he will not satisfy the conditions for this Case to apply. The potential result is that he will remain taxable in the UK on his worldwide income until 5 April following his departure from the UK, despite being non-resident for the following tax year under another test of the SRT.

Even if the individual managed to satisfy the sufficient hours worked overseas test (see **Appendix 5**) for the tax year after the tax year of departure, and made minimal visits to the UK, if there was a break of more than 30 consecutive days between the two employments then again the sufficient work overseas test will not have been satisfied. This is because there would have been a significant break in the overseas employment (a break of at least 31 consecutive days where no overseas work has been performed and the individual is not on annual, sick or parental leave).

Example 2

Continuing the above example, say in the tax year following the year of his departure from the UK 2019-20, Frank was headhunted and offered another job overseas which he accepts. He decides to delay the start of his new employment overseas and takes the opportunity to travel for a couple of months. He visits the UK during 2019-20 for 14 midnights.

Even though Frank is not resident for 2019-20 under the first automatic overseas test (see **2.2.2(1)**), he does not satisfy the third automatic overseas test (see **2.2.2(3)**) and so Case 1 will not apply to split the 2018-19 tax year. If Case 3 split-year treatment (see below) does not apply, then he will remain taxable in the UK on his worldwide income (including his earnings overseas) and gains until 5 April 2019, unless exemption can be obtained under a double tax treaty.

As can be seen, problems can occur in respect of the filing of self-assessment tax returns, by not knowing whether or not an individual has satisfied all the conditions for Case 1 by the time the tax return needs to be filed.

Law: FA 2013, Sch. 45, Pt. 3, para. 44
Guidance: HMRC's RDR3 para. 5.9 to 5.15 (pages 53 to 57)

Case 2 – partner of an individual commencing full-time work overseas

The individual must:

- have been resident in the previous tax year;
- be not-resident under any of the SRT tests for the tax year following the year of departure;

- have a partner who qualifies for Case 1 split-year treatment either in the tax year of the individual's departure from the UK or in the previous tax year;
- on a day during the tax year, leave the UK to live with his or her partner while he or she is working overseas;
- have been living together with his or her partner in the UK either in the current or previous tax year; and
- for the period from the deemed departure day (see below) to the following 5 April, have no home in the UK (or if he or she has homes in both the UK and overseas, must spend the greater part of his or her time in the overseas home) and must not spend more than the permitted level of days in the UK during this period (see above HMRC table as this is the same as for Case 1).

A partner includes a spouse or civil partner and includes circumstances where individuals are living together as husband and wife or as civil partners.

The deemed departure day depends on when the working partner qualifies for split-year treatment. If it was in the previous tax year, then this day will be the day that the individual moves overseas to live with his or her partner. If it is in the same tax year, then the deemed departure day will be the later of when the individual leaves the UK and the first day of the overseas part of the year for the individual's partner.

Case 2 split-year treatment will equally not apply to an individual if Case 1 does not apply to the individual's partner.

Example 3

So, following on from the above example, if Frank were suddenly to be made redundant, such that he is no longer eligible for Case 1 split-year treatment, then this will have a knock-on effect with regards to Betty his wife if she were to move overseas with him, insofar as she will then not be eligible for Case 2 split-year treatment.

Issues may arise if an individual spends a significant amount of time living in the UK whilst also living in the country where his or her partner is working, or potentially in other countries. For instance, it is common for wives of employees assigned to work in the Middle East to live with their husband for part of the year and then return to live in the UK during the heat of the Middle Eastern summer. This could pose problems with the last condition above, where the wife needs to spend the greater part of her time living in the overseas home where her husband is working, particularly if she visits other countries, as the greater part of her time refers to the home in the country where her husband is working. This could also be problematical in the situation where the working partner makes numerous business visits to other countries and is accompanied by his or her partner.

If all the conditions for this Case are satisfied, then the overseas part of the year will be from the deemed departure day until the following 5 April, with the UK part being from the previous 6 April until the day before the deemed departure day.

Law: FA 2013, Sch. 45, Pt. 3, para. 45

Guidance: HMRC's RDR3 para. 5.16 to 5.21 (pages 57 to 59)

Case 3 – leaving the UK and ceasing to have a home in the UK

The individual must:

- must have been resident for the previous tax year;
- be not resident for the following tax year;
- at the beginning of the tax year of departure, have at least one home in the UK and must cease to have one in the UK at some point during the tax year, and continue not to have one from this day until the following 5 April;
- spend fewer than 16 midnights in the UK from the date he or she ceases to have a home in the UK until the following 5 April; and
- (i) within the six-month period commencing from this date, have his only home(s) in a country overseas or be regarded as tax resident in a country overseas, or (ii) spend every midnight in one overseas country during this six-month period.

The last requirement is particularly onerous to meet, as the individual needs to spend every single night in this six-month period in just one overseas country. Therefore he will not satisfy this if he were to visit another country, say on holiday or on a business visit, and spent a midnight there. Similarly, if there was a gap between the individual ceasing to have a home in the UK and then moving to the host country (the country the individual is moving to), then again this Case will not apply, e.g. if the individual leaves the UK and holidays in another country on his way to the host country. In this scenario, for Case 3 to apply, the individual will need to make sure he satisfies one of the other sufficient link tests of either having his or her only home in a country overseas or becoming tax resident in a country overseas within six months. This will be difficult if the country does not tax individuals and so has no rules on tax residence – e.g. many Middle Eastern countries – or if the country's rules for establishing tax residence mean that the individual is not a tax resident until after this six-month period.

Another issue may be what constitutes a "home". Generally, holiday homes do not; however, this could become an area of dispute with HMRC as to whether or not a property is a home, especially for properties in different countries. The above 16-day rule remains the same regardless of when the individual leaves the UK. Therefore, it will potentially be more difficult to satisfy for individuals who have left the UK earlier in the tax year.

The individual is required under this Case to cease having a home in the UK. Many expats moving abroad, especially those working overseas, often retain their home in the UK and do not rent it out while away, so it remains available for the individual's own use. This is particularly common with individuals who are working in the Middle East, where the individual's spouse and family may have remained living in the family home in the UK. The individual will not then have ceased to have a home in the UK and so will not satisfy this Case. In this scenario the only Case under which split-year treatment may apply is Case 1, where it is important to ensure that the third automatic overseas test is satisfied for the tax year following the tax year of departure.

The overseas part of the split year will be from when the individual ceases to have a UK home until the following 5 April, with the UK part being from the previous 6 April until the day before he or she ceases to have a UK home.

Example 4

Peter has been assigned to Dubai for a few years by his UK employer and departs the UK during 2018-19, remaining resident for this year under the SRT. His wife and family remain living in the family home in the UK, where he stays when visiting the UK.

During 2019-20, his UK employer goes through difficult times and has to make staff redundant, Peter being one of them. He remains living overseas and is not resident for 2019-20 under the sufficient ties test. He eventually finds new employment with another employer in Dubai and commences working for them two months after being made redundant.

Even though Peter is not resident for 2019-20, he has not satisfied the third automatic overseas test of working sufficient hours overseas, as there was a significant break in his overseas employment of more than 30 consecutive days, meaning that Case 1 split-year treatment does not apply for 2018-19.

Because he has maintained his home in the UK, Case 3 split-year treatment will also not apply, resulting in his Dubai earnings and any other overseas income and gains (including UK gains after leaving) remaining taxable in the UK until 5 April 2019. This would be a particular issue if Peter's salary reflected the fact that he is not taxed in the UAE.

As can be seen, careful planning will be required to try and avoid earnings after leaving the UK remaining taxable in the UK, especially if there is no double tax treaty between the UK and the host country, and so no possibility of treaty exemption / relief from UK tax (see **2.3.3**). This may be of particular concern to individuals who are working in a country where their earnings etc. are not taxed, such as in the Middle East.

If more than one Case above applies, then the legislation sets out which Case takes priority – Case 1 always takes precedence over the other two Cases, with Case 2 taking priority over Case 3.

Law: FA 2013, Sch. 45, Pt. 3, para. 46 and 54
Guidance: HMRC's RDR3 para. 5.22 to 5.25 (pages 59 to 60)

2.2.8   Relevant Cases for those arriving in the UK

Case 4 – starting to have a home only in the UK

This Case will apply if the individual:

- was not resident in the tax year prior to the year of arrival;
- has his or her only home in the UK (or all homes in the UK if more than one home) some time during the tax year and continues to do so for the rest of the tax year, not having met the test at the start of the tax year; and
- does not meet the sufficient ties test (see **2.2.4**) for the overseas part of the tax year, i.e. from the previous 6 April to the day before the individual starts to satisfy the only home test.

The only home test in this respect is different to the only home test under the automatic UK tests under **2.2.3(2)** above. The test is satisfied if the individual has only one home and that is in the UK or if more than one home and they are all in the UK. This means that if someone has a home overseas that takes them time to dispose of after moving to the UK, i.e. there are delays in selling the overseas home, then this Case may not be met depending on the circumstances.

Example 1

Frank, from the previous example, returns to the UK during 2021-22 after his time working overseas, during which he purchased a home abroad. If he decided to rent this out once he moved out of it, then it will cease being a home for him. If he sold it, it would potentially remain a home for him until it is sold. If he kept it for his own use and used it as a holiday home then, as mentioned above, a holiday home is not regarded as a home. However, Frank may well find he is in dispute with the Revenue over this, especially if he is relying on this Case to split 2021-22 and establishing when, if at all, it turns into a holiday home.

The UK part is from when the individual first meets the only home test, the overseas part being from 6 April to the day before this.

Law: FA 2013, Sch. 45, Pt. 3, para. 47
Guidance: HMRC's RDR3 para. 5.26 to 5.29 (pages 60 to 62)

Case 5 – starting full-time work in the UK

This Case is satisfied if:

- an individual was not resident in the tax year prior to the tax year of arrival;
- there is a period of 365 days falling in the tax year (in full or part of) where the full-time employment in the UK test as explained in **2.2.3 (3)** is satisfied; and
- the individual has not met the sufficient ties test (see **2.2.4**) in the overseas part of the tax year, i.e. from 6 April to the day before he or she starts working full-time in the UK.

The UK part starts on the first day of the above 365-day period when the individual does more than three hours' work in the UK, the overseas part being from 6 April to the day before this day.

Law: FA 2013, Sch. 45, Pt. 3, para. 48
Guidance: HMRC's RDR3 para. 5.30 to 5.32 (pages 62 to 64)

Case 6 – ceases full-time work overseas

This is for when an individual returns to the UK following a period of working full-time abroad and when he:

- is resident in the tax year following the tax year of arrival;
- was not resident in the previous tax year because he satisfied the sufficient hours worked overseas test (the third automatic overseas test under **2.2.2(3)**), but was resident in one or more of the four tax years prior to this previous tax year (e.g. for an employee returning to the UK during 2018-19, it will be in respect of the tax years 2013-14 to 2016-17);
- satisfies the sufficient hours worked overseas test under **2.2.2(3)** (see **Appendix 5**) during the period from 6 April to the last day the employee performs more than three hours' work overseas. In this respect, the limits of days worked in the UK and visits generally to the UK during the overseas part of the year are modified as per the HMRC table below, as well as the permissible gap between any

overseas employments. There must be no significant breaks in the overseas work.

UK part of tax year starts on						
	6 to 30 Apr	1 to 31 May	1 to 30 June	1 to 31 July	1 to 31 Aug	1 to 30 Sept
Permitted limits in the overseas part of the tax year for (i) days in the UK where more than 3 hours' work is performed per day and (ii) the maximum number of days that can be subtracted for gaps between employments for the purposes of the sufficient hours worked overseas test (see **Appendix 5**)	2	5	7	10	12	15
Permitted limit on days spent in the UK in the overseas part of the tax year	7	15	22	30	37	45

	1 to 31 Oct	1 to 30 Nov	1 to 31 Dec	1 to 31 Jan	1 to 29 Feb	1 Mar to 5 Apr
UK part of tax year starts on						
Permitted limits in the overseas part of the tax year for (i) days in the UK where more than 3 hours' work is performed per day and (ii) the maximum number of days that can be subtracted for gaps between employments for the purposes of the sufficient hours worked overseas test (see **Appendix 5**)	17	20	22	25	27	30
Permitted limit on days spent in the UK in the overseas part of the tax year	52	60	67	75	82	90

The overseas part of the year is from 6 April until the last day the individual performs more than three hours' work per day overseas, the UK part being from the day after this.

This Case is intended to be for employees who are usually living in the UK, who have been working overseas for a few years and who are returning to the UK. If an individual has been working for a number of years overseas, then it is very likely he or she will not be eligible for Case 6 split-year treatment, because despite having been working full-time overseas, the employee was not resident in any of the four tax years prior to the tax year before the tax year of arrival.

Example 2

Frank, from Example 1 above, ceased working overseas and returned to the UK in August 2025, so during the 2025-26 tax year. He would not satisfy this Case even if he was not resident for 2024-

25 under the third automatic overseas test, because he would have been not resident for all the tax years 2020-21 to 2023-24. If, say, he had come back during 2022-23 then he would have been resident in one of the four tax years prior to 2021-22 and so satisfy this four-year rule.

Law: FA 2013, Sch. 45, Pt. 3, para. 49
Guidance: HMRC's RDR3 para. 5.33 to 5.39 (pages 65 to 67)

Case 7 – partner of someone ceasing to work full-time overseas

This Case applies where the individual:

- returns to the UK with his partner who has been in full-time work overseas, but ceases to work overseas and relocates to the UK and satisfies Case 6 above for either the current or previous tax year;
- was not resident for the previous tax year;
- during the tax year concerned, returns to the UK so that he and his partner can continue to live with each other;
- is resident for the following tax year;
- for the period from 6 April to the day before the deemed arrival day (see below), has no home in the UK or, if he does, spends the greater part of his time living in an overseas home; and
- during this period does not exceed the permitted number of days in the UK (see HMRC table above).

The term "partner" for this Case has the same meaning as that under Case 2 (see **2.2.7**).

The deemed arrival day is the later of (a) the day the individual returns to the UK to live with his or her partner or (b) the start of the UK part of the tax year in respect of the individual's partner under Case 6.

The overseas part is from 6 April to the day before the deemed arrival day, the UK part being from this day until 5 April.

This Case would not apply to an individual who returned before his or her partner in an earlier tax year to that of the partner.

Example 3

Betty, Frank's wife, returned to the UK on 15 February 2022 to prepare for their move back to the UK and was resident for 2021-22 by satisfying the only home in the UK test under **2.2.3(2)**. Frank did not return until 21 April 2022, after his overseas employment ceased, which means that Betty would not qualify for Case 7 split-year treatment for 2021-22, even if Frank qualifies for Case 6 split-year treatment for 2022-23, because she returned in a tax year prior to the tax year in which Frank returned (2022-23).

Law: FA 2013, Sch. 45, Pt. 3, para.50
Guidance: HMRC's RDR3 para. 5.40 to 5.43 (pages 67 to 69)

Case 8 – starting to have a home in the UK

This Case will apply if the individual:

- was not resident in the previous tax year;
- does not have a home in the UK at the start of the tax year, but acquires one during the tax year and continues to have one until the following 5 April and throughout all of the following tax year;
- remains resident for the following tax year and does not qualify for split-year treatment for this following year; and
- does not meet the sufficient ties test (see **2.2.4**) during the overseas part of the tax year, i.e. from 6 April to the day before first acquiring a home in the UK.

This case is subtly different to Case 4 in that this is just to do with acquiring a home in the UK as opposed to having a home *only* in the UK. Care needs to be taken that there are no gaps in between different homes acquired in the UK, otherwise this Case will not apply even if another home is acquired later in the tax year (e.g. if someone first lives in rented property and then purchases a property, but a gap appears in between for whatever reason).

For individuals who have maintained a home in the UK while living overseas, this Case will not apply.

Example 4

For instance in example 4 at **2.2.7**, involving Peter, if he were to return to the UK to live, Case 8 would not apply because he has maintained a home in the UK throughout his time living overseas.

The overseas part of the year is 6 April to the day before first acquiring a home in the UK, the UK part being from this day until 5 April.

Law: FA 2013, Sch. 45, Pt. 3, para. 51

Guidance: HMRC's RDR3 para. 5.44 to 5.46 (pages 69 to 70)

Split-year date

In respect of all the Cases 4 to 8, reference is made to "the split-year date" which is the last day of the overseas part of the split tax year. This date is then used to establish which Case takes priority if more than one applies.

- Generally Case 6 has priority over the other Cases unless Case 5 has an earlier split-year date;
- if Case 6 does not apply, then Case 7 will take priority unless again Case 5 has an earlier split-year date; and finally
- if Cases 6 and 7 do not apply, then the Case with the earliest split-year date will apply.

Below is an HMRC table which shows the permitted level of days an individual can spend in the UK in the overseas part of the tax year when looking to see if the sufficient ties test (see **2.2.4**) has been met or not.

Law: FA 2013, Sch. 45, Pt. 3, para. 55

HMRC table in respect of modified limits for day count tests in respect of Cases 4, 5 and 8

Day before satisfying only home, having a home or full-time work in the UK tests						
	6 to 30 April	1 to 31 May	1 to 30 June	1 to 31 July	1 to 31 Aug	1 to 30 Sept
For 15 substitute	1	2	4	5	6	7
For 45 substitute	4	7	11	15	19	22
For 90 substitute	7	15	22	30	37	45
For 120 substitute	10	20	30	40	50	60

Day before satisfying only home, having a home or full-time work in the UK tests						
	1 to 31 Oct	1 to 30 Nov	1 to 31 Dec	1 to 31 Jan	1 to 28 Feb	1 March to 5 April
For 15 substitute	9	10	11	12	14	15
For 45 substitute	26	30	34	37	41	45
For 90 substitute	52	60	67	75	82	90
For 120 substitute	70	80	90	100	110	120

Example

Jane returned to live in the UK during October 2018, having been not resident for UK tax purposes for the previous five tax years (so an arriver), and not having performed any work in the UK during this time. Assume that her overseas home ceased during October

2018 and her split-year date also falls in this month. If, say, she had two ties during the overseas part of 2018-19, then from the above table she can spend fewer than 71 midnights in the UK during the overseas part of the tax year (for the full tax year the requirement would be in the UK for up to 120 midnights to satisfy the sufficient ties test as an arriver with two ties) and still satisfy the requirement that she does not have any sufficient ties in the UK during the overseas part of 2018-19.

For all the Cases above, when looking at the sufficient ties test for the overseas part of the tax year, only the ties in existence during this part of the year are considered, except for the family tie which needs to be looked at for the whole tax year and not just the overseas part of the year. Any day count tests are modified for the overseas part of the year.

Generally an individual can have two successive tax years that are split years, unless specifically excluded (such as for Case 8).

The legislation on split-year treatment sets out the rules for taxing different types of income in a split year. In the absence of any special rules for a specific type of income or gains, that income or gain will be taxed as if the individual is resident for all of the tax year.

With regards to capital gains, prior to 6 April 2013, split-year treatment, as for income, was given under a Revenue concession, ESC D2. Unlike ESC A11, though, it was much harder for an individual to qualify for split-year treatment. Such treatment was only available if he or she had been not resident in all the previous five years when coming to the UK or, if leaving, had been not resident and not "ordinarily resident" (a concept abolished since 6 April 2013) for four of the previous seven tax years. In addition, there was always doubt as to whether or not a gain in the non-residence part of the split tax year, especially if a large gain, would be taxed as the Revenue could have denied the concession on the grounds that ESC D2 was just being used to avoid tax.

The new split-year treatment in place since 6 April 2013 applies equally to both income and capital gains, meaning that an individual will not be taxed on any gains accruing during the overseas part of a tax year (any losses accruing in the overseas part will not be allowable). This gives more certainty than was the case before with ESC D2.

Both income and gains in the overseas part of a tax year will be subject to the temporary non-residence rules (see **2.2.11**).

If split-year treatment does not apply, then a person's income or gains may be taxed in both the UK and the host country where he or she is living. In this scenario, any double tax treaty in place between the UK and the host country will need to be looked at to see if treaty exemption or relief is available to alleviate any double tax that may arise (see **2.3.3**). When looking at double tax treaties, split-year treatment does not apply, so an individual is regarded as being resident for all of the UK tax year when looking at the residence of an individual under a double tax treaty.

Example

Kulvinda and Meena left the UK to live permanently in Australia on 11 November 2018. They kept their property in the UK and decided not to rent it out, as they will be visiting family at least once a year and so want to stay in it while visiting the UK. For the first few years, they also want to be able to move back to the UK easily, in case the move to Australia does not work out for them.

After leaving the UK, they visit family and friends in Asia and make a holiday of their journey to Australia. So they do not arrive in Australia until 6 January 2019. They initially live in temporary accommodation until 31 January before finding a more permanent place to live which is rented.

It takes them a while to find suitable jobs and neither of them has a job until after 5 April 2019. Under the SRT, Kulvinda and Meena are both resident in the UK for 2018-19, so they need to see if split-year treatment applies.

Case 1 will not apply as they did not start work in Australia until after 5 April 2019, so during the 2019-20 tax year.

Case 2 will, therefore, not apply either.

This just leaves Case 3, leaving the UK and ceasing to have a home there. However, this Case will also not apply because they still have their home in the UK available to them after leaving.

Had they rented out their UK home when they left, so that it was no longer available to them, then assuming they did not visit the UK before 6 April 2019, Case 3 may have applied. This would also have been on the basis that their only home was in Australia before 11 May 2019, six months from leaving the UK, or that they became tax resident in Australia within this time. In this situation, they would not be able to rely on the condition that they spent every midnight in Australia for this six-month period after leaving on 11 November 2018, as they visited and holidayed in Asia on their way out to Australia. Had either of them found work in Australia prior to 6 April 2019, then Cases 1 and 2 would need to be considered, as well as Case 3. If Cases 1 or 2 applied then these would take precedence over Case 3 in establishing when 2018-19 is split.

In the first scenario, when none of the Cases apply, then Kulvinda and Meena will both remain taxable in the UK on their worldwide income until 5 April 2019, assuming they are not resident for 2019-20. If their only real source of income is earnings then this may not be such an issue. However, if they had other income outside the UK, such as investment income, then they would need to look at the double tax treaty between the UK and Australia (or with the country in which the income/gain is sourced) to see if any tax relief is available.

2.2.9 Record keeping

HMRC's RDR3 sets out in a lot of detail the records they expect individuals to be keeping for the purposes of the SRT, which can be quite onerous, especially with regards to hours worked. Detailed evidence must be kept in respect of work days and hours, and where these are performed and what work activity was performed, including training and travelling, as it is likely HMRC will scrutinise this area in great detail.

The location of work for tax purposes is where it is physically performed by the individual, regardless of where the employee is employed, from where he is paid, or where the employer is located. It has, therefore, always been good practice for expats to keep a travel diary that shows where they have been and what they were doing on each day, e.g. whether any given travel was undertaken for work purposes or for personal reasons such as holiday. Under the SRT more detailed records are required, including the number of hours per day worked, so that it can be established whether or not a person has worked for more than three hours either in the UK or overseas. This level of record keeping does require a certain amount of diligence and discipline on the part of the individual, which can be difficult for busy expats, so may well be a challenge for many. To get round this, expats will sometimes arrange for their PA to keep these travel diaries and so effectively keep a timesheet.

Such a timesheet may have the following headings:

• Date • Activity i.e. whether work, holiday, sick etc. • Hours worked • The country where the above hours are worked • Days in the UK at midnight – for any reason	• Days worked in the UK for more than three hours per day • Days on annual, sick or parental leave • Non-working days while on annual, sick or parental leave, e.g. weekends, public holidays etc. • Employment gaps • Any days spent in the UK as a result of exceptional circumstances – *including details of what these circumstances are*

Such a timesheet, if in a spreadsheet format, may also calculate whether sufficient hours are being worked overseas (see **Appendix 5**), so that action may be taken if it looks like this may not be achieved for the tax year concerned.

In addition, records will need to be kept if working while travelling to and from the UK. Any work done on a journey to or from the UK will be regarded as overseas work:

(i)   for journeys to the UK, the overseas work ceases when a person disembarks his or her plane, ship, train etc. that takes them into the UK;

(ii)   for journeys from the UK, the overseas work starts when an individual embarks on their plane, ship, train, etc.

Records will therefore need to be kept to be able to show when a person embarks or disembarks his or her plane, ship, train, etc., together with the entry and exit points to and from the UK. Internal journeys within the UK will need to be recorded separately.

The above details are necessary for the purposes of the automatic overseas and UK tests and will help to determine whether a person is performing full-time work overseas or in the UK if he or she were to return there. An employee may well think he is working full-time without the need to keep records, but the employee needs to be able to back this up with documentary evidence in case HMRC were to query it, especially if the individual is relying on Cases 1, 5 or 6 for split-year treatment (see **2.2.7** and **2.2.8**). In addition, because of the way the legislation is drafted, some surprising and unexpected results may arise whereby someone is not regarded as working full-time, even though the individual may be convinced otherwise. For instance:

(i) an employee on a rota basis of working a few weeks and then having a few weeks off, where the individual's time off is not regarded as annual leave in his employment contract, may not have worked enough time while working to satisfy the sufficient hours worked test; or

(ii) employees working a typical 9-to-5 day, five days a week, are unlikely to satisfy the sufficient hours worked test.

It will be particularly important to keep documentation showing when something has *not* been done, e.g. that an individual has not worked more than three hours a day in the UK. HMRC can request documentation such as emails, notes, correspondence, agreements, etc., so it is important to keep these types of documents. This is especially true if an employee moves from one employer to another, as it will be more difficult to obtain such documentation from a previous employer should HMRC request this at a later date.

In addition to a travel diary, individuals need to keep travel documentation such as travel itineraries, boarding cards and tickets, as well as documentation such as bank and credit card statements, and mobile phone bills, which show where a person has been using ATMs, debit and credit cards and mobile phones, etc. This documentation must obviously back up what the individual says! So if an individual is claiming that he was absent from the UK on a particular day, his bank statements may prove otherwise by showing that he was withdrawing cash from an ATM (automatic teller machine) in the UK, or his phone bill or credit card statements may show that he must in fact have been in the UK, and so on.

Particular care needs to be taken if working in both the Republic of Ireland and in Northern Ireland and travelling between the two countries. Should border controls arise between the two countries as a result of Brexit, then records of trips across the border may be available to both commuters and HMRC, thereby helping to establish either non-residence or residence.

Where an individual stays will also need to be recorded to help establish where his home is (or, as the case may be, where his homes are). HMRC would be looking for evidence to establish whether his home is in the UK or overseas and RDR3 lists the details and documents HMRC would be expecting individuals to keep. What is regarded as a home for these purposes is another area that is expected to cause future disputes with HMRC, as the legislation in this respect is not clear cut, so it is important that the details listed in RDR3 are kept.

As can be seen from the above and RDR3, numerous details and documents need to be kept to be able to show where an individual performs his or her work, how many hours per day the individual works, details of what work is performed, details of the person's travelling, where his or her home is, and details of the individual's lifestyle, and so on. As mentioned above, this may prove to be a challenge for some expats.

It will be difficult in negative situations to show that something has not been done, e.g. that an employee has not done more than three hours' work in the UK. Any documentation that can show this must be kept, as it is anticipated this may be an area of the SRT which may cause disputes with HMRC.

Good records will help considerably when establishing a person's residence status for a tax year and will potentially enable the individual to take action sooner, if it looks like he or she may become resident again in the UK, especially when unexpected events occur such as visiting the UK for family emergencies.

Guidance: HMRC's RDR3 chapter 7 (pages 80-82)

2.2.10   *Dual residence*

Each country's domestic tax legislation establishes an individual's residence status for its own tax purposes – regardless of that person's residence status elsewhere – and countries around the world have very different rules for establishing where and from what date an individual is resident. This often leads to individuals being dual residents, i.e. resident for tax purposes in two countries at the same time, usually in the individual's home country (where he normally lives and which he has perhaps just left) and the host country (the country to which he has moved). The individual is then in a potential double tax situation, with his income and gains taxed in both countries, as most countries tax their residents on their worldwide income and gains. In practice, expats are often surprised (and sometimes in utter disbelief!) that this can happen. In this situation, an individual would need to look and see if there is a double tax treaty (see **2.3.3**) between the two countries concerned, which:

(i)   will establish which country he is resident in *for treaty purposes only* (and not for domestic tax purposes); and

(ii)   will potentially provide partial or complete relief from any double taxation.

For UK tax purposes, as was mentioned above, a person is resident for all of a tax year, which means from 6 April to the following 5 April. This can very often lead to individuals being dual resident until 5 April after leaving the UK, or from 6 April before he or she arrives if coming to the UK. The date from which the person is regarded as resident in the country to which he is moving, and the date from when the individual ceases to be resident in the country he has left, will both depend on that country's domestic tax legislation – it may be from when the individual arrives or leaves or it may be for all of that country's tax year (which will invariably be different to the UK's tax year) or from some other point.

In the UK a dual resident may be rescued from double taxation by the application of the split-year treatment (see **2.2.6**). However, this may not always be the case, in which case the person would then need to look at any relevant double tax treaty to establish if relief from any double tax is available (see **2.3.3**).

Example

Liz left the UK on 8 August 2018 and moved to Australia, arriving there on 12 August 2018, from which date she became resident for Australian tax purposes.

Under the statutory residence test (SRT), Liz establishes that she remains resident in the UK for all of the 2018-19 tax year, with split-year treatment not applying as she does not satisfy any of the Cases for leaving. She therefore remains taxable in the UK on her worldwide income and gains until 5 April 2019, i.e. she is a tax resident in both the UK and Australia from 12 August 2018 until 5 April 2019 and so a dual resident for this period.

Liz is a permanent resident in Australia for immigration purposes and so is taxed in Australia on her worldwide income and gains from when she arrived there on 12 August 2018, meaning that Liz is in a double tax situation from 12 August 2018 until 5 April 2019 on her worldwide income and gains. She therefore needs to look at the double tax treaty between the UK and Australia to see if treaty relief /exemption is available to relieve this double tax.

A common situation in which a person may become a dual resident is a retiree (say) who decides to spend six months of the year in the UK and the other six months in sunnier climes, for example Spain, to avoid the UK winter. This to most people would sound like an idyllic situation. Sadly, from a tax perspective, it is anything but idyllic, as the individual could very well find himself or herself as a dual resident and so potentially in a double tax situation.

In this scenario, the individual would need to look at any double tax treaty that may be in place, to see whether he or she can claim treaty exemption or relief. If no such treaty is in place, then relief for any double tax may be available under the UK's tax legislation, but this can still cause significant cash flow issues if both countries' tax liabilities need to be settled before relief for the double tax can be obtained, very often via the person's tax returns. Even if treaty exemption or relief is available, it will complicate a person's tax situation as he or she will need to obtain residence certificates from tax authorities and claim the treaty relief, as it is not given automatically.

2.2.11   Temporary non-residence

Anti-avoidance legislation exists in respect of non-residents who return to the UK within a certain time of leaving. The main aim of this legislation is stop individuals becoming non-resident for a short time during which they receive income or gains that escape taxation because the person was non-resident. For example, an individual might sell assets other than UK residential property while non-resident, and whilst therefore outside the scope of UK capital gains tax, before returning to the UK.

Anti-avoidance legislation existed prior to the introduction of the SRT on 6 April 2013, but was amended as a consequence of the SRT coming into effect, when new rules were also introduced.

The previous legislation still applies to departures from the UK prior to 6 April 2013, whereas the new legislation covers later departures. For example, TCGA 1992, s. 10A was the legislation in place prior to 6 April 2013 with regards to non-residents disposing of assets while non-resident, and s. 10AA was introduced with effect from 6 April 2013. Section 10A still applies to non-residents who left the UK prior to 6 April 2013, whereas s. 10AA applies to those non-residents who left the UK thereafter.

An individual will be treated under the legislation as a temporary non-resident if:

(a)   the individual has sole UK residence for a residence period;

(b)   immediately following that period (referred to as "period A"), one or more residence periods occur for which the individual does not have sole UK residence;

(c)   at least four out of the seven tax years immediately preceding the year of departure were either:

   (i)   a tax year for which the individual had sole UK residence, or

   (ii)   a split year that included a residence period for which the individual had sole UK residence; and

(d)   the temporary period of non-residence is five years or less.

When looking at tax years before 2013-14, and at (c) above, the legislation goes on to state:

> "(1) This paragraph applies in determining whether the test in paragraph 110(1)(c) [of FA 2013, Sch. 45] is met in relation to a tax year before the tax year 2013-14 (a "pre-commencement tax year").
>
> (2) Paragraph 110(1) is to have effect as if for paragraph (c) there were substituted—
>
>> '(c) at least 4 out of the 7 tax years immediately preceding the year of departure was a tax year meeting the following conditions—
>>
>> (i) the individual was resident in the UK for that year, and
>>
>> (ii) there was no time in that year when the individual was Treaty non-resident (see paragraph 112(3)).'
>
> (3) Whether an individual was resident in the UK for a pre-commencement tax year is to be determined in accordance with the rules in force for determining an individual's residence for that pre-commencement tax year (and not in accordance with the statutory residence test)."

The residence period referred to in the legislation above is either:

(i)   a tax year which is not a split year; or

(ii)   the overseas or UK parts of a split year.

Sole UK residence for the residence period is when the individual is resident in the UK for all of the tax year or the UK part of a split year and at no time during these periods is treaty non-UK resident. An individual is treaty non-resident if he is dual resident (see **2.2.10**) and is regarded as resident in another country other than the UK under the relevant double tax agreement as a result of the tie breaker clause (see **2.3.3**).

The temporary period of non-residence is from the end of period A until the start of the next period of residence for which the individual has sole residence in the UK.

In order for these anti-avoidance provisions not to apply, the individual's period of non-residence must be for more than five years (i.e. at least five years plus one day).

Example

Ella had spent all her life living in the UK and so had always been resident for UK tax purposes. Her UK employer assigned her to work in Belgium for a few years and she left for her overseas assignment on 1 September 2017, but visited friends in France first over the weekend before arriving in Belgium and starting work there on 4 September 2017.

Split-year treatment applied under Case 1 with the overseas part of 2017-18 starting on 4 September 2017. (Two residence periods therefore exist, (i) the UK part of 2017-18 up until 3 September and (ii) the overseas part from 4 September 2017 until 5 April 2018).

Ella returned to the UK after her overseas assignment finished on 30 November 2020, with Case 6 split-year treatment applying to split 2020-21, the UK part of the year starting on 30 November 2020, the day after she stopped working overseas.

While working in Belgium she satisfied the third automatic overseas test and working full-time overseas. As a result she is non-resident for 2018-19 and 2019-20 for UK tax purposes. She was regarded as resident for tax purposes in Belgium from when she arrived there, so from 4 September 2017, and so was a dual resident for treaty purposes from this date until 5 April 2018. Under the tie breaker clause of the double tax treaty between the UK and Belgium, she was regarded as treaty resident in Belgium from 4 September 2017 and so treaty non-resident in the UK from this date until 5 April 2018.

Ella was a sole resident in the UK up until 3 September 2017 (the end of Period A which is from 6 April to 3 September 2017). Therefore the maximum temporary period of non-residence is from 4 September 2017 until 3 September 2022. As Ella returned to the UK within this five-year period, she will be temporarily non-resident and any income or gains she received while living and working in Belgium, if covered by these provisions (see **2.2.12**), will become taxable in the UK in the tax year of her return when she becomes a sole resident again in the UK, so during 2020-21.

For temporary non-residence legislation that was in place prior to 6 April 2013, the five-year period is different – it is five full tax years. In order to avoid being temporarily non-resident, the individual under these rules therefore had to be non-resident for five complete tax years. This may still be relevant for individuals whose tax year of departure (as defined below) is before 2013-14.

Example

Say, in the above example, that Ella instead left the UK on 1 September 2012. In order to avoid being caught by these provisions, she would need to be non-resident up until 5 April 2018 and so would not be able to return and become resident until after this date if she wanted to avoid being temporarily non-resident.

The legislation refers to the "year of departure". However, for the purposes of temporary non-residence, this may be before the individual actually leaves the UK, as shown in the example below, as it is defined as the tax year consisting of or including period A. It is this "year of departure" which is relevant when establishing which temporary non-residence rules to apply, i.e. either those before or after 6 April 2013.

One such scenario is if an individual does not qualify for split-year treatment for the tax year he leaves the UK, in which case the start of the period of temporary non-residence may be dependent on when he becomes resident in the country he has moved to and the effect of any double tax treaty in place.

Example

Say that Ella in the above example left the UK on 1 September 2017. She kept her home in the UK available for her own use while away and did not satisfy the third automatic overseas test, working full-time overseas, so did not qualify for split-year treatment (so the residence period is all the 2017-18 tax year as opposed to the UK part up until 3 September 2017) and did not become resident in Belgium until 1 January 2018. If she is treaty resident in Belgium from this date (and so treaty non-resident in the UK) her period of temporary non-residence will commence on 6 April 2017, the start of 2017-18, as she will have been treaty non-resident for part of the 2017-18 tax year, the residence period, and so did not have sole UK residence for all of this residence period, the 2017-18 tax year.

Ella's "year of departure" for these provisions is therefore 2016-17. Her period of temporary non-residence is from 6 April 2017 until 30 November 2020. If, say, Ella was not resident in Belgium until after 5 April 2018, then she would have sole residence in the UK for all of 2017-18 and so the start of the period of temporary non-residence would not start potentially until after 5 April 2018.

Example 42 of RDR3 (on page 73) also shows the effect of not qualifying for split-year treatment in the year of departure from the UK.

Tax treaties may also have an effect even when split-year treatment is applicable. For example, an individual moved overseas and became treaty non-resident in the UK before the start of the overseas part of the split tax year, then for part of the UK part he would have been treaty non-resident and so cannot be a sole resident for the UK part.

The "period of return" is defined in the legislation as "the first residence period after period A for which the individual has sole UK residence". Again, as with the year of departure, this may not be in the same tax year as the individual's actual return to the UK, depending on the situation.

These anti-avoidance rules are likely to affect individuals who live overseas for a short time, so anyone intending to live overseas for potentially less than six years and with any of the income below (at **2.2.12**), or intending to sell any assets, may need to consider if he or she will be affected.

Law: TCGA 1992, s. 10A, 10AA; FA 2013, Sch. 45, Pt. 4 and Pt. 5, para. 157
Guidance: HMRC's RDR3 Chapter 6

2.2.12   *Impact on income tax, CGT and IHT*

The effect of the temporary non-residence rules is that certain types of income and capital gains which arise or accrue during a period of temporary non-residence, that are normally not taxable in the UK because the individual is non-resident, will become taxable in the UK when the individual returns to the UK. They will be taxed in the period of return. This also means that the limit of tax paid by non-residents (see **2.3.20**) does not apply.

For the effect of temporary non-residence on inheritance tax (IHT) see section **2.1.3**. The following applies to the effect of temporary non-residence for income and capital gains tax purposes.

During a period of temporary non-residence any exemption from UK tax under a double tax treaty is generally denied.

The types of income caught by these provisions include:

- certain types of pension income;
- income that is taxable under the disguised remuneration regime;
- distributions from close companies, including companies that would be close if UK resident, and write-off or release of loans to participators;
- chargeable events from life insurance policies;
- offshore income gains; and
- if an individual is a non-UK domicile and was taxed on the remittance basis while resident in the UK, the remittance of relevant foreign income during a period of temporary non-residence will be treated as remitted to the UK in the individual's period of return.

With regards to some of the more common types of income British expats may receive while non-resident:

(i) *Pensions*

HMRC's RDR3 lists at 6.14 the types of pension income affected by these provisions. The result is that if an individual receives or is entitled to such income during a period of temporary non-residence, he will be treated as having received or been entitled to the income during the individual's period of return.

See example 45 of RDR3.

(ii) *Dividends/distributions from close companies*

These were new provisions introduced at the same time as the SRT and so only apply for individuals whose year of departure from the UK is the 2013-14 tax year or later.

Any dividends or other distributions from a close company in the UK received by a "material participator" (as defined by CTA 2010, s. 457 – someone (including associates such as a spouse, child, sibling etc. (CTA 2010, s. 448)) with an interest of more than 5%) during a period of temporary non-residence will be taxed in the period of his or her return. This is also the case for any dividends/distributions received from an overseas company that would be classed as close in the UK if it were resident there.

Normally the taxation of this type of income may be affected by double tax treaties. However, the treaty provisions will be disregarded if the individual is caught by the temporary non-residence rules and taxed in the period of return. Relief will be available for any tax paid, and dividends received which relate to "post departure trade profits" as defined by ITTOIA 2005, s. 401C (basically profits arising after the individual became non-resident) will not be taxed, although this may be difficult to establish if the individual became non-resident during a period of account. Any tax credit associated with such dividends will be allowed in the period of return.

Write-offs of loans to participators during a period of temporary non-residence will also be caught and taxed as if they had occurred during the period of return, including loans made after the participator has become non-resident.

(iii) Gains from life insurance contracts

If a chargeable event gain arises from a life insurance policy when the individual is temporarily non-resident, which would have been taxable had it arisen when the individual was resident, then this will be taxed in the period of return, although there are exceptions such as gains on death. No tax liability will arise if the policy was taken out after the individual became non-resident during a period of temporary non-residence.

(iv)   Capital gains

Prior to the introduction of the SRT in April 2013, anti-avoidance measures were previously in place for capital gains made during a temporary period of non-residence. These existing measures were amended for 2013-14 onwards, but the previous provisions still apply for anyone whose year of departure from the UK is before 2013-14. For individuals whose year of departure is 2013-14 or later, the new rules apply.

Under both the old and new rules, if a non-resident sells an asset during a period of temporary non-residence, which would otherwise not be taxable in the UK because the individual is non-resident, then the gain will be taxed when the individual returns to the UK. When they are taxed depends on which set of rules they fall under.

Rules prior to 2013-14

For an individual whose year of departure from the UK is before 2013-14, the period for which he needs to be non-resident to escape being taxed on any gains that arise after leaving the UK and becoming non-resident is five full tax years. This was on the basis that he had been resident for at least four out of the seven tax years prior to the tax year of departure.

Example

Sheila left the UK during September 2012, so during the 2012-13 tax year. In order to avoid being taxed on any assets she sold after she left the UK and became non-resident, she needs to be non-resident for the five tax years 2013-14 through to and including 2017-18. If she returned to the UK and became resident after 5 April 2018, then she would not be taxed on any gains that arose during her period of non-residence. If she returned to the UK and became resident before 6 April 2018, then she would be taxed on any gains that arose while she was non-resident during the tax year of her becoming resident again. There is no concept of sole residence with the old rules.

Rules for 2013-14 onwards

For individuals whose year of departure is 2013-14 or later, their period of temporary non-residence is as explained above at **2.2.11**. Again, if an individual sells an asset while a non-resident during this period, he will be taxed on the gain during his period of return.

For both sets of rules, an individual will not be taxed on gains arising from assets purchased after leaving the UK at a time when the individual was non-resident, even if the disposal is during a period of temporary non-residence. Any losses that arose during the period of temporary non-residence will also be treated as having accrued during the period of return or the tax year in which the individual became resident again under the old rules.

With regards to the interaction of the above temporary non-residence rules and the NRCGT regime (see **3.2**), any part of the gain not subject to the NRCGT charge will be taxed under the above rules.

Law: TCGA 1992, s. 10A, 10AA, 86A; ITEPA 2003, s. 394A, 554Z4A, 554Z11A, 572A, 576A, 579CA; ITTOIA 2005, s. 368A, 401C, 408A, 413A, 420A, 465B, 689A, 832A; ITA 2007, s. 812A

2.3   Income tax

2.3.1   Rates of tax

For income that is taxable in the UK, and where relief or exemption from UK tax is not available under a double tax treaty, the same rates of tax apply to non-residents as they do to resident taxpayers. There are no special tax rates as a result of the individual being a non-resident, unlike in some countries (e.g. Australia). These income tax rates and thresholds in the UK are as follows:

	Band of taxable income (after the personal allowance) (see **2.3.2**)		Tax rates	
	2017-18	**2018-19**	**2017-18**	**2018-19**
Basic rate	£1 to £33,500	£1 to £34,500	20%	20%
Higher rate	£33,501 to £150,000	£34,501 to £150,000	40%	40%
Additional rate	Over £150,000	Over £150,000	45%	45%

Scottish rules

For 2017-18 onwards, Scottish income tax rates and bands are as follows:

	Band of taxable income (after the personal allowance) (see **2.3.2**)		Tax rates	
	2017-18	**2018-19**	**2017-18**	**2018-19**
Starter	-	£1 to £2,000	-	19%
Basic rate	£1 to £31,500	£2,001 to £12,150	20%	20%
Inter-mediate	-	£12,151 to £32,423	-	21%
Higher rate	£31,501 to £150,000	£32,424 to £150,000	40%	41%
Additional /top	Over £150,000	Over £150,000	45%	46%

The above rates and tax bands apply to Scottish taxpayers' non-dividend and non-savings income, with the UK rate thresholds and tax rates still applying when calculating the tax due on dividend and savings income.

A Scottish taxpayer can only be someone who is a UK tax resident under the SRT, so if an individual is non-resident for UK tax purposes, he will not be a Scottish taxpayer and so will not be subject to Scottish income tax. In addition to being a UK tax resident, the individual will also need to meet the following conditions if he is to be treated as a Scottish taxpayer:

- he must have a close connection with Scotland; or
- he must not have a close connection with the rest of the UK and must spend more days in Scotland than in the rest of the UK. (In this respect, a day in a part of the UK is when the individual is present in that part at midnight.) For this purpose Scotland includes the adjacent UK territorial waters up to 12 nautical miles from the shore, but not the adjacent UK continental shelf. Days spent on the latter, e.g. on an oil rig, are not days spent in any part of the UK for these purposes.

A close connection is a place of residence where the individual lives for at least part of the tax year and does not include a holiday home or a property that an individual owns but does not occupy. There needs to be a degree of continuity and it does not necessarily have to be owned by the individual, so could include rented or employer-provided property. If a person has put in a second home election nominating a residence in Scotland to be his or her main residence for CGT private residence relief purposes (see **3.2.7**), this will not make it a residence for establishing if a person is a Scottish taxpayer.

If an individual has more than one place of residence during a tax year, and one is in Scotland and another in another part of the UK, then he will be a Scottish taxpayer if his main place of residence has been in Scotland for at least as long as it has been in any other part of the UK. STTG 5000 lists what sort of evidence HMRC will look at to establish where a person's place of residence or main residence is.

If a person is regarded as a Scottish taxpayer then this will be for all of the year, although split-year treatment (as described at **2.2.6** above) will still apply in this respect for an individual who leaves or arrives in the UK during a tax year.

An individual can be either a Scottish or UK taxpayer, but cannot be both.

Rates and allowances – complicating factors

Various allowances and rates can complicate an individual's UK tax liability, one of which is the savings rate.

If an individual's taxable non-savings income is below £5,000 for 2018-19, then his or her savings income will be taxed at 0% up to this limit (which is reduced for any non-savings income, so if non-savings income is (say) £1,500, then savings income up to £3,500 is taxed at 0%) and then at the basic, higher and additional rates as normal, depending on the level of the individual's income.

The nil rate savings band of £5,000 forms part of the basic rate band, e.g. for 2018-19, the basic rate band is £34,500 so if an individual had only savings income which was more than £5,000, then he will have £29,500 left of his basic rate band for any savings income in excess of £5,000 to be taxed at basic rate.

The personal savings allowance (see **2.3.12**) works in conjunction with the starting rate for savings and does not replace it, although the savings rate band takes priority.

When establishing what rates of tax are applicable, savings income is treated as the top slice of income, but below dividend income.

Savings income includes:

- interest (per ITTOIA 2005, s. 369 to 381);
- income from purchased life annuities (per ITTOIA 2005, s. 422 to 426);
- deeply discounted securities (per ITTOIA 2005, s. 427 to 460);
- income chargeable under the accrued income scheme; and
- chargeable event gains on life policies etc. which are liable to income tax.

Prior to 2016-17, banks and building societies deducted basic rate tax from interest paid to account holders. From 2016-17, this is no longer the case, so interest is now paid gross. A repayment may be claimed of any tax that was deducted at source but which is not due, say because the interest is taxed at the savings starting rate of 0%.

Dividends in excess of the dividend allowance (£2,000 for 2018-19 – see **2.3.12**) are taxed at the following rates depending on the individual's level of taxable income:

Individual taxed at:	Rates for 2018-19
Basic rate	Dividend ordinary rate of 7.5%
Higher rate	Dividend upper rate of 32.5%
Additional rate	Dividend additional rate of 38.1%

Law: *Scotland Act 1998*, s. 80D to 80F; ITA 2007, Pt. 2
Guidance: HMRC manual *Scottish Taxpayer Technical Guidance* (STTG)

2.3.2   *Personal and other allowances*

The personal allowance is an amount of taxable income that an individual (including Scottish taxpayers – see **2.3.1**) can receive before he or she starts paying tax in the UK. For the 2018-19 tax year, the personal allowance is £11,850.

For individuals whose "adjusted net income" is more than £100,000, the personal allowance will fall by £1 for every £2 in excess of £100,000, meaning that a person will not be entitled to a personal allowance once his or her taxable income reaches £123,700 for 2018-19.

In this respect, an expat returning to work in the UK should make sure that his PAYE tax code does not include the personal allowance, if he thinks his taxable income for the year of his return will be at such a level that he will not be entitled to the allowance, or adjusted to reflect the fact that he may only receive part of the personal allowance. Failure to do this may mean that the taxpayer finds himself facing a tax liability that needs to be paid depending on his circumstances generally.

Adjusted net income

Adjusted net income for this purpose is defined by ITA 2007, s. 58 and is basically taxable income less certain reliefs for items such as pension contributions and Gift Aid payments. HMRC explain what adjusted net income is on their website at https://www.gov.uk/guidance/adjusted-net-income.

From 2016-17, all resident taxpayers are entitled to the basic personal allowance shown above, subject to the above limit. Previously, there used to be higher allowances (commonly known as age allowances), for individuals who were aged over 65 for tax years prior to 2013-14, and for those born before 6 April 1948 for the tax years 2013-14 to 2015-16.

An individual needs to be resident to be entitled to the personal allowance. However, s. 56(3) of ITA 2007 lists certain non-residents who are entitled to it, such as EEA nationals and Crown employees. Presumably, this will be changed with regards to EEA nationals following Brexit.

Prior to 2010-11, Commonwealth citizens were also entitled to the personal allowance as a non-resident, but this has no longer been the case since 6 April 2010.

Non-residents may also be entitled to the personal allowance via a double tax treaty. In this respect the individual usually needs to be a national or resident (or both) in the country with which the UK has the treaty. Not all double tax treaties enable the non-resident to claim the personal allowance, the most notable one being the treaty with the US.

HMRC's double tax digest shows whether the personal allowance can be claimed under a specific double tax treaty and, if so, the digest sets out what requirements must be met under each treaty for a non-resident to be able to claim the personal allowance. In this respect, if a non-resident is not entitled to a personal allowance under the tax legislation, then if the relevant double tax treaty requires the individual to be both a national and resident in that country to be entitled to the personal allowance and he or she is just resident and not a national or vice versa, then the non-resident will not be entitled to the personal allowance.

Example

Douglas and Florence have moved to Australia and are non-resident for 2018-19. They jointly own a rental property in the UK, which for 2018-19 produced a taxable profit of £10,000. They have no other UK sourced income. Douglas is a British citizen and so is entitled to the personal allowance as a non-resident by being a national of an EEA state. Florence is an Australian citizen, but is entitled to the personal allowance under the double tax treaty between the UK and Australia, as she is both a national and resident in Australia. This means that there is no tax liability in the UK for either of them, as their share of the taxable rental income is covered by their personal allowances.

Douglas is assigned by his Australian employer to New Zealand for a few years and Florence moves with him. Douglas will continue to be entitled to the personal allowance as an EEA citizen. Florence, however, will no longer be entitled to the personal allowance under the double tax treaty between the UK and New Zealand, as the treaty states that she must be a New Zealand national as well as resident there in order to be able to claim the personal allowance. She cannot claim the personal allowance under the treaty between the UK and Australia, as she needs to be resident there. This means that her share of the taxable income will be taxed in full, producing a tax liability of £2,000 if her 50% share is £10,000.

If, say, Douglas and Florence had instead moved to the US, and Florence was a US national rather than an Australian citizen, then in this situation, even though Florence is a national and resident in the US, under the double tax treaty between the US and the UK she is not entitled to claim the personal allowance. Once again, her share of the taxable rental income would therefore be taxed in full in the UK. As above, Douglas would still be entitled to the personal allowance being an EEA national.

HMRC have previously released a consultation document proposing that entitlement to the personal allowance be restricted for all non-residents. At the time of writing this proposal had gone on the back burner, but whether this will come to the forefront again remains to be seen, especially if the legislation needs to be changed with regards to EEA nationals following Brexit.

When calculating an individual's tax, the personal allowance is treated as reducing different types of income in a manner which produces the lowest tax liability. This is particularly important when looking at the order of set-off for investment income where the taxpayer is entitled to the dividend and savings allowances etc. (see **2.3.12**).

Transferable marriage allowance

Since 2015-16, married couples and civil partners have been able to transfer part of their personal allowance to one another subject to satisfying certain conditions. The amount of this transferable marriage allowance is set by the legislation and is 10% of the personal allowance, rounded up to the nearest £10, so for 2018-19 is £1,190. The transferable amount reduces the transferor's personal allowance, while the transferee is entitled to a reduction against his or her tax liability for this amount at basic rate. The conditions that need to be satisfied are:

- the transferor needs to make an election;
- the transferee must only be taxed at basic rate and must either be resident in the UK or entitled to the personal allowance as a non-resident (see above); and
- neither spouse or civil partner has made a claim for the married couple's allowance (see below).

In order for the transferor to be able to make an election, the individual must:

- at the time the election is made, be married to, or in a civil partnership with, the same person for all or part of the tax year;
- be entitled to the personal allowance;
- be taxed at a rate no higher than the basic rate (ordinary dividend rate); and
- (if eligible for the personal allowance as a non-resident) have hypothetical net income less than the personal allowance.

The legislation defines hypothetical net income as follows:

"(3) For the purposes of subsection (2), an individual's "hypothetical net income" is the amount that would be that individual's net income calculated at Step 2 of section 23 if that individual's income tax liability were calculated on the basis that the individual—

(a)   was UK resident for the tax year concerned (and the year was not a split year),

(b)   was domiciled in the United Kingdom for that tax year,

(c)   in that tax year, did not fall to be regarded as resident in a country outside the United Kingdom for the purposes of double taxation arrangements having effect at the time, and

(d)   for that tax year, had made a claim for any available relief under section 6 of TIOPA 2010 (as required by subsection (6) of that section).

(4) An individual's hypothetical net income for a tax year is, to the extent that it is not sterling, to be calculated by reference to the average exchange rate for the year ending on 31 March in the tax year concerned."

The above election needs to be made within four years of the end of the relevant tax year if it is made after that tax year and only applies to that tax year. If made during the relevant tax year then it remains in force until either withdrawn or the above conditions are not met or there is no matching tax reduction.

Married couple's allowance

Previously, there was a married couple's allowance available to all married couples. However, this is now only available for married couples and civil partners where one spouse/civil partner was born before 6 April 1935, so is not so common now. It is available to non-residents who are eligible for the personal allowance (see above). The relief is given as a reduction against the individual's tax liability and is restricted to the lower of:

- 10% of the allowance; and
- the individual's total income tax liability.

For marriages before 5 December 2005, the relief is given to the husband. For marriages/civil partnerships on or after this date, the relief is given to the individual with the highest total income.

Law: ITA 2007, s. 35, 45, 46, 55A-55E, 56, 58

Guidance: https://www.gov.uk/guidance/adjusted-net-income; https://www.gov.uk/government/publications/double-taxation-treaties-territory-residents-with-uk-income; https://www.gov.uk/government/consultations/restricting-non-residents-entitlement-to-the-uk-personal-allowance

2.3.3 *Double tax treaties*

Double tax treaties (sometimes referred to as conventions) are agreements between two countries (referred to as "contracting states"). The treaties do not give new taxing rights but try to allocate taxing rights between the states. They also seek to alleviate double taxation which may arise where an individual (or an entity such as a company) is taxed in two countries on the same income. (This is known as juridical double taxation, as opposed to economic double taxation where a stream of income is taxed twice, but on two separate persons, e.g. dividends where the company pays tax on the profits from which the dividends are paid and which are then taxed again on the person who receives them.)

In a federal system, consideration needs to be given to whether all the states making up the federation actually acknowledge double tax treaties. For example, some states in the US do not recognise double tax treaties.

Many countries (but not, for example, the US, which taxes its nationals on their global income regardless of where the individual is resident) tax their resident taxpayers on their worldwide income and their non-resident taxpayers on the income sourced in that country. For British expats living overseas, there is a good chance that the individual will be taxed on his worldwide income in the country where he is living (although if in the Middle East the individual is unlikely to be taxed there on his or her income). The individual will also, though, be taxed in the UK on any UK sourced income he may have, such as rental income from a UK property, meaning that this income is potentially double taxed. In this situation, an individual needs to turn to the relevant double tax treaty to see if there is exemption, or at least partial relief, from one of the country's taxes. This is often referred to as treaty relief/exemption.

The UK has numerous treaties in place with countries around the world, most of which follow the OECD model treaty – a template for treaties between developed countries. Even though the basics of a treaty may follow the OECD model, it is vital that the actual treaty is referred to, as many of the UK's various treaties differ in some way from the OECD model treaty (see commentary following the table below).

Commentary on the OECD model exists, which explains how the various articles of the treaty are to be interpreted generally and which sets out any different interpretations that specific countries may have. This commentary is therefore useful for interpreting what an article means and what it covers. A UN model treaty together with relevant commentary also exists, which is a template used more for agreements with developing nations.

Double tax treaties are made up of a number of articles on various issues, such as:

- who is covered (usually someone who is resident in one of the countries involved);
- the taxes covered by the agreement (social security (such as National Insurance contributions (NIC)) is not covered; nor is inheritance tax (IHT) (though the UK has a few specific IHT agreements with countries); nor are US state taxes);
- the residence status of a dual resident individual/entity for treaty purposes (often known as the tie-breaker clause);
- how various types of income and gains will be taxed with regard to the countries involved; and
- how double tax relief will be given.

Some of the latest double tax treaties, based on the OECD model from July 2014, will have the following articles:

Article number	Description
Chapter I – Scope of the convention	
1	Persons covered
2	Taxes covered*
Chapter II – Definitions	
3	General definitions
4	Resident (commonly referred to as the "tie-breaker clause")*
5	Permanent establishment
Chapter III – Taxation of income	
6	Income from immovable property (covers rental income from property)*
7	Business profits
8	Shipping, inland waterways transport & air transport
9	Associated enterprises
10	Dividends*
11	Interest*
12	Royalties*
13	Capital gains*
14	Deleted from latest OECD convention dated July 2014. However, many older double tax treaties will have this, often as "Independent personal services"
15	Income from employment (sometimes described as "Dependent personal services" in older treaties)*
16	Directors' fees*

Article number	Description
17	Entertainers and sportspersons
18	Pensions*
19	Government service*
20	Students (some treaties will also include details on how visiting lecturers, professors, teachers, etc. are to be taxed, sometimes in a separate article)*
21	Other income (UK's state pension often covered by this article)*
Chapter IV – Taxation of capital	
22	Capital
Chapter V – Methods of elimination of double taxation	
23A	Exemption method*
23B	Credit method*
Chapter VI – Special provisions	
24	Non-discrimination (It is this article which will state whether or not a non-resident who is not eligible for the personal allowance under UK tax legislation, is able to claim the personal allowance under the treaty – see **2.3.2**)
25	Mutual agreement procedure
26	Exchange of information
27	Assistance in the collection of taxes
28	Members of diplomatic missions and consular posts
29	Territorial extension

Article number	Description
Chapter VII – Final provisions	
30	Entry in force
31	Termination

*Articles mostly commonly used by British expats living overseas.

The above is the July 2014 OECD model convention, and gives a good indication as to what sort of issues are covered by the newer double tax treaties in place, though an updated version was published in December 2017 so future treaties will be based on the 2017 model treaty. Any reference to the OECD model treaty in this publication is in respect of the 2014 model treaty. However, many of the UK's double tax treaties have been in place for many years and so are based on earlier versions of the OECD or UN models. This will mean they do not have exactly the same articles as shown above, so it is important that the relevant double tax treaty is always referred to.

If a British expat is potentially liable to UK tax on a UK source of income or gain, one of the first steps, therefore, is to look and see if there is a relevant double tax treaty in place and – if there is – whether treaty exemption or relief is available in respect of the UK tax potentially due.

Some of the more common articles used for British expats overseas are in respect of:

- the residence tie-breaker;
- income from immovable property – rental income – see **3.1**;
- dividends – see **2.3.12**;
- interest – see **2.3.12**;
- employment income – see **2.3.9**;
- pensions – see **4.1**; and
- double tax relief – see below.

If treaty relief or exemption is available under the treaty, this needs to be claimed via the individual's self-assessment tax return using forms HS302 (if treaty relief is claimed by a dual resident) or HS304 (if a non-resident with double taxed income/gain is claiming treaty relief). For both forms a certificate of residence is required from the tax authority of the residence state, i.e. the country the individual is regarded as being resident in for treaty purposes (often known as treaty residence) except where the residence state is the US, in which case HMRC accept that a residence certificate from the US's IRS is not required.

This certificate should cover the UK tax year concerned and confirm that the individual was resident in that country for the purposes of the double tax treaty. In practice, it can take some tax authorities months to produce this certificate, if at all(!), which can very often mean that the individual's self-assessment tax return needs to be filed without the relevant certificate if the online filing deadline of 31 January is to be met. In this situation, it is advisable to have a note on the tax return stating the certificate has been applied for and will be forwarded to HMRC once received.

Treaty relief or exemption can be obtained at source by completing form DT-Individual, although this is just in respect of pension, interest and royalty income.

If treaty exemption or relief is not available for a particular type of income or gain, then double tax relief should be available. Under the treaty, it is usually the residence state (the country in which the individual is regarded as treaty resident) which must give relief for any double tax, thereby giving the source state what are known as primary taxing rights.

Double tax relief is usually given by 3 methods: exemption, credit or deduction. The method used depends on the country concerned.

Under the **exemption method**, there are two ways this is achieved:

(i) full exemption, where the income is treated as being completely exempt from tax in the residence state and is not included when establishing the person's tax rate for his other income; or

(ii) exemption with progression, where the income is exempt from tax but is included with other income to establish which rates of tax are to be used to tax the individual's other income.

The second of these is by far the more common, especially in European countries.

The **credit method** is used in the UK. Under this method, the double taxed income is included with the individual's other income and taxed as normal in the residence state. The foreign tax paid in the source state is then set off against the residence state's tax. In the UK this is restricted to the lower of (i) the foreign tax paid and (ii) the UK tax due on the double taxed income – see the notes to the foreign pages of the self-assessment tax return (SA106) and helpsheets 261 for capital gains tax and 263 for income tax on how to calculate this.

Care needs to be taken that only non-refundable foreign tax paid is set off against the residence state's tax. For instance, in the UK, it is a common error for people to set off, against the UK tax due, foreign tax that has been paid but which is later refunded, say when the individual files his foreign tax return (which may be after the taxpayer has filed his UK return). This then means that not enough tax was paid by the due date and so late filing penalties and interest will arise. This point may also arise in other countries.

Under the **deduction method**, the double taxed income is included as taxable income in the residence state and then the source state's tax is deducted as an expense against that income. This method is also available in the UK, but is used more rarely than the credit method.

If there is a situation where there is no double tax treaty in place, then the individual needs to see if the residence state gives relief for any double tax under its domestic tax legislation.

Care needs to be taken, when looking at double tax relief, that the tax paid in the source state is actually due. In the UK, for instance, relief for foreign tax is on the basis that that tax was actually due in the source state and that the income was not exempt or partially relieved from tax under that country's domestic tax legislation or under one of the articles of the relevant double tax treaty. If it was, then double tax relief is not available in the UK for any tax that was paid in error and was not actually due. The individual would then need to obtain a repayment of the tax from the source state rather than claim double tax relief in the UK. This point may well apply in other countries.

Example 1

Freda is a British citizen who is working both in the UK and Germany for a German employer. She travels to Germany on a Monday morning to work there until Thursday evening when she flies back to the UK and works from home on the Friday. Her partner and children, who are also British citizens, have remained living in the family home in Berkshire.

While working in Germany she stays in various short term serviced apartments, so all of her possessions have remained in her home in Berkshire, other than a few items she needs for work such as her laptop, tablet, smartphone, clothing etc. which she takes with her while working in Germany. She has a bank account in Germany, into which she is paid, and a German credit card for use while she is in Germany, as well as some investments in that country. The majority of her investments, savings, assets etc. are in the UK.

Under the domestic tax legislation of both the UK and Germany, it has been established that she is regarded as resident in both countries for tax purposes and so is a dual resident, resulting in her being taxed on her worldwide income and gains in both countries.

In this scenario, Freda needs to turn to the double tax treaty and the tie-breaker clause (article 4) to see which country she is regarded as being resident in *for treaty purposes only*. (It is important to realise that the tie-breaker clause establishes which country an individual is resident in for the purposes of the double tax treaty only and not for a country's domestic tax legislation. It is commonly mis-understood that a double tax treaty establishes a person's residence status for all purposes including for domestic tax law and regulations.)

Article 4 under the Germany/UK treaty in respect of individuals reads as follows:

"Article 4 Resident

(1) For the purposes of this Convention, the term "resident of a Contracting State" means any person who, under the laws of that State, is liable to tax therein by reason of his domicile, residence, place of management, place of incorporation or any other criterion of a similar nature, and also includes that State and any political subdivision or local authority of a "Land" or a Contracting State. This term, however, does not include any person who is liable to tax in that Contracting State only if he derives income or capital gains from sources therein or capital situated therein.

(2) Where by reason of the provisions of paragraph 1 an individual is a resident of both Contracting States, then his status shall be determined as follows:

   (a) he shall be deemed to be a resident only of the Contracting State in which he has a permanent home available to him; if he has a permanent home available to him in both Contracting States, he shall be deemed to be a resident only of the Contracting State with which his personal and economic relations are closer (centre of vital interests);

   (b) if the Contracting State in which he has his centre of vital interests cannot be determined, or if he does not have a permanent home available to him in either Contracting State, he shall be deemed to be a resident only of the Contracting State in which he has an habitual abode;

(c) if he has an habitual abode in both Contracting States or in neither of them, he shall be deemed to be a resident only of the Contracting State of which he is a national;

(d) if he is a national of both Contracting States or of neither of them, the competent authorities of the Contracting States shall settle the question by mutual agreement."

Under the treaty, Freda will be regarded as resident in the UK for the purposes of the treaty, as her permanent home has remained in the UK and it can be argued that she does not have one in Germany. If, say, she also owned a flat in Germany and had done so for many years and had visited it frequently with her family and lived there while working in Germany, such that it could be argued to be a permanent home, then Freda would then need to look at where her economic and personal ties were to establish where her centre of vital interests was. Again, if this cannot be established in just one of the countries, then she would need to see where she habitually resides.

If Freda did not have a permanent home in either the UK or Germany, say because she was Swedish and normally lived there, but her employment situation meant she was resident in the UK and Germany and travelling around a lot within those countries, then in this scenario she would not look at where her centre of vital interests was, but instead would go straight to looking at where her habitual abode was. If this was in Sweden, then her nationality would be looked at, but if she was Swedish and not German or British, then HMRC and the German tax authority would need to agree between themselves, as to where she would be treated as resident for the purposes of the treaty. This scenario, however, is rare in practice.

Freda pays German salary tax and social security on her earnings, together with a church tax and solidarity surcharge. She is also liable to UK income tax on her earnings. Returning to the original scenario in this example, as Freda is resident in the UK for treaty purposes (because her permanent home is there), this means the UK, as the residence state, must give her relief for the German tax she has incurred against the UK tax due on her earnings. But which German taxes?

Previously, HMRC used to give a useful list of which German taxes could be set off against UK tax and which could not (at DT 7903 of their *Double Taxation Relief* manual and their *Guidance by countries of double tax treaties*). However, the updated version of DT 7903 is not so helpful and just repeats what article 2 of the Germany/UK treaty states, with no guidance from HMRC as to what taxes can be included.

According to HMRC's previous version of DT 7903, it was the case that the solidarity surcharge along with the salary tax could be included to set off against the UK tax due, but not the church tax. However, DT 7903 now states at the time of writing that German income tax together with "supplements levied thereon" can be included in the German tax credit set off against UK tax, which suggests that the church tax can now be included as this is a percentage of the income tax due by a person, just as the solidarity charge is.

This highlights how it is not always straightforward to determine which taxes can be included in the foreign tax credit. DT18102 with regards to Swiss taxes highlights how complex this can be at times.

Returning to Freda, it would seem now – according to HMRC's manual on double tax relief – that she can include the German church tax she has paid in her German tax credit to set off against the UK tax on her earnings, although previously HMRC's view was that she could not. The German social security she has paid will not be included in this credit.

One issue to be wary of is non-residents thinking that just because they are paying tax in the source country, they do not need to pay tax in the residence state, and they may question why it matters which country the tax is paid in on a particular type of income. In this scenario, the residence state's tax authority, if aware of the income, will certainly want to tax it. If this is a number of years after the income arose, say as part of a tax audit, then the individual may find himself in the situation whereby he has to pay tax in the residence state, but even if the tax was exempt from the source state's tax under a double tax treaty, the individual may be too late to make a treaty relief claim and claim back the tax in the source state. He may therefore end up in a double tax situation with no relief for this.

Example 2

Fred is a British national resident in Australia and receiving a pension in the UK, which under the UK and Australia double tax treaty is just taxable in Australia, the country where he is treaty resident.

Tax had automatically been deducted from his pension in the UK under PAYE. Fred did not claim this back from HMRC and did not declare the income in Australia, because he mistakenly thought it did not matter which country the tax had to be paid in. He thought it was OK as tax had been paid somewhere.

A few years later, he was unfortunately subject to a tax audit in Australia, as a result of which he ended up with an Australian tax liability on his UK pension income. He tried to set off the UK tax he had paid against his Australian tax liability, but as this was not due in the UK the Australian Tax Office would not allow a credit for the UK tax. He tried to obtain a repayment from HMRC of the tax that had been deducted under PAYE, but this was five years after the end of the relevant tax year and so HMRC refused to repay him the tax, because it was beyond the fourth anniversary of the end of the relevant tax year and so too late to make a treaty relief claim. Fred therefore ended up paying tax in both the UK and Australia with no relief for the double tax.

Guidance: https://www.gov.uk/government/collections/tax-treaties; *International Manual* at INTM 150000; *Double Taxation Relief Manual* (DT)

OECD model tax convention and commentary: https://www. keepeek.com//Digital-Asset-Management/oecd/taxation/model-tax-convention-on-income-and-on-capital-condensed-version-2017_mtc_cond-2017-en#page1

UN model tax convention and commentary: http://www.un.org/esa/ ffd/documents/UN_Model_2011_Update.pdf

2.3.4   *Gift Aid donations*

It is quite common for non-residents to pay donations in the UK under the Gift Aid scheme. This may have arisen because the individual had set up a monthly direct debit while living and resident in the UK and never cancelled it when he or she left the UK, or perhaps the individual made a donation while visiting the UK which he or she did not realise was made under Gift Aid.

In this scenario, if the non-resident is not paying tax in the UK, perhaps because all his taxable income is covered by the personal allowance, then the tax claimed on the donation by the charity is clawed back from the non-resident donor rather than from the charity concerned. As a result, the non-resident will have to pay tax in the UK despite all his taxable income being covered by the personal allowance.

Example

Denise lived in and was resident in the UK, during which time she had set up a direct debit of £20 per month to her favourite cat charity under Gift Aid. She then left the UK for a life in New Zealand during 2017-18 and became non-resident for UK tax purposes. However, when she left she did not cancel this direct debit, or change it to be no longer paid under Gift Aid, so the monthly direct debits continued as before under Gift Aid.

Denise rented out her property in the UK, with her only other UK sourced income being a small amount of interest from her UK bank account. For 2018-19, her income was as follows:

- rental income after allowable expenses £8,000; and
- bank interest £50.

Her total UK sourced income was therefore £8,050, which is completely covered by her personal allowance for 2018-19, so no tax is due in the UK, or so she thought!

As she did not cancel or amend her monthly direct debit to the cats' charity, she ends up with a tax liability for 2018-19 of £60 which has been calculated as follows:

Total donations Denise paid during 2018-19 amounted to £240 (12 times £20pm).

This is the net amount after basic rate tax, so needs to be grossed up to £300.

This gross amount of £300 is then taxed at basic rate of 20% to give a tax liability of £60.

2.3.5 Repayment of tax

If an individual leaves the UK part way through a tax year, and was an employee paid under PAYE, then it is often the case that, because of the way the PAYE system works, the individual is due a repayment of tax depending on his circumstances and on what other income or gains he may have. The individual needs to claim this repayment and it is common for taxpayers not to realise that they are in a repayment situation, so the position should always be checked when an individual leaves the UK: he or she should complete a P85 departure form (see **2.3.6**) or file a self-assessment tax return. Unfortunately, individuals in this situation often do not realise that a repayment of tax is due until more than four years from the end of the relevant tax year, when it is too late to claim a repayment. HMRC are determined not to make repayments of tax after this four-year limit.

Example

Martin was an employee working in the UK and so taxed under PAYE. While working in the UK, he had no other source of income.

He left the UK to work in Dubai during May 2018. He rented out his UK home while working in Dubai, but did not complete a P85 form when he left the UK and was a bit remiss and did not file self-assessment tax returns. During July 2025 he decided to review his UK tax situation as he had purchased a property in the UK to rent out and so sought advice from a UK tax adviser on this purchase. His adviser established that Martin was due a repayment of £4,000 for 2018-19. However, it was too late to claim this back, so Martin ended up overpaying tax for 2018-19 by £4,000.

This scenario may not arise so often now that HMRC issue P800 calculations. However, it is something that should always be checked when an individual leaves the UK and a repayment for other reasons may arise which may not be picked up by HMRC issuing a P800 calculation. If the individual completes a P85 departure form, then any overpayment of tax will be repaid to him if he includes his P45 with the form. Similarly, if a person files self-assessment tax returns, then any repayment due can be claimed via the individual's tax return.

If an individual realises he has overpaid tax due to a mistake on his self-assessment tax return, he can amend his return for this error within 12 months of the 31 January filing deadline (if filed online) and claim back the tax overpaid. If the individual discovers the error after this 12-month period, or does not file self-assessment tax returns but believes he has paid too much tax, he will need to make an overpayment relief claim to HMRC.

The deadline for making this claim is four years after the end of the relevant tax year. As mentioned above, HMRC are very strict in this respect and will not make repayments in respect of tax years beyond this deadline. TMA 1970, Sch. 1AB, para. 2 lists the various scenarios where an overpayment relief claim cannot be made.

HMRC state, in their *Self Assessment Claims Manual* at SACM 12150, that the claim must be made in writing and must state that it is a claim for overpayment relief, the amount overpaid, the tax year concerned and the grounds on which the overpayment of tax has occurred. Documentary proof of the tax paid must be included with the claim and the claim must include a declaration by the claimant stating that the claim is correct and complete to the best of his knowledge and belief, and this must be signed by him.

Law: TMA 1970, Sch. 1AB
Guidance: SACM 12000ff.

2.3.6   P85 completion

If an individual leaves the UK and does not file self-assessment tax returns at the time, then he either needs to tell HMRC of his departure (in which case HMRC will then decide if he needs to complete a P85 departure tax form or self-assessment tax return) or complete a P85 form if he wishes to claim back any tax which may

109

be due for the tax year of his departure. He will need to include the P45 with the form.

A P85 may need to be completed if the individual is applying for an NT PAYE code, e.g. if an employee of a UK employer has been assigned overseas and remains on the UK employer's payroll, but is not liable to UK tax and so no tax should be deducted from his salary under PAYE (see **2.3.19**).

In practice, many individuals leaving the UK submit a P85 form just to inform HMRC of their departure from the UK. It is common for HMRC not to respond to the submission of a P85, especially if no tax is due back to the individual concerned.

If an individual is filing self-assessment tax returns, he should not complete a P85, although he should still write to HMRC to inform them of his departure from the UK, so that HMRC can update their records.

Guidance: EIM 42940

2.3.7   64-8 and gateway account

When an adviser commences acting for a person, a 64-8 form needs to be in place to allow the adviser (called "agent" by HMRC) to liaise with HMRC on the person's behalf and to gain access to his self-assessment account online. This authorisation to act on the individual's behalf is extremely useful in respect of individuals who are living overseas and who are non-resident, particularly if they live in a country with a poor postal system such that it is difficult to receive HMRC correspondence in a timely manner, if at all (see example below). An agent in the UK is therefore obviously an advantage for the non-resident.

A 64-8 paper form can be sent in the post to HMRC's Central Agent Authorisation team at:

> National Insurance Contributions and Employer Office
> HM Revenue and Customs
> BX9 1AN
> United Kingdom

HMRC only accept the original signed form and do not accept copies, which for non-residents can cause issues if they live in a country with a particularly poor postal system (see example below).

Agent authorisation can also be achieved online. However, for individuals living overseas this is often not the fastest way as, at the time of writing, part of the process involves HMRC sending out in the post to the individual concerned an authentication code, which the individual then passes on to his or her adviser, who then has to input this code to finalise the online authorisation process. The issue with this method is that the adviser needs to input the code within a time limit which is usually 28 days. This limit for many non-resident individuals is impossible to meet, as the code often arrives with the non-resident after the deadline to input it, even when they live in a country with a relatively good postal system.

Example

Peter, a British citizen, lives in Sierra Leone and has been living overseas for many years, working for a major mining company. He has been having problems receiving mail from HMRC – some of it arrives, but many months later, and some never arrives.

It seems that after years of not having to file tax returns in the UK, Peter for some reason has been issued with notices to file a tax return, even though his circumstances have not changed, so this is something he was not expecting. He did not receive these notices and the only reason he knows about the requirement to file a tax return is because he did receive a penalty notice for many hundreds of pounds several months after it was issued.

He tried to resolve the matter by registering to file self-assessment tax returns online, but this was not possible as HMRC send out a code in the post, which needs to be inputted by him within a short deadline. He never received the code so was unable to register for online filing via HMRC's website (although he would not be able to use this service in any case, as it does not include the "Residence, Remittance basis etc." pages that he needs to file to claim non-residence status and the personal allowance as a non-resident – see **2.8.1**) . He decides that he needs help from a professional with his UK taxes and so engages a suitably qualified adviser based in the UK.

However, arranging for the relevant agent authorisation to be in place is still proving to be a challenge, if not impossible! The online authorisation is just not an option, due to the deadline of inputting the authentication code, which just leaves the option of submitting a paper 64-8 form in the post. This latter option (i) may never happen as there is a very high chance the form will never reach HMRC in the post and (ii) even if it is delivered it may take many months to reach HMRC, although his adviser in the UK can still file self-assessment tax returns for him via his or her own tax return software without a 64-8 form, thereby stopping further late filing penalties from arising.

Fortunately for Peter, a colleague was returning to the UK for a business trip and so was able to take the form with him and post it in the UK. This meant then that his adviser in the UK was able to liaise with HMRC and successfully appeal against the late filing penalties that Peter had incurred, on the grounds that Peter had not received the notice to file a tax return.

The above example shows how difficult it can be arranging for agent authorisation to be put in place for individuals living overseas. It does not help either that 64-8 forms can often go missing within HMRC and clients can suddenly disappear with alarming frequency from an agent's list of online self-assessment clients! It is the author's understanding that HMRC are looking into this area to try and improve the situation.

The Government Gateway allows individuals to use the UK government's online services and an account therefore needs to be set up: a Government Gateway account, whereby specific services can be activated, such as access to a person's self-assessment account.

Personal tax accounts have now been introduced by HMRC which enable individuals to access their tax accounts in real time and to perform various functions. However, agents do not (at the time of writing) have access to clients' personal tax accounts. This, again, is an area that HMRC are looking into.

Personal tax accounts show various details regarding a person's tax and National Insurance position, including their:

- self-assessment situation;
- National Insurance record, and whether there are any gaps in this – particularly useful for non-residents who are looking to protect their UK state pension and potentially need to make voluntary contributions while overseas (see **2.7.5**);
- PAYE situation, including PAYE codes in place – useful for non-residents who have been assigned overseas by their UK employer and so are still on a UK payroll and under PAYE;
- benefits such as tax credits and child benefits;
- state pension forecast;
- and so on.

A personal tax account can be set up at https://www.gov.uk/personal-tax-account. A Government Gateway account also needs to be set up.

At the time of writing, HMRC state that the following services can be performed via a person's personal tax account:

- check an individual's tax estimate and tax code;
- fill in, send and view a personal tax return, although non-residents, at the time of writing, are unable to do this as the "Residence, remittance basis etc." supplementary pages, which they need to complete and file, are not available via HMRC's website;
- claim a tax refund;
- check and manage tax credits;
- check his or her state pension;
- track tax forms that have been submitted online;
- check or update his or her marriage allowance;
- tell HMRC about a change of address;
- check or update benefits he or she get from work, for example company car details and medical insurance, although again this may not be relevant for non-residents who are not taxed in the UK on their earnings and benefits and who have not been performing any work in the UK.

HMRC state that more services will be added in the future.

Guidance: Links to HMRC's website re: agent authorisation and Government Gateway accounts: https://www.gov.uk/government/publications/tax-agents-and-advisers-authorising-your-agent-64-8; https://www.gov.uk/ government-gateway

HMRC online guidance on personal tax accounts: https://www.gov.uk/government/publications/your-personal-tax-account/your-personal-tax-account

2.3.8 Typical UK sources of income for non-residents: introduction

As mentioned previously, the residence status of an individual dictates what income he or she will be taxed on in the UK. For non-residents this is the individual's UK sourced income. Some of the more common forms of UK sourced income that a British expat overseas may have, are as follows.

2.3.9 Earnings from UK work days

The source for earnings is where the work is performed. If a non-resident physically performs some work in the UK, then he is liable to UK tax on these earnings from UK work days, regardless of where his employer is located, where he is paid from or the location of the bank account into which the payment is made.

Non-residents commonly think that they are not liable to UK tax on earnings from work performed in the UK, because they are employed by an overseas employer, or because they are paid from overseas and/or into an overseas bank account. These factors are irrelevant, as the deciding factor is where the work is physically performed.

Incidental duties

If the work can be described as "merely incidental" to the individual's overseas duties, then the earnings from these incidental duties will not be liable to UK tax (as opposed to substantive duties, which are taxable in the UK).

Incidental duties are not defined and so disputes can arise with HMRC in this respect. HMRC describe incidental duties as work which is "subordinate or ancillary to that done overseas." If the UK work is "the same kind as that done overseas, or if not the same, of equal importance, it will not be 'merely incidental' ". HMRC consider that a duty that "forms part of the essential or fundamental requirements of the employment could not be incidental." Therefore, if the UK duties are the same as, or similar in nature to, those performed overseas, HMRC are unlikely to agree they are merely incidental to the overseas duties, even if performed for only a very short time.

HMRC guidance (in the *Employment Income Manual* at EIM 40204) provides examples of what incidental duties may include (e.g. arranging a meeting or business travel while in the UK) and what will likely be regarded as substantive duties (e.g., depending on the circumstances, responding to a business email while in the UK). HMRC used to say that classroom-based training in the UK, as in attending a course or conference as opposed to presenting a course or at a conference, was usually regarded as an incidental duty. This is no longer included in HMRC's internal guidance, but it is believed this is still HMRC's view and the example is still referred to in HMRC's RDR1 as potentially constituting incidental duties.

Robson v Dixon is a key case in respect of incidental duties. In this case it was held that an airline pilot of international flights was not performing incidental duties when in the UK to land and take off planes. This was because his duties in this respect were the same in whichever country he was landing and taking off from, even though the UK ones were few in number compared to his total take-offs and landings. This case showed that the important factor in deciding whether duties are incidental is the *nature* of the duties in the UK in relation to the overseas duties and not necessarily the length of time doing the duties or the quantity of those duties. As such, the facts of each case need to be considered on their merits. Having said that, HMRC are unlikely to accept that duties are incidental if they amount to more than three months in a year.

If HMRC were to look into whether a person is performing incidental or substantive duties in the UK, they would be looking at details such as a person's employment contract, what his role and job title is, and what his duties entail both in the UK and overseas. HMRC might also ask for the individual's travel diaries, so all this documentation should be kept.

When directors perform their statutory duties, such as attending a board meeting in the UK, these will not be regarded as incidental as they are considered part of the person's duties as a statutory director.

Earnings from UK work days that are taxable in the UK (from substantive duties as opposed to incidental duties) are usually calculated on a days worked apportionment basis, i.e. the total earnings for a tax year are calculated and are then apportioned between UK and overseas work days. If, however, earnings can specifically be associated with UK work only, then there should be no apportionment and all these earnings would be taxed in the UK.

Earnings can also be apportioned on some other reasonable basis, but generally the work days apportionment described above is used (see EIM 40110). Individuals should keep documentation, such as a diary, to show where they have been working and for how long per day. This ties in with the documentation needed for SRT purposes (see **2.2.9**).

Example

Norma has been non-resident for UK tax purposes for a number of years. She is an accountant and, during 2018-19, she visited the UK to attend a course for three days on international tax and accounting as part of her CPD requirements.

While in the UK she arranged to have meetings with two of her clients in London to discuss their accounts. This occurred on two days. She also spent a day responding to emails from clients, most of which resulted in her responding to specific points/queries raised. She spent the weekend visiting family and friends and then returned to the US, where she lives and is resident.

The total number of days she worked during 2018-19 was 240 days. Her total earnings for 2018-19 amounted to US$100,000.

When looking at what earnings are potentially taxable in the UK, the two days having business meeting are unlikely to be regarded as incidental duties, as is the day spent replying to clients' emails. There are grounds to argue that Norma's three days attending her CPD course are incidental duties.

In summary, there are potentially three days when she did substantive duties in the UK, the earnings from which are taxable. To calculate what her taxable earnings are, an apportionment is done using work days, so as follows:

Total work days	240
UK work days	3

Taxable earnings in the UK:

$100,000 x 3/240   = $1,250

Double tax treaties

If a non-resident's earnings become taxable in the UK, then he or she may be able to claim exemption from UK tax under a double tax treaty, usually article 15, para. 2, which very often will read along the following lines:

> "(1) Subject to the provisions of Articles 16, 18 and 19 of this Convention, salaries, wages and other similar remuneration derived by a resident of a Contracting State in respect of an employment shall be taxable only in that State unless the employment is exercised in the other Contracting State. If the employment is so exercised, such remuneration as is derived from that exercise may be taxed in that other State.
>
> (2) Notwithstanding the provisions of paragraph 1 of this Article, remuneration derived by a resident of a Contracting State in respect of an employment exercised in the other Contracting State shall be taxable only in the first-mentioned State if—
>
> > (a) the recipient is present in the other State for a period or periods not exceeding in the aggregate 183 days in any twelve month period commencing or ending in the fiscal year concerned; and
> >
> > (b) the remuneration is paid by, or on behalf of, an employer who is not a resident of the other State; and
> >
> > (c) the remuneration is not borne by a permanent establishment which the employer has in the other State."

However, it is important that the relevant double tax treaty is referred to as many of the UK treaties differ in some way from the above.

For non-residents with taxable earnings from UK work days, para. 2 above may enable exemption from UK tax on these earnings, providing the individual is not present (for any part of a day) in the UK for the 183-day period mentioned in (2)(a) above. This requirement refers to any 12-month period ending or finishing in the UK's tax year, so for 2018-19 the period 7 April 2017 to 4 April 2020 needs to be considered. In some older treaties, the year to be considered is just the source state's tax year, but this is becoming rarer as these older treaties are replaced with newer treaties that stipulate the above requirements or may refer to a 12-month period. Note that presence in the source state is for any reason and not just for work.

For treaty exemption under (2) above against UK tax, the individual's remuneration must be paid by an employer who is not resident in the UK (some treaties state the employer must be resident in the resident state, i.e. the country the employee is treaty resident in, as opposed to the source state where the work has been performed) and the remuneration must not be borne by a permanent establishment in the source state (i.e. the UK if trying to claim exemption from UK tax on earnings). Care needs to be taken if there are management charges or costs being recharged between entities that may include an element in respect of the individual's remuneration. With regards to the meaning of "permanent establishment", an article in the relevant treaty (usually around article 5) will define what this is for the purposes of the treaty; it is normally a fixed place of business through which the business operates and it normally includes such entities as a branch, office, factory, workshop or place of management.

When looking at the 183-day rule in (2)(a) above, any part of a day is counted as a day of presence (as opposed to just presence at midnight for the SRT) and days when an individual was resident in the source state are ignored. This is particularly relevant for individuals who were resident in the UK and then have to work overseas, but may visit the UK for work, the duties of which are not incidental and so are potentially taxable in the UK.

Example

Norman had been living and working in the UK all his life and so was resident in the UK.

On 10 April 2018, his UK employer assigned him to South Africa for a few years and he was regarded as not resident for UK tax purposes for the 2018-19 tax year and so from 6 April 2018, as he met the third automatic overseas test and working sufficient hours overseas (see **2.2.2(3)**). He became resident in South Africa from when he arrived there.

Norman was required to visit the UK for various meetings with customers and suppliers for a few days every quarter. In 2018-19 he visited the UK for 15 days (including part days). This work was not regarded as incidental to his overseas work and so the earnings from these UK work days are potentially taxable in the UK.

When looking at the double tax treaty between the UK and South Africa, and in particular at article 14, income from employment, para 2(a) is the same as above, i.e. the period over which the 183-day presence is considered is any 12-month period ending or commencing in 2018-19. However, as Norman was resident in the UK up until 5 April 2018, these days in the UK can be ignored when looking at whether he spent more than 183 days in the UK. Assuming he visited the UK for a similar number of days for the following tax years, then he should satisfy the 183-day presence test in (2)(a) above.

When looking at the residence of the individual's employer for treaty purposes, HMRC follow the OECD's view of taking into account the "economic employer" in this respect and not the legal employer (see the *Double Taxation Relief Manual* at DT 1922). If an entity in the UK bears the costs and risks and benefits of the employee working in the business, then that entity may be regarded as an economic employer for the employee, even though his or her employment contract has remained with the overseas employer. In this situation, the conditions of para. 2 above will not be met and exemption from UK tax will not be due.

HMRC will not treat a UK entity as the economic employer if the employee continues to work in the business of the non-resident employer, or if the employee is in the UK for less than 60 days in the tax year and this is not part of a substantial period in the UK. This is known as the 60-day concession.

This economic employer concept may be more of an issue for non-resident individuals who have been living overseas and working for an overseas employer and who are sent over to work in the UK for a short time (say a few months).

If treaty exemption is available, then the individual needs to claim this via form HS304 (if non-resident) or HS302 (if a dual resident), which is attached to the self-assessment tax return. A residence certificate from the tax authority in the country of residence is also needed (except for the US where no certificate is required by HMRC). This certificate confirms the individual's tax residence in the residence state for the UK tax year concerned.

Law: ITEPA 2003, s. 27, 39

Case Law: *Robson v Dixon* (1972) 48 TC 527

Guidance: EIM 40110, 40201, 40203, 40204, 77020; DT 1920-1924; RDR 1; *Tax Bulletin* 68; see also HMRC's guidance on dual contracts which includes interpretation of incidental duties https://www.gov.uk/government /publications/dual-contracts

2.3.10 Deferred earnings

Very often, an individual who has been working in the UK, and has (say) been assigned to work overseas by his or her UK employer, will continue to receive earnings relating to previous UK work, even after leaving the UK and becoming non-resident. This typically includes earnings such as bonuses and income from employee share options or awards.

The taxation of bonuses will depend on the employee's circumstances during the period to which they relate and not at the time they are received. If it is a straightforward bonus for a particular year, paid in respect of the individual's work generally throughout that period, then the bonus will remain taxable in the UK if it relates to work when the individual was a UK tax resident, or to work performed in the UK.

If the employee left part way through the period, so that there is both UK and overseas work, with the latter performed as a non-resident and so not taxable in the UK, then the bonus will normally be apportioned on a work days basis to establish the taxable amount in the UK.

Example

June has worked for many years for J Blogs Limited in the UK, part of a US group, J Blogs Inc.

On 1 September 2018, June was seconded to the US for a number of years. On this date, her employment contract was transferred from the UK subsidiary to the US company and so she ceased being paid by the UK payroll and was paid instead via the US payroll. She left the UK on 25 August 2018, spending a week settling in before commencing work in the US on Monday 3 September 2018. She did not perform any work in the UK from leaving until 31 December 2018.

June is resident for all of 2018-19. However, she is eligible for split-year treatment under Case 1 (see **2.2.7**) and is treated as if a non-resident from 3 September 2018.

In February 2019 she was paid an annual bonus of US$20,000 by her US employer and so was paid through the US payroll. This bonus related to all her work for the year to 31 December 2018. US tax was withheld from this bonus.

The element of June's bonus which is taxable in the UK is the part which relates to the time she was resident in the UK, so from 1 January to 2 September 2018. June performed work on 240 days during the year to 31 December 2018, of which 162 were performed while she was resident in the UK.

The UK taxable element is, therefore, $20,000 x 162/240 = $13,500.

As this bonus was paid through the US payroll, PAYE was not operated on it and so no UK tax has been withheld from it. June will, therefore, need to declare the bonus on her self-assessment tax return and pay the tax due via the self-assessment system.

Even if June had remained on the UK payroll, UK tax may still not have been deducted from her bonus if she had been issued with an "NT" code (see **2.3.19**).

June will also need to check that not too much US tax has been withheld from her bonus, if US tax was not due on the UK element.

For the year to 31 December 2019, June received a bonus from her US employer of $25,000. During the year June had visited the UK for work and attended various business meetings there. The total number of days she worked in the UK was 10. Again she performed in total 240 days and she continued to be non-resident for UK tax purposes.

The taxable bonus in the UK is $25,000 x 10/240 = $1,041.67. However, she may be able to claim exemption from UK tax under the double tax treaty between the UK and the US (see **2.3.3**).

If, in February 2019, June had been paid a bonus of say $20,000 for her time while working for the UK company and $10,000 in respect of her work for the US company, then no apportionment would have been necessary and all of the $20,000 would be taxed in the UK.

The taxation of bonuses becomes more complicated for deferred bonuses and similar remuneration where conditions may need to be met before the employee is entitled to receive the bonus. In addition, long term incentive plans (LTIPs) often involve a mixture of both cash and shares, further complicating the situation. For these types of bonus, a review of the bonus plan and other documentation is vital to establish the nature of the bonus, and hence how it will be taxed in the UK.

The difficulty in these circumstances is establishing the period to which the bonus relates. An important case in this respect is *Bray v Best* where it was stated that the period to which earnings relate depends on the facts of the case, including the employer's intentions and the source of the earnings. HMRC take this view (although they used not to, before February 2008) and will look at the facts of each case. If these, together with any bonus documentation, show that the bonus was for a particular period, then they will treat the bonus as having been "earned" for this period and tax it accordingly. Otherwise, the bonus will be taxed in the tax year in which all the conditions are fulfilled such that the employee is then entitled to the bonus unconditionally.

Similarly, an employee may have been working overseas and have been non-resident, may then return to live in the UK and may receive a bonus once resident again in the UK. In this case, if the bonus relates to the individual's time working overseas, when a non-resident, it will not be taxed in the UK. However, a UK tax liability will arise if part of the bonus related to work performed in the UK while the employee was a non-resident, when the earnings from these UK work days were taxable in the UK, unless exemption is available under a double tax treaty (see **2.3.3**).

HMRC's quite detailed guidance on bonuses, including various examples, may be found at EIM 40002 to 40016.

Employee shares

The taxation of employee share remuneration is explained more fully in section **8.2**.

Briefly, the UK taxation of employee share schemes depends on whether or not the scheme is approved for UK tax purposes.

In the case of approved schemes, specific rules apply (depending on the type of scheme) to give relief from both UK income tax and capital gains tax, assuming certain conditions are satisfied.

The UK taxation of unapproved schemes was simplified from April 2015 with the introduction of special rules for taxing share-related remuneration for internationally mobile employees (IMEs). If the employee concerned has been not resident for at least one of the tax years since the grant of his options, or award of RSUs (restricted share units) or similar share award, then the individual will fall under these rules, regardless of whether or not he is resident in the UK at the time of vesting.

From 6 April 2015, share-related remuneration in respect of IMEs is time apportioned between taxable UK and non-taxable foreign income for the relevant period, which will be from the grant of the options (or award of RSUs, etc.) to the time they vest. (For options this is the date they are exercisable, as opposed to the date they are actually exercised if different.)

This time apportionment will be based on the total number of days in the relevant period. The number of days when the employee is not resident (including the overseas part of any split year), and has not performed any work in the UK, will relate to the non-taxable foreign element that is deducted from the total share-related income, leaving the amount that is taxable in the UK. This will be taxed in the tax year the income arises.

If the shares are kept and sold later, these will be subject to capital gains tax like any other shareholding. If the individual is non-resident at the time of sale, then these will be outside the scope of UK CGT unless the five-year rule under the temporary non-residence rules applies (see **2.2.12 (iv)**).

The above is on the assumption that there are conditions that the employee must satisfy before the share options or awards vest, so that the tax rules applying are those of the specific share-based remuneration legislation. If an employee is granted or awarded share-based remuneration which is not conditional (e.g. salary, cash-based bonus, etc.) then this is taxed as general earnings. If this is the case, then if the employee is non-resident at the time and the remuneration relates to work not performed in the UK, he will not be taxed in the UK. The first step, therefore, is to establish whether the share-based remuneration is taxable as general earnings or whether it falls under the specific legislation for share-based remuneration.

The timing of the grant or award is also important, as this will dictate which part of the legislation is relevant.

Relief from any double tax may be available under the employment article of a double tax treaty, but reference must be made to the relevant treaty to ensure that share-based remuneration is included as earnings for the purposes of this article.

The taxation of share-based remuneration is complex, especially when taken in the international context. The above is likely to be most relevant to employees who have been assigned within a global group, commonly a US group.

Law: ITEPA 2003, s. 6, 7, 16, 29, 41F-41L, 62, and Pt. 7
Case: *Bray v Best* [1986] STC 96, 61 TC 705
Guidance: EIM 40002-40016; ERSM 160000-163200

2.3.11   Termination/redundancy

See **8.2.5** for a detailed explanation of the taxation of termination payments.

Prior to 6 April 2018, foreign service relief was potentially due on any termination payments which related to a period when the employee was non-resident and working overseas. This is no longer the case if the individual is resident for the tax year in which his or her termination of employment happens and if the payment is in respect of terminations which occur after 5 April 2018.

2.3.12 Savings and investment income

The taxation of investment income in the UK has become more complex over recent years, due to the introduction of various rates and allowances specifically relating to savings income and dividends.

Savings

If non-savings income is less than the starting rate limit, which for 2018-19 is £5,000 (as has been the case since 2015-16), then any savings income below this limit is taxed at the starting rate of 0% for 2018-19 and then at the usual rates on savings income above this limit.

The tax rates on savings income for Scottish taxpayers are the same as for the rest of the UK and in this respect reference is made to UK tax rates and thresholds as opposed to Scottish thresholds.

The personal allowance, if available to the non-resident, can be set off against different types of income in a way which minimises a person's tax liability (per ITA 2007, s. 25(2)).

ITA 2007, s. 18 defines what is included as savings income and includes interest, income from purchased life annuities, profits from deeply discounted securities, accrued income profits and chargeable event gains on life policies subject to income tax.

When establishing whether savings income has exceeded the above limit, it is treated as the highest slice of income apart from (a) dividends and (b) employment termination payments and benefits.

In addition, from 2016-17, a personal savings allowance (PSA) is now available of £1,000 for basic rate taxpayers (individuals who do not have any income taxable at the higher or additional rates or dividend upper or additional rates – see below) and of £500 for higher rate taxpayers (individuals who do not have any income taxable at the additional and dividend additional rates – see below). There is no allowance for additional rate taxpayers, i.e. those individuals paying tax at either the additional or dividend additional rate (see below). These are still the amounts for 2018-19.

The UK tax thresholds, rather than the Scottish ones, are relevant when establishing what PSA is applicable to Scottish taxpayers.

This allowance is given regardless of what an individual's other income is and is not restricted like the savings starting rate. It works in conjunction with the starting rate of tax for savings, but the latter takes priority. The allowance is not a deduction against a person's taxable income, but is a nil rate tax band – the savings nil rate.

Dividends

From 2016-17, a dividend allowance was introduced at £5,000, but reduced to £2,000 for 2018-19. This replaced the 10% tax credit that was previously associated with dividends and is a nil rate tax band for dividends, as opposed to a deduction against taxable income. Any dividends in excess of the dividend allowance are taxed at the following rates:

Dividend ordinary rate (for individuals taxed at basic rate)	7.5%
Dividend upper rate (for individuals taxed at higher rate)	32.5%
Dividend additional rate	38.1%

Example

Brian is a British citizen living and working in Brazil and has been non-resident for many years. He rents out a few properties in the UK, from which he received taxable profits of £15,000 for 2018-19. He has interest arising in the UK of £6,000 for 2018-19 and dividends from UK companies of £2,500.

Ignoring for this example the disregarded income rules (see **2.3.20**), Brian's UK tax liability for 2018-19 will be as follows:

	£
Rental profits	15,000
Interest	6,000
Dividends	2,500
	23,500
Less: Personal allowance	(11,850)
Taxable income	11,650

Tax due:

£1,850	@ 0% (savings) – see below	Nil
£1,000	of savings covered by PSA	Nil
£3,150	of savings at 20%	630.00
£2,000	dividend allowance	Nil
£500	@ 7.5% ordinary dividend rate	37.50
£3,150	@ 20% on taxable rental profits	630.00
£11,650		£1,297.50

Brian is able to set off the personal allowance against his rental income first, leaving £3,150 which is taxable. As this is below the starting rate limit of £5,000, he is entitled to use the savings starting rate of 0%.

Note, however, that account is taken of the non-savings income (other than dividends) when establishing what amount of the starting limit is available for Brian's savings income to be taxed at 0%, i.e. £5,000 less the excess of rental income above the personal allowance of £3,150, leaving £1,850 of the starting rate limit at which Brain's savings income can be taxed at 0%.

Brian is able to set off the personal allowance against his rental income first, leaving £3,150 which is taxable. As this is below the starting rate limit of £5,000, he is entitled to use the savings starting rate of 0%.

As a basic rate taxpayer, Brian is also entitled to the personal savings allowance of £1,000 and the £2,000 dividend allowance. His excess dividends above this are taxed at the dividend ordinary rate of 7.5%.

The remaining rental income of £3,150 not covered by his personal allowance is taxed at 20%.

The situation might become more complex if Brian were a higher rate taxpayer. It would then be necessary to establish how best to set off his personal allowance to achieve the lowest tax liability.

Interest from UK bank and building societies used to have basic rate tax deducted at source by the bank or building society. Since 2016-17, this has no longer been the case and the interest is now paid gross with no deduction of tax.

Many of the UK's double tax treaties stipulate what the maximum rate of tax is that a source state (the UK for non-residents) can use. This is typically 10% for interest (see article 11 of the OECD model treaty) and 15% for dividends (see article 10 of the OECD model treaty). If a non-resident's situation is such that the rates of UK tax charged on his interest or dividend income are higher than the rates stipulated under a double tax treaty, then he can claim treaty relief in this respect. However, the disregarded income rules (see **2.3.20**) need to be considered first, which can sometimes mean that a treaty relief claim is not necessary.

Law: ITA 2007, s. 7-8, 11D-19
Guidance: HMRC's *Savings and Investment Income Manual*

2.3.13   *Property letting*

See **3.1** for a detailed explanation of the taxation of rental income from the letting of property.

Any income a non-resident receives from UK property will be taxable in the UK and it is rare that exemption from UK tax on this can be claimed under a double tax treaty. The OECD model treaty at article 6 – "Income from Immovable property" – states the income may be taxed in the source state. It is likely, therefore, that a non-resident may face double taxation of his UK rental income, i.e. it is taxed both in the UK and the country where he is living. In this situation, the individual would then claim relief for the double tax in the country where he is living and resident.

2.3.14   Pensions

See **4.1** for a detailed explanation of the taxation of pensions.

UK-sourced pensions received by a non-resident remain taxable in the UK, although treaty relief may be available. The OECD model treaty states under article 18:

> "Subject to the provisions of paragraph 2 of Article 19, pensions and other similar remuneration paid to a resident of a Contracting State in consideration of past employment shall be taxable only in that State."

Article 19 refers to government service and paragraph 2 reads as follows:

> "2. a) Notwithstanding the provisions of paragraph 1, pensions and other similar remuneration paid by, or out of funds created by, a Contracting State or a political subdivision or a local authority thereof to an individual in respect of services rendered to that State or subdivision or authority shall be taxable only in that State.
>
> b) However, such pensions and other similar remuneration shall be taxable only in the other Contracting State if the individual is a resident of, and a national of that State."

Very often the pension received for past non-government employment by non-residents is taxable only in the country where the individual is resident for treaty purposes. Pensions in respect of government service are generally taxable in the country where that service was performed, unless the individual is a national of the other state and resident there, in which case the pension is then taxed in that state. There are exceptions to this, one of which is the Australia/UK double tax treaty, where *all* pensions, including government pensions, are only taxed in the country of treaty residence, as the extract below from the Australia and UK double tax treaty shows:

"1) Pensions (including government pensions) and annuities paid to a resident of a Contracting State shall be taxable only in that State."

The UK's state pension is generally taxed under the "other income" article of double tax treaties (article 21 of the OECD model treaty) and so will generally be taxed only in the country where the individual is treaty resident.

Some treaties also cover pension contributions, such as the UK/US treaty under article 18.

2.3.15   Introduction to certain occupations

Certain occupations/situations have specific tax rules. Some of the most common ones are as follows.

2.3.16   Self-employment and directors

The taxation of the self-employed is a large and complex area and so a detailed explanation is beyond the scope of this publication. The following, therefore, just highlights some of the key issues a non-resident individual should watch out for.

If a non-resident is a sole trader overseas, and does not carry out any of his business in the UK, then none of his profits will be taxable in the UK. If the individual does carry out some of the business in the UK, then the profits from this will be taxable in the UK.

With regards to whether or not an individual carries out business in the UK, there is a distinction between carrying out the business *within* the UK as opposed to *with* the UK. The profits from the latter are likely to fall outside the scope of UK taxation, whereas the profits from the former are likely to be taxable in the UK. Care needs to be taken if agents or representatives are used in the UK.

Care is also needed over the question of whether any contracts are concluded in the UK. If so, this may cause part of an individual's business to be taxable in the UK. For a company, this may present permanent establishment (PE) issues, again with the result that some of the company's profits may become taxable in the UK.

If the business is initially carried out when the individual is resident in the UK, but if he or she then becomes non-resident and continues that business overseas while non-resident, the specific rules on cessation and commencement of a business will apply. The individual is deemed to have ceased one business and commenced another when he or she becomes non-resident, which is the end of the last UK tax year of residence (or the UK part if split-year treatment applies).

If the individual's sole trade had unused losses when he or she became non-resident, then these losses may be set off against any profits that are subject to UK tax from the "new" overseas business when the individual is non-resident. However, if the change in the business location results in (say) a different structure, customer base and/or employees, HMRC's view is likely to be that the business has in fact ceased and that a new one started in the country to which the sole trader has moved. This would be likely to be the case if, for example, a business is run via a shop or factory.

In contrast to this, the business may not be constrained to one location but can be run anywhere (such as a person providing professional advice). This type of business has probably not ceased as a result of the individual moving overseas but rather continues as before, only in a different country. If the facts support that conclusion then any losses arising from the time the individual was operating in the UK can be carried forward and set off against any future taxable UK profits.

With regards to double tax treaties, articles 7 (business profits) and 5 (permanent establishments) of the OECD model treaty will be relevant.

Generally the employment parts of the SRT will also apply to the self-employed. There are some exceptions though, such as the "sufficient hours worked" tests for both overseas and UK work and the deduction for gaps in employments when looking at the number of days in the reference period (see **Appendix 5**). This deduction is not applicable for self-employed individuals.

If an individual returns to live in the UK and decides to set up as a self-employed individual, then he will need to register with HMRC in this respect (see https://www.gov.uk/set-up-sole-trader). The individual will also need to consider if he needs to register for VAT and, if employing staff, will have to set up a PAYE scheme.

Directors

If an individual decides to operate through a UK limited company, probably as a director, then he or she may be regarded both as an employee and a statutory director. The income from the two roles may potentially be taxed differently under both UK domestic tax legislation and (particularly) under double tax treaties.

The director's fees paid in respect of a non-resident individual's statutory duties as a director, such as attending board meetings in the UK, remain taxable in the UK, unless *all* the duties are performed overseas. HMRC regard a director's statutory duties for a UK company not to be incidental duties to his or her overseas duties and so they are taxable in the UK (see **2.3.9**). This also includes a director who is present in the UK and is involved in a board meeting held overseas by phone or video conferencing.

There is usually a separate article in double tax treaties covering directors' fees. This is article 16 of the OECD model treaty which states:

> "Directors' fees and other similar payments derived by a resident of a Contracting State in his capacity as a member of the board of directors of a company which is a resident of the other Contracting State may be taxed in that other State."

Some treaties do include directors' fees in the employment income article so that they are treated like any other earnings, whilst others have a separate article but tax the fees in the country of the individual's residence for treaty purposes.

Care needs to be taken when statutory directors are tax equalised or protected, as this can be regarded as a loan to the director and so illegal unless appropriate shareholder approval has been obtained.

In addition, if the company is a close company for UK tax purposes, then a director (including an associate of the director) of such a company is regarded as a "participator" and so may be deemed to receive a distribution – rather than earnings from an employment – and taxed accordingly, i.e. the income is taxed in the same way as a dividend.

The question of whether a Class 1 NIC (National Insurance) liability arises on directors' fees, as a result of the non-resident director being "present" in the UK, will depend on the facts of the case. In particular, HMRC will take into account the extent and purpose of the individual's visits to the UK, the place at which he performs his work and the location of his home. By concession, under paragraph 66 of CA44, HMRC will ignore visits to the UK for the purposes of deciding whether Class 1 NIC is due on a director's fees if either:

(i)   the non-resident director makes no more than 10 visits to the UK per tax year to attend board meetings and each visit is no more than two nights; or

(ii)   the non-resident director only makes one visit to attend one board meeting in the tax year and this visit does not exceed two weeks.

HMRC will not apply this concession if the above conditions are not satisfied and give the example of a director who attends 11 board meetings in a tax year but only stays one night for each of them. HMRC have also stated that the director's visits to the UK cannot be averaged out, even if the result is that he did not spend more than two nights per visit in the UK on average.

If a director visits the UK from an EEA country, or a country with which the UK has a social security reciprocal agreement (see **Appendix 3**), then the EU social security regulations or the relevant social security agreement (see **2.7**) would need to be referred to first. Only if, under these, NIC is due will the above concession then need to be considered. Para. 66 of CA44 includes a table which explains the social security implications of directors both coming to work in the UK and leaving to work overseas.

The status of directors under the EU regulations can become complex, as some EEA countries regard directors as self-employed whilst others regard them as employees. In this situation, the general rule under these regulations is that the social security liability falls in the state that treats the director as an employee. This will obviously be an area that changes following Brexit.

If a director is liable to Class 1 NIC on his or her director fees, then employer's NIC will also be due on the fees.

Quite often, non-resident individuals who are self-employed consultants or contractors will set up a limited company through which to operate in the UK. The provisions of IR35 may need to be considered in these situations, although these provisions should not apply to non-resident individuals who would not have been taxable in the UK on their earnings had they been in a normal employment relationship.

If an individual operates through a UK registered company, the basic rule is that a company incorporated in the UK is considered resident in the UK for UK corporation tax purposes and so is taxable in the UK on its worldwide profits. However, if the company is treaty resident in another country under a tie-breaker clause, normally using the "place of effective management" test (usually where the central management and control of the business is), then the company is regarded as resident in that country and not resident in the UK for corporation tax purposes. It follows that the company's profits will not be subject to UK corporation tax. These are known as "treaty non-resident" (TNR) companies.

If a company was originally UK resident, but then becomes treaty non-resident as described above, it is regarded as a migrating company. This can occur if an individual was living in the UK and was (say) working as an IT contractor operating through a UK registered company, of which he was the sole director and shareholder. The company would be resident in the UK for corporation tax purposes. If the individual were to obtain a contract to work overseas, for example in Germany, but continued to operate through the UK company, then under article 4 of the UK/Germany double tax treaty (the tie-breaker clause) it would be regarded as treaty resident in Germany if the effective management of the company moved to Germany. When this happens the chargeable assets of the migrating company are deemed to be sold and reacquired at their market value and HMRC need to be informed of any resultant tax liability at the time of migration.

Under TMA 1970, s. 109B there are various compliance requirements that a migrating company needs to meet before it migrates and which can potentially lead to hefty penalties if not done. These requirements are to:

- notify HMRC of its intention to cease to be resident, and migration time;
- provide a statement of its tax liabilities;

- make arrangements for the settlement of these liabilities in due course; and
- obtain HMRC's approval of the arrangements.

HMRC's *Company Tax Manual* at CTM 34195 explains the procedure for meeting the above requirements.

Under TMA 1970, s. 109C, the penalty for failing to do the above is up to the amount of the company's outstanding tax liabilities at the date of migration. The directors of the company may themselves also be liable to a similar penalty under s. 109D. If any tax due by the migrating company is not paid within six months, then s. 109E enables HMRC to recover the amounts due from the director(s).

The above will be particularly relevant for UK registered companies that have been resident in the UK for corporation tax purposes, but that have become treaty non-resident as a result of the shareholders and directors leaving the UK and becoming non-resident. This might apply, for example, to an individual who is the sole director and shareholder, or to a husband and wife who are the only directors and shareholders, but who continue to operate through the UK company while living overseas or who keep the company but let it become dormant.

The VAT implications also need to be considered, in particular with regards to NETP (non-established taxable person) – see sections 9 to 13 of VAT notice 700/1: *Should I be Registered for VAT?*

If the non-resident director is also a shareholder of the company, as is often the case, then any dividends from the UK company will remain taxable in the UK, as they are from a UK source, but subject to the dividend allowance (see **2.3.12**) and also to the disregarded income rules (see **2.3.20**) under which dividends may be excluded when calculating the maximum tax due by a non-resident.

A double tax treaty may also limit the tax due in the UK. A salary from the company may not be taxable in the UK if it does not relate to any work performed in the UK by the director concerned and is not in respect of directors' fees. Subject to the disregarded income rules (again, see **2.3.20**), this latter route may be a more beneficial way for the director to pay himself if he has not performed any work in the UK, although it will also be necessary to consider the tax consequences in the country in which the individual is living and resident.

Law: TMA 1970, s. 109B-109F; TCGA 1992, s. 185; ITEPA 2003, s. 48-59; CTA 2009, s. 14, 18

Guidance: HMRC's CA44 *National Insurance for Company Directors,* para. 66; CTM 34000; INTM 120000ff. (esp. 120070); NIM 12013; VAT Notice 700/1

2.3.17 Seafarers and transport workers

Due to the nature of their employment and working across various borders, specific rules apply to international transport workers and seafarers, including workers in the oil and gas industry.

International transport workers

Under the statutory residence test (SRT: see **2.2**), special rules apply to international transport workers when establishing their residence status. The legislation refers to "Relevant jobs on board vehicles, aircraft or ships" rather than international transport workers and states:

"(1) P has a "relevant" job on board a vehicle, aircraft or ship if condition A and condition B are met.

(2) Condition A is that P either—

(a) holds an employment, the duties of which consist of duties to be performed on board a vehicle, aircraft or ship while it is travelling, or

(b) carries on a trade, the activities of which consist of work to be done or services to be provided on board a vehicle, aircraft or ship while it is travelling.

(3) Condition B is that substantially all of the trips made in performing those duties or carrying on those activities are ones that involve crossing an international boundary at sea, in the air or on land (referred to as "cross-border trips").

(4) Sub-paragraph (2)(b) is not satisfied unless, in order to do the work or provide the services, P has to be present (in person) on board the vehicle, aircraft or ship while it is travelling.

(5) Duties or activities of a purely incidental nature are to be ignored in deciding whether the duties of an employment or the activities of a trade consist of duties or activities of a kind described in sub-paragraph (2)(a) or (b)."

If an individual has such a job as described above and, during the tax year, at least six of his trips as part of this job are cross border trips (condition B above) that either start or end in the UK, then he is excluded from the third "automatic overseas test" (see **2.2.2**) and cannot be automatically non-resident because of this test. In addition, such a worker is excluded from the "full-time work in the UK" test under the automatic UK tests (see **2.2.3**) and again cannot be automatically resident in the UK because of this test.

With regards to work performed in the UK by an individual who is not resident, HMRC exclude from incidental duties (see **2.3.9**) any work performed in the UK by a crew member of a ship or aircraft, so the earnings from these UK workdays will be taxable in the UK.

If employment duties are performed on a voyage that does not extend to a port outside the UK, then the earnings will be taxed in the UK (regardless of the individual's residence status), as will the earnings for work done by a UK resident on a voyage or journey, on a vessel or aircraft, which starts or ends in the UK (or if part of such a voyage or journey starts or ends in the UK) where the work is considered as having been performed in the UK.

For individuals working in the UK sector of the Continental shelf, this work will be regarded as from UK duties if in respect of the exploration or exploitation of the seabed or subsoil and their natural resources.

Deduction for seafarers

For seafarers with *general earnings* subject to UK tax under ITEPA 2003, sections 15, 22 or 26, or 27 if resident in another EEA state and liable to tax there, a 100% deduction against these earnings may be available subject to certain conditions being satisfied. This deduction is not available against *specific employment income* such as share-based remuneration like share options that are taxed elsewhere under ITEPA 2003. If the conditions are met, the seafarer's earnings may be free of UK tax even though the individual may spend up to half his time in the UK (see EIM 33000).

Since 2011-12, this deduction has also been available to seafarers who are resident in an EU/EEA state (other than the UK) and who have taxable earnings in the UK as a result of working in UK waters. This may well change following Brexit.

Non-resident seafarers outside the UK and EU/EEA are not entitled to the deduction. If such individuals work for a UK shipping company, and have had PAYE operated on their salary and so UK tax deducted from their salary, they may be able to reclaim this tax if it is not due, using tax form R43M.

Meaning of "seafarer"

A seafarer (for this purpose) is defined in the legislation as an individual whose employment consists of the performance of duties on a "ship" (see below) or of such duties and others incidental to them. HMRC indicate that this can include not just sailors, but anyone who works on a ship, including cooks, entertainers on cruise ships, etc. Currently, the definition excludes anyone in Crown employment, e.g. working for the Royal Navy, although the autumn Budget 2017 announced legislation to allow employees of the Royal Fleet Auxiliary to claim seafarer status for the purposes of this earnings deduction.

Meaning of "ship"

There is no statutory definition of "ship", but HMRC state that it must be capable of navigation and must be used in navigation, with navigation meaning ordered movement across the water. Therefore, structures that do not normally move about are not generally regarded as ships as they are not used in navigation. These include fixed production platforms, accommodation barges, light and weather ships, etc.

Offshore installations

Offshore installations that can use navigation, such as mobile drilling rigs in the oil and gas industry, are specifically excluded under the legislation (ITEPA 2003, s. 385); it follows that workers on such installations are not regarded as seafarers and so are not eligible for the deduction.

ITA 2007, s. 1001 defines an offshore installation as follows:

"(1) In the Income Tax Acts "offshore installation" means a structure which is, is to be, or has been, put to a relevant use while in water (see subsections (3) and (4)).

(2) But a structure is not an offshore installation if—

(a) it has permanently ceased to be put to a relevant use,

(b) it is not, and is not to be, put to any other relevant use, and

(c) since permanently ceasing to be put to a relevant use, it has been put to a use which is not relevant.

(3) A use is a relevant use if it is—

(a) for the purposes of exploiting mineral resources by means of a well,

(b) for the purposes of exploration with a view to exploiting mineral resources by means of a well,

(c) for the storage of gas in or under the shore or the bed of any waters,

(d) for the recovery of gas so stored,

(e) for the conveyance of things by means of a pipe, or

(f) mainly for the provision of accommodation for individuals who work on or from a structure which is, is to be, or has been, put to any of the above uses while in water.

(4) For the purposes of this section references to a structure being put to a use while in water are to the structure being put to a use while—

(a) standing in any waters,

(b) stationed (by whatever means) in any waters, or

(c) standing on the foreshore or other land intermittently covered with water.

(5) In this section "structure" includes a ship or other vessel."

In addition, there are a number of cases which cover what is and what is not an offshore installation. The following have been found to be offshore installations (thus preventing the workers on these from claiming the 100% deduction):

- fixed and floating production platforms;
- floating production storage;
- offloading vessels;
- floating storage units;
- mobile offshore drilling units (e.g. semi-submersibles, jack-up drilling rigs, drill ships); and
- floating accommodation units ("flotels").

Vessels qualifying as ships

EIM 33104 shows that HMRC do not accept that any of the above are ships. On the other hand, HMRC may accept the following as being ships, potentially making the 100% deduction available to workers on these, provided the vessel is not standing or stationed if engaged in a relevant use as defined above under the tax legislation:

- anchor handling vessels;
- construction and maintenance vessels;
- diving support vessels;
- heavy lifting vessels;
- pipe laying barges;
- platform support vessels;
- safety standby vessels;
- seismic survey vessels;
- shuttle tankers; and
- well service vessels.

HMRC point out that whether a vessel is a ship for the purposes of the seafarers' deduction depends on the facts of each case, including the nature of the duties performed by the vessel.

Mechanics of giving tax relief

The 100% deduction is available if the seafarer's employment duties are performed either wholly or partly outside the UK, in the course of an "eligible" period that falls wholly or partly in the tax year and which consists of at least 365 consecutive days of absence from the UK or is a "combined period" as per ITEPA 2003, s. 378(3).

It is a deduction against the seafarer's non-UK earnings during the period (or the part of the period that falls in the tax year concerned) and so results in none of these earnings being taxed in the UK.

The United Kingdom for tax purposes includes:

- England;
- Wales;
- Scotland;
- Northern Ireland; and
- the territorial sea extending 12 miles out from the shoreline.

Detailed guidance and examples can be found in the *Employment Income Manual*, starting at EIM 33000. HMRC helpsheet HS205 is also produced to help seafarers establish if they qualify for the deduction.

Relief is given by way of a deduction from the seafarer's taxable earnings and does not exempt the income. The relief does not extend to NIC.

A seafarer who is resident for UK tax purposes, and entitled to the above 100% earnings deduction, can still contribute into a UK registered pension scheme and obtain tax relief at basic rate.

Expenses claims by international workers

There are specific rules with regards to expenses that international transport workers and those working on vessels, including offshore installations, can claim.

Offshore gas and oil workers are exempt from tax under ITEPA 2003, s. 305 on their transfer costs from mainland Great Britain and Northern Ireland to the offshore installation they are working on (whether or not this is a permanent workplace). The exemption extends to related accommodation and subsistence costs, and local transport costs, and also covers the payment or reimbursement of the employee's expenses in respect of these, providing they are reasonable.

Where an employee works partly on a vessel outside the UK, a deduction may be made from his or her taxable earnings for certain travel costs paid or reimbursed by the employer, subject to conditions being satisfied (ITEPA 2003, s. 370(5)). Tax relief may also be available for travel expenses of the employee's spouse and family visiting the worker, if these have been borne by the employer. Again, these are subject to certain conditions being satisfied (ITEPA 2003, s. 371).

National Insurance

For NIC purposes, seafarers are referred to as mariners but the term also includes workers on offshore installations who are not eligible for the seafarers' earnings deduction. Because this is a complex area, a specific group within HMRC has been set up to deal with mariners and their NIC liability, the Marine Group at S0970, Newcastle NE98 1ZZ. A mariner can have his NIC situation assessed each year by the Marine Group by completing a "Mariners' Questionnaire" (see https://www.gov.uk/government/publications /mariners-national-insurance-questionnaire) each tax year.

As with all employee situations, the NIC implications may be divided into three (see **2.7**):

- The EEA and the EU social security regulations;
- Social security reciprocal agreements the UK has with various countries around the world (see **Appendix 3**); and
- UK domestic legislation.

A mariner will first see if the EU regulations apply to his or her situation. If not covered by the EU regulations, then it may be that a country with which the UK has a reciprocal agreement is involved. If so, that agreement needs to be referred to. But if neither the EU regulations nor a reciprocal agreement is relevant, then UK domestic legislation will apply to establish the mariner's social security liability.

Under the EU social security regulations, if the vessel the mariner is working on is flying the flag of an EU state, that will normally be the country in which the mariner will pay social security, regardless of his or her residence or domicile status (though there are exceptions as shown in NIM 29004 and 29005).

HMRC give the following example:

Example

Albert is a French national and is employed on board a vessel flying the flag of the UK. Even though he is resident in France, Albert is liable for Class 1 NICs under UK legislation.

This is very likely to be an area that will change following Brexit and it may well be the case that the reciprocal agreements that are still in place with various EU countries, but which have become largely redundant because of the EU regulations, may come into play again (see **Appendix 3**). However, this is just the author's opinion and only time will tell what the effect of Brexit will be in this respect.

When looking at reciprocal agreements, the relevant agreement needs to be referred to, so as to establish the mariner's social security situation. In this respect, the following factors may be taken into account when establishing where the mariner pays social security:

- where the mariner, employer, payer of wages or ship-owner lives;
- the place of business of the employer, payer of wages or ship-owner; and
- the place where the ship is registered, the voyage pattern of the ship and the flag it flies.

If neither the EU nor social security reciprocal agreements apply, then the UK domestic legislation will apply. According to HMRC (in the *National Insurance Manual* at NIM 29008, but with spellings corrected):

"A person is defined as a 'mariner' if they are or have been employed under a contract of service as:

- a master, member of the crew or radio officer of any ship or vessel, or
- in any other capacity (commonly referred to as a supernumerary) on board a ship or vessel where the:
  - employment in that other capacity is for the purpose of that ship or vessel or her crew or

143

> any passenger or cargo or mails carried by the ship or vessel, and
>
> o the contract is entered into in the United Kingdom, with a view to its performance (in whole or in part) while the ship or vessel is on her voyage."

For a liability to pay a primary Class 1 contribution (employee's NIC) the mariner has to be domiciled or resident in Great Britain, whereas a liability to pay a secondary Class 1 contribution (employer's NIC) arises if the employer is resident or has a place of business in Great Britain. For the latter HMRC will look at:

- contracts of employment;
- agreements with shipping unions;
- disciplinary agreements, payroll procedures;
- establishing who remains liable for the payment of earnings if the ship owner or cruise operator were to default on fees due to the offshore entity; and
- establishing who holds employers' liability insurance.

NIM 29014 has a flowchart to help establish if UK NIC is due when the mariner is working on a British ship and NIM 29015 has an equivalent flowchart if the mariner is working on a foreign ship. There are other flowcharts to assist in establishing a mariner's NIC situation if the individual is working as a supernumerary or radio officer.

This a complex area and NIM 29002 to 29034 has detailed guidance on the NIC implications for mariners.

For the NIC implications of aircrew see NIM 27002 to 27010, and for employees working on the Continental Shelf see NIM 28002 to 28007, together with regulations 111 to 124 of SI 2001/1004.

Law: ITEPA 2003, s. 40, 41, 305, 370(5), 371, 372, 378-385; ITA 2007, s. 1001; FA 2013, Sch. 45, para. 9(3), 14(4), 30; *Social Security Contributions Regulations* 2001 (SI 2001/1004), reg. 111 to 124

Guidance: EIM 33000, 34090, 34110; NIM 27000-29034; HMRC Helpsheet HS205; HMRC website https://www.gov.uk/guidance/seafarers-earnings-deduction-tax-relief-if-you-work-on-a-ship

2.3.18   Commuting employees

This section covers the situation where an employee commutes, perhaps on a weekly basis, from his or her home in the UK to work in another country, very often in Europe.

Example

George is a British national and lives in London with his family. He works in the Netherlands for a Dutch IT company and flies from London to Amsterdam on a Monday morning and then returns home on a Thursday evening, working from home in London on the Friday. So he spends four nights a week in the UK and three in the Netherlands. His home and family remain in the UK, and he lives in temporary accommodation while working in the Netherlands. He typically spends 200 midnights in the UK per tax year and so is automatically resident in the UK under the 183-days test (see **2.2.3**).

George will remain taxable in the UK on his worldwide income. The Netherlands may also treat him as a resident there for tax purposes and tax him on his worldwide income, although he may be eligible for a specific scheme for expats working in the Netherlands that may give him relief from Dutch tax (this is beyond the scope of this book). Even if George is not resident for tax purposes in the Netherlands, the earnings from the work he performs in that country may still be taxable there, subject to any relief that may be available to him under any special expat scheme.

In this scenario, George would need to look at the double tax treaty between the UK and the Netherlands. The first step would be to see which country he is regarded as being resident in for the purposes of the treaty under article 4, the tie-breaker clause. Assuming he is resident in both the UK and the Netherlands, then as his permanent home is in the UK he will be regarded as treaty resident in the UK. Even if he is not regarded as resident in the Netherlands, he will still be regarded as treaty resident in the UK, as he is regarded as resident in the UK under the UK's domestic tax legislation.

Under article 14 of the double tax treaty, George will not be able to claim exemption from Dutch tax under article 14(2), because his employer is resident in the Netherlands. He will, therefore, be taxed both in the UK and the Netherlands on some or all of his earnings, depending on his residence status in the Netherlands and on what tax reliefs are available to him under Dutch tax law.

Assuming the Dutch tax is less than the UK tax, the UK will have to give George relief for the Dutch tax he has paid on his earnings by way of a credit against his UK tax on the double taxed income, usually via a claim on his UK tax return. In this respect, George will need to be careful as to the credit he claims against his UK tax for the Dutch tax he has paid.

It is a common mistake for employees in this situation to deduct all the Dutch tax that was deducted from their salary under the Dutch equivalent of PAYE. They file their UK tax return first and then file their Dutch tax return later, at which point they discover that too much Dutch tax was deducted from their salary and so they are due a refund. In this situation, too much credit will have been taken against the UK tax, so an amendment needs to be made to the UK tax return, resulting in more UK tax being due. As this will invariably be after the payment deadline for outstanding tax for a tax year, it will result in late payment penalties and interest arising on a daily basis.

George will, therefore, need to make sure that he only deducts, against his UK liability, Dutch tax that is due and not refundable.

With regards to NIC, George will be covered by the EU social security regulations (see **2.7**). As he is working in two EU states, the UK and the Netherlands, the multi-state provisions will apply. Under these provisions, George can continue paying into the UK NIC system as this is where he resides, but only if he performs 25% or more of his work in the UK. On the basis that he works only one day a week in the UK, he may well not satisfy this test, in which case he would then be liable to Dutch social security as this is where his employer's registered address is.

With regards to PAYE, George's Dutch employer (being a foreign employer) may not have an obligation to operate PAYE on George's salary. Strictly speaking, George should operate a PAYE scheme himself. However, he can request agreement from HMRC that he can pay his UK tax via self-assessment rather than having to set up a PAYE scheme.

As can be seen from the above example, the taxation of such commuters can be complicated, with double tax commonly arising.

The social security implications can also potentially be complicated depending on whether the EU regulations, a reciprocal social security agreement (see **Appendix 3**) or UK domestic legislation applies. It is quite possible for double social security liabilities to arise with no relief for these, if the individual is working in a country not covered by the EU regulations or by a reciprocal agreement.

The introduction of the statutory residence test (SRT) in 2013-14 has meant that, in practice, weekly commuters and the like now remain resident in the UK. (This was not always the case prior to 2013-14 and, to counter this, HMRC took the view that internationally mobile workers who made frequent and regular trips overseas for their work, whilst maintaining their home and domestic life in the UK, remained resident in the UK. HMRC's views on this were given in the April 2001 *Tax Bulletin*.)

For such commuting employees, tax relief may be available for their travel and accommodation expenses. Relief for these costs under the standard employee travel rules (ITEPA 2003, s. 337 and 338) is unlikely to apply to such employees, as their travel expenses will most likely be to a permanent workplace. (If it is available, however, then the travel expenses do not need to be borne by the employer, so the employee can obtain relief for travel and subsistence expenses incurred and not reimbursed by the employer.) Nevertheless, seeing if relief is available under these sections is only the starting point before moving on to the following tax reliefs.

Under ITEPA 2003, s. 341, a resident employee may be able to claim tax relief for the cost of his travel at the beginning and end of his time working overseas. However, the employee must perform all his work overseas, so none must be performed in the UK. This may prove difficult, with more and more employees performing work from home in the UK (as in the George example above). Incidental duties in the UK (as tightly defined – see **2.3.9**) will be treated as performed overseas for the purposes of this relief.

If the employee works for a foreign employer then he or she must be UK domiciled to be able to claim this relief. However, the employer does not need to have borne the cost of these for the employee to be able to claim the tax relief.

A claim under ITEPA 2003, s. 370 can be made for resident employees' travel expenses to their overseas work, the cost of which has been borne by their employer. The work can be performed partly in the UK and so does not need to be wholly performed overseas. However, the employee must be absent from the UK wholly and exclusively to perform his or her work overseas, and the duties must be such that they can only be performed overseas. There is no limit to the number of journeys for which the resident employee can claim relief, but each journey must relate wholly and exclusively to the employee's work overseas, which can only be performed overseas. If there is any private reason for the trip then none of the expenses for the journey will be an allowable deduction.

Under ITEPA 2003, s. 376, a resident employee may be able to claim tax relief for the provision by his employer of accommodation and subsistence while he is working overseas, or the reimbursement of this by his employer. Relief is only available if the accommodation or subsistence is paid for or reimbursed by the employer, so no relief is available if the employee bears the cost of these. The employee must work wholly overseas, so this relief will not be available if the employee works partly in the UK, such as in the George example above. If the employer is foreign, then the employee must have a UK domicile (see **2.1**). Again, as with s. 341 claims, any incidental duties performed in the UK will be treated as performed overseas.

Under ITEPA 2003, s. 371, tax relief may also be available for the travel costs from the UK of a resident employee's spouse (or civil partner) and minor child to visit him or her while working overseas, up to a maximum of two return trips per tax year per person. Again, the employer (and not the employee) must bear the cost of these expenses. However, in the situation such as that of George in the example above, it is unlikely he will satisfy one condition for this relief, which is that there must be a continuous period of at least 60 days' absence from the UK for the purposes of his or her work (see EIM 34060 for examples).

Law: ITEPA 2003, s. 341, 370, 371, 376; EU *Social Security Regulations* 883/2004
Guidance: EIM 34001-34080

2.3.19 PAYE implications of moving overseas

The PAYE implications for an employee moving overseas will depend on the individual's circumstances.

If an employee has been assigned overseas by his UK employer, and remains on the UK payroll, then PAYE will continue to be operated as normal on his salary. In this scenario, the employee will need to consider whether or not he should apply to HMRC for an "NT" PAYE code, which means no tax is deducted from his salary. This would be necessary if the individual becomes non-resident and does not perform any of his work in the UK and so is not liable to UK tax on his earnings. If relevant, an "NT" code should be applied for in plenty of time prior to leaving the UK, to avoid cash flow issues if both UK tax and the host country's tax need to be withheld from the employee's salary (see PAYE 81665 to 81680).

Returning to the UK

If an employee returns to the UK after a time assigned overseas, then his or her employer does not need to submit new starter information or forms P45 or P46, but must inform HMRC of the individual's return, so that any "NT" code can be altered as necessary and an appropriate PAYE code issued (see PAYE 81545). This is also important from the employee's perspective, so that he or she is not faced with a large underpayment of tax that needs to be paid by the 31 January self-assessment payment deadline and which has arisen as a result of insufficient tax being collected under PAYE. This is a common issue for individuals arriving in the UK and can cause significant cash flow issues, especially if the individual has left the preparation and filing of his self-assessment tax return until the last minute. It is important, therefore, that an employee returning to the UK checks that the correct PAYE code is being applied, to avoid large underpayments of tax arising. The inclusion of a personal allowance in an employee's PAYE code that is not due, as a result of the individual's taxable income being at such a level that he or she is no longer entitled to it, often causes underpayments to arise.

Non-resident employees

If a non-resident employee is partly performing some of his work in the UK, the income from which is taxed under ITEPA 2003, s. 27, then a direction from HMRC under ITEPA 2003, s. 690 may need to be obtained. This will reduce the amount of tax collected under PAYE, failing which the employer is obliged to operate PAYE on all the non-resident employee's salary (see PAYE 81545 and 81555-81565 and also https://www.gov.uk/government/publications/paye-apply-for-a-section-690-or-informal-treaty-direction-s690).

Even though the employee can claim back a repayment of tax that is not due on his or her self-assessment tax return, this will obviously cause cash flow issues for the employee, as it is most likely that the host country will have a similar withholding obligation in respect of tax on the employee's salary. The application must be made by the employers or their agent and not by the employee. The employee will then declare the actual amounts of taxable and not taxable earnings on his self-assessment tax return. One point to highlight is that HMRC may refuse a s. 690 application if the employee is not up to date with his self-assessment tax affairs.

Tax equalisation

Employees assigned overseas who are tax equalised will have hypothetical tax (often referred to as "hypo tax") deducted from their salary. Assuming the individual is not resident in the UK and not taxed on his or her earnings in the UK, this hypo tax is not actual tax and so is not paid over to HMRC. It is the tax (and sometimes the NIC depending on the employer's tax equalisation policy) that the employee would have paid had he continued to live in the UK and not been assigned overseas. The employer deducts this hypo tax from the assignee's earnings and keeps this to pay for the host country's tax that the employer has agreed to pay for the employee. What this tax is on will again depend on the employer's tax equalisation policy; for example, some employers will pay the tax due on the exercise of share options whereas others will not. The situation becomes more complex if the individual remains resident in the UK or part of his or her earnings remain taxable in the UK.

Tax credit relief arrangements

For employees who remain resident in the UK but are working overseas, the PAYE code may be amended to take account of any foreign tax that is withheld from the individual's earnings, i.e. double tax relief is given via the individual's PAYE code. This is known as a net-of-tax credit relief arrangement (see PAYE 81715 and 82001).

National Insurance

A non-resident employee who is assigned overseas may remain liable to UK NIC only (and not to UK income tax) on his or her earnings. In such a case, the employer can apply for a modified NIC arrangement under PAYE 82004.

Law: ITEPA 2003, s. 690
Guidance: PAYE 81500

2.3.20   Limit on tax liability for non-residents

For non-residents, legislation is in place which limits the amount of tax the individual pays in the UK, known as the "disregarded income" rules (previously the "excluded income" rules). These rules apply to individuals who are non-resident for the whole of the tax year, so they do not apply to the overseas part of a split year (see **2.2.6**).

Basically two tax computations need to be prepared:

(i)   the first calculates the tax due as normal on all the non-resident's taxable income in the UK, taking account of the personal allowance if the individual is entitled to this as a non-resident (and any other personal reliefs the individual may be entitled to as a non-resident, as per ITA 2007, s. 811(6)).

(ii)   The second computation calculates the tax due excluding certain types of income (disregarded income: see below) and also the personal allowance (and any other personal reliefs available), and adds to this liability any tax which has been deducted at source on the disregarded income (and, prior to 2016-17, the tax credits associated with dividends).

Whichever computation produces the lower tax liability is used.

ITA 2007, s. 813 defines disregarded income, to include:

- interest;
- income from annual payments such as royalties;

151

- dividends from UK-resident companies;
- purchased life annuity payments;
- profits from deeply discounted securities;
- income from unit trusts;
- some social security benefits (such as the state pension);
- retirement annuities.

From 2016-17 tax credits are no longer associated with UK dividends. However, dividends are still treated as disregarded income for the purposes of this limit.

Example

Georgina is a British national who is non-resident, living in New Zealand, and has the following income for 2018-19:

	£
Dividends from UK companies	25,000
Rental income from a UK property (after allowable expenses)	15,000
Bank interest (gross, no tax deducted)	1,000

Her tax liability will be as follows:

1. Ignoring the above s. 881 limit:

	£
Dividends	25,000
Rental income	15,000
Bank interest	1,000
	41,000
Less: Personal allowance	(11,850)
Taxable income	£29,150

Tax due:

£1,000	bank interest covered by personal savings allowance	Nil
£2,000	dividends covered by dividend allowance	Nil
£23,000	taxed at ordinary dividend rate of 7.5%	1,725
£3,150	rental income (after personal allowance) taxed at basic rate 20%	630
Total tax due		**£2,355**

2. Using the disregarded income rules and s. 811 limit

	£
Rental income	15,000
Tax at 20%	3,000

As can be seen, the limit under s. 811 does not apply to Georgina as her tax liability is higher under the disregarded income rules, so her tax liability for 2018-19 will be £2,355.

If her rental income had been £5,000 rather than £15,000 then the above calculations would be as follows:

1. Ignoring the above s. 881 limit:

	£
Dividends	25,000
Rental income	5,000
Bank interest	1,000
	31,000
Less: Personal allowance	(11,850)
	£19,150

Tax due:

£1,000	bank interest covered by personal savings allowance	Nil
£2,000	dividends covered by dividend allowance	Nil
£16,150	taxed at ordinary dividend rate of 7.5%	1,211
Total tax due		**£1,211**

2. Using the disregarded income rules and s. 811 limit

	£
Rental income	5,000
Tax at 20%	1,000

In this scenario, s. 811 would apply to limit Georgina's tax liability to £1,000.

If she had made a loss in respect of her rental income, then no tax would arise in the UK for 2018-19, as the only taxable income Georgina would have in the UK would be dividends and bank interest, which are disregarded income and so can be excluded when calculating her tax liability.

See also section **6.2.4**.

Law: ITA 2007, s. 810-814, 825, 826
Guidance: INTM 269180; SAIM 1170

2.4 Capital gains tax

2.4.1 Introduction

Subject to the temporary non-residence rules (see **2.2.11** and **2.2.12(iv)**), the general rule is that a person who is non-resident is outside the scope of UK CGT. If a gain or loss arises during the overseas part of a split year, then this will also be outside the scope of UK CGT. As always, there are exceptions, one of which is the sale of residential property under the non-resident capital gains tax (NRCGT) regime, when a taxable gain or allowable loss arises from 6 April 2015 (see **3.2**).

It was announced in the 2017 autumn Budget, that from April 2019 the NRCGT regime would be extended to cover the disposal of all types of immovable UK property held by non-residents, so commercial properties as well as residential ones and also all land, no matter how the property or land is held. It will, therefore, include such entities as non-resident companies that are currently excluded from the current NRCGT regime (companies that are not close and which are referred to as "widely-held companies" by HMRC), meaning that this change will have an effect for not just UK CGT, but also for corporation tax. A consultation document called "Taxing gains made by non-residents on UK immovable property" was issued at the time of the Budget. At the time of writing, this consultation is still ongoing.

This consultation document refers not just to direct disposals, but also to "indirect disposals" by non-residents via entities that are "property rich", i.e.:

> "broadly where 75% or more of its gross asset value at disposal is represented by UK immovable property. ... Such

disposals will trigger the charge only where the person holds, or has held at some point within the five years prior to the disposal, a 25% or greater interest in the entity."

The consultation document states that for such "indirect disposals there will be a reporting requirement on certain third-party advisers who have sufficient knowledge of the transaction." If this reporting requirement is in point it needs to be carried out within 60 days of completion. (See paragraphs 7.12 to 7.15 of the consultation document). Advisers involved in such transactions should therefore keep abreast of these changes.

With regards to reporting requirements on the seller, then as with the existing NRCGT regime (see **3.2.12**) sellers will need to report the disposal within 30 days of it being completed (usually the completion date) for both direct and indirect disposals, if the disposal falls to be taxed under the capital gains tax regime. If it falls to be taxed under the corporation tax regime, then the non-resident will need to register for corporation tax self-assessment, if not already registered, and report the disposal under this regime.

It is proposed that the same penalty regime as for the current NRCGT and self-assessment regimes will apply for the seller. For third party reporting, the penalties will be those described under FA 2011, Sch. 23.

Rebasing of properties (using the market value as the base cost) will need to be done for April 2019, by obtaining valuations at this time for the properties and land concerned, although for non-residents already within the NRCGT regime, April 2015 will remain the relevant date for rebasing purposes for residential properties.

For direct disposals by non-residents the consultation proposes that they should have the option to compute the gain or loss using the original acquisition cost. This would be beneficial if the non-resident makes a loss overall. For indirect disposals, the consultation states that only the rebasing method of calculating the gain or loss can be used. The current option of using the straight line time apportionment method under the NRCGT regime for residential properties (see **3.2.10**) will not be available for either direct or indirect disposals of commercial properties, but will remain an option for the disposal of residential properties.

Any losses arising to non-residents subject to CGT will be treated in the same way as those under the current NRCGT regime, although losses and gains from this new regime and the existing NRCGT regime can be set off against each other. Losses that a company incurs under this new regime, under corporation tax, will be treated in the same way as any other losses the company incurs.

The consultation document includes an anti-forestalling rule that came into effect at the time of publication, 22 November 2017, and that prevents arrangements being put into place to avoid the new rules. From April 2019, when the rules come into effect, a targeted anti-avoidance provision will also be introduced.

As the above is an ongoing consultation at the time of writing, it is likely that some aspects of it may change before it becomes legislation.

Another exception to the general rule above – about non-residents being outside the scope of UK CGT – is if a non-resident carries on a trade, profession or vocation in the UK through a branch or agency. In this situation, that individual would remain liable to UK CGT on any gains arising from the disposal of assets situated in the UK and used in the trade, profession or vocation. Furnished holiday lets are, however, excluded from this rule.

Law: TCGA 1992, s. 2, 10, 10A, 10AA, 14B-14H, Sch. B1; FA 2015, s. 37, Sch. 7

Guidance: https://www.gov.uk/government/consultations/taxing-gains-made-by-non-residents-on-uk-immovable-property

2.4.2 Rates of tax

If a non-resident is liable to UK CGT then the rates of tax are as below for both 2017-18 and 2018-19. The Scottish taxpayer basic rate bands do not apply.

		Rates
Chargeable gains arising from (i) the disposal of residential property and (ii) carried interest	For an individual up to income tax basic rate band* Above basic rate band	18% 28%
As above	Trusts and personal representatives	28%
Other gains	For individual up to income tax basic rate band* Above basic rate band	10% 20%
As above	Trusts and personal representatives	20%

* £33,500 and £34,500 for 2017-18 and 2018-19 respectively

If a residential property qualifies for private residence relief (PRR) then the higher rates of 18% and 28% do not apply, as the gain will be exempt from tax anyway. For residential properties that are only partially exempt from tax under PRR, HMRC have confirmed that any chargeable gain remaining will be taxed at the higher rates of 18% and 28%.

Law: TCGA 1992, s. 4

2.4.3 Allowances

Non-residents, like residents, are entitled to the CGT annual exemption (£11,700 for 2018-19, £11,300 for 2017-18). This means that any chargeable gains up to this amount in a tax year are not taxed.

Any gains in excess of this are taxed at the rates in **2.4.2** above. This is the annual exemption for individuals and personal representatives. For trusts the annual exemption is lower at £5,850 for 2018-19 (£5,650 for 2017-18).

It is a common misunderstanding among individuals that they think the personal allowance (see **2.3.2**) can also be set off against chargeable gains. This is not the case. The personal allowance applies for income tax purposes only.

The above annual exemption is per person, and each owner of a jointly held asset (e.g. a husband and wife) will be entitled to the exemption.

Example

Married couple, Boris and Theresa, are non-residents living in Russia, where Boris has been assigned by his UK employer for a number of years. They rented out their home in the UK and then decided to sell it during 2018-19, as they plan to continue living overseas for the foreseeable future. The property is in their joint names.

A chargeable gain under the NRCGT regime arises of £30,000, after PRR and letting relief. This gain will be split 50:50 between them and so each will have a chargeable gain of £15,000.

Their taxable income in the UK is £45,000 each, which is rental income from their UK investment property portfolio. Boris is an American citizen so is not entitled to the personal allowance as a non-resident. Theresa is a British citizen and so is entitled to the personal allowance.

The amount of tax each of them will pay is as follows:

	Boris £	Theresa £
Income tax		
Income	45,000	45,000
Less: personal allowance	Nil	(11,850)
Taxable income	£45,000	£33,150
Tax at 20% on £34,500/£33,150	6,900	6,630
at 40% on £10,500	4,200	Nil
Total income tax due	£11,100	£6,630
Capital gains tax		
Share of gain	15,000	15,000
Less: annual exemption	(11,700)	(11,700)
Taxable gain	£3,300	£3,300
Tax at 18% on £1,350 (£34,500 less £33,150 see above)	Nil	243
at 28% on £3,300/£1,950	924	546
Total capital gains tax due	£924	£789

In HMRC's guidance notes on page CGN 1, they list certain situations where an individual must complete the capital gains pages and file a self-assessment tax return. One such situation is where the proceeds from the sale of a chargeable asset is more than four times the annual exemption, regardless of whether a taxable gain is made or not. For example, for the tax years 2015-16 and 2016-17 this limit was £44,400, for 2017-18 £45,200, and for 2018-19 £46,800.

Law: TCGA 1992, s. 3

2.4.4   Five-year rule

See **2.2.11** and **2.2.12** for a more detailed explanation.

An individual needs to be not resident for more than five years in order to escape UK CGT on assets which he owned at the time of departure and which he disposes of after leaving the UK. This five-year period depends on when the individual left the UK. If before 6 April 2013, then this needs to be for five full tax years, if after 5 April 2013 then it is five years from when his sole UK tax residence ceases.

If a non-resident becomes resident again in the UK during this five-year period, then any assets he sells after leaving the UK will be taxed in the UK when he returns. If the individual becomes resident again after this five-year period, then any assets he disposed of after leaving while non-resident will not be subject to UK CGT.

When disposing of assets, the individual will need to consider the tax implications in the country in which he is resident for tax purposes.

2.4.5   Non-residence clawback

An individual, whilst resident in the UK, has the opportunity to claim CGT "gifts relief" in certain circumstances but this is often subject to a requirement that the recipient does not become non-resident within a certain time period. Both transferor and transferee must elect for this treatment (using form HS295).

The relief shifts the taxable gain onto the transferee but, when the transferee leaves the UK to live or work abroad, it may therefore become chargeable. It may be the last thing on the expat's mind that CGT held over using gifts relief in a previous year of residence can now become chargeable on the transferee. HMRC are mindful of potential avoidance of tax on a rolled over or held over gain if someone then becomes non resident because they will not then be subject to CGT on UK assets (other than UK property). See the example at **1.3.7** (Taking independent advice).

It is only in certain circumstances that there will be a clawback of relief where someone has claimed rollover/holdover relief and subsequently become non resident within a certain time frame. These circumstances are considered in turn below.

Gift relief

This relief was once widely available (in the 1980s) on the transfer of assets from one individual to another. However, it is now generally limited to gifts of assets used in a trade or business (see "Gifts of business assets" below) and to gifts that are immediately chargeable to inheritance tax as a chargeable lifetime transfer (e.g. gifts into a discretionary trust).

For instance, where the donee is UK resident when the gift is made into discretionary trust, but becomes non resident within six years after the end of the tax year in which the gift was made, that individual will become subject to tax on the gain held over or rolled over on clawback. If the asset on which the claim was made was disposed of prior to the non residence then the anti avoidance provision will not apply.

These clawback provisions will not apply if the individual is going abroad for *full time employment* purposes and then takes up UK residence again within three years of leaving the UK: see again the example at **1.3.7** (Taking independent advice) and see also the Carl example below.

Schedule 7 of FA 2015 provides that where UK residential property is the asset, and is disposed of as a gift from a UK resident to a non-UK resident, holdover relief is not denied where the asset is chargeable to NRCGT in the hands of the transferee and the full amount of the held over gain accrues as a chargeable NRCGT gain for the transferee on subsequent disposal. Section 261 of TCGA 1992 would normally deny holdover relief for gifts to non-UK residents but this is now subject to this new s. 261ZA.

Example – Carl

Grandfather Bert is wealthy and goes into a retirement home where his company pension is sufficient to pay the care home fees. He knows he will not be returning to his four bedroomed family home and gifts it into discretionary trust for his grandson Carl and any future grandchildren, at the same time excluding himself from future benefit.

As it was his main residence there is no CGT liability on the gift into trust but there is a very small IHT charge as the value is slightly over the £325,000 nil rate band. The property is rented out by the family trustees and increases in value over eight years to £500,000. At that time, grandson Carl, who is now 18 years old and still the only grandchild, states to the trustees that he needs his trust fund to pay fees and accommodation costs for his three year university degree course.

The trustees, under the terms of the trust deed, decide to transfer the property to him so that he has a source of income whilst at university and they jointly hold over the gain of £150,000. However, after one year at the university, Carl decides to give up his degree course and goes travelling abroad, ending up in a commune in Goa where he becomes permanently resident. Carl sells the UK property and remits the proceeds to the commune, which means the deferment of the gain now becomes chargeable under the NRCGT rules.

The held over gain normally becomes taxable under TCGA 1992, s. 168(1) where the individual becomes non-resident without having disposed of the asset in question. However, where the asset is property it comes under the NRCGT rules and a tax charge then arises only on actual disposal, which applies to Carl when he takes the decision to dispose of the property (s. 14D, 167A).

The capital gains tax will be at 18%/28%. If Carl does not pay within twelve months the transferor (i.e. the trustees) will become liable and they would have recourse to recover the amount from Carl. However, they have not retained sufficient assets and it may prove difficult to obtain the funds from Carl to pay the tax. The trustees should have retained an amount to pay any potential tax liability on the held over gain becoming liable.

Enterprise investment scheme

A gain on the disposal of any asset can be deferred wholly or partly if there is a qualifying subscription for EIS shares. The subscription must be made in the period from one year before to three years after the disposal giving rise to the capital gain. However, the gain becomes chargeable if the EIS investor then becomes non resident within three years of the EIS shares being issued.

Interestingly, the rules regarding the seed enterprise investment scheme (SEIS) do not have a non-resident clawback exclusion although, of course, the investment limits are lower with SEIS, i.e.

£100,000 compared with £1 million for EIS. Similarly, the relatively new social investment relief (SIR) and the older venture capital trust (VCT) £200,000 investment schemes do not have non-resident clawback rules.

Gifts of business assets

This relief is now generally limited to gifts of assets used in a trade or business, farmland and farm buildings, shares and securities in unlisted companies, gifts of heritage property, and heritage property maintenance funds.

A person who is resident in the UK can roll over a gain from the disposal of qualifying business assets against the acquisition of new qualifying assets wherever they are situated in the world. Relief will not be denied where the person has ceased to be UK resident if all other conditions for relief are met and the person had ceased to be resident when the new qualifying assets were acquired.

Even if the replacement business asset, on which holdover relief was claimed, is disposed of whilst the individual is abroad there will be no clawback of the held over gains unless the individual is resident by design or default (under the temporary residence rules). However, it should be borne in mind that where the asset is UK residential property special rules apply regarding the introduction of NRCGT charges.

An election can be made so that the held over gain on a business asset that is residential property does not attract an NRCGT charge, but the full amount of the NRCGT in addition to any gain that has accrued will be charged on a subsequent disposal.

Law: TCGA 1992, s. 165, 166, 168, 168A, 260, 261

2.5 VAT and GST

2.5.1 Invoicing

Many countries throughout the world now charge value added tax (VAT) or goods and services tax (GST), including now the Middle East countries, e.g. Saudi Arabia and UAE at 5% from 1 January 2018. This is pertinent to the internationally mobile employee who may have furniture in storage, may employ the services of a local accountant, and may import furniture to the foreign country to which he or she is being posted (see below), etc. The question is: will VAT and GST apply?

The main problem a British expat is likely to come across VAT-wise is in connection with the letting of his or her property (or properties) in the UK. These are usually let on a shorthold tenancy agreement and, as such, are VAT exempt, so there is no need to register for VAT in most cases and the current VAT threshold of £85,000 would not be in point. The letting agent's charges would be subject to VAT at 20% on that particular portion.

However, if the property is let as furnished holiday lettings then this is treated as a business and as the expat is located abroad he or she is classed as a "non-established taxable person" (NETP) and has no £85,000 threshold to play with, so VAT is effectively chargeable on all turnover at 20%. To avoid this it is normal to appoint a letting agent in the UK to facilitate lettings for the expat, so that the agent's establishment in the UK supersedes the NETP position and then VAT will only be due on the agent's fees/commissions.

However, if annual lettings exceed £85,000 (e.g. if the expat has a number of buy-to-lets which are let as furnished holiday lettings) then VAT registration will be required. If the expat lets holiday accommodation during the off-season (see below), the expat should treat that letting as exempt from VAT provided:

- it is let as residential accommodation;
- it is let for more than 28 days; and
- holiday trade in the area is clearly seasonal.

The holiday season normally lasts from Easter to the end of September, although some popular tourist areas, such as London and Edinburgh, receive substantial numbers of tourists at all times throughout the year and are therefore not regarded as having a seasonal holiday trade.

Airbnb lets will usually (but not always) be rooms in the family home, i.e. the host is in residence and no VAT is applicable. Airbnb will charge a fee for finding the guest and this will have a VAT charge attached to it on that portion. Where the expat is not in residence (and this is more likely where couples tend to go on foreign assignment together) the NETP rules need to be considered as detailed above. Other relevant reliefs that may be relevant are the

£1,000 per annum "micro entrepreneurs' relief" and the VAT fixed rate scheme option – VAT is complex in many respects and specialist VAT practitioner advice is advised, especially concerning expats.

If the place of supply of the service is not in the EU the business does not have to charge EU VAT, but the supplier would include the sale in box 6 on his VAT return. If the supplier is supplying services relating to land and property, the place of supply is always where the land or property is located. Land and property includes the land itself plus any buildings or other structures.

Land and property services include:

- construction, refurbishment, conversion, repair, maintenance and demolition;
- professional services of estate agents, architects, surveyors, etc., but also see **3.1.8** (Airbnb and furnished holiday lettings);
- property management and maintenance services.

A pertinent example of this for UK expats is the storage of furniture/possessions whilst the individual is on overseas duty:

"190. For the particular example of storage of goods, the legislator has fixed the requirement that a specific part of the immovable property where the goods are stored must be assigned for the exclusive use of the customer (i.e. that the space where the goods are stored is identified, known by the customer and is allocated exclusively to his needs during the whole duration of the contract) for the storage to be seen as connected with immovable property."

The following services are treated as supplied in the place where the customer belongs, when provided to non-EU non-business customers:

- services of consultants, engineers, consultancy bureaux, lawyers, accountants, and other similar services – data processing and provision of information, other than any services relating to land;
- banking, financial and insurance services;
- supply of staff.

Examples of services that are not directly land-related include accountancy or tax advice, even when that relates to tax on rental income. Also, if Kris in the example below lets his house unfurnished and places his furniture in storage he would be charged VAT as the supply services directly relate to land. The place of supply of those services is where the land itself is located, notwithstanding that Kris is situated abroad. If the service of storage is provided to multiple specific sites in different countries it may still be directly related to land. Where this occurs, and the service is land-related, a suitable apportionment between countries should be made.

Other exceptional examples of VAT charged to expats are detailed in the examples below:

Example 1

Kris is going abroad to work for two years in Kenya. He now has rental income arising in the UK from renting out his UK home.

The UK managing agents, Big Letters Ltd, are deducting tax at basic rate on the rents and charging him a 10% management fee each year of £1,200. The storage company, Self Store UK Ltd, is charging £80 per month for 270 square feet of space excluding VAT. (Note that the application of VAT to storage was changed in October 2012 to apply VAT at standard rate.) Kris also needs to appoint an accountant to deal with claiming back the tax deducted on his rental income. He appoints Wiltons Accountancy, who indicate that the annual bill will be £500 per annum.

Company	Fee £	VAT £ pa
• Big Letters Ltd	• 1,200	• 240
• Wiltons Accountancy	• 500	• Nil
• Self Storage UK Ltd	• 960	• 192

Note: Wiltons Accountancy would require Kris's personal address in Kenya for the invoice so that the charges are outside the scope of VAT.

Services that are land-related include property management services carried out on behalf of the owner, such as by Big Letters. Under article 31a(2)(o), the concept of property management encompasses the administrative services provided to ensure the proper running, maintenance and use of immovable property. Typically, these services consist in coordinating the supervision, cleaning, and maintenance of the property; collecting rents; keeping records and managing payments of ongoing expense; advertising the property; enforcing the terms of the lease; taking responsibility for the mitigation and resolution of conflicts between the property owner and service suppliers and/or tenants.

Example 2

An expat resident is working in Japan and is insured there on a comprehensive worldwide motor insurance policy for the whole family. He receives news that his daughter has crashed the family car in the UK. The UK garage repairs the car, so the work is performed in the UK and the car is registered for use in the UK. The garage repairs have the effect of discharging the insurer's obligation to the insured party for the car and the place of the supply of the repairs is the UK. Therefore VAT is charged even though the insured is not resident in the UK but in Japan.

When freight transportation and related services are supplied to customers who are not "in business" it is necessary to consider the place of supply of the freight transportation, i.e.

- transportation from the EC to a third country takes place where the transportation is performed, in proportion to the distances covered;
- intra-EC transportation takes place wholly where the transportation begins; and
- the place of supply of related services takes place where physically performed.

Example 3

A UK individual who is being posted to Australia has arranged to have goods exported to there from Heathrow airport. The cargo facilitator is asked merely to arrange for a haulier to take the goods to the airport. The cargo facilitator is therefore acting as an intermediary in the making of arrangements of international freight transport with a haulier. The haulier is making supplies of transport in connection with an export and the cargo facilitator's supply is zero-rated. The haulier's supply is also zero-rated.

Subsequently, the cargo facilitator is asked to arrange for goods to be imported from Australia on behalf of the individual whose contract has ended. The cargo facilitator arranges the international transport, insurance, customs clearance, and payment of import duty, and secures the cost of transport from Australia to the individual's home in the UK. The cargo facilitator is considered to be making a single supply of international transport. The supply is therefore zero-rated to the extent that the transport takes place in the UK and the remainder of the journey is outside the scope of UK VAT. The payment of import duty is a disbursement and is outside the scope of VAT. The disbursements, such as payment of customs duty, are outside the scope of VAT and should normally be identified separately on the invoice. Expenses such as postage and telephone costs form part of the consideration for the cargo facilitator's supply even if separately itemised on the invoice.

Law: EU Council Directive 2006/112/EC; VATA 1994, Sch. 1A

Guidance: Explanatory notes on EU VAT place of supply rules on services connected with immovable property that entered into force in 2017; VAT notice 741A *Place of Supply of Services;* VAT notice 709/3; VAT notice 744B

2.5.2   GST/VAT abroad

Most countries in the world are now looking towards introducing VAT or the equivalent GST. In the Middle Eastern countries, the drop in oil revenues has perhaps precipitated the introduction of VAT and GST in order to supplement Treasury receipts.

Many Far East countries, not previously subject to VAT and GST, are also now introducing this tax, which adds to the cost for a posting to these countries. Relatively recently, for example, Malaysia introduced 6% GST, based on the UK's VAT system, and the latest of these countries to introduce VAT will be Saudi Arabia (see below) and Brazil. Countries that are working towards, or have recently implemented, a VAT and GST system include:

- Afghanistan, Bahamas, Bhutan, Kiribati, Marshall Islands, Micronesia, Palau, Sao Tome and Principe, Syria;
- Gulf Cooperation Council (Bahrain, Kuwait, Qatar, Saudi Arabia, Oman and the United Arab Emirates); and
- China and India – to have a uniformed GST system.

169

Example

Saudi Arabia has introduced VAT and Janine is moving there to be a theatre nurse at the main hospital in Jeddah. She is being provided with accommodation, as well as travel to and from the country two times a year, but the accommodation is unfurnished so she is taking furniture and personal possessions. She is concerned about whether she will be subject to VAT on importing her possessions.

Article 40 of the Saudi Arabian Customs Procedures Manual (exempt imports) states:

> "Imports of personal items and gifts carried in travellers' personal luggage are exempt from tax on importation, provided these fall within the limits set by the Customs Department for relief from collection of customs duty upon entry, in accordance with Unified Customs Law and the Customs Procedures Manual applying to the Kingdom."

Should she be registered to make importation to the Kingdom? Article 9 (registration provisions applying to specific circumstances) states:

> "Employed and other persons in so far as they are bound to an employer by contract or by any other legal ties creating the relationship of employer and employee as regards working conditions, remuneration and the employer's liability, are not considered to be carrying on an economic activity for the purpose of registration under the Law and these Regulations."

2.5.3   Digital services

In the EU where digital services are supplied on a B2C basis, the supplier is responsible for accounting for VAT on the supply; this must be to the tax authority at the VAT rate applicable in the consumer's EU member state.

The rules only apply where a UK business meets all of the following criteria:

- customers are charged for digital services (but those provided free of charge are not affected by the rules);
- services are supplied from the UK to private consumers in another EU member state;
- the EU customers are not VAT registered businesses; and
- digital services are not sold through a third party platform or market place.

Businesses outside the EU (for example, in the USA) that supply digital services to consumers in one or more EU member states are also affected by the changes. They will either have to register for VAT Mini One Stop Shop (MOSS) in a member state, or register in each member state where they have non-business customers.

The business needs to identify the place where the consumer is based, has his permanent address, or usually resides. This will be the member state where VAT on the digital services supply is due. For example, if a UK citizen is an expat who works or lives most of his time in Spain, then the business supplying digital services to that consumer should charge Spanish VAT on those services and not UK VAT.

Using the internet, or some electronic means of communication, just to communicate or facilitate trading does not always mean that a business is supplying e-services. For instance, using the internet for the services of lawyers and financial consultants who advise clients through email does not come within the meaning of "digital services".

Law: *Council Implementing Regulation* (EU) 1042/2013
Guidance: HMRC's *VAT: businesses supplying digital services to consumers*

2.5.4 Vehicle export outside Europe

The personal export scheme (PES) allows visitors and UK nationals to buy a motor vehicle in the UK free of VAT for export outside the European Union (see also **3.3.3** Motor vehicles). There are, of course, some restrictions but the motor car / motorcycle / motor caravan can be used for a limited period in the EU before it is exported. There is no need to use the scheme if the vehicle is not going to be used in the UK before it is exported from the EU.

The vehicle provider can zero-rate the supply of the new or second hand motor vehicle for export by the purchaser providing:

- the supply is as a direct export and the vehicle is not used or delivered in the EC before its export;

- the supply is as an indirect export, provided that the vehicle is not subsequently used except for the trip to the place of departure from the EC; or

- if the vehicle is sold to a private individual under the terms of the personal export scheme.

The DVLA will send a registration certificate which will allow the exporter to re-register the vehicle in the foreign country, providing that country allows imported cars. However, if the individual is planning to leave the UK less than 14 days after buying the vehicle he or she should notify the dealer before purchase so that the dealer can tell the DVLA or DVA about the export.

For second hand cars, owners will need to take the vehicle registration certificate (which will be in the previous keeper's name) with them when they leave. Shipping arrangements need to be made in good time, unless the dealer will be organising this for the purchaser, in which case the dealer can make sure that the vehicle is exported by the due date.

Factory-fitted or dealer-fitted extras are VAT-free if they're included on the initial invoice for the supply of the vehicle at the time it is purchased.

Example

Grant and his wife Georgina are selling their UK home and retiring to Malaysia under the "Malaysia My Second Home" (MM2H) scheme, which allows such retirees to import a car tax/duty free. This makes sense to them as cars purchased in Malaysia have a substantial importation loading.

Grant asks the dealer to organise some modifications, such as replacing the heater unit with a factory-modified air conditioning/climate control unit at a cost of £1,634 excluding VAT. The Range Rover 4x4 SD4 HSE 5 door automatic costs £59,460 but the free on board price (FOB) price is £51,135. The cost, insurance and freight (CIF) price will be extra on top of the FOB price, of course. In Malaysia the price for the equivalent Range Rover car would be £81,800 with the foreign car import duties, etc.

If Grant wants urgent delivery of the car, the dealer would get him to complete the certificate for urgent delivery, which confirms certain matters as follows:

Vehicle details:

Make:... Model:......................................

Chassis number:...................... Registration number:................

I hereby certify that I have this day personally interviewed
.... [name of applicant]
who assures me that he has not applied for or acquired a
VAT free motor vehicle under the Personal Export Scheme,
as described in Notice 705, within the last 6 months.

I have also inspected his passport, number:............................,
issued by .... [name of authority] and
the following documents: [see * below]......................................

I have no reason to doubt his status as an overseas
visitor/entitled EU resident [delete as appropriate] or his
declared intention to leave the European Union with the
vehicle on [date] .... [see ** below] and to
remain abroad with the vehicle for at least 6 consecutive
months.

Signed:..

Position in company:..

Date:...

* Example: details of car ferry tickets, overseas residence
   permit, return tickets, confirmatory letters or such
   evidence as was seen.

** This date must not be later than one month from the date
   of application.

Guidance: VAT Notice 707: *Personal Export Scheme;* VAT Notice 703:
Export of Goods from the UK; VAT Notice 728: *New Means of Transport*

2.6 Inheritance tax and will planning

2.6.1 Gifts

UK domiciled individuals are chargeable to inheritance tax in respect of property anywhere in the world irrespective of their residence status at the time of death.

There are three main ways in which an individual may mitigate or eliminate inheritance tax on death:

- by making substantial gifts during lifetime and surviving for a period of at least seven years after the date of the gift;
- by dissipating wealth during lifetime, by making lifetime gifts; and
- by altering his or her domicile from a UK domicile to a domicile of choice in the new foreign jurisdiction of retirement and residence (see **2.1** – Domicile).

As stated above, it is possible for an individual to reduce his or her estate effectively for inheritance tax purposes by making lifetime gifts. Some examples of exempt lifetime gifts are as follows:

Normal expenditure out of income

This method would apply to, say, life assurance policy premiums paid for the benefit of someone else, as long as such premiums form part of the individual's normal expenditure.

Other gifts out of income require the personal representatives/ executors to complete form IHT403, which requires comprehensive details of income and expenditure of the deceased for the eight years prior to death. Unless such records have been kept this requirement is difficult to meet and very time consuming in terms of historical research for the personal representatives/executors.

Law: IHTA 1984, s. 21

Gifts for family maintenance

This applies for married couples, and for the education/ maintenance of children (including illegitimate children) up to the age of 18, and for the care and maintenance of a dependant relative.

Law: IHTA 1984, s. 11

175

Small gifts to the same person

Any outright gifts to any one person in any one tax year, provided the total gifts to that person do not exceed £250 in that year. If the requirement is not met, even by £1, the exemption will not be available (but the gift will use up part of the annual allowance reduction, as below, if available).

Law: IHTA 1984, s. 20

Gifts in consideration or contemplation of marriage

Up to £5,000 may be gifted by a parent, £2,500 by a grandparent or £1,000 by anyone else. Note that if the marriage does not go ahead the gift will not count as exempt.

Law: IHTA 1984, s. 22

Transfers between husband and wife

These are exempt if both husband and wife have the same domicile or if the donee spouse is UK domiciled.

A non-domiciled spouse can elect to be treated as UK domiciled for IHT purposes by making an election (see **9.1.3** Advantages of electing for UK domicile). If the non-domicile spouse lifetime exemption is not available, any gift in excess of the annual exemption (and not covered by any of the other exemptions) will be a potentially exempt transfer (PET). It may therefore become taxable if the donor dies within seven years, and if the threshold of £325,000 is exceeded in total.

So a gift of £350,000 to a non-domiciled spouse would result in £25,000 being a PET and after seven years this becomes a "successful" PET. Alternatively, if the donor dies within seven years, the £25,000 would become a "failed" PET and would be allocated against any available nil rate band of £325,000.

Law: IHTA 1984, s. 18

Annual transfers not exceeding £3,000

The first £3,000 of lifetime transfers in any tax year are exempt. Any unused portion of an annual exemption may be carried forward for one year only, which effectively means that the individual could transfer up to £6,000 in one tax year (but the current year allowance is used first).

Law: IHTA 1984, s. 19

Exempt gifts

Certain gifts are exempt, including those made to charities or political parties, and gifts of land to registered housing associations. Gifts to charity exceeding 10% of the net estate after the nil rate band can reduce the overall IHT charge to 36%.

Most of the transfers made by an individual in his or her lifetime are either wholly exempt or potentially exempt (PET) unless those gifts are a chargeable lifetime transfer (CLT) (e.g. gifts into discretionary trusts – see **7.2.5** Offshore trusts). However, PETs are potentially subject to tax if the donor dies within seven years of making the gift, unless there is a CLT followed by a PET as detailed in the example below.

Even on death there may be no tax to pay on the PET unless, when added to reckonable chargeable transfers in the seven years before it, it exceeds the nil rate band threshold available at death. PETs that become chargeable are taken into account to decide how much, if any, of the nil rate threshold is available to set against the value of the estate at death.

If a PET does become chargeable to tax due to the death of the donor within seven years, taper relief is available to reduce the tax on that gift if the gift was made more than three years before death. The taper rate effectively reduces the liability to tax by 20% for each year after the first three years, so that an 80% reduction to the tax charge is available if death occurs between six and seven years after the gift.

The PET seven-year "look back" rule can in certain circumstances be extended almost to 14 years. This is likely to happen where there has been a chargeable lifetime transfer (such as the setting up of a discretionary trust, say for the grandchildren) and the gift into trust is followed by a PET. Therefore the net effect of this is that the CLT made more than seven years prior to death reduces the available nil rate band and therefore can result in tax payable on a later PET within seven years of death.

For this reason, any questionnaire checklist by an adviser (see **Appendix 2**) should include a reference to the set up date of any trusts in the previous 14 years. A case could arise such as that below.

Example

Angelina set up a discretionary trust for her grandchildren in August 2010 for £300,000 after advice from her financial adviser regarding "assets protection" (see the table at **2.6.2** below). She then made a gift of stocks and shares, valued at £150,000, to her son in October 2015.

Angelina dies in November 2018 with an estate comprising quoted stocks and shares of £500,000. The nil rate band during this period is a constant frozen £325,000.

The computation of the IHT on the lifetime gifts will proceed as follows:

- the discretionary trust CLT made in August 2010 is made more than seven years prior to her death and is therefore not subject to IHT; but
- the PET made in October 2015 is now chargeable as the donor has died within seven years in November 2018.

At first sight, the PET would seem to be covered by the nil rate band of £325,000. However, even though the CLT discretionary trust gift was more than seven years ago it affects the calculation of tax on the PET in October 2015:

	£	£
Nil rate band on death		325,000
Deduct previous CLT	300,000	
Less two annual exemptions	(6,000)	294,000
Nil rate band available for use against PET		31,000

	£	£
The IHT payable on the PET will then be calculated as:		
Gift in October 2015		150,000
Deduct two annual exemptions		(6,000)
		144,000
Deduct nil rate band as above		(31,000)
Total now subject to tax		113,000
IHT @ 40% on £113,000	45,200	
Less taper relief year 3-4 (20%)	9,040	
IHT payable by son		36,160

Therefore, in this case, the CLT that was made more than eight years before the donor's death has resulted in a £36,160 tax charge on the subsequent PET. This will be payable by the recipient of the gift, in this case her son.

Angelina only has an estate consisting of a stocks and shares portfolio of £500,000 which will not be impacted by this, and the IHT tax charge would be calculated ignoring the earlier CLT transfer. The estate would suffer IHT calculated as:

Angelina's total estate		500,000
Deduct nil rate band	325,000	
Less failed PET Oct. 2015	(144,000)	181,000
Taxable estate		319,000
IHT due @40%		127,600

Note: the additional residence nil rate band of £125,000 is not available as Angelina has no home, merely stocks and shares (see **2.6.2** – RNRB).

A PET which becomes chargeable because of death within seven years is brought into account at the value of the gift when it was made. The nil rate band threshold and rate of tax used are, however, those in force at the date of death, as in the example above.

It is therefore possible to fix the value of the transfer by making gifts during lifetime, and this may be useful where there are appreciating assets, as any later growth in value is in the hands of the donee. So in the example above the £150,000 stocks and shares may have risen to £165,000 but tax is paid on the original £150,000 value.

The capital gains tax position must also be considered by the donor because lifetime gifts of chargeable assets could be liable to CGT (depending on whether the donor is resident or temporarily not resident in the UK at the time of the gift). If an asset is held until death the increase in value escapes capital gains tax as the asset passes on to beneficiaries at probate value. Any CGT paid on a gift that is a PET cannot be offset in calculating the inheritance tax on the gift, if it becomes liable to inheritance tax. Of course the wealth of the donor will have been depleted by the capital gains tax paid, thereby reducing the inheritance tax payable out of the estate.

Gifts by a UK domiciled individual to a non-domiciled spouse during lifetime up to £325,000 are exempt, as stated above, and any amount thereafter is treated as a PET. However, if the UK domiciled spouse donor dies within seven years of the gift there will be a potential charge to IHT at 40% (after the £325,000 nil rate band has been offset if not already utilised).

Law: IHTA 1984, s. 3A, 23ff.

2.6.2   Trusts

The practical use of trusts is well rehearsed in the Claritax Books publication *Financial Planning with Trusts* and reference can usefully be made to that book. However, the UK trust structures – such as bare trust, discretionary trust, discounted gift trust, loan trusts, as well as some other overseas variations – form key areas of planning for the internationally mobile employee or retiree, and further uses of these options and others are therefore detailed at **7.2** – Offshore trust options.

See **7.2.1** for a table providing an overview of the different types of trust.

2.6.3   Residence nil rate band (RNRB)

From April 2017, a new residence nil rate band is available, rising to £175,000 per person by 2020-21, where the individual has a family home that is passed on to children and/or grandchildren. The exemption applies only to a "family home" transferred by a married couple or those in civil partnerships and is calculated before the nil rate band.

Therefore by 2020-21 a married couple with a family home and the full available nil rate band of £325,000 could benefit from £1 million, i.e. £500,000 x 2 as detailed below. The property / family home can be in the UK or abroad for these purposes for UK domiciled individuals but the exemption only applies to UK property for non-UK domiciles.

Those who can benefit are married couples with children, grandchildren, step children or foster children, who will inherit the family home on their parents' demise. So updating wills will now be a priority so that the children/grandchildren are specifically included as inheritors, and also to include adopted children, step children, foster children and illegitimate children, according to circumstances.

The £1 million joint total allowances for a married couple include the unutilised nil rate bands of the husband and wife together, i.e. £325,000 each, and the addition for the residence nil rate band (RNRB) of £175,000 each. By 2020-21 this joint RNRB saving is worth £140,000 in tax on death of the last spouse (i.e. £350,000 @ 40%).

This family home allowance is being phased in in cumulative tranches, the first tranche being £100,000 in 2017-18, with an additional £25,000 in 2018-19, £25,000 in 2019-20 and finally £25,000 in 2020-21, up to the full £175,000 per spouse / civil partner. The inheritance tax nil rate band remains at £325,000 for the estate of each individual after first using the RNRB, so this creates an effective £500,000 inheritance tax threshold for each in 2020-21, providing there have been no previous lifetime gifts made that were potentially chargeable, or indeed chargeable, transfers.

The new family home nil rate band is also available when downsizing occurs on or after 8 July 2015 and assets of an equivalent value, up to £175,000 in 2020-21, are passed on death to direct descendants. They will only be liable to inheritance tax if the total estate exceeds £500,000 per individual.

If the total family assets held jointly exceed £2 million the "family home" benefit starts to reduce by £1 for every £2 over that amount. So with joint assets of over £2 million the penalty starts to apply. The limit of taper in 2020-21 for a married couple would be £2.7 million when the allowance is dissipated completely. Consideration should be given to moving direct assets above this amount out of the estate at an early opportunity.

The following will not benefit (or will not fully benefit) from this family homes relief:

1. those with a family home abroad that is owned by a non-UK domicile with other non-property assets in the UK;

2. companies and certain trusts (e.g. discretionary trusts) owning the property (but see note below):

3. expatriates who have never lived in their UK home but rent it out;

4. family homes that are valued below the RNRB (i.e. these will not benefit fully);

5. those with only extended family, such as nieces and nephews;

6. those who transfer or gift the property during lifetime, as it is a relief on death only;

7. farmers whose farmhouse exceeds the agricultural value and that excess value, when added to the taxable estate, exceeds £2.4 million in 2017-18 (£2.5 million in 2018-19, £2.6 million in 2019-20, £2.7 million in 2020-21) (and see note below);

8. spouses of direct descendants who have since married someone other than the deceased's lineal descendant.

Notes

At point (2) above it may benefit from the RNRB if the trust is for a disabled beneficiary, for orphaned children under 18, or for any children under 25, as these trusts are treated differently for IHT purposes.

At point (7) above see also the Gerrard example at **9.4.2** (ATED) regarding the value exceeding the agricultural value of a farmhouse.

There is no need for the family home to be actually held by the direct descendants after inheriting it. For instance the estate's personal representative can sell the home as part of the administration of the estate and pass the sale proceeds to the direct descendants. Also, once the direct descendants have inherited the home, there is no restriction on what can be done with it. The estate will still qualify for the additional family home allowance, even if the direct descendants decide to sell the home after inheriting – there would, of course, be little or no CGT liability at that stage.

"Downsizing" relief applies in cases where the married couple have disposed of their family home on or after 8 July 2015 in certain circumstances, such as moving to a smaller property or going into a care home. To this end they can still benefit from the RNRB, no matter how long the interval between disposal and death, as if they had owned it until death and the downsized residence (or assets) is left to their direct descendants. It may be appropriate to include a clause in the will along the lines below stating:

> "I give free of tax a cash sum equal to the downsizing addition within the Residence Nil Rate Band amount to my children/grandchildren in equal shares absolutely."

The suggestion at the beginning of this section was for old wills to be updated to take into account the RNRB requirements that the family home or downsizing assets be left to lineal descendants. If this does not happen and, say, the property is left a non-lineal descendant such as a brother and his children, the RNRB will not be available. A deed of variation can be implemented to pass the property to the children, so taking advantage of the RNRB. See **2.6.8** below.

Example 1

Jon and his brother Nick now share their parents' family home since their death years ago. They both have children to whom they will leave their other assets. Each has a will that allows the surviving brother to live in the home until his death (i.e. an immediate post-death interest (IPDI)) and then each brother's half share of the family home goes to his own children. No RNRB would be due but if the survivor brother effects a deed of variation so as to leave the half share to the deceased brother's children then the RNRB will be due.

Example 2

Robert and Liz, British citizens, retired to Bali, Indonesia in January 2011, having sold all their assets in the UK. They bought a beach villa there, now worth £600,000. Note that in Bali foreigners cannot own land but can lease a property on Balinese land.

They also have a joint bank account in Jersey, with £500,000, into which pensions are paid monthly. Robert died in 2015 and left all his assets to Liz in his mirror will. Neither of them made efforts to change their UK domicile.

Liz dies in March 2018 and leaves her assets to their daughter Clara. Even though Robert died before the RNRB was introduced his RNRB amounting to £100,000 (i.e. the first instalment phase in 2017-18) will be added to that of his wife on claim. This RNRB is available in respect of their Bali property, together with 100% of the £325,000 nil rate band, which is transferable as he left all his assets to his wife (form IHT 436). Liz also has the same RNRB and nil rate band allowances available to add to those of her late husband, form IHT 435.

The property and bank assets are left to her daughter under the provisions of the mirror will. Therefore total allowances amount to £850,000 available to set against the Bali property and bank account in Jersey, leaving £250,000 taxable at 40%. Had Liz survived to 2020-21 the full £1 million (£325,000 + RNRB £175,000 x 2) would have been available for offset.

Clara sells the Bali property within six months for £610,000 and has no CGT liability. Had she sold the property for £650,000, HMRC may have raised questions as to the true value of the Bali property as reported for IHT purposes.

Law: IHTA 1984, s. 8D, 8FA-8FK (re downsizing relief)
Guidance: IHTM 27041*ff.*, 46000*ff.*; forms IHT435 and 436

2.6.4   *Will preparation*

Prior to departure from the UK, an internationally mobile individual and his or her trailing partner should have wills in place. This is vital if the estates are to be distributed on death as the couple would wish and not fall within the intestacy rules.

The intestacy distribution rules, which changed on 1 October 2014 following the 2014 *Inheritance and Trustees' Powers Act*, can have unfortunate consequences, some of which will be:

- If married without children, assets devolve to the surviving spouse/civil partner and not to relatives, charities or others whom the deceased may have wished to benefit.

- In the case of the married couple dying together (*commorientes* circumstances – see below), where the couple have children, there will be no provision for who will act as guardian for the surviving children. (Note: In Dubai, guardianship of minor children residing there with their parents will, if both parents die, pass automatically to the husband's family unless there is a valid DIFC will registered that states otherwise. See **6.7.4** and the will review section of the questionnaire at **Appendix 2**).

- If the couple are unmarried then the surviving cohabitee partner will not benefit in any part from the estate of the deceased unless the surviving cohabitee/partner is a joint tenant in the property.

- The loss of the opportunity to set up tax-efficient and asset protection trusts, charitable donations, and bequests to friends.

- See **Appendix 2** for an example of a will preparation questionnaire and **Appendix 4** for the intestacy asset distribution rules now applying under the *Inheritance and Trustees Powers Act*.

Example

Sam has been sent to Dubai on a two year construction project contract. His long-time girlfriend Angela cannot receive a dependent pass as she is not married and has remained in the UK but makes regular trips to Dubai to see Sam. Neither has a will in place. They share assets but it is Sam who owns their UK property and chattels.

On a weekend "dune bashing" excursion the vehicle turns over and Sam is killed. Under the intestacy rules applying from the revised distribution rules in the *Inheritance and Trustees' Powers Act* 2014, Sam's assets will go initially to his parents if they are alive and, if not, to his immediate relatives under the *Administration of Estates Act* 1925. Angela will not benefit and may have to vacate their family home unless she has a tenancy in common or is a joint tenant in property.

Further problems arise in Dubai if Sam has assets situated there under the laws of succession in the UAE. See "Foreign wills" in the example at **6.7.4** below.

It has always been advisable for an individual (testator), however small his or her estate, to draw up a clear and precise will, especially where there may be persons who are either left out of the will or given less than they consider is their due. Under the *Inheritance (Provision for Family and Dependants) Act* 1975, a UK court can order financial provision for family, civil partners and a wide range of dependants.

In addition, with the death duties imposed in many countries like the US, France and the UK on estates in excess of certain specific thresholds, then estate planning is a priority in conjunction with the drawing up of a will.

Also, dying intestate (without a recognised will), or abroad without a local will, becomes even more costly and complicated, and a "re-sealing" process is required in the latter case.

Even when the individual has a will it may still be contested. This can arise through sloppy or confused drafting or where the individual has drawn up his own will by using an "off the shelf" variety. See the *STEP code for will preparation in England and Wales*.

The Law Commission published a consultation paper in the summer of 2017 reviewing the law of making wills. One of the suggested new proposals was for the acceptance of new technological wills such as video wills and electronic signatures. Also being considered is reducing the minimum age for making a will from 18 to 16 and other diverse matters such as treatment of digital assets and mental capacity to make a will (e.g. in cases of dementia). The consultation ran from 13 July to 10 November and the outcome is awaited at the time of writing.

In the US, typewritten wills are the norm but holographic (handwritten) wills are recognised by some States and also oral (nuncupative) wills made in front of witnesses. Where a valid will has been made then, excepting any invalid execution of the will, the beneficiaries should benefit. However, on intestacy a surviving spouse is entitled to the grant of letters of administration in priority to all others and will receive all personal chattels, £250,000 absolutely, and a life interest in one half of the residue (See **Appendix 4** for Table). The children will receive one half of the residue at age 18.

In these cases, where the surviving spouse or civil partner (being UK domiciled or deemed domiciled, or having elected for UK domicile) benefits from the deceased spouse's estate under intestacy (see **Appendix 4**) the interspouse exemption will also apply. However, children and non-domiciled spouses / civil partners will potentially be chargeable to tax at 40% after deduction of any available nil rate band, residence nil rate band and debts. Any lack of a tax-efficient will or valid marriage certificate could result in a heavy IHT bill.

Under the *Inheritance (Provision for Family and Dependants) Act 1975* a court may order financial provision for family, civil partners and dependants of a deceased person out of his net estate. This provision in the 1975 Act has led to a raft of cases coming before the courts in recent years contesting the wills of deceased persons. This is evidenced by the recently concluded Supreme Court case of *Heather Ilott* which involved an estranged adult child who was partly successful in claiming from her mother's estate which had been left to certain charities.

In some cases brought before the courts the perceived injustice by a family member is deemed to be "totally without merit" – as in the case of *Ashcroft* – and the litigant is issued an extended civil restraint order. To counteract appeals against the terms of the will by disgruntled beneficiaries, a "forfeiture clause" can be inserted into a will to disinherit the legatees if the potential beneficiaries decide to prevent them from making a claim. However, this will not necessarily work with a litigious beneficiary or someone who has been excluded from the will altogether.

Law: *Wills Act* 1837, s. 1; *Administration of Estates Act* 1925, s. 25, 46; *Inheritance (Provision for Family and Dependants) Act* 1975; *Inheritance Tax Act* 1984, s. 18(3), (4); *Inheritance and Trustees Powers Act* 2014, s. 1

Cases: *Ilott v The Blue Cross and Others* [2017] UKSC 17; *Ashcroft v Webster* [2017] EWHC 887 (Ch)

2.6.5   *Mirror or mutual wills?*

The "mirror will" is one that replicates another and is usually the type of will a husband and wife agree should put in place. The wills are drawn under similar terms so that a husband leaves everything to his wife and *vice versa*. So, if either predeceases the other then, on the survivor's death, the assets are usually left to the children.

This type of will is simple and relatively easy to understand. The danger, though, is that the survivor of the couple can revoke the will, directing assets to someone else, and this can lead to litigation within families where parties have been disinherited.

The "mutual will", by contrast, is a binding agreement between (say) husband and wife which prevents the parties from changing the wills. In this connection, there is the "doctrine of mutual wills" dating back to the eighteenth century, which will apply where two testators (say, husband and wife) make identical wills regarding the distribution of their estates and agree that there will be no revocation of same.

The mutual will is difficult to draw up and make watertight. It cannot be dispensed with by only one party and the survivor is restricted on the destination of assets when circumstances change. There is, oddly, little case law, but see the recent case of *Legg v Burton*. If either party (usually the survivor) tries to revoke his or her will then under the law of equity an attempt at revocation will be prevented as the law creates a trust of the survivor's assets. At this point the Court will require clear proof that there was a binding agreement between the parties that their wills were not to be revoked by either party on the death of the other. An understanding would not be sufficient proof and evidence would need to be in the form of an express clause of such an understanding between the parties.

See *Charles v Fraser*, where paragraph 59 states in the judgment that an agreement may be incorporated in the will by extraneous evidence which is oral or written. In that same case, the wills concerned were very detailed as to their terms and in the estates, each allocated equal proportions to each party's friends and relatives. Persons concerned in the drawing up of mutual wills would be advised to look at the case and the nine points on the law of mutual wills. It was commented in the case that:

"I think it was the plain duty of any solicitor, then as now, faced with two sisters wishing to make reciprocal wills, to ascertain their intentions as to revocation, to advise as to the effect of making mutual wills and to ensure that any agreement the testatrices wished to make was clearly and accurately recorded. The fact that Mr. Collins does not appear to have done this in 1991 is a powerful point in Miss Da Costa's favour. It cannot, however, be conclusive because it is perfectly possible that Mr. Collins did not have the requirements of the law clearly in mind, did not do a very good job or did make some record which has been lost (no notes from the original file survive)."

Example

Bill and Gertrude have both been married before and only Bill has children from his first marriage. They create mirror wills so that on either death the survivor will inherit the assets of the deceased spouse and the assets will pass on to Bill's children subsequently.

Bill dies and Gertrude, after one year of mourning, meets "the love of her life", a trainer down at the gym. They marry. He is much younger than her and she is concerned that whilst he is currently employed he has little income and no pension provision for old age. Bill's children from his previous marriage are doing very nicely in secure, well paid jobs. Gertrude, mindful of these facts, changes her will and leaves everything on her death to her new husband.

Had Bill and Gertrude created mutual wills, and made them irrevocable by inserting such words in the wills, and had notes been kept by a solicitor at the time, then Gertrude would have been necessarily bound by the doctrine of mutual wills. The mutual will may have been as follows:

"Gertrude and I make this day's wills in similar terms under a binding agreement that these wills will remain in force until we both die. If the wills become ineffective, identical wills under identical binding terms will apply unless:

1. We agree otherwise;
2. One of us has given written consent to the other to withdraw from the agreement; or
3. One of us accepts, even implicitly, the other's repudiation of the agreement."

Point 2 above will become ineffective if the recipient is not able to make a new will or through no fault of his or her own became unable within 28 days of receipt of the notice without having made a new will.

Note: the rest of the will adds further terms and conditions.

Cases: *Charles v Fraser* [2010] EWHC 2154 (Ch); *Legg v Burton* [2017] EWHC 2088 (Ch)

2.6.6   *The survivorship clause*

Where a clause is inserted in a UK will which states "provided that [...] survives me for a period of twenty-eight days" then this 28-day clause insertion in mutual/mirror wills results in each estate passing as though the other mutual party had already died.

This means that, for instance in such disastrous circumstances as simultaneous deaths, or for couples who are not married or in second marriages, each party may wish his (or her) estate to go to his own family members by inclusion of the survivorship clause rather than to the family of whichever party outlives the other. For instance, in partnerships (i.e. co-habiting couples who are not married) each individual may wish to pass his or her own estate to family members so as to make use of the inheritance tax nil rate band of £325,000 together with, in rare circumstances, the residence nil rate band. (Normally unmarried couples living together share the house as joint tenants so on one partner's death his or her half share in the property goes to the survivor automatically and, as they are not married, the residence nil rate band would not be due. A tenancy in common in the property gifted to children/grandchildren would get round this but most couples have a joint tenancy for this very reason and never go to the trouble of securing tenancy in common.)

Law: *Law Reform (Succession) Act* 1995, s. 1

2.6.7 *Commorientes circumstances*

Where there is the rare case of spouses / civil partners who die simultaneously (*commorientes* circumstances) then the situation is complicated for inheritance tax purposes by the transfers-on-death legislation and inter-spouse exemption under the *Inheritance Tax Act* 1984, sections 4(2) and 18 respectively. The older spouse's estate can escape UK inheritance tax completely.

Because of this potential tax saving, a survivorship clause, which is normally desirable as mentioned above, is deliberately excluded in the event of the spouses dying simultaneously. This view is confirmed by HMRC in the IHT manual at IHTM 12197, and is illustrated by the following example:

Example

Gordon (37) leaves his estate to his younger wife, Wendy (34), by will, without any survivorship requirement. Wendy's will leaves her estate to Gordon under the mutual wills provision but if he does not survive her it passes to their children.

Gordon and Wendy are killed in a plane crash travelling to their overseas posting. The order of their deaths cannot be established so devolution comes into play according to the *Law of Property Act* 1925. Gordon is the elder and therefore is deemed to have died first (even though it cannot be known if this was the case or not) so his assets pass into Wendy's estate. Wendy's estate passes to their children who are at boarding school in England. Guardianship of the children goes to Wendy's sister.

The position for Inheritance Tax (IHT) is determined as follows:

- Gordon's death: His estate is spouse or civil partner exempt because it passes to Wendy and IHTA 1984, s. 4(2) does not prevent s. 18 applying.

- Wendy's death: Section 4(2) has effect to exclude Gordon's death estate from Wendy's death estate for the purposes of the charge on her death. Since Gordon and Wendy are treated as having died at the very same moment, tax is only charged on Wendy's estate.

Therefore Gordon's estate escapes IHT on both deaths. So it reaches the children, the beneficiaries under Wendy's will, without incurring a tax charge.

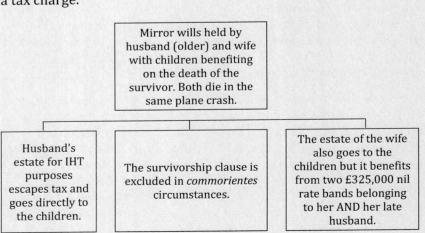

The position would have been very different if Gordon's will had required Wendy to survive him by a certain number of days, say 28, before she could inherit, or if he had died intestate. Gordon's estate would then have passed directly to the children and thereby would not be spouse or civil partner exempt.

Note that simultaneous deaths in Scotland and in Northern Ireland are treated differently and no spouse or civil partner exemption is available in these circumstances.

In the case of *Jump*, Mabel and John Minson had executed mirror wills and devolved their estates along the lines of:

- their estates to each other on the first to die; then
- pecuniary legacies of £234,500 to 23 beneficiaries; then
- the residuary estates passing to their nieces.

However, the wills did not address what would happen in the event of both dying together at the same time. Mabel and John died in circumstances such that it could not be determined who had died first. As John was the younger he was deemed to have died after Mabel.

The gifts under both wills were deemed effective. It was held that the survivorship clause used in the wills was wide enough in scope to apply so that the younger spouse, John's, failure to survive by 28 days after Mabel's death meant that the gift to him from her did not take effect.

In this case, therefore, the primary gifts under both wills failed and the wills had to be administered in accordance with the substitute provisions in the event that the original gifts fail. As a result, all of the gifts under both wills were valid so doubling up those bequests!

In summary, the problem was with the use of a standard precedent clause by the solicitors preparing the mirror wills. If the correct clause/wording had been used, the gifts would not have taken effect twice. Evidence in court suggested that John Minson had concern about a doubling up of the gifts and his fears had been allayed by the will drafter. This is why it is so important to instruct solicitors experienced in drafting effective mirror wills and gifts that only take effect on the survivor's death. See above.

Law: *Law of Property Act* 1925, s 184; *Inheritance Tax Act* 1984, s. 4(2), 18
Case: *Jump v Lister* [2016] EWHC 2160
Guidance: IHTM 12101, 12197

2.6.8   Deed of variation / disclaimer

An instrument varying a will must clearly indicate the dispositions that are the subject of the variation, and vary the relevant destinations as laid down in the will, or the law of intestacy, or otherwise, e.g. a disposal of property passing on survivorship. It is not necessary that the instrument should seek to vary the will or intestacy provisions themselves: it is sufficient if the instrument identifies the disposition to be varied and varies its destination. See the example below.

The statutory tax provisions for this relief arise under IHTA 1984, s. 142 and TCGA 1992, s. 62. HMRC have also specified certain conditions which they consider must be satisfied before an instrument of variation can come within IHTA 1984, s. 142.

The practicalities of a deed of variation are such that the instrument must contain a statement made by all of the "relevant persons," i.e. those persons who are going to give up the benefit of assets under the terms of the original will and the personal representatives where there is *additional* IHT payable arising from the change. It would be strange from a tax planning point if there was additional IHT but there may be family or other non-tax circumstances that apply to the particular variation and that result in additional tax.

If there is any alteration in the tax payable, beneficial or otherwise, as a result of the variation then a copy of the deed should be sent to HMRC. There is no substitute for getting the will drafting right in the first place but at the moment, at least, there is another option in the form of a deed of variation.

Example 1

Gerald, who is English domiciled, dies in Australia where he has a manufacturing business. He owns 100% of the share capital in OZ Air Conditioners Pty Ltd and leaves the shares to his wife, along with the other assets in the UK. He and his wife Angela have two sons.

Angela has no desire to make regular trips to Australia to monitor the business and wishes to pass the shares on to the sons. The assets being passed to Angela by her late husband benefit from the inter-spouse exemption under IHTA 1984, s 18. However, a deed of variation passing the shares to the two sons equally would benefit from the business property relief (BPR) exemption under IHTA 1984, s. 105(1). The deed is executed within the two years following Gerald's death.

The fact that the business is situated in Australia does not preclude BPR but if the business had been farming then the agricultural property relief (APR) would not be due as APR is restricted to the UK, Channel Islands, Isle of Man and EEA. See IHTA 1984, s. 116(8).

A deed of variation might therefore be drawn up on the following lines:

THIS DEED OF VARIATION is made 2018

BETWEEN

1. 'the Mother', Namely.......................of...

2. 'The Sons', Namely..........of............... and ....of.................

3. 'The Executors', Namely (1)...........................of...............,
    (2)...............of....................., and (3).............of...........................

WHEREAS

A.   ....of.....................('the Father') died on
        ....2018;

B. The Father's will dated ....('the Will') appointed
    Executors to be executors and trustees of his estate;

C. The Executors obtained probate of the will from the
    [...............] District Probate Registry on 2017;

D. Under the Will the Mother is by Clause 3 entitled wholly to
    100% of the shares in Oz Air Conditioners Ltd and a net
    income of the company after expenses and disbursements;

E. The property detailed in the Schedule ('the Property')
    comprises the assets and liabilities of OZ Air Conditioners
    Ltd;

F. The Mother wishes to vary the dispositions of the Will as
    follows:

NOW THIS DEED WITNESSES

1. The Will shall be deemed to read and always to have read as if
    the Property has been left (subject to tax) to the Sons as
    tenants in common in equal shares absolutely.

2. The parties elect for section 142 of the Inheritance Tax Act
    1984 and section 62 of the Taxation of Chargeable Gains Act
    1992 as amended to apply to this deed.

Note: The UK/Australia double tax treaty, at article 13, states under
Alienation of Property that "income and gains derived by a resident
of a Contracting State from the alienation of real property situated

in the other Contracting State may be taxed in that other State". This implies that there would be taxation imposition in Australia on the disposal by gift or otherwise, but Australia does not impose estate taxes. This deed would need to be confirmed as acceptable by a tax lawyer in Australia.

Example 2

Trevor and his wife Trish have both been married before. They both have two children from their first marriages but none themselves in the current marriage. Both are wealthy in their own right, each having assets amounting to £2.5 million.

Their mirror wills leave 50% of their estates to each other on death and the remaining 50% to be distributed equally to both sets of children so each gets 12.5% of the estate. The survivor spouse will leave their assets to all four children equally.

Trish dies suddenly and £1.25 million before nil rate band is to go to the four children, giving an IHT liability of £370,000. Trevor's children decide to sign a deed of variation relinquishing their shares in favour of their father, which reduces the taxable estate to £625,000 on which IHT tax is due of £120,000, so Trish's children's after tax entitlement increases by £32,500. Trevor's children are confident that they will benefit from his estate at a later date.

There is no written or verbal agreement or understanding between Trevor and his children (and solicitors), merely an expectation. HMRC would inspect the deed of variation (DoV) / instrument of variation (IoV) to check:

- whether there had been any discussion between the parties before the DoV/IoV was made about how the benefit redirected to Trevor should be dealt with; and

- whether subsequent to the DoV/IoV Trevor has made any transfers to the original chargeable beneficiaries, or is contemplating making any such transfers.

The expectation by Trevor's children that they will eventually benefit from their father's will is merely that, an expectation.

An expectation is not a written or verbal agreement or an understanding within the first bullet point above. In fact s. 142(3) states:

> "Subsection (1) above shall not apply to a variation or disclaimer made for any consideration in money or money's worth other than consideration consisting of the making, in respect of another of the dispositions, of a variation or disclaimer to which that subsection applies."

In the case of *Lau* the deceased's step-son disclaimed £665,000, which then passed to the deceased's widow as part of the residuary estate. Soon after receiving the money from the estate, the widow passed £1m back to the step-son, which would have normally been treated as a PET but for s. 142(3) above. The widow argued that the £1m was nothing to do with the step-son disclaiming the legacy and it was a combination of:

- a wedding present; and
- partly a payment to set the step-son up in business, which she had promised long ago.

This evidence was rejected by the Judge, partly due to the fact that a solicitor had advised that the children could save IHT by disclaiming the legacies and receiving the money as potentially exempt transfers instead. He commented:

> "The £1 million payment was not connected with Mr Harris' marriage. The Appellant's explanations for the wedding gift were inconsistent and contradictory which together with her failure to explain not making the payment either on or before the dates of the proposed wedding or the actual wedding significantly undermined her assertion that the payment was a wedding gift in part or in full."

Clearly, therefore, subsequent gifts made by the beneficiary of the deed of variation will be scrutinised by HMRC and if there is any "agreement" may be nul and void.

Oddly, in cases regarding the *Mental Capacity Act* an application to the Court of Protection to change an existing will can be successful as "it may authorise gifts beyond the scope of what is permitted by section 12(2) (for example for tax planning purposes)". From the point of view of tax planning it is also always judicious to keep in mind the General Anti Abuse Rule (GAAR) which states that:

> "Where taxpayers set out to exploit some loophole in the tax laws, for example by entering into some contrived arrangements to obtain a relief but suffering no equivalent economic risk, they will fall into the target area of the GAAR."

In certain cases, potential beneficiaries may not wish to benefit from a will and may wish to disclaim their benefit. See the case of *Lau* above. A disclaimer must also be made in writing within two years of the date of death of the testator. It will be void if consideration is given in money or money's worth.

A disclaimer deed is unilateral, and the personal representatives are not party to the disclaimer (unlike a deed of variation), but see the example below. In the case of a potential beneficiary's interest in settled property a disclaimer may apply whereas a variation may not. See IHTM 35161 onwards.

Example 3

If Alec dies leaving property to Brenda, who does not want ownership for personal reasons, then the property can be excluded from Brenda's estate for IHT purposes by a disclaimer. Brenda has not received the property from the estate of Alec or received any benefit from it, e.g. use of the seaside holiday home. Brenda's personal representatives and beneficiaries agree, within the rules of IHTA 1984, s 142(1).

THIS DEED OF DISCLAIMER is made by .... of .... ('Ms Brenda X')

WHEREAS

A.   [.........] died on ....2018 ('the Testator');

B.   The Testator left a Will dated .... ('The Will');

C.   Under clause 4 of the Will the Testator leaves the property called 'Sea Breeze' (land Registry number ....) at the address .... to Ms Brenda X;

D.   Ms Brenda X wishes to disclaim the gift.

NOW THIS DEED WITNESSES as follows:

1.   Ms Brenda X disclaims the afore-stated gift; and

2.   Ms Brenda X confirms that she has accepted or received no benefit from the gift.

Law: IHTA 1984, s. 142, 143, 144; TCGA 1992, s. 62

Cases: *Lau v HMRC* [2009] STC (SCD) 352; *Vaughan-Jones v Vaughan-Jones* [2015] EWHC 1086

Guidance: IHTM 35000ff.

2.7   NIC and social security

2.7.1   Introduction

An area that is often forgotten by those leaving the UK is their NIC (National Insurance contributions) and social security position. It is possible for an individual not to be liable to UK tax, but still liable to NIC on his or her earnings.

When an individual is looking at his social security situation, his entitlement to benefits – and any interruption in his contributions record – should be considered, as well as the cost element. For example, an individual paying social security on his earnings in his host country should consider whether he wishes to pay UK NIC on a voluntary basis as well (if he can), in order to protect his entitlement to a full state pension in the UK, and potentially other UK state benefits too (see **2.7.5**).

The NIC world is divided into three:

(i)   the EEA (European Economic Area) and the EC social security regulations;

(ii)   countries with which the UK has reciprocal social security agreements (see **Appendix 3**); and

(iii) the rest of the world, which is covered by the UK's domestic legislation.

When an individual moves overseas, the first step, therefore, is to see whether the EC regulations apply and, if not, whether a reciprocal agreement is in place. It is only when neither of these applies that the UK domestic legislation is referred to.

Unlike the position with tax, there are neither specific agreements between countries nor relief under UK domestic legislation, to alleviate any double social security contributions charges that are due in the UK and the host country on the same earnings. It is therefore very possible for an individual to be in this situation if the individual's NIC liability is determined under UK domestic legislation, although this is unlikely to be the case under the EC regulations or a reciprocal agreement.

With employment, NIC is split into two types – an element paid by the employee (employee's NIC, also known as primary contributions) and another element paid by the employer (employer's NIC, known as secondary contributions). The first step is to see what the employee's liability is and, in most countries, the employer's liability will then follow the employee's liability.

There are various classes of NIC, as follows:

Type of income	Class of NIC	Who pays
Employment – salary and similar	Class 1	Both employees and employers
Employment – benefits in kind	Class 1A	Employers only
Employment – PAYE settlement agreement (PSA)	Class 1B	Employers only
Self-employed	Class 2, Class 4	Self-employed individuals (both classes); also overseas employees on a voluntary basis (Class 2 only)
Voluntary	Class 3	Individuals wishing to pay NIC on a voluntary basis

The rates of NIC and relevant thresholds are as follows:

Class 1 NIC

	2017-18	2018-19
Weekly lower earnings limit (LEL)	£113	£116
Weekly primary threshold (PT)	£157	£162
Weekly secondary threshold (ST)	£157	£162
Upper earnings limit (UEL)	£866	£892
NIC rates		
Employee's Class 1 NIC (primary)		
Below the LEL	0%	0%
Between the LEL and PT	0%	0%
Between the PT and UEL	12%	12%
Above the UEL	2%	2%
Employer's Class 1 NIC (secondary)		
Below the ST	0%	0%
Above the ST	13.8%	13.8%

Class 2 NIC

	2017-18	2018-19
Small profits threshold (SPT)	£6,025pa	£6,205pa
NIC rates		
Below the SPT (n/a for employees working overseas and paying Class 2 on voluntary basis)	0%	0%
Above SPT or an employee working overseas and paying on a voluntary basis	£2.85pw	£2.95pw

Class 3 NIC

	2017-18	2018-19
Weekly rates	£14.25	£14.65

Class 4 NIC

	2017-18	2018-19
Lower profits limit (LPL)	£8,164	£8,424
Upper profits limit (UPL)	£45,000	£46,350
NIC rates		
Below LPL	0%	0%
LPL to UPL	9%	9%
Above UPL	2%	2%

Guidance: NIM 33000; HMRC leaflet NI38 *Social security abroad*

2.7.2   The EC social security regulations

The EC regulations take priority over social security reciprocal agreements the UK has with various countries and over the UK's domestic NIC legislation. These regulations apply in respect of EEA states which, at the time of writing, are:

Austria	Greece	Norway
Belgium	Hungary	Poland
Bulgaria	Iceland	Portugal
Croatia	Ireland (The Republic)	Romania
Cyprus	Italy	Slovakia
Czech Republic	Latvia	Slovenia
Denmark	Liechtenstein	Spain
Estonia	Lithuania	Sweden

Finland	Luxembourg	Switzerland (not an EEA country but applies EC social security regulations)
France	Malta	UK (includes Gibraltar, but not the Channel Islands or Isle of Man)
Germany	The Netherlands	

These regulations also apply to any EEA citizen, and so will apply if (say) a British citizen who normally lives outside the EEA returns to work in the UK or another EEA country.

The basic rule under these regulations is that an individual only pays social security in one country at any one time on the same earnings, which is the place where he or she is physically performing the work. This is the case regardless of where the individual lives and of the location of the employer's registered office or business.

Example 1 – Nigella

Nigella, a UK citizen, has been assigned for at least six years to France by her UK employer. Her employment contract has remained with her UK employer, but she performs all her work in France. She will therefore be liable to French social security on her earnings rather than UK NIC, from the time she starts working in France. Her NIC liability will cease when she stops working in the UK.

Her employer in the UK will also pay French social security on her French earnings from the date she started working there and employer's NIC will cease when she stops working in the UK.

There are exceptions to the above rule.

Under article 12 of EC regulation 883/2004, if an employee is assigned temporarily by his UK employer to work in an EEA country for less than two years (known as a "posted worker"), then he can remain in the UK NIC system rather than having to pay social security in the country he is working in, providing he is not replacing another posted worker. There are various conditions that need to be satisfied (see article 14 of EC regulation 987/2009).

Article 16 of EC regulation 883/2004 allows for a longer period than 24 months to remain in the UK NIC system by mutual consent between HMRC and the host country social security authority, if it is in the interests of the individual concerned (see NIM 33115).

An employer should apply to HMRC online for an A1 (certificate of coverage), using forms CA3821 and CA3822. This application should occur before the assignment starts, though HMRC will issue certificates retrospectively after the secondment has started. A copy of the A1 should be kept by the employee as proof of his or her continuing liability in the UK and another copy should be kept by the host country employer, to back up the non-payment of contributions in the host country. At the same time as issuing an A1 certificate, HMRC will issue European health insurance cards (EHIC) for the individual and his or her family to enable them to access medical treatment in the host country.

Another exception is if the employee is working in more than one EEA country simultaneously, referred to as "multi-state employ-ment". In this situation, article 13 of EC regulation 883/2004 states that the employee will pay contributions in the country in which he resides (i.e. his habitual residence – his centre of vital interests), providing a substantial amount of his work is performed in that country. "Substantial" here means that at least 25% of his work must be performed in the country or at least 25% of his remuneration must come from working in that country. If that is not the case, then he will pay contributions in the EEA state in which his employer's registered office or place of business is located.

Example 2 – Bernard

Bernard is a British national who is employed by a German employer whose registered office and place of business is in Berlin. Bernard is a senior manager for marketing in Europe and so travels extensively within the EEA, but he remains living in his home in Richmond, Surrey. He spends on average one day a week working in the UK and the rest of his time working in other EEA states. This one day's work is less than 25% of his work time and so, as his remuneration relates evenly to all his work, he will pay German social security rather than UK NIC, on the grounds that his employer's registered office is in Germany.

If Bernard wishes to pay UK NIC rather than German social security he would need to increase the number of days he works in the UK to at least 25% of his total work days.

If the individual works for more than one employer, whose registered offices are in different EEA states, then he will pay contributions in the country in which he habitually resides.

If the individual works in two or more EEA states for an employer whose registered office and place of business are outside the EEA, then he will pay contributions in the country where he is resident.

If the employee does not reside in any of the EEA states in which he works, then he will pay contributions in the country where the employer's registered office or place of business is located.

Where the above multi-state rules apply, a certificate needs to be obtained via form CA8421i.

Article 11 of EC regulation 987/2009 details the criteria for establishing which EEA state is the individual's state of residence and if agreement on this cannot be reached between EEA social security authorities, article 6 of the same regulations lays down where the employee will pay social security contributions in this scenario.

The advantage of the EC social security regulations is that, in certain situations, they allow an employee who is working in the EEA to remain within the UK NIC system and so to continue to be entitled to benefits in the UK, such as the state pension. This may be particularly important for an employee who is coming up to retirement.

This is perhaps one of the more significant areas where a British expat may be affected by Brexit, if he or she is living and/or working in another EEA country, or has done so in the past. At present, there is no indication as to what may happen in this respect, but it is the author's opinion that the reciprocal agreements that are still in place with various EEA countries may come into effect again once Brexit occurs. At present, these agreements, although still in existence, have largely been overridden by the EC regulations unless a certain aspect of an expat's situation is not covered by these regulations, in which case reference is made to any reciprocal agreement that may be in place. This is only the author's opinion as to what may happen after Brexit and only time will tell what will actually happen.

Law: EC regulations 883/2004, 987/2009 (1408/71, 574/72 for before 1 May 2010)

Guidance: NIM 33020 (NIM 33300 for before 1 May 2010)

2.7.3   UK reciprocal social security agreements

Appendix 3 lists the countries with which the UK has the above agreements. As with the EC social security regulations, these agreements override UK domestic NIC legislation. Some agreements (such as the one with New Zealand) only cover benefits and not contributions.

In general, the agreements are based on similar terms, although there are some differences and so, as with double tax treaties, it is important to look at each agreement.

Some of the common elements are that the employee generally pays contributions in the country he is working in, although there are exceptions in respect of employees:

- who have been seconded between the two countries;
- who are international transport workers or mariners; or
- of the Crown, some other statutory body or armed forces.

For employees seconded between the two countries, the rules are very similar to those under the EC regulations (at **2.7.2** above), i.e. they remain in the home country system. So British expats assigned overseas remain in the UK NIC system for a certain period of time, which varies between the different agreements (e.g. the UK/USA agreement stipulates five years). In this situation, the employer will apply to HMRC for a certificate of coverage. See NIM 33425 for an HMRC flowchart for individuals going abroad.

Guidance: NIM 33400, 33425

2.7.4   UK domestic rules

The domestic legislation covering NIC is different to tax legislation. Terms such as "residence" are not defined in the same way as for tax, meaning that residence for NIC purposes is not defined under the statutory residence test (see **2.2**). In addition, the concept of ordinary residence still exists for NIC purposes while it no longer does for tax purposes (see NIM 33555 and 33560 and HMRC leaflet NI38 page 6).

Whether NIC is due depends on certain factors.

First, the individual needs to be regarded as an "employed earner", which the legislation (at SSCBA 1992, s. 2(1)) defines as being "a person who is gainfully employed in Great Britain either under a contract of service, or in an office (including elective office) with earnings". HMRC's view in this respect is that it is where the employee physically performs the work that dictates whether or not NIC is due on his or her earnings, so if an employee is not physically performing work in the UK, there is no NIC liability. The legislation refers to Great Britain, which excludes Northern Ireland, but there is legislation in place for Northern Ireland which mirrors that for Great Britain. An individual is gainfully employed if he is paid for the work he does (or hopes/wishes to obtain remuneration or profit from his employment) or is under a contract of service.

The individual also needs to be either resident or ordinarily resident (for NIC and not tax purposes) or present in the UK (based on the facts of each case).

For employees leaving the UK, the "52-week rule" may be applicable under regulation 146 of *The Social Security (Contributions) Regulations* (SS(C)R) if he or she:

- is ordinarily resident in Great Britain and Northern Ireland for NIC purposes;

- was resident in Great Britain or Northern Ireland immediately prior to the overseas employment starting; and

- is working overseas in what would have been employed earner's employment had it been in Great Britain or Northern Ireland, for an employer who has a place of business in Great Britain or Northern Ireland.

If the above applies, then the employee will continue to be liable to Class 1 NIC for 52 contribution weeks commencing from the beginning of the contribution week in which the overseas employment commences (see NIM 33530 to 33535 and flowchart at NIM 33550). A "contribution week" is defined by SS(C)R 2001, reg. 1

as "a period of seven days beginning with midnight between Saturday and Sunday", so this 52-week period will start on the Sunday prior to the date the employee leaves the UK to start his overseas employment and will stop on the Saturday of the 51st contribution week following the contribution week in which the employee left the UK.

Example – Kevin

Kevin is a UK citizen and has lived in the UK all his life. His UK employer, of a number years, sends him on secondment to Australia for three years. He leaves the UK on Wednesday 7 November 2018 to start work in Melbourne the following Monday, 12 November. As he is ordinarily resident in the UK, and resident (for NIC purposes) immediately prior to leaving the UK, and as his employer has a place of business in the UK, the above 52-week rule applies starting from Sunday 4 November 2018 and ceasing on Saturday 2 November 2019. During this period, both Kevin and his employer are required to pay Class 1 NIC (including employer's Class 1A and 1B if relevant).

As to whether a change of employment during this 52-week period causes this rule to cease, HMRC state that this depends on the facts of the case and give the following example at NIM 33535:

HMRC example – Ralph

- Ralph was posted by the UK company to work in Australia for a period of 2 years as a General Manager of the Sydney office
- After 6 months he applied for promotion as an Overseas Sales Executive with a separate department of the UK company
- He was successful and immediately took up his new position in Malaysia

The subsequent posting from Australia to Malaysia would be considered to arise in connection with the new employment with the UK Company. The 52-week period would cease.

Had the UK employer simply posted him to Malaysia in connection with the original occupation/employment as a General Manager then the 52-week period would have continued in full.

If an employee were to return to work temporarily in the UK after the above 52-week period has finished, he or she could then work in the UK for up to six continuous contribution weeks before NIC becomes due again. If the individual returned to the UK on either paid annual or sick leave, then after 26 weeks of such leave NIC will become due; if he then leaves the UK again to work overseas, a new 52-week period will start.

If the employee returns to live in the UK, whether during the above 52-week period or after it has ceased, NIC will start being due immediately once he starts working in the UK again.

Under regulation 145 of SS(C)R 2001, NIC may not be due for the first 52 weeks of an individual's assignment to the UK if he normally works overseas for a foreign employer, he is not ordinarily resident, and he works in the UK for a time on a temporary basis (see NIM 33515 and flowchart at 33545).

The question of whether or not an employer has a place of business in the UK will, as HMRC state, depend on the facts of each case. HMRC will look at various factors, including whether the employer is registered under the UK's *Companies Act* 2006 or whether there is a place in the UK from which the business or its agent can operate. Other factors include letter headings using a UK address, UK phone directory entries, the existence of lease/rental agreements for UK premises, and so on.

It is important to realise that this 52-week rule does not apply if the EC regulations or a reciprocal agreement apply.

Law: SSCBA 1992; SI 2001/1004, reg. 1, 145, 146
Guidance: NIM 33500; HMRC leaflet NI38

2.7.5   *Voluntary NIC*

If a non-resident individual is not liable to Class 1 NIC, he or she may nevertheless wish to pay NIC on a voluntary basis to protect entitlement to certain state benefits, the main one being the UK state pension.

An individual needs to have 35 years of contributions to be entitled to the full state pension. Consideration should therefore be given to making voluntary contributions while living overseas, to make up any gaps in the contribution record. If an employee is only living overseas on a temporary basis, and intends to return to live and work in the UK, then it may be the case that he or she will have enough contribution years by working in the UK without the need to pay voluntary contributions while overseas. An individual working longer term overseas may need to pay voluntary NIC to protect entitlement. However, this is very much a personal choice and the individual may be happy to rely on private pension provision and may not be bothered about making up any gap in his or her NIC record.

Many British expats have lived and worked abroad for long periods of time and have not kept up with their voluntary contributions and will, therefore, have insufficient amounts for a full UK state pension. In most cases a cost-to-benefit analysis suggests that settling missing contributions is a good idea and the adviser should point this out as a matter of priority. See "new state pension" at **4.1.2** and HMRC leaflet NI38.

An individual considering making voluntary contributions should first check his National Insurance records via his personal tax account (see **2.3.7**) to see what gaps there are in his contribution record and should also obtain a state pension forecast.

If an individual wishes to pay voluntary NIC, the normal route is via Class 3 NIC. However, if he is working overseas it may instead be possible to pay Class 2 NIC on a voluntary basis. The advantage of this is that Class 2 is much cheaper than Class 3 (£2.95 per week as opposed to £14.65 per week for Class 3 NIC for 2018-19), for potentially more state benefits.

If an individual is living in a country that is not covered by the EC regulations or a reciprocal agreement, then reg. 147 of SS(C)R 2001 sets out the conditions that need to be satisfied for payment of Class 3 NIC. These are that the individual:

- has been resident (for NIC purposes) in Great Britain or Northern Ireland at any time for a continuous period of at least three years prior to the period for which voluntary contributions are to be paid (the relevant period);

- has paid at least 156 contributions of any Class of NIC; or
- has paid contributions which have an earnings factor of at least 52 times the Class 1 Lower earnings limit (LEL):

    (i) in each of any three years ending prior to the relevant period;

    (ii) for each of two such years, plus 52 contributions of any Class of NIC; or

    (iii) for one such year, plus 104 contributions of any Class of NIC.

If the individual paid Class 1 NIC under the 52-week rule in **2.7.4**, then he can apply to pay Class 3 NIC without the need to satisfy the above conditions if he is working overseas (SS(C)R 2001, reg. 146(2)(b)).

As mentioned above, if an individual is working overseas it is usually more beneficial to pay Class 2 NIC on a voluntary basis. To be eligible to do so, the individual not only needs to satisfy the above conditions for Class 3, but must also have been employed, self-employed or seeking work in Great Britain or Northern Ireland immediately prior to moving overseas. However, it is intended that Class 2 NIC will be abolished from 6 April 2019, meaning that only the more expensive Class 3 NIC can then be paid by individuals working overseas. Individuals should therefore consider their NIC record sooner rather than later and decide whether or not they wish to make up any potential gaps.

The normal rule regarding payment of voluntary NIC is that this can be paid for the previous six tax years, the deadline being the following 5 April. So, for example, contributions for the tax years 2012-13 to 2017-18 need to be made by 5 April 2019. However, voluntary Class 2 and 3 NIC for the tax years 2006-07 to 2015-16 can be paid up until 5 April 2023, for individuals whose state pension age is after 5 April 2017.

An application by individuals who are overseas, and who wish to pay Class 2 or 3 voluntary NIC, can be made on form CF83 at the back of HMRC's leaflet NI38.

If an individual is covered by the EC regulations or a reciprocal agreement, then the above does not apply and he needs to refer to article 14 of the current EC regulations or the relevant reciprocal agreement to establish his position in respect of voluntary contributions.

Law: SI 2001/1004, reg. 146(2)(b), 147, 148
Guidance: NIM 25000, 33600; HMRC leaflet NI38

2.8   Self-assessment compliance

2.8.1   Overview

Self-assessment has been in existence since 1996-97, so for over 20 years. It is the system whereby individuals (and also trustees and partnerships) file tax returns every year which include a self-assessment of how much tax is owed. As this self-assessment is the amount of tax paid, it eliminates the need for HMRC to raise tax assessments.

The self-assessment tax return is made up of various elements. There is a core return, pages TR 1 to TR 8 (SA100), with guidance notes (SA150). Depending on the individual's circumstances, various supplementary pages can be added to this core return and it is his or her responsibility to complete and file the relevant pages for those circumstances. The most common supplementary pages for non-residents are:

- **Additional information (SA101)** – covers various items such as share scheme remuneration, termination payments and relief from UK tax on foreign earnings, which is particularly important for employees who have remained on a UK payroll, and so under PAYE, but who are not taxed in the UK on their earnings.

- **Employment (SA102)** – particularly relevant for employees assigned overseas by their UK employer, who have therefore remained on a UK payroll and under the PAYE system.

- **UK property (SA105)** – where rental income from UK properties is declared.

- **Foreign (SA106)** – these pages will not be relevant for an individual who is non-resident for a tax year, but non-residents can often be under the misunderstanding that this section needs to be completed. These pages are only required if the individual is resident for a tax year (including the UK part of a split year) and has overseas income which needs to be declared. Any claim for foreign tax paid is made on these pages.

- **Capital gains summary (SA108)** – for declaring gains on UK residential properties which have arisen following the introduction of the NRCGT regime.
- **Residence, remittance basis etc. (SA109)** – see below.
- **Tax calculation summary (SA110)**.

Individuals who are non-resident certify this status on the above "Residence, remittance basis etc." pages. These pages are not available to be filed via HMRC's tax return filing service on their website, so commercial tax return software has to be used. It is very common for non-residents filing self-assessment tax returns themselves, not to file these pages or, if they are filed, not to tick the relevant box claiming the personal allowance as a non-resident. The failure to claim the personal allowance results in the individual incurring an unexpected tax liability. If entitled to the personal allowance, the individual needs to appeal against any tax calculation raised by HMRC that excludes the allowance and then amend his or her self-assessment tax return accordingly (see **2.3.2**).

For all supplementary pages, HMRC provide notes to assist individuals completing them. HMRC have also issued various helpsheets to assist the taxpayer with the completion of the tax return and tax calculation. Some of the more common ones for non-residents are:

- **HS300** – non-residents and investment income. There is also a working sheet which assists non-residents calculate their UK tax liability, particularly in respect of the disregarded income rules (see **2.3.20**).
- **HS302** – claiming treaty relief against UK tax if a dual resident (see **2.2.10**).
- **HS304** – claiming treaty relief against UK tax if non-resident.

Any claims or elections that need to be made can be made via the individual's tax return.

There is a short tax return (SA200). However, a non-resident cannot file this and must file a full return (SA100).

Requirement to file a return

An individual first has to establish whether or not he is required to file a tax return. HMRC's website has a tool which assists a person in establishing this (see https://www.gov.uk/check-if-you-need-a-tax-return). HMRC state that the following are required to file a tax return for a tax year:

- the self-employed;
- a company director – unless it was for a non-profit organisation (such as a charity) and the director did not get any pay or benefits in kind;
- an individual who receives:
    o £2,500 or more in untaxed income;
    o income from savings or investments that was £10,000 or more before tax;
    o income from dividends that was £10,000 or more before tax;
    o profits from selling assets such as shares, a second home etc. and who needs to pay capital gains tax;
    o taxable income over £100,000;
    o state pension which was more than the individual's personal allowance and was his or her only source of income;
    o income (or partner's income) which was over £50,000 if one of them claimed child benefit;
    o overseas income upon which tax is due;
- an individual who lives abroad and receives income in the UK;
- a trustee of a trust or registered pension scheme;
- a taxpayer who received a P800 tax calculation from HMRC stating there was an underpayment of tax for a tax year if the individual did not pay this through his or her PAYE tax code or via a voluntary payment.

Registering with HMRC

If it is established that a tax return has to be filed, then the individual will need to register for self-assessment if he or she has not already done so. This can be done via form SA1 online or by completing the form online, printing it off and then sending it in the post (see https://www.gov.uk/government/publications/self-assessment-register-for-self-assessment-and-get-a-tax-return-sa1).

This registration needs to be done by 5 October following the relevant tax year. Once registered, HMRC will send the individual a UTR (unique taxpayer reference) which is a 10 digit reference; a tax return cannot be filed without a UTR.

The individual is then in a position to file a return. For non-residents, this can only be done through commercial tax return software. (There is a facility on HMRC's website to file tax returns online. However, as mentioned above, the Residence, remittance basis etc. pages that non-residents need to complete and file are not included under this facility and HMRC specifically state that non-residents cannot use this facility to file their tax return.)

Once registered there is no need to re-register every year and HMRC will issue a notice to file a tax return immediately after the end of the relevant tax year, unless a tax return is not filed for a previous tax year. In this case, HMRC state on their website that re-registration will be necessary, although care should be taken to ensure that there are not two UTRs for an individual, which can then lead to complications, particularly in respect of late filing penalties.

Filing returns

Once issued, there is a legal obligation on the individual to file a tax return even if it is a nil return. However, it is possible to request HMRC to withdraw their notice to file a return, if they agree a tax return is not required for a particular tax year.

A tax return can be filed either online or in paper format, although HMRC encourage the former by having different filing dates – 31 January for online returns and 31 October for paper returns (see **2.8.2**). An individual has up to four years following the end of the relevant tax year to file a tax return, after which it will no longer be possible.

Self-assessment statements are issued by HMRC showing transactions on an individual's self-assessment account. These are sent in the post and can also be accessed online.

At the time of writing, HMRC intend to abolish the need to file self-assessment tax returns over the next few years and instead introduce digital tax accounts. The idea is that, through these, taxpayers will be able perform the various functions currently dealt with by tax, including declaring income, claiming any relevant tax reliefs and allowances, certifying non-residence status, and so on.

Tax payments

Any outstanding tax for a tax year needs to be paid by 31 January following the tax year concerned. This is known as a balancing payment.

In addition, two payments on account (also known as interim payments) need to be made for the following tax year, if the tax due for the current tax year (less tax that has been deducted at source) is either (i) £1,000 or more or (ii) at least 20% or more of the tax collected at source. These payments on account will be the tax liability less any tax deducted at source for the current year, with 50% due for payment by 31 January in the tax year to which the liability relates and 50% by 31 July after that tax year.

Example 1

Jacob is non-resident and receives royalty income from the UK during 2018-19 which has had UK tax withheld from it at source of £10,000. His total tax liability in the UK for the 2018-19 tax year is £19,200 before deducting the above tax that was withheld at source.

Jacob has to pay a balancing payment of £9,200 for 2018-19 plus the first payment on account for 2019-20 of £4,600 by 31 January 2020, so a total due of £13,800. The second payment on account for 2019-20 will be another payment of £4,600, which needs to be paid by 31 July 2020.

Jacob's outstanding tax liability for 2018-19, after the deduction of tax withheld at source, is above £1,000. Also, less than 80% of the tax liability for 2018-19 was collected at source. Therefore, he falls under the payments on account regime.

If an individual believes that his tax liability will be lower for the following tax year, he can make a claim to decrease the payments on account. However, if these are decreased by too much, interest on the late payment of tax will arise from the due dates of the payments on account. This claim can be made either on form SA303 or on page TC1 of the self-assessment tax return. The grounds for believing the tax liability may be less need to be given and there are penalties for making an incorrect statement in this respect on a fraudulent or negligent basis, the maximum penalty being the amount of tax that should have been paid had the incorrect statement not been made.

Individuals need to be aware of the cash flow consequences of falling under the payments on account regime, as significant amounts of tax may need to be paid by the 31 January payment deadline, especially in the first year of having to make payments on account.

Example 2

In the above example, Jacob has to pay £13,800 by 31 January 2020 and then a further £4,600 by 31 July 2020, so a total of £18,400 in a six-month period.

If, say, Jacob's balancing payment for 2019-20 was £10,000, then his payments on account for 2020-21 will be £5,000 each. A total of £15,000 will be due for payment by 31 January 2021. However, from this he can deduct the payments on account he made for 2019-20 of £9,200, leaving £800 to pay for 2019-20 and so a total of £5,800 to be paid by 31 January 2021. His second payment on account for 2020-21 of £5,000 will need to be paid by 31 July 2021.

If a taxpayer is unable to pay his tax, he can contact HMRC's business payment support service on (at the time of writing) +44 (0)300 200 3835, to see if he can agree to pay the tax under a payment plan, and pay by instalments. Even though this is the business support payment service, it is available to individuals not in business. This should be done before the filing deadline for tax returns.

Errors and overpayments

If an individual discovers that he has made an error on his tax return, he can amend this up to a year after the filing deadline. After this, he can still make an overpayment relief claim if he believes he has overpaid tax (see SACM 12000). A claim has to be made within four years of the end of the relevant tax year, e.g. for the 2018-19 tax year an overpayment relief claim needs to be made by 5 April 2023. In this respect HMRC are very strict and will not allow a claim beyond this time limit.

SACM 12065 sets out exclusions, i.e. circumstances in which overpayment relief claims cannot be made, and SACM 12150 sets out what must be included in a claim.

HMRC have a right to enquire into a self-assessment tax return. They have "a process now, check later" approach to tax returns, so initially while processing the tax return, they will amend any obvious mistakes such as arithmetical errors. Once the tax return has been processed, HMRC may then raise an enquiry. This can be done simply on a random basis, though there is usually a specific reason why HMRC raise an enquiry, such as requiring more information to back up items shown on the return.

Enquiries, penalties, appeals

HMRC must raise an enquiry within 12 months of the return being delivered to them and must give the taxpayer written notice of their intention to open an enquiry into his or her return. If, however, HMRC have reason to believe there has been a loss of tax through carelessness or deliberate action on the part of the taxpayer, or that there has been an incomplete disclosure of information, then they can raise a discovery assessment after this 12-month period, which can be up to 20 years after the relevant tax year, depending on the circumstances.

Penalties for inaccuracies found during an enquiry can be up to 100% of the additional tax found to be due (but up to 200% if overseas income or gains are involved).

Example 3

Jacob (from the first two examples above) purchases a buy-to-let property during 2018-19 and renovates it to a high standard. He then sells it for a gain of £40,600, on which he pays 28% CGT on 31 January 2020 after allowances of £11,700.

HMRC raise an enquiry into the circumstances of the gain and, after investigation, Jacob acknowledges that he never let the property out, but immediately sold it following renovation. HMRC state that the gain is to be treated as trading income and taxed as such at his marginal income tax rate of 40%, instead of 28%, and without the benefit of the annual CGT exemption of £11,700. This will result in the late payment of tax and so penalties and interest in this respect will be incurred, along with penalties for an inaccurate return (see *Wisdom v Chamberlain* (1969) 45 TC 92).

A taxpayer has a right to appeal against HMRC decisions or amendments under self-assessment, usually within 30 days, which could be to the Tax Tribunal (First-tier and Upper). The individual needs to make an appeal first to HMRC and only then, if he still disagrees with HMRC's decision, can the appeal proceed to the Tax Tribunal, although he may first want to consider the alternative dispute resolution (ADR) facility offered by HMRC. This is where another HMRC member of staff, not involved with the case, reviews the situation and acts as a neutral, third party mediator.

Records

All records supporting a tax return must be kept, and HMRC have a right to request these records. Penalties are in place for not doing so or if they are not accurate, complete or readable (see **2.8.2**). There is no prescribed way of keeping these records.

If the individual filed his return on time, the records need to be kept for at least a year after the 31 January filing deadline, so for 2018-19 records need to be kept until 31 January 2021. If the tax return was filed late, then the records need to be kept for at least 15 months after filing. If an individual is self-employed then the records need to be kept longer – for five years after the filing deadline. If the return is filed four years or more after the filing deadline, then records need to be kept for at least 15 months after the return is filed.

For employees the following should be kept:

- P60 – tax form an employer should give to an employee after each tax year, showing the gross pay he was paid and the tax that was deducted under PAYE;
- P45 – tax form given to an employee when he leaves an employer. This will show the above information and also the date of leaving amongst other things;
- P11D – tax form showing what benefits in kind were provided to an employee during a tax year and also any taxable expenses. Again, this form is given to the employee after the end of the tax year;
- any certificates or documentation regarding employee remuneration schemes, e.g. share schemes, deferred bonus schemes, etc., along with any scheme rules and documentation explaining how the scheme works;
- documentation and details, including any agreements, upon redundancy or termination of employment; and
- records of expenses incurred in respect of the individual's employment duties.

Non-residents who are working for a foreign employer, and so not paid via a UK payroll, will not have some of the above documentation (P60, P45 and P11D) so they should keep the equivalent in their host country, as well as items such as salary slips and details of where they have worked (see **2.2.9**). The latter will be particularly important for individuals who partly work in the UK and for whom an apportionment of their earnings needs to be made between their UK and overseas work days.

For savings, investments and pensions, HMRC suggest the following should be kept:

- bank or building society statements and passbooks;
- statements of interest and income from savings and investments;
- tax deduction certificates issued by banks, although this will be less relevant now that banks and building societies have stopped deducting tax at source from interest;
- dividend vouchers from UK companies;

- unit trust tax vouchers;
- documents that show the profits made from life insurance policies (called "chargeable event certificates");
- details of income from a trust;
- details of any "out-of-the ordinary" income received, like an inheritance.

For pensions, HMRC suggest the following should be kept:

- form P160 (Part 1A) which is received when a pension starts;
- form P60, which the pension provider sends to the pensioner every year;
- any other details of a pension (including state pension) and the tax deducted from it.

For rental income, the following details should be kept:

- the dates when property is let;
- all the rent received, including details of deposits withheld from tenants;
- any income from services given to tenants (e.g. charging for maintenance or repairs);
- rent books, receipts, invoices, letting agent and bank statements;
- expenses incurred in running the rental property. (It's advisable to keep details of all expenses incurred, even if the expense is not deductible – say because it is a capital expense – when it may be deductible for capital gains tax purposes when the property is sold.);
- lease agreements;
- insurance claim documentation;
- certificates, from the lender, of mortgage interest paid.

For capital gains that are taxable in the UK the following should be kept:

- Receipts, bills and invoices that show the date and the amount:

- o paid for an asset;
- o of any additional costs, like fees for professional advice, stamp duty, improvement costs, or to establish the market value such as valuation reports;
- o received for the asset – including details of any deferred consideration, such as payments received later in instalments or when conditions are satisfied;
- o of compensation if the asset was damaged;
- o of selling costs on the sale, such as estate agent fees.
- Also any contracts for buying and selling the asset (for example from solicitors or stockbrokers) and copies of any valuations. Completion statements should be kept and, with property, the date of exchange.
- With regards to shareholdings, a record should be kept of when each holding is acquired and sold, together with details of any rights or bonus issues etc.

If an individual is liable to UK tax on his or her **overseas income**, as well as the above (if relevant) the following should be kept:

- evidence of income earned from overseas, such as payslips, P60/P45 equivalents, bank statements or payment confirmations;
- receipts for any overseas expenses which may be allowable deductions;
- dividend certificates from overseas companies; and
- certificates or other proof of the tax paid overseas.

As mentioned at **2.2.9**, detailed records need to be kept for the purposes of the statutory residence test, and for establishing a person's residence status.

Law: TMA 1970 (esp. Pt. II)

Guidance: HMRC manuals *Self Assessment: The legal framework (SALF); Self-Assessment Claims Manual (SACM);* https://www.gov.uk/topic/personal-tax/self-assessment

2.8.2   *Deadlines and penalties*

Deadlines

Task	Deadline	Law
Filing of online self-assessment tax return	31 January following end of relevant tax year.	TMA 1970, s. 8
Filing of paper self-assessment tax return	31 October following end of relevant tax year.	
Filing of online self-assessment tax return when notice to file is issued after 31 October following relevant tax year	3 months from issue date of notice to file.	
Filing of paper self-assessment tax return when notice to file is issued after 31 July following relevant tax year	3 months from issue date of notice to file.	
Filing of electronic return where taxpayer wishes any eligible underpayment of tax to be collected via his or her PAYE tax code	31 December following relevant tax year.	SI 2003/2682, reg. 186
Filing of paper return where taxpayer wishes any eligible underpayment of tax to be collected via his or her PAYE tax code	31 October following relevant tax year.	
Notify HMRC of chargeability to tax if no notice to file a tax return is issued	5 October following relevant tax year.	TMA 1970, s. 7
Payment of tax due for a tax year (balancing payment)	31 January following end of relevant tax year.	TMA 1970, s. 59B
First payment on account for a tax year	31 January in the tax year concerned.	TMA 1970, s. 59A
Second payment on account for a tax year	31 July following the end of the relevant tax year.	

Penalties

Task	Penalty	Law
Filing of online self-assessment tax return	a. Initial late filing penalty of £100. b. Continued failure to file for more than 3 months, £10 per day penalty up to a maximum of 90 days, i.e. £900. c. Failure to file within 6 months, penalty of the higher of (i) £300 and (ii) 5% of the tax due. d. Failure to file within 12 months, same penalty as above unless there has been deliberate withholding of the tax return, in which case the following applies: Deliberate withholding – 70% of the tax due. Deliberate and concealed withholding – 100% of the tax due. Reductions are available for unprompted disclosure resulting in the minimum penalty being between 20% and 30%, and between 35% and 50% where there has been prompted disclosure.	FA 2009, Sch. 55
Filing of paper self-assessment tax return		
Filing of online self-assessment tax return when notice to file issued after 31 October following relevant tax year		
Filing of paper self-assessment tax return when notice to file is issued after 31 July following relevant tax year		

Task	Penalty	Law
Notify HMRC of chargeability to tax if no notice to file a tax return is issued	Based on potential lost revenue, so if tax due is not paid by the due date of 31 January the following applies: Failure to notify – 30%. Deliberate but not concealed – 70%. Deliberate and concealed (i.e. makes arrangements to conceal the situation) – 100%. Reductions in the above penalties are available as follows: <table><tr><td>Standard %</td><td>Min. % if unprompted disclosure</td><td>Min. % if prompted disclosure</td></tr><tr><td>30%</td><td>Nil if disclosure within 12 months, otherwise 10%</td><td>15%</td></tr><tr><td>70%</td><td>20%</td><td>35%</td></tr><tr><td>100%</td><td>30%</td><td>50%</td></tr></table>	FA 2008, Sch. 41
Payment of tax due for a tax year (balancing payment)	31 days late – 5% (3 March unless a leap year when 2 March). 6 months late – an additional 5%. 12 months late – a further additional 5%.	FA 2009, Sch. 56
First payment on account for a tax year	No penalties for late payment, but interest charged on a daily basis.	
Second payment on account for a tax year		

Task	Penalty	Law
Inaccuracy in return	Based on potential lost revenue on the following basis: |	Standard %	Min. % if unprompted disclosure	Min. % for prompted disclosure
---	---	---	---
Careless inaccuracy	30%	Nil	15%
Deliberate but not concealed	70%	20%	35%
Deliberate and concealed	100%	30%	50% | "Careless" means a failure to take reasonable care.	FA 2007, Sch. 24, para. 1, 2
Failure to notify HMRC of an error in an assessment within 30 days of the date of the assessment	30% of potential lost revenue with reductions to a minimum of nil if unprompted disclosure or 15% if prompted.	FA 2007, Sch. 24, para. 2
Failure to keep adequate records	Up to £3,000.	TMA 1970, s. 12B(5)
Making a fraudulent or negligent claim to reduce payments on account, which is incorrect	Up to the additional amount that would have been due had a correct statement been made.	TMA 1970, s. 59A(6)
Failure to correct by 30 September 2018 irregularities in undeclared tax liabilities of offshore interests	200% of the potential lost revenue, with reductions available but minimum penalty 100%.	F(No.2)A 2017, Sch. 18

Task	Penalty	Law
Fraudulent evasion of income tax	On summary conviction, imprisonment of up to 12 months or a fine of up to the statutory maximum (£5,000), or both. On conviction on indictment, imprisonment of up to 7 years or a fine or both.	TMA 1970, s. 106A
Offences involving an offshore matter	Potentially up to 200% of tax due in the UK, depending on country ("territory") involved.	HMRC complian ce checks factsheet CC/FS17

For further HMRC guidance, see compliance checks factsheets CC/FS7a, CC/FS11, CC/FS18a.

For all tax paid late, interest is also charged on a daily basis until the date of payment – see https://www.gov.uk/government/publications/rates-and-allowances-hmrc-interest-rates-for-late-and-early-payments/rates-and-allowances-hmrc-interest-rates for appropriate rates of interest charged by HMRC. Repayment supplements (interest received) are paid on overpaid tax refunded by HMRC.

Example 1 – penalties where no tax due

Barnaby is a non-resident and has been a bit remiss with the filing of his UK tax returns and has fallen behind with these. He has been issued with notices to file tax returns for 2015-16 and 2016-17 which are still outstanding and have not been filed (not an unfamiliar situation for a number of non-residents!).

Barnaby has various sources of UK income but these do not exceed his personal allowance and so he owes no UK tax for either year. He eventually files both returns online in September 2018.

His penalty situation will be as follows:

227

		£
Late filing of 2015-16 tax return	Initial penalty	100
	Daily penalties for being over 3 months late (max.)	900
	Penalty for being 6 months late	300
	Penalty for being 12 months late	<u>300</u>
		<u>£1,600</u>
Late filing of 2016-17 tax return	Initial penalty	100
	Daily penalties for being over 3 months late (max.)	900
	Penalty for being 6 months late	<u>300</u>
		<u>£1,300</u>
	Total penalties due	<u>£2,900</u>

As can be seen from the above, Barnaby's late filing penalties total £2,900, despite there being no tax due.

Example 2 – penalties where tax due

Suppose, instead, that Barnaby's taxable income in both years exceeded his personal allowance, so that he owed tax of £15,000 in 2015-16 and £12,500 in 2016-17. In this case, his penalty situation would be as follows:

		£
Late filing of 2015-16 tax return	Initial penalty	100
	Daily penalties for being over 3 months late (max.)	900
	Penalty for being 6 months late 5% of £15,000	750
	Penalty for being 12 months late (assuming that Barnaby just did not think and there was no deliberate action on his part not to file his returns)	750
		£2,500
Late filing of 2016-17 tax return	Initial penalty	100
	Daily penalties for being over 3 months late (max.)	900
	Penalty for being 6 months late 5% of £12,500	625
		£1,625
Late payment of tax for 2015-16	Penalty for being more than 31 days late, at 5% of tax due	750
	Same penalty for being 6 months late	750
	Same penalty for being 12 months late	750
		£2,250
Late payment of tax for 2016-17	Penalty for being more than 31 days late at 5% of tax due	625
	Same penalty for being 6 months late	625
		£1,250
	Total penalties due	£7,625
Payments on account (PoA) for 2016-17	1st PoA due 31 January 2017	7,500
	2nd PoA due 31 July 2017	7,500
Payments on account (PoA) for 2017-18	1st PoA due 31 January 2018	6,250
	2nd PoA due 31 July 2018	6,250

It can be seen that the penalties Barnaby incurs when he owes tax are quite significant, at £7,625, and need to be paid along with the tax due and the payments on account, so the amount he has to pay in September is:

	£
Balancing payment for 2015-16	15,000
PoA for 2016-17 – with the benefit of hindsight he can put in an election to reduce these to £12,500	12,500
Balancing payment for 2016-17 (covered by payments on account) Balancing payment for 2016-17 (covered by payments on account)	Nil
PoA for 2017-18	12,500
Penalties	7,625
Total payment due in September 2018	£47,625

This is not an insignificant amount, which could be considerably worse if (say) Barnaby's wife was in the same position, which can often be the case, and also if he was further behind with tax returns and had more outstanding tax years for which to file tax returns. Even with no tax due, the penalties can soon mount up to substantial amounts. The moral of the story is for individuals to be up to date with filing UK tax returns, as the penalties for not doing so are hefty.

On top of Barnaby's penalties above, he will also have to pay interest on the late payment of tax on a daily basis from the due date until the day the tax is paid.

HMRC's view is that the late filing penalties for being six and twelve months late is a minimum of £300 on each occasion. However, whether the decision in *Jackson* (an FTT case on the late filing penalties for a NRCGT return – see **3.2.12**) will change this view remains to be seen. In this case, the tribunal judge held that HMRC had not taken into account the provisions of FA 2009, Sch. 55 para. 1(3) and 17(3). These state that where penalties arise under more than one paragraph of Sch. 55, and reference needs to be made to the individual's tax liability to establish them, then the total of these penalties cannot exceed his or her tax liability.

Case: *Jackson v HMRC* [2018] UKFTT 64 (TC)

Warning!

Individuals who, at the end of 2016-17, have undeclared UK tax liabilities in respect of offshore interests, have until 30 September 2018 to correct this situation. On this date, countries under the common reporting standard will start exchanging information, enabling HMRC to establish which individuals have not been declaring taxable overseas interests.

Individuals in this position should review their situation urgently and make appropriate disclosures before 30 September 2018 to avoid significant penalties (200% of the potential tax lost).

For non-residents, this will be a concern for those who have only just become non-resident and were resident for 2016-17 and had overseas interests. As the legislation (F(No.2)A, Sch. 18) does not distinguish between simple carelessness and deliberate action, it is advisable for individuals generally to review their situation to make sure they are not caught out by this new legislation.

2.8.3   Simple assessment

"Simple assessment" has recently been announced by HMRC and is key to the transition from phasing out self-assessment tax returns to the use of digital tax accounts and third party information.

From September 2017, HMRC are removing some taxpayers from self-assessment, meaning that those individuals are no longer required to file self-assessment tax returns but will instead pay their tax via simple assessment.

A simple assessment tax liability will be raised on form PA302, which will replace HMRC's tax calculation currently shown on form P800. A PA302 will be sent in the post and will also be available via the individual's personal tax account. If the taxpayer does not agree to the simple assessment tax liability, then he or she will have 60 days to appeal against this, either in writing or by phone. A new simple assessment tax liability will then be raised, which the individual will have 30 days to appeal against if he or she still does not agree to the liability. This appeal will need to be made in writing.

The payment of tax will need to be made before 31 January following the relevant tax year or, if the simple assessment is raised after 31 October following the year of assessment, three months after this. The payment of tax will be made via the individual's personal tax account (see **2.3.7**) or, at the time of writing, can be made by cheque.

A PA302 will only be raised if there is a liability of tax. If an overpayment of tax has arisen, the taxpayer will receive a P800 tax calculation.

HMRC will contact taxpayers in writing, explaining that they have been removed from self-assessment and no longer need to file a self-assessment tax return. Nevertheless, taxpayers will still be able to file self-assessment tax returns if they prefer, in which case any simple assessments will be cancelled by HMRC. If HMRC incorrectly remove an individual from self-assessment, and a self-assessment tax return is required to be filed, then it is the taxpayer's responsibility to inform HMRC of this.

The 5 October deadline for notifying HMRC of chargeability to tax will still apply.

At the time of writing, simple assessment is limited to individuals who are:

- in receipt of the state pension only and this exceeds the personal allowance (quite a rare occurrence); and
- under PAYE and who have an underpayment of tax which cannot be collected via the PAYE tax code.

Law: TMA 1970, s. 28H to 28J, 31, 31A, 31AA, 59BA; FA 2009, Sch. 56

Guidance: https://www.gov.uk/simple-assessment

3. Selling or letting the UK property

3.1 Property letting

3.1.1 Significance

It is very common for individuals who move overseas to keep their UK properties and rent these out while they are living abroad, particularly if they intend to return to live in the UK, for example if their employer has sent them on an overseas assignment for a set number of years or if they have been unable to sell their property. The rental income from these properties will remain taxable in the UK, even if the individual is non-resident for tax purposes, as it is from a UK source. As such, it will need to be declared on an individual's self-assessment tax return on SA105, the UK Property pages. With regards to exemption or relief from UK tax under a double tax treaty most treaties do not allow this; however, it is still important that the appropriate treaty is referred to in case some form of relief is available.

It can be common for expats living overseas to think that the income is not taxable in the UK, perhaps because they are no longer living in the UK and it is taxed in the country they are living in. or because they have obtained HMRC's agreement that the rental income can be paid gross (see **3.1.4** below) and they misunderstand this to mean the income is exempt from UK tax. If rental income has not been declared by an individual, then he or she should be making a voluntary disclosure to HMRC as soon as the error is discovered.

Law: ITTOIA 2005, Pt. 3 (income tax); CTA 2009, Pt. 4 (corporation tax)
Guidance: HMRC's *Property Income Manual* (PIM)

3.1.2 Let property campaign

Individuals who, for whatever reason, have not been declaring their rental income to HMRC and not paying any tax that is due, now have (at the time of writing) the opportunity to come forward and declare the income and pay any tax due via the "let property campaign". This applies equally to non-resident taxpayers as well as resident ones, so overseas landlords who have not declared their UK rental income now have the opportunity to declare this via this campaign. For husband and wives who have undeclared income from one property they jointly own, each of them must make a separate declaration.

One of the benefits of declaring under the let property campaign is that the penalties charged are less than would normally be the case. The campaign cannot be used for declaring income for the current or previous tax year; this must be done via a self-assessment tax return, so individuals not yet registered for self-assessment must do so. If an individual is registered for self-assessment and has been issued with notices to file tax returns, then if a self-assessment tax return is outstanding and is within the four-year rule for being able to file tax returns (see **2.8.1**), then the individual must declare the income via his outstanding tax return. The effect of this is that the individual will be subject to the normal self-assessment penalties rather than the potentially less severe penalties under the let property campaign.

If an individual has filed all of his or her tax returns on time, but did not pay enough tax because of a careless mistake, then another benefit of using the let property campaign is that he only has to pay underpaid tax for a maximum of six years. If some tax, however, has deliberately been underpaid, then tax due for up to 20 years will have to be paid.

See HMRC's website for more detailed guidance on which tax years need to be declared under the let property campaign, which is dependent on an individual's situation.

Use of the let property campaign can sometimes, in certain situations, lead to interesting outcomes.

Example

A husband and wife, Donald and Hilary, rent out their UK home while they are living and working in the US. They are both non-resident and so applied for their rental income to be paid gross and received HMRC's agreement to this (see **3.1.4** below). In the following tax years Hilary was issued with notices to file self-assessment tax returns, whereas Donald was not, despite his taxable income being above his personal allowance and so tax being due in the UK for most tax years. Because of this lack of notices to file tax returns, Donald mistakenly thought that HMRC's agreement for his share of the rental income to be paid gross meant they were agreeing to this income being exempt from UK tax (despite HMRC's standard letter saying otherwise!). He therefore did not inform HMRC that he owed tax and should be filing tax returns.

Meanwhile Donald prepared and filed Hilary's tax return for her each tax year (he did not seem to question why she was required to file tax returns and he was not). Unfortunately tax was not his forte and he made a few errors with the result that in one year, 2008-09, he did not claim the personal allowance for Hilary as a non-resident (see **2.3.2**). He also overstated her taxable rental income, which resulted in poor Hilary having a tax liability in the UK of £2,000, which was not actually due. In addition he was late filing Hilary's tax return and paying the above tax for this tax year and so she also incurred late filing and payment penalties of £1,800, so a total due for 2008-09 of £3,800 with interest also due on this amount.

Hilary tried to rectify the situation, but unfortunately did not do this until after the four-year deadline for being able to put in an overpayment relief claim (see **2.3.5** and **2.8.1**) and so HMRC refused her claim and she ended up having to incur the above liability.

After seeking advice from a qualified tax adviser, however, Donald was able to use the let property campaign to declare his share of the rental income for a number of tax years, as he had not been issued with notices to file tax returns. 2008-09 was beyond the four-year deadline mentioned above. Nevertheless, when calculating the tax due he was able to take into account the personal allowance for 2008-09 and the correct amount of taxable income. This meant that he ended up with no tax liability for 2008-09 (the correct situation) and no penalties as there was no tax due. As a result, his liability for 2008-09 under the let property campaign was nil, compared to Hilary's liability of £3,800 (plus interest).

As can be seen from the above example, if an individual wishes to come forward and make a voluntary disclosure of rental income that should have been declared previously, being able to use the let property campaign can sometimes be more beneficial depending on the individual's circumstances and so should always be considered. It is a way for individuals to bring their tax affairs up to date on a voluntary basis and provides more favourable terms than would

235

otherwise be the case. An individual does not have to use the let property campaign to make a voluntary disclosure, but will in that case not benefit from the more favourable terms given under the campaign.

There is currently no time limit for using the let property campaign, unlike other similar campaigns HMRC have run, and at the time of writing it is still available. The campaign can only be used by individuals for declaring rental income from residential property (not commercial property) and cannot be used by companies or trusts or individuals who are already under enquiry or a compliance check by HMRC or who have been notified of this by them. There is a let property questionnaire on HMRC's website which shows whether or not an individual is eligible to use the campaign.

The initial step is for an individual to notify HMRC that he wishes to use the campaign to declare his rental income and he then has 90 days in which to declare everything and to calculate and pay over all tax and penalties that are due (all done online).

The level of penalties charged depends on the reason why the individual did not declare the income (see HMRC guidance on their website). A key element of being able to benefit from lower penalties is how much the individual co-operates with HMRC and the accuracy of the information he provides to HMRC.

Once an individual has settled with HMRC any tax due under the let property campaign, HMRC expect that individual to keep his or her tax affairs in order in the future and to file any future tax returns accurately and on time.

Guidance: https://www.gov.uk/government/publications/let-property-campaign-your-guide-to-making-a-disclosure/let-property-campaign-your-guide-to-making-a-disclosure

3.1.3   *Lettings while abroad*

Once an individual starts living overseas, he will fall under the non-resident landlord scheme (NRLS). The name of this scheme is a bit of a misnomer, as an individual does not actually need to be not resident to fall under the scheme, just living overseas – i.e. his or her usual place of abode is outside the UK. HMRC regard someone as falling under the scheme if the individual is absent from the UK for six months or more, so someone who is a tax resident in the UK can still fall under this scheme.

Example

Husband and wife, Terry and June, are living in Dubai, where Terry is working full-time. They have two children who attend boarding school in the UK. June lives in Dubai with Terry, but visits the UK each year between June and September to avoid the Middle Eastern summer and to be with their children over the school summer holidays. She stays in the family home which is always available for their own use and she has three ties (accommodation, family and 90 days) under the "sufficient ties test" (see **2.2.4**). June remains resident in the UK under the sufficient ties test of the statutory residence test, but is regarded as a non-resident landlord under the NRLS, as she is absent from the UK for at least six months (October to May).

For rental properties that are jointly owned, for example by husbands and wives, if one is a non-resident landlord (in this respect for the purposes of the NRLS and not for the SRT) and the other is not, then the letting agent or tenant only needs to deduct tax at 20% from the share of the net rental income of the non-resident landlord and not from the share of the other owner who is not a non-resident landlord.

Under the NRLS, a tenant (or a letting agent if one is engaged) is obliged to deduct tax at source from the non-resident landlord's rental income at the basic rate of tax, before paying over the rental income to the landlord, and must account for this tax to HMRC on a quarterly basis. Technically, anyone who pays rent to or collects rent for a non-resident landlord is obliged to deduct basic rate tax from the rental income. In practice, however, it largely applies to letting agents and tenants although tenants do not need to deduct tax if the weekly rental income is £100 or less.

The letting agents (or tenant if no agent is involved) should calculate the tax due on the rental income received for the landlord (or paid to the landlord if there is no agent involved) and after taking into account various allowable expenses they have paid for. However, the reality is that many letting agents do not do this and just calculate the tax due on the gross rental income before allowable expenses. This will often result in too much tax being deducted, which the landlord can claim either:

(i)   as a refund of the tax on his annual self-assessment tax return if he does not owe any UK tax for the tax year concerned (say because all his taxable income is covered by his personal allowance); or

(ii)   if he does owe tax, the tax deducted under the NRLS can be set off against his tax liability for the year.

However, in cases where non-declaration has occurred for a number of years and then the position is rectified by declaration, the period that the individual may go back is four years and, therefore, that individual may lose out on tax refunds due for years earlier than the previous four years!

If the letting agent or tenant deducts tax from a landlord's rental income, they should provide the landlord with a certificate of tax liability (NRL6) which will show the tax they have deducted during the tax year concerned. They should give this certificate to the landlord by 5 July following the year ended 31 March.

It is common for letting agents, and especially tenants, to be unaware of the NRLS and so they often fail to deduct tax from the landlord's rental income as they should. In this situation, HMRC will seek to recover the tax that should have been deducted and accounted for from the letting agent or tenant and not from the landlord. If the letting agent or tenant can show that the landlord has paid the tax due, say via his or her self-assessment tax return, or that there is no tax due, then HMRC may agree to collect only penalties and interest, and not tax, from the letting agent or tenant.

3.1.4   *Forms NRL1, 2 and 3*

As mentioned above, an individual who has been living overseas for at least six months is covered by the NRLS and so the tenant or letting agent is obliged to deduct UK tax at basic rate from the rental income before paying it over to the landlord.

The landlord can apply to HMRC for his rental income to be paid gross with no deduction of tax at source. If agreed by HMRC, it should be remembered that if a further property is purchased and let out, another application should be made for that particular property, otherwise basic rate tax (at the time of writing 20%) should be deducted until agreement is received from HMRC. Individuals apply on form NRL1, companies on form NRL2 and trustees on form NRL3. This is now done online in one of two ways, either via a Government Gateway account (see **2.3.7**) or via an online form that is then sent to HMRC in the post. HMRC will no longer accept any earlier versions of the forms.

There is no deadline for submitting the above forms, but it can take HMRC some time to send their agreement, during which time the letting agent or tenant is obliged to deduct tax until they have been informed by HMRC that they are no longer required to do this, although the Revenue will usually agree that tax does not need to be deducted from the beginning of the quarter in which the application for gross rents to be paid is made. If the tax deducted is not due then it can be claimed back by the individual on his self-assessment tax return. HMRC will not consider applications made more than three months before the landlord leaves the UK.

Under the NRLS, if the individual obtains HMRC agreement that his rents can be paid gross, then strictly he should file self-assessment tax returns. However, in practice it is quite common for HMRC to agree that no returns are required if they are happy that no tax is due, e.g. if the gross rental income before deductions is well below the personal allowance and the individual has no other taxable income.

For husbands and wives who own property jointly which is rented out, each of them needs to complete and submit an NRL1 form, if they are both considered to be non-resident landlords for the purposes of the NRLS.

An individual can apply to HMRC for his rental income to be paid gross if:

- his UK tax affairs are up to date;
- he has not had any UK tax obligations before he applied; or
- he does not expect to be liable to UK income tax for the year in which he applies.

Once agreement has been obtained from HMRC (they will confirm this to the landlord in a letter), it is important to realise that the income is not exempt from UK tax. It is still liable to UK tax and so needs to be declared on the individual's self-assessment tax return and any tax due must be paid by the normal due date under self-assessment of 31 January. However, it is a common misunderstanding amongst landlords that HMRC are agreeing that the rental income is exempt from UK tax, which is not the case – they are just agreeing that the income can be paid gross with no deduction of tax at source. This is stated in HMRC's standard letter to landlords confirming their agreement to rental income being paid gross.

If the landlord changes agents, then there is no need to reapply on form NRL1, but he should inform HMRC of the change in agents. HMRC will then contact the new agent to confirm that no tax needs to be deducted. Prior to this the new agent will need to deduct tax from the non-resident landlord's rental income.

The rental income from UK property may well be liable to tax in the country where the individual is living and so it may potentially be double taxed if UK tax also arises. In this situation, the individual needs to see if relief is available under a double tax treaty between the UK and that country. If not, then it is likely that the country in which the landlord is living and resident for tax purposes, will give relief for any double tax.

Law: ITA 2007, s. 971, 972; SI 1995/2902

Guidance: INTM 370000, PIM 4800; HMRC *Guidance Notes for Letting Agents and Tenants on the Non-resident Landlords Scheme*

3.1.5   Appointing UK letting agents

There are many letting agents who will manage the letting of the UK home, or of buy to let properties, if the expat is working or living abroad. However, the competence of these letting agents is varied – big does not necessarily mean competent in dealing with expats. It is best to carry out due diligence on the prospective letting agent as follows:

- Is the letting agent a member of the Association of Residential Letting Agents (ARLA), subject to verification?
- Is it a well established business (circa 10 years)?

- Is it a nationwide or family run business? If the latter there may be a more personal attention paid to the expat's property.

- Does it have a solid social media presence?

- How many properties do the agents have available on their website for let and what is the modal number of lets staff deal with?

- How many properties are let against the number advertised (to ascertain the percentage vacancy)?

- Are the agents members of the Property Ombudsman, subject to verification?

- Are they a member of the Propertymark CMP scheme, subject to verification?

- Is their business of lettings only or also sales (as this can affect the service provided)?

- Do they provide an out of hours emergency service?

Example

Gerry is moving abroad and wishes to rent out his three bedroom flat on shorthold tenancy agreements of six months. He has approached two letting agents who have stated they will be pleased to handle the lettings for him whilst he is abroad. Big Letters Ltd is a large national chain (12% fees) and Stavely Lets (8% fees) which is a six man team based locally. He undertakes a due diligence research on both and notices:

- Stavely Lets marketing. They are listed on www.rightmove.co.uk, along with various social media platforms. Should they also be on Zoopla & Primelocation but they may in any case have short void periods (i.e. quick replacement of tenants) – check further!

- Transparency. Big Letters Ltd has no information on its website about the company registration number, etc. Why?

- Stavely Ltd website is very basic and social media traffic is low – this may be because of local passing customers using the office rather than the website or enquiries coming from weekly advertising in the regional paper?

241

- Stavely Ltd has no mention of a complaints procedure on its website and the Big Letters Ltd complaints procedure has many exclusions.

- Neither is a member of NAEA (more difficult than ARLA). Considering they have both been in business for over a decade why is this?

- Neither is a member of SafeAgent ... (red flag)! Both have advised that from 1 April 2018 the energy efficiency regulations state that the minimum energy performance rating must be at least 'E' for all energy performance certificates for all new lets and renewals of leases.

- Big Letters Ltd makes no mention of Legionella Risk Assessment ... (red flag)! This is a legal requirement so why not?

- They both use the Dispute service to register deposits, and the name implies exactly what it is. This is time consuming, in the eventuality of a dispute.

Gerry's further enquiries show that Stavely Lets have 13 properties available for rent on Rightmove, and notably most of them are 2/3 bed flats, whereas the Big Letters Ltd properties cover a much wider range including HMOs and large detached properties.

Although there are a few red flags for Stavely Lets, Gerry likes the reduced management fees, the fact they seem to have a specialism in 2/3 bed flats and that they are familiar to the local population. Stavely Lets also has six members of staff, and they are managing around 275 properties. This fits in with the number that can be managed without standards of management and care dropping.

One factor of concern with Big Letters Ltd was the fact that although Gerry mentioned he was moving abroad the non-resident landlord requirements (form NRL1) were not mentioned although this point was mentioned by Stavely Lets.

3.1.6 Tenancy agreements

When letting a UK property whilst on assignment, a tenancy agreement should be drawn up between the landlord and tenant so that possession of the property is enabled at the end of the assignment. Normally the agreements will be an "assured tenancy" or an assured shorthold tenancy. There are important distinctions between the two as shown in the Table below. The advantage of the assured shorthold tenancy agreement is that the landlord can give notice to repossess the property on the last day of the fixed term or (more usually) two months before the term ends.

Assured tenancy agreements. Housing Act 1988, Chapter 1	• Period: fixed term or monthly. • Rent can be varied. • Possession: owner occupation and notice given. • Occupant: as only or principal property. • Tenant's recourse: rent assessment committee. • Landlord recourse: mandatory possession order.
Assured shorthold tenancy agreements. Housing Act 1988, Chapter 2	• Period: minimum six months duration and two months notice thereafter. • Rent is fixed. • Possession: two months notice. • Occupancy as only or principal property. • Tenant's recourse: rent assessment committee. • Landlord's recourse: two months and then possession grant.

Assured and assured shorthold tenancies will continue as a statutory periodic tenancy after the end of the contractual fixed term under the Act. Periodic assured shorthold tenancies can be ended at any time after service of a statutorily drafted "section 21" notice. It is this right under s. 21 of the *Housing Act* 1988 for the landlord to recover possession of the property after the end of the fixed term. The landlord must follow the correct procedure, i.e. service of the section 21 notice and then via the courts.

The following clause 5 is taken from the "Model Agreement for an Assured Shorthold Tenancy and Accompanying Guidance" published by the Department for Communities and Local Government:

"**5.1** If the Landlord wants the Tenant to leave the Property at the end of the Tenancy, the Landlord must:

(a) give the Tenant at least two months' notice in writing before the end of the fixed term in accordance with section 21 of the Housing Act 1988 (this is known as a "section 21 notice"); or

(b) seek possession on one or more of the grounds contained in Schedule 2 to the Housing Act 1988 (if any of those grounds apply).

5.2 If ground 1 of Schedule 2 to the Housing Act 1988 applies in relation to the Property ... then the Landlord should complete the notice in Annex 2 of this agreement and give it to the tenant(s) prior to the date on which this agreement is entered into."

The guidance goes on to explain that the purpose of clause 5.2:

"is to alert landlords who have previously occupied the property as their only or principal home or who may need to occupy the property as their home at the end of the fixed term tenancy, to the fact that they should give tenants the notice [of this] before entering into this agreement. This is necessary if a landlord wants to be able to rely on this reason (i.e. ground 1 of schedule 2 to the Housing Act 1988) to get possession of the property at the end of the fixed term and is also relevant if the property is mortgaged."

Most landowners are reluctant to let a tenant into their property if it means that the tenant will be almost impossible to evict. However, if they can evict them within six months of the end of the contractual fixed term, that is a different matter.

An assured shorthold tenant's security is only either as long as his fixed term lasts, or – if it has ended with no section 21 notice being served – the notice period of a section 21 notice, plus (in both cases) however long it takes to get a possession order through the courts. Taking action through the courts can be time consuming and expensive as in this example:

Example

Irina is seconded to work abroad by her employer and advertises in one of the London evening newspapers. She gets many applicants for her central London flat, one of which is a high ranking diplomat with a foreign embassy in London. He seems very nice and well spoken and shows her his recent salary notice which adequately covers the rent. A shorthold tenancy agreement is signed and Irina goes abroad.

After a year abroad Irina's job is terminated and she returns to London. The shorthold tenancy agreement has now expired and she gives notice for the tenant to leave. He does not leave within the time stipulated and now does not pay his rent of £4,000 per month.

Irina has to move into a cheap hotel and she finds that the diplomat has immunity from eviction under the *Diplomatic Privileges Act 1964*. The Act provides that a diplomatic agent (meaning the head of the mission or a member of the diplomatic staff of the mission) is entitled to immunity from the civil and administrative jurisdiction of the British courts except in a case of article 31 (1) which concerns "a real action relating to private immovable property situated in the territory of the receiving state unless he holds it on behalf of the sending state for the purposes of the mission". So perhaps Irina can bring a claim for possession of the property against the diplomat on the grounds that he has not paid his rent, but this is unlikely to be successful.

Irina not only has to find the court costs to pay but she also has the advance payment on her self-assessment rental statement to pay as well!

A section 21 notice does not actually end the tenancy – i.e. rents are still payable – but it simply means that the Judge at Court has to grant a court order in possession proceedings.

The current laws have created an opportunity for landlords to enter the market, as in the case of Irina in the example above, and they can charge very good rents as there is a housing shortage. However, when things go wrong there is no easy recourse and costs can mount up as Irina's case illustrates. Insurance is a must in these situations and a lack of it can prove very costly.

Law: *Housing Act* 1988 (as amended by subsequent deregulation Acts)

3.1.7 *Accounting for rental receipts and allowable expenses generally*

When calculating the taxable profit from a rental property, the profit is calculated like any other trade and so normal accounting principles are used, i.e. the accruals basis whereby income and

245

expenses are matched to the period they relate to. If an individual's gross rental income is below £15,000, then HMRC may allow the cash basis to be used instead, i.e. with income and expenses accounted for when they are received or paid (PIM 1101). In this situation the cash basis needs to be applied consistently and overall it must give a reasonable result that does not differ substantially from the accruals basis.

From 2017-18, the cash basis is used by all unincorporated businesses whose total receipts are below £150,000 per annum (pro-rated for part years) as the default way of accounting for rental profits. However, an individual can elect for generally accepted accounting principles (GAAP) to apply instead to his property business if he so wishes.

From 2017-18, a £1,000 property income allowance is available. An individual's gross rental income receipts (see "Airbnb" below), before the deduction of expenses (excluding rent-a-room receipts), are not taxed if the amounts are less than £1,000, and they do not need to be declared. In addition, if the income received is above this limit, the individual can elect to use the £1,000 property income allowance as a deduction (rather than expenses actually incurred) to calculate the taxable profit.

The basic rule for allowable expenses is that they are incurred wholly and exclusively for the property business and are revenue and not capital in nature (ITTOIA 2005, s. 33; CTA 2009, s. 53). Revenue expenses are in respect of items with a short term benefit such as maintenance, insurance, loan interest (but not capital repayments), letting agent fees, etc.

HMRC describe capital expenditure as the cost of buying, installing, building, altering, or improving fixed assets used in the rental business. It has a more long term benefit than revenue expenditure. Depreciation of assets cannot be deducted from the rental income, unlike in some countries (e.g. Australia) where this is possible. However, capital allowances for plant and machinery may be an allowable deduction, but generally only for:

  (i)   furnished holiday lettings located in the UK and the EEA (the European Economic Area – whether this will change after Brexit remains to be seen); or

(ii)   the letting of commercial properties.

Allowances are not generally given for residential properties as (per CAA 2001, s. 35) these are regarded as "dwelling houses" (but furnished holiday lets are not regarded as dwelling houses). HMRC's *Capital Allowances Manual*, at CA 11520, defines a dwelling house as a property with the "ability to afford to those who use it the facilities required for day-to-day private domestic existence". Revenue and Customs Brief 45/10 also discusses what a dwelling house is.

Complications can arise from premises that comprise of more than one dwelling house, such as blocks of flats, where the block is not regarded as a dwelling house, but each individual flat is, so the capital expenditure incurred for communal areas may attract capital allowance deductions, whereas that incurred within a flat will not, although expenditure for the benefit of the block as a whole may qualify for capital allowances, e.g. fire and air-conditioning systems, lifts, security systems and so on. Student accommodation may also cause complications with regards to qualifying expenditure for allowable capital allowances.

For residential properties that are dwelling houses, allowances in respect of depreciation included the wear and tear allowance for fully furnished properties and the renewals basis, both of which have been replaced with the replacement domestic items relief from 6 April 2016 (see **3.1.8**). This loss of the 10% wear and tear allowance deduction from 2016-17 can make a big difference in the profit assessable, especially if there are no replacement domestic items in that particular year on which to claim allowances (see further below).

The individual should keep all evidence that shows an expense was incurred wholly and exclusively for the rental business. This may include documents, such as invoices and agreements etc., and a record of the purpose of incurring the expense should also be kept. The sole purpose of the expense should be for the rental property business; however, if it can be shown there is a clear distinction between an element that relates solely to the rental property, and an element that relates to some other purpose, then it may be possible to apportion the expense between the two elements on a reasonable basis. For example, a non-resident may visit his rental property and rent a car while visiting the UK. If he can show the

247

mileage for travelling to the property to inspect it or carry out some other task purely for the rental property business, then he may be able to claim a deduction for this travelling cost.

Some of the most common types of expenses are considered below.

Law: ITTOIA 2005, s. 34; CTA 2009, s. 54; F(No.2)A 2017, Sch. 2 (Pt. 2), Sch. 3
Guidance: PIM 1900

3.1.8   *Repairs and renewals*

When looking at repairs and renewals to a residential property, the whole property is regarded as the asset. Therefore, anything replacing an item which is attached to or part of the property – e.g. changing units in a fitted kitchen – may normally be regarded as a repair to the fabric of the property as a whole, as it is only replacing part of the asset, whereas the replacement of a whole asset would be regarded as a capital expense. On the other hand, if a refurbishment or alteration to a property results in substantially the whole of the property being altered, then this cost may be regarded as capital expenditure. The invoices for capital expenditure incurred should be kept, as these items may be treated as enhancement of capital expenditure when claiming capital gains tax (CGT) relief later.

The main issue is establishing whether the expense is capital or revenue expenditure. A key question, therefore, when looking at whether repair or renewal expenditure is an allowable deduction, is whether or not it improves the item concerned. If it merely replaces the item with a modern day equivalent, using modern technologies and materials for essentially the same item, with no other improvement or upgrade, then the cost should be regarded as a repair and so allowable. If there is another improvement or upgrade, then it is unlikely this will be treated as an allowable repair expense.

Up until 5 April 2016 (31 March 2016 for corporation tax purposes), landlords of a fully furnished property (defined at PIM 3215 as a dwelling house that has sufficient furniture, furnishings and equipment for normal residential use), had the choice of either claiming a wear and tear allowance or the renewals basis. The wear and tear allowance was calculated as 10% of the net rent from the property (i.e. rent received less council tax, water rates, gas, electricity and any other usual tenant liabilities born by the landlord). The renewals basis was the replacement of items on a like-for-like basis. Once the choice was made, the landlord had to continue using the same method each year and so could not swap between the two alternatives.

The 10% wear and tear allowance was in respect of moveable furniture and furnishings and covered items such as sofas, white goods, TVs, beds, carpets, crockery, cutlery, linen, etc. It did not cover fixtures, so a landlord who was claiming the wear and tear allowance could also claim deductions for other repairs and replacements to fixtures not covered by the allowance (such as wash basins, sinks, toilets, fitted kitchens and bathrooms). He could not, however, claim the actual renewal of furniture and furnishings which were covered by the wear and tear allowance.

For expenditure incurred from 6 April 2016 (1 April 2016 for corporation tax), both the wear and tear allowance and the renewal basis have been replaced by the replacement domestic items relief, which provides relief for the cost of replacing items that are used for domestic use by tenants such as furniture and furnishings (e.g. sofas, beds, freestanding wardrobes, curtains, carpets and other floor coverings, linen), household appliances (e.g. freestanding white goods, TVs) and kitchenware (e.g. crockery and cutlery). This newer relief applies to all landlords, not just to those of fully furnished rental properties. It should also be noted that the relief applies to freestanding items only, and not to fixed items such as integrated appliances like an oven in a fitted kitchen, fitted or walk-in wardrobes and so on.

This new relief basically replaces the old renewals basis and is very similar:

- the original cost of providing the item cannot be claimed;
- where the replacement item is the same as the original item, then the full replacement cost is allowable, but where this is not the case then the cost that can be deducted is that for replacing the item with a similar one;

Example

In respect of the latter point, HMRC give the example of a sofa being replaced with a sofa bed, where a new sofa would have cost £400 but a sofa bed costs £550. In this situation only £400 can be claimed as a deduction and no relief is available for the £150 difference.

If the sofa bed is replaced later, then as long as there is no improvement and the bed is used in the dwelling house that is rented out, the full cost of the replacement will be allowed.

When considering if a new item is an improvement of the old asset, HMRC consider that the test is whether or not the replacement item is the same or substantially the same as the old item. In their view, changing the functionally (from a sofa to a sofa bed in the above example) means the replacement is not substantially the same as the old item. In addition, they take the view that changing the material or quality of the item also means that the replacement is not substantially the same as the old item. HMRC give the example of upgrading from synthetic fabric carpets to woollen carpets, where they consider the replacement is not substantially the same as the old item and so there has been an improvement.

However, if the replacement item is a reasonable modern equivalent, for example a fridge with improved energy efficient rating compared to the old fridge, HMRC would not consider this to be an improvement and the full cost of the new item should be eligible for relief.

- incidental capital expenditure in replacing the item, and costs of disposing of the item, can be included, but any consideration from disposing of the item or in respect of its part-exchange will reduce the amount that can be claimed;

- if, during a tax year (or accounting period, for corporation tax purposes), the property was a furnished holiday letting, or if rent-a-room relief was claimed, then replacement domestic items relief is not available for that tax year (or accounting period).

The legislation stipulates four conditions which must be satisfied in order for the relief to apply. These are:

- *Condition A* is that a person ("P") carries on a property business in relation to land which consists of or includes a dwelling-house.

- *Condition B* is that—

    (a) a domestic item has been provided for use in the dwelling-house ("the old item"),

    (b) P incurs expenditure on a domestic item for use in the dwelling-house ("the new item"),

    (c) the new item is provided solely for the use of the lessee (a person who is entitled to use the dwelling-house under a lease or other arrangement under which a sum is payable in respect of the use of the dwelling house),

    (d) the new item replaces the old item, and

    (e) following that replacement, the old item is no longer available for use in the dwelling-house.

- *Condition C* is that a deduction for the expenditure is not prohibited by the wholly and exclusively rule, but would otherwise be prohibited by the capital expenditure rule (see **3.1.7**).

- *Condition D* is that no capital allowances may be claimed in respect of the expenditure, meaning that landlords of furnished holiday lettings will not be entitled to this relief.

The above relief does not apply to fixtures of a rented residential property. However, as the property as a whole is regarded as the asset, the replacement of such items should be regarded as repairs (subject to the above improvement rule) and so relief should be available. This will not apply to commercial properties where capital allowances will be available instead.

As mentioned above, originally the renewals basis was very similar to the replacement domestic items relief, in so much the original cost of the item was not allowable, but any subsequent replacement was subject to the above improvement rule.

With the withdrawal from 6 April 2013 of ESC B47 "Furnished lettings of dwelling houses: wear and tear of furniture", the Revenue started denying relief for the replacement of any freestanding items on the basis that, in their view, the renewals basis was never intended to apply to large and expensive items and that it only applied to items of small value with a short useful economic life that required regular replacement due to wear and tear, such as crockery and rugs. HMRC therefore took the view that it did not apply to items such as carpets, which were of much higher value, or to freestanding white goods unless they were an integral part of a fitted kitchen and so part of the property. This HMRC view (which much of the profession disagreed with) largely affected landlords of unfurnished or partly furnished residential properties, who were unable to claim the wear and tear allowance that was available to landlords of fully furnished properties.

With the introduction of replacement domestic items relief, relief is once again available to all landlords of residential properties for the replacement of freestanding items, regardless of the amounts involved (leaving just the period from 6 April 2013 to 5 April 2016 when relief was not available).

In certain circumstances, extensive repairs to a building which has just been acquired with the view to being rented out may not be allowable repair expenses, such as when a property is not in a fit state to be rented out or the price paid reflected the dilapidated state it is in. PIM 2030 sets out circumstances in which HMRC would regard such costs as capital rather than revenue.

The FTT case of *C Wills v HMRC* held in favour of the taxpayer, that substantial repairs carried out to an old property that was then let to tenants were indeed repairs, so a revenue deduction was available, based on the principles laid down in *Conn v Robins Bros Ltd*.

If repairs are covered by insurance, then only the excess costs above the amount received from the insurance policy can be deducted. Similarly, any grants received towards repairs must be taken into account.

In some situations a tenant may pay for maintenance or repair costs which are the landlord's responsibility and perhaps receive a period of reduced rent as a result. In this situation, the amounts paid by the tenant need to be brought in as income and taxed accordingly. Similarly, if the tenant makes a contribution towards maintenance or repair costs then this contribution needs to be included with income rather than against the cost deduction.

Law: ITTOIA 2005, s. 308A-308C, 311A; CTA 2009, s. 248A-248C, 250A; FA 2016, s. 73

Cases: *Conn v Robins Bros Ltd* (1966) 43 TC 266; *C Wills v HMRC* [2010] UKFTT 174 (TC)

Guidance: PIM 2020, 3200

3.1.9   *Finance costs generally*

Relief for these costs differs depending on whether the landlord is subject to income tax or corporation tax. If the latter then the relief is covered by the loan relationship regime under CTA 2009, Parts 5-6 and is outside the scope of this publication. The following applies to landlords who are subject to income tax.

Fees and commissions in respect of obtaining loan finance or providing security are generally an allowable expense as long as they are wholly and exclusively in respect of the letting of property on a commercial basis. This will include loans for the purchase of the property and for any other items for the rental property business, such as repairs, alterations and improvements. BIM 45815 details the kind of expenses that are usually allowable and BIM 45820 details those that are excluded from tax relief. Typical allowable costs would include:

- loan interest paid, including interest paid under hire purchase, overdraft etc.;
- loan/mortgage application or arrangement fees;
- legal fees for arranging a loan/mortgage;
- financial adviser or mortgage broker fees in respect of arranging the loan/mortgage and also any re-mortgaging; and
- early repayment fees.

For tax years up to and including 2016-17, the tax relief was given as a deduction against rental income. From 2017-18 the tax relief is given as a reduction in the individual's tax liability up to a maximum of basic rate tax, which is to be introduced gradually over four tax years – See **3.1.10** immediately below.

Guidance: BIM 45800; PIM 2105

3.1.10   Finance costs from 2017-18

Tax relief for loan interest is available, as long as the borrowing is to fund the rental property business and satisfies the wholly and exclusively rule explained above. The source of the borrowing and the security of the loan, together with the residence of the lender, are not normally relevant when deciding whether or not tax relief is available. Example 2 at BIM 45700 shows how a landlord can withdraw funds from the property business, and use those for some reason other than in respect of the rental business, including for private purposes, but still receive tax relief for the interest. The key point is that the individual's capital account does not become overdrawn and, to be able to show this, a balance sheet will need to be prepared.

When looking at loan interest, it is important to make sure that the amount only relates to interest and that there is no element relating to capital repayment.

For tax years up to 2016-17, the tax relief was given as an allowable deduction in full against rental income. For 2017-18 onwards a restriction in tax relief is gradually being phased in, whereby the relief is restricted to just basic rate tax relief and is set off against an individual's tax liability, rather than as a deduction against rental income as was the case previously. This new regime only applies to rental property businesses subject to income tax, so covers individuals (including those in partnership), trusts and estates, but not companies and also not furnished holiday lets (FHL) in the UK, though property located overseas will be covered by the new restriction. The restriction relates to finance costs, and not just loan interest, and therefore includes costs associated with obtaining a loan.

In respect of these new rules, the legislation refers to costs of a "dwelling related loan" i.e. an amount that has been borrowed for the purposes of the property business and is in respect of generating income from land which consists of a dwelling house or part of a dwelling house or an estate, interest or right in or over

254

such land. The term "dwelling house" is for these purposes given its ordinary meaning and includes its garden and grounds. Where the amount borrowed is only partly used for the above purpose, for example a dwelling house and some other letting like a residential flat above a shop, it should then be apportioned on a just and reasonable basis.

As mentioned, this new method of relief is being phased in. This is taking place over the four tax years 2017-18 to 2020-21 as follows:

	Old rules	New rules			
Total amount of allowable interest	**2016-17**	**2017-18**	**2018-19**	**2019-20**	**2020-21**
% as a deduction against rental income	100%	75%	50%	25%	0%
% as a basic rate reduction from individual's tax liability	0%	25%	50%	75%	100%

Example 1

Bert is a non-resident living and working in Dubai, having been assigned there by his UK employer for a number of years. He has a number of rental properties in the UK and these provide his only source of UK income. This was £25,000 per tax year before mortgage interest of £5,000 per year. Using 2017-18 rates and allowances for each year, his tax liability under both the old and new rules is as follows:

	Old rules	New rules			
	2016-17 £	2017-18 £	2018-19 £	2019-20 £	2020-21 £
Rental income before mortgage interest	25,000	25,000	25,000	25,000	25,000
Less: mortgage interest	(5,000)	(3,750)	(2,500)	(1,250)	Nil
	20,000	21,250	22,500	23,750	25,000
Less: personal allowance	(11,500)	(11,500)	(11,500)	(11,500)	(11,500)
Taxable income	£8,500	£9,750	£11,000	£2,250	£13,500
Tax at 20%	1,700	1,950	2,200	2,450	2,700
Less 20% rental reduction (amount not relieved by deduction x 20% (BR))	Nil	(250)	(500)	(750)	(1,000)
Total tax due	£1,700	£1,700	£1,700	£1,700	£1,700

As can be seen, as Bert is a basic rate taxpayer the new rules will not have any adverse effect on him and he continues paying the same amount of tax as a result. This is likely to be the case for a number of British expats living overseas, with (say) one or two rental properties in the UK and no other UK sourced income.

Suppose, however, that Bert had performed some work in the UK, the earnings from which are taxable in the UK as he is unable to obtain exemption from UK tax under the double tax treaty between the UK and UAE. He also receives some deferred bonuses which related to his UK work before leaving, and some restricted share units vest which were awarded to him while he was still working in the UK, resulting in some of these becoming taxable in the UK (see **8.2** on share options). As a result, he becomes a higher rate taxpayer and so the new rules will start having a negative impact on his tax liability. If it is assumed his taxable earnings each tax year amount to £50,000, then his tax liability, again using 2017-18 tax rates and allowances, will be as follows:

	Old rules	New rules			
	2016-17 £	**2017-18** £	**2018-19** £	**2019-20** £	**2020-21** £
Earnings	50,000	50,000	50,000	50,000	50,000
Rental income after allowable mortgage interest	20,000	21,250	22,500	23,750	25,000
	70,000	71,250	72,500	73,750	75,000
Less: personal allowance (see note)	(11,500)	(11,500)	(11,500)	(11,500)	(11,500)
	£58,500	£59,750	£61,000	£62,250	£63,500
Tax at 20% on £33,500	6,700	6,700	6,700	6,700	6,700
Tax at 40%	10,000	10,500	11,000	11,500	12,000
	16,700	17,200	17,700	18,200	18,700
Less 20% rental reduction	Nil	(250)	(500)	(750)	(1,000)
Total tax due	**£16,700**	**£16,950**	**£17,200**	**£17,450**	**£17,700**

As can be seen, when Bert is a higher rate taxpayer his tax liability will increase as a result of the new rules.

NOTE: The personal allowance is taken as a straight £11,500 throughout for comparative purposes only.

The new rules on tax relief for finance costs will, therefore, have an adverse effect for taxpayers who are higher or additional rate taxpayers.

The new rules could also have a detrimental effect for a non-resident whose interest deduction under the old rules meant he was a basic rate taxpayer or where it reduced his taxable income such that it was covered by his personal allowance. Without this deduction he may end up having a tax liability because his personal allowance no longer covers all of his taxable rental income or it could push him into the higher tax rate bracket. Similarly, if a non-resident has been in a loss situation because of the deduction of interest, then again this may reduce the losses available or the individual may find himself in a profit situation which is not fully covered by the personal allowance.

It should also be noted that there has been a consultation on the withdrawal of personal allowances for non-residents and, whilst a decision has been deferred, this could still be in the government's armoury for tax collection in the future (see **2.3.2**).

The legislation refers to the above tax reduction being available when the individual has "relievable amounts" – amounts of finance costs which have not been allowed as deductions against rental income and which can include both current year and brought forward amounts. Where not all the relievable amount is used in a tax year, the amount unrelieved can be carried forward indefinitely or until the rental property business ceases, even if the loan to which the finance costs relate to is repaid.

HMRC guidance on their website states that this tax reduction (which is designed so that there is no tax reduction against the tax on savings income such as bank interest and dividends) is the basic rate of tax times the lowest of:

i.   finance costs which have not been deducted from rental income for the current year and any amounts brought forward – the relievable amount;

ii.   profits of the rental property business after any losses brought forward; and

iii. the individual's adjusted total income (ATI). This is calculated as total income excluding savings and dividends income *less* losses, reliefs, personal allowances and (where appropriate) blind persons' allowances.

If the tax reduction is based on (ii) or (iii) above, then the excess of finance costs can be carried forward.

For individuals who have more than one property business, e.g. a non-resident returning to live in the UK who has both UK and overseas rental properties, the legislation sets out a complicated calculation (ATI/S x L) for establishing what the tax reduction is to be in this scenario for each property business.

"L" referred to in the legislation's calculation is the lower of (i) and (ii) above. "S" is the sum of "Ls" when an individual has more than one property business.

The tax reduction cannot be used to produce a tax refund.

Example 2

Gordon is non-resident, but has kept his home in London while he is working overseas. He rents it out and his taxable profit for the tax year is £30,000, before mortgage interest he has paid during the year of £7,500. He had spent quite a bit renovating the property before renting it out and so has losses brought forward of £8,000.

The personal allowance for the year is £11,500 and none of his mortgage interest can be deducted against his rental income.

Gordon's other UK taxable income is an army pension of £15,000 and interest and dividends of £10,000.

As such:

    i.   his relievable amount is £7,500;

    ii.   his rental profits are £22,000 (£30,000 less losses brought forward of £8,000);

    iii.   his ATI is £25,500 (£22,000 rental income after losses brought forward, plus his army pension of £15,000 less his personal allowance of £11,500).

In this example Gordon's tax reducer is based on the relievable amount, so the reduction in his tax liability is calculated as 20% x £7,500 = £1,500. No amount is carried forward.

If a violent storm caused a tree to fall onto Gordon's UK property, resulting in a new roof and other substantial repairs, so that his rental profit before mortgage interest fell to £15,000, then:

259

    i.   as before, his relievable amount is £7,500;

    ii.   his rental profits are £7,000 (£15,000 less £8,000 losses brought forward);

    iii.   his ATI is £10,500 (£7,000 rental profits, after losses brought forward, plus £15,000 army pension, less his personal allowance of £11,500).

In this scenario the tax reducer will be £7,000 x 20% = £1,400, so interest he paid of £500 will be carried forward to the next year.

Further complications can arise when ITA 2007 s. 25(2) is considered, i.e. a taxpayer can deduct reliefs and allowances in such a way that reduces his or her tax liability in the greatest way.

As to what can be done to mitigate the negative effects of this new regime, much comment on this is often centred around incorporation, as a company can still obtain full tax relief for allowable finance costs. However, care needs to be taken when considering whether or not a landlord should incorporate his rental property business and both wider tax issues and non-tax issues should be considered. For example, a landlord may obtain private residence relief, if it has been his main residence at some stage during his ownership of the property, and so (in turn) letting relief. These reliefs will be lost if the property is transferred to a limited company, which may not be in the landlord's interests if he moves back into the property to live in it, as his only or main residence, after a period of living and working overseas, which is regarded as a deemed period of occupation under s. 223(3) of TCGA 1992 (see **3.2.6**).

Other options may include:

- increasing the rent charged;
- for spouses, if not already the case, consider the property being jointly owned between them;
- consider the timing of expenditure and potentially paying off capital.

As mentioned above, non-tax issues also need to be considered.

Law: ITTOIA 2005, Pt. 3, Ch. 3 (s. 272A, 272B, 274A, 274AA)

Guidance: BIM 45650; PIM 2050, 2105; www.gov.uk/guidance/changes-to-tax-relief-for-residential-landlords-how-its-worked-out-including-case-studies

3.1.11   Interest paid to overseas lenders

Relief for interest is available regardless of where the lender is located. However, care needs to be taken when dealing with overseas lenders to ensure that there is no obligation on the individual to withhold tax at basic rate from the interest payments he makes to an overseas lender and to account for these to HMRC.

The rule in this respect is that if *yearly interest* from *a UK source* is paid to *a non-resident*, then the payer must deduct UK tax at basic rate from this interest and account for this to HMRC.

Yearly interest

The legislation refers to yearly interest, but there is no statutory definition of this. HMRC confirm (in their *Savings and Investment Manual*) that there is a presumption that if a loan is for less than a year, then the interest on this is regarded as being short and there will be no withholding obligation. They then go on to say that if, at the outset, the loan is for more than a year, then the interest paid on this loan is likely to be regarded as being yearly interest and so there is potentially a withholding obligation, although the facts of the case need to be considered to establish if this is the case or not, as the situation may not be so clear cut. The intentions of the parties involved will be an important factor in determining if the interest is short or yearly.

One of the leading cases on yearly interest is *Cairns v MacDiarmid*.

Law: ITA 2007, s. 874
Case: *Cairns v MacDiarmid* (1982) 56 TC 556
Guidance: PIM 2064; SAIM 9070-9110

UK source

This will depend on a number of factors, one of the key ones being where the payer is resident and the location of his or her assets. Residence for this purpose is not the same as for tax, but is the individual's residence for jurisdiction purposes, i.e. under which jurisdiction the lender would take action against the payer, e.g. for payment of interest or the repayment of the loan. HMRC will also look at the following factors when establishing if the payment of interest is from a UK source:

- the place of performance of the contract and the method of payment;
- the residence of any guarantor;
- the location of any security for the loan;
- the source from which the interest is paid; and
- where the interest is paid.

However, HMRC regard an individual's residence for jurisdiction purposes, and where the lender will enforce the debt, as being the most important factors when establishing the source of interest.

If the individual is resident in the EU, then the Council Regulation (EC) 44/2001 on *Jurisdiction and the Recognition and Enforcement of Judgments in Civil and Commercial Matters*, and the 1968 Brussels Convention, may have an impact on the above, though this may well change once Brexit has occurred. Under these EU rules, legal action will take place in the state where the person's domicile is (as defined by the States concerned: see SAIM 9090 for the UK definition of this).

One of the leading cases on the source of interest is that of *Westminster Bank*.

Case: *Westminster Bank Executor and Trustee Company (Channel Islands) Ltd v National Bank of Greece SA* (1968) 46 TC 472
Guidance: PIM 2064; SAIM 9070-9110

A non-resident

This is a person whose usual place of abode is outside the UK.

The above withholding obligation will be particularly relevant for non-residents returning to the UK who arranged a foreign loan, perhaps whilst living outside the UK, which continues once they return to live in the UK.

If there is a withholding requirement, then exemption from this requirement may be available under a double tax treaty and for the interest to be paid gross with no deduction of tax (or at a lower rate of tax). However, in this scenario it is the lender, not the borrower, who has to apply to HMRC and who will be required to deduct and account for tax until they are told otherwise by HMRC. If the interest is paid gross, without deduction of tax, and without HMRC's authorisation, then the tax that should have been deducted will still have to be paid to HMRC.

Guidance: PIM 2064; SAIM 9070-9110

3.1.12   Travel costs

The purpose of the journey will be important in establishing whether the costs of that journey are an allowable deduction. The cost of travelling to a rental property will be allowable if the sole purpose of the journey is in respect of the rental business. Costs such as flights to the UK are unlikely to be allowable, as there is very likely to be a dual purpose of the journey, i.e. if an individual is visiting the UK for another reason as well, such as seeing relatives, friends, to perform work in the UK (a business meeting and so on). It will then be difficult to distinguish an element that relates solely to the rental business, from other reasons such as visiting family and friends. In rare cases where, say, a non-resident owning UK property has no agent and travels to the UK to oversee renovations, repairs, tenant eviction or signing leases, there may be a case for claiming a standard economy airfare as travel expenses.

For journeys that are solely for the purposes of the rental business, e.g. visiting the rental property for maintenance or inspection reasons or meeting letting agents or tenants, mileage records should be kept if an individual uses a car or any other vehicle, so as to show the mileage in respect of the allowable journey. Other running costs can be included as well as fuel. Since 6 April 2017, landlords (individuals and partnerships, but not companies) can claim the fixed rate mileage rates of 45p per mile for business mileage up to 10,000 miles per year (and then 25p per mile above this), rather than claiming the actual costs.

If public transport, or some other form of transport like a taxi, is used then receipts and tickets should be kept in respect of journeys purely for the rental business.

Relief may not be available for travel from the individual's home, but this depends on the circumstances and on where the property business "base" is.

Guidance: PIM 2220

3.1.13 Salaries

With regards to salaries paid, the same rule applies as for other businesses, i.e. only the amounts paid during the tax year or within nine months of the year end can be included as an allowable expense.

Care should be taken if salaries are paid to family or relatives to ensure the amounts paid are commercial and reflect the work actually done. The recipient could be taxed on the amounts received. Landlords cannot claim a deduction for their time spent on their rental business.

Normal payroll rules apply and so PAYE and NIC, and also pension regulations, need to be considered and operated as with any other employer/employee relationship.

Guidance: PIM 2210

3.1.14 Professional and management fees

Professional fees are an allowable expense if they are revenue in nature and not capital. Revenue expenses include accountancy fees for the preparation of the rental business accounts, agreeing tax liabilities (consideration should be taken of overseas accountancy fees as well as UK fees) and fees in respect of the renewal of leases (if for less than 50 years) or the first lease if for less than a year, but not the fees in respect of the initial lease if for more than one year, as this would be regarded as a capital expense. Fees in respect of a replacement lease with a different tenant should be allowable if the replacement lease is similar to the previous lease in place. If there is a substantial change, such as changing to a long lease from a short lease, then the fees may not be allowable.

Premiums paid in respect of leases are not allowable expenses.

Letting agent fees should be allowable if in respect of the normal day to day management of the property, as well as other costs such as advertising and marketing for new tenants, collecting rents and evicting tenants.

Guidance: PIM 2120

3.1.15   Service charges

Service charges for blocks of flats, etc. may include both running costs of common areas and capital expenditure. Therefore a breakdown of the charge will be needed to establish which costs are allowable and which are not. As mentioned above, capital allowances may be available in respect of capital expenditure incurred in common areas.

3.1.16   Cost of providing services

These would include such items as gardening, cleaning, waste disposal, light and heat, water and so on and should be allowable if solely for the rental business. If the costs are incurred only partly in respect of the rental business, then an apportionment should be made on a reasonable basis to establish the allowable element.

Guidance: PIM 2076

3.1.17   Expenses on commencement and cessation of a property business

Expenses may be claimed for periods before and after the rental business has started and ceased.

For expenses incurred prior to the business starting, which meet the "wholly and exclusively" rule and which are not capital in nature, all of the following conditions need to be satisfied for the expense to be an allowable deduction:

- the expense must have been incurred within a period of seven years before the date the rental business started;
- it must not be otherwise allowable as a deduction for tax purposes; and
- it must be a type of expense that would have been allowed as a deduction if it had been incurred after the rental business had started.

265

Qualifying pre-commencement expenses are treated as having been incurred on the first day the rental business starts.

For expenses incurred after the rental business has ceased (e.g. when the individual moves back into the property to live and he has no other rental property), the manner of giving relief will depend on whether or not there were any post cessation receipts (e.g. collection of bad debts that had previously been written off), which would be taxed in the year of receipt. If there are, then they can be deducted against these. If not, then certain expenses, such as the cost of collecting bad debts, can be relieved sideways and against other taxable income and gains in the same tax year. In this respect the claim for relief needs to be made by 31 January following the relevant tax year.

Again, as with pre-commencement expenses, only post-cessation expenses up to seven years after the property business has ceased can potentially be relieved.

Law: ITTOIA 2005, s. 57; ITA 2007, s. 125
Guidance: PIM 2500

3.1.18   Other expenses

Other common allowable expenses include:

Insurance, which will cover premiums paid for damage to buildings and contents and loss of rent.

Council tax and rates, although this is usually the tenant's responsibility and so would normally only be incurred by the landlord during a period in between tenancies.

Bad debts. If the accruals basis has been used in preparing the rental business accounts, then relief for bad debts is available, but only in respect of specific debts as opposed to a general provision. As landlords have been able to start using the cash basis from 2017-18, the write off of bad debts will become less common.

Ground rent is allowable, although this will need to be apportioned if it also relates to an element which is not rented out.

Guidance: PIM 2072, 2110, 2140, 2205

3.1.19   *Properties not rented out at a market rent*

Strictly speaking, in this scenario (e.g. where a property is used by a friend or family member free of charge or at a reduced rent) no expenses can be deducted: HMRC view these expenses as probably having been incurred for personal or philanthropic purposes, to provide that person with a home, and so they would fall foul of the wholly and exclusively rule. However, HMRC permit the deduction of allowable expenses, but not to the extent that a loss arises, and any excess expenses not deducted cannot be carried forward for use in the future.

Allowable expenses in respect of properties that are both let on a commercial basis and provided free to friends or relatives to stay in, such as holiday homes, need to be apportioned on a reasonable basis between the commercial and uncommercial use, with any excess elements relating to the latter not being allowed to be carried forward for future relief.

Guidance: PIM 2130

3.1.20   *Deposits*

Any deposits withheld from tenants, and either fully or partially kept at the end of the tenancy, need to be declared as income, and associated costs can be deducted as expenses if allowable.

3.1.21   *Overseas rental properties*

If an individual living abroad acquires a property overseas which is rented out, then while the person is non-resident the income will not be taxed in the UK. Once he or she returns to the UK and becomes tax resident, and so taxable on his worldwide income, the rental income from this overseas property will be taxable in the UK. It will be treated as a separate overseas rental business to any rental income from UK properties he may have. The income will need to be declared on the foreign pages (SA106) of the self-assessment tax return and the taxable income will be calculated in the same way as with UK rental income. Relief will be available for any foreign tax paid, which may be either in the form of a tax credit against the UK tax due on the income or a deduction against the rental income. This latter method may be more appropriate if a loss is being made on the rental property and the foreign tax credit method is then lost, as there is no UK tax against which to offset it.

Law: ITTOIA 2005, s. 265
Guidance: PIM 4700

3.1.22 Losses

Any loss made for a tax year cannot be set off against any other taxable income arising in the same tax year (except in very limited circumstances), as is the case in some countries like Australia. It is first set off against any other taxable profits that have arisen in the same tax year from the UK rental business and any excess is then carried forward to set against future profits from the UK rental business. No claim is needed for this loss relief as it applies automatically and the losses can be carried forward indefinitely.

Losses from a UK rental property business cannot be set off against any profits from an overseas property business. This will not be relevant when an individual is not resident in the UK as the profits from overseas properties are not then taxable in the UK, but if he were to return to the UK and become resident again, this may need to be considered.

Law: ITA 2007, s. 117-126
Guidance: PIM 4200

3.1.23 Airbnb, furnished holiday lets, etc.

Expats moving abroad can obtain lettings relief for CGT purposes when letting out their family home (see paragraph **3.2.5**). These lets may be for short or long tenancy agreements depending on the period of assignment abroad.

However, those who are unsure of the time they will spend abroad – but require income whilst abroad – may consider lets on a shorter term basis, such as those provided by becoming an Airbnb host or by offering furnished holiday lettings (FHLs). See the comparison of income and expenses for both in sections **3.1.24** and **3.1.25** below. The demand for both of these has risen substantially over the last few years; in the case of the former, hotel accommodation for people is expensive and no longer the vogue with travellers wanting a "home from home". In the case of the latter, the weakness of the pound since Brexit has meant that more holiday makers are spending their holidays in the UK now and the demand for holiday lets is rising.

In both cases, on average, the rental payments are substantially more than the individual can get for a standard shorthold tenancy agreement and there is the added advantage that the expat's property can be used when he or she is back in the UK for holidays, whereas this would not be possible with shorthold tenancy agreements.

3.1.24   Airbnb

Having a good location for the property, such as in the major tourist cities or near the coast, is an advantage, but even other areas do attract visitors on a regular basis who are passing through. Airbnb hosting relies on a regular turnover of guests and therefore the host (i.e. property owner) is going to need to have regular reliable meet-and-greet/changeover support, which will be an additional expense for the expat who is abroad.

There is a fee payable to Airbnb for securing the visitor. There will also be the need to consider income tax, VAT and in some countries an occupancy tax. VAT in the UK is to be considered but thankfully occupancy tax is not currently applicable to UK hosts, but the government may perceive Airbnb hosts as an area of tax loss and choose to alter this in the future. Airbnb rents are subject to tax after expenses but may be covered by the expat's personal allowance of £11,850 if unused. Note that VAT would also be charged on the commission deductions in the examples below (see **2.5 VAT and GST**).

Two types of scenario exist, first where the host is "on site" (i.e. letting out a room to visitors) or second where the host is not on site and the whole property is available for the guest. In the case of the former the rent-a-room relief (see below) may apply, giving tax relief up to £7,500 per year, but this will possibly be restricted to long Airbnb lets following a consultation document issued on 1 December 2017. However, most expats will be abroad when the letting occurs and the income and expenses will be reportable on the SA105 property income pages in boxes 20-29.

Example

Rental statement for Airbnb income and expenditure for Four Seasons, Barton on Sea, Hants.

	£	£
Total gross Airbnb payments 2019-20 (240 days @ £75 per day)		18,000
Less allowable expenses:		
Airbnb commission at 3%.	540	
Water rates/council tax, etc.*	698	
Insurance*	182	
Accounting	250	
Gardening*	160	
Welcome packs (160 x £11)	1,760	
Maintenance/repairs	325	
Cleaning (160 days x £30 per changeover)	4,800	
Gas/electric/etc.*	240	8,955
Total net income		9,045

*Apportioned for periods of non-occupation.

3.1.25   *Furnished holiday lettings (FHL)*

In order to qualify as an FHL the property should be:

- in the UK or in the European Economic Area (EEA) (but also including Iceland, Liechtenstein and Norway); and
- furnished.

All FHLs in the UK, if there is more than one, are taxed as a single UK FHL business and all FHLs in other EEA states are taxed as a single EEA FHL business. Separate records are required for each of these because the losses from one FHL business cannot be used against profits of the other. See SA 105 boxes 5-19.

The FHL property should be commercially let with the intention of making a profit but if the lets during winter months merely cover costs then that will not necessarily exclude the FHL commerciality condition from being met over the whole year. It would be expected that summer lets would be at a more commercial figure of weekly rent than winter lets.

There are a number of requirements to the letting as follows:

1. The FHL must be available for letting as such for at least 210 days in the year.
2. Days of occupation by the owners are not counted as days available for letting.
3. The property must be let to the general public for at least 105 days in the year.
4. If the FHL is closed for part of the year due to lack of customers, e.g. perhaps Cornwall in the winter months, expenses such as insurance and loan interest can be deducted for the whole year, provided the FHL owner does not live there.
5. Where the owner uses part of the property for part of the year the expenses claimed need to be apportioned on a just and reasonable basis, typically by reference to the number of days the owner is using the FHL personally.

Properties that are let as FHLs are treated differently to ordinary let properties, so that:

- CGT reliefs for traders can be claimed, such as business asset rollover relief, entrepreneurs' relief, relief for gifts of business assets and relief for loans to traders.
- Plant and machinery capital allowances are allowed for items such as furniture, equipment and fixtures.
- The profits count as earnings for pension purposes.

Example

FHL rental statement for income and expenditure for Four Seasons, Barton on Sea, Hants.

	£	£
Total gross FHL payments 2019-2020 (34 weeks @ £500 per week)		17,000
Less allowable expenses:		
Seaside Cottages Ltd commission at 10%	1,700	
Water rates/council tax, etc.*	946	
Insurance*	250	
Accounting	250	
Gardening *	256	
Welcome packs (34 weeks x £11)	374	
Maintenance/repairs	775	
Cleaning (34 weeks x £30)	1,020	
Gas/electric/etc.*	642	6,213
Total net income		10,787

*Expenses during winter months of non-occupation allowed.

The gross income from the FHL over the year is less than Airbnb but the expenses are less because of the weekly turnover compared to many daily changeovers with Airbnb. Also, the fact that pension payments could be made with FHL net income is an important factor. With both Airbnb and FHLs the expat can reoccupy the property on visits to the UK, whereas the tenancy agreements of an ordinary letting of the individual's main property would not allow this.

3.1.26   Rent-a-room relief

Sometimes a non-resident may only rent out a room in his UK home while living overseas, with the rest of the property being available for his own use. In this scenario, rent-a-room relief is unlikely to apply to most expats overseas, as the property needs to be the individual's only or main residence at some point during the tax year. The relief may be of some value where, say, the husband works abroad and the wife stays in the UK but this is not a common scenario.

However, there will be circumstances where the rules can be used to advantage by expats, especially if they have children at University (see the example below). The relief allows owner occupiers and tenants to receive tax-free rental income of £7,500 per annum if they provide furnished accommodation in their only or main home.

If someone else receives income from letting accommodation in the same property, such as a joint owner, then the limit is divided but oddly the limit is the same even if the accommodation/rooms are let for less than 12 months. Gross receipts will also include any amounts received for meals, goods and services, such as cleaning or laundry.

There are two methods of paying tax on gross receipts as follows:

Method A

Tax is paid on actual profit less any expenses and capital allowances, similar to the examples of Airbnb and FHLs above. HMRC will automatically use the actual profit (Method A) to work out the tax.

Method B

Under this method, tax is paid on gross receipts over the rent-a-room limit of £7,500, i.e. on gross receipts minus £7,500 (or £3,750 if divided between two individuals). Expenses and capital allowances cannot be deducted if this method is chosen. This method must be elected for and, once that is done, HMRC will continue to use this method until otherwise advised.

Using Method B automatically stops if rental income drops below the £7,500 limit.

Example

Alexandra's parents live in Hong Kong. She is aged 18 years, is in her first year of a five-year course at Cambridge University and her father does not wish to pay large amounts for her accommodation in the city over five years (or more if she goes on to do a masters/doctorate). Instead, he provides the funds by gift into a bare trust for his daughter to acquire a three bedroomed property. The advantages of this are that Alexandra will:

- have accommodation available rent free;
- pay the reduced SDLT rate because the purchase is her first and only property in the UK or anywhere else (see SDLT at **9.5.2**);

- obtain tax-free income up to £7,500 (or more) per annum, depending on bedrooms let to fellow students, from rent-a-room relief;

- obtain capital gains tax main residence relief on the eventual sale (see **3.2.3**).

See also the sections on lettings relief, CGT and SDLT.

In the 2018-19 tax year Alexandra rents out two of the bedrooms to university students at £500 per month each, sharing the home and yearly expenses amounting to £750 per annum for heat and light contribution. The gross income is £12,750 per annum minus £7,500 allowance so under Method B she would pay tax of £1,050 (£5,250 @ 20%). By Method A she would deduct all total expenses of, say, £4,500 to give £8,250, giving a tax liability of £1,650 (£8,250 @ 20%). Method B is more attractive and Alexandra must tell HMRC she wants to use this method by 31 January 2020.

Law: ITTOIA 2005, s. 309, 784-802
Guidance: PIM 4000

3.1.27   HMRC toolkit

When completing self-assessment tax returns, it is advisable to use HMRC's toolkit on rental properties which is available on their website.

Guidance: https://www.gov.uk/government/publications/hmrc-property -rental-toolkit

3.2   Capital gains on selling UK property

3.2.1   Introduction

The general rule is that non-residents are outside the scope of UK capital gains tax (CGT) and so will not be liable to UK CGT on any assets they sell while non-resident. This is subject to the five-year rule and temporary non-residence where capital gains during such a period are assessed in the period of return to the UK (see **2.2.12**).

There are exceptions to the general rule, one of which is with regard to the sale of residential property in the UK. As from 6 April 2015, a non-resident person selling UK residential property will be liable to

UK CGT on the gain arising from this date. This is known as the non-resident capital gains tax (NRCGT) regime. This regime does not apply to resident persons who sell UK property, just non-resident persons, including those who are treated as non-resident during an overseas part of a split year (see **2.2.6**).

NRCGT covers:

- non-resident individuals;
- personal representatives of non-resident deceased persons;
- non-resident trustees;
- certain non-resident companies (generally those controlled by five or fewer persons); and
- any such person who is a partner in a partnership.

For the purposes of this publication, the following will concentrate on non-resident individuals only.

A non-resident individual is one who is not resident under the statutory residence test (SRT) (see **2.2**). A dual resident (see **2.2.10**) should not be covered by these rules if he or she is not resident in the UK for treaty purposes.

Residential property is an interest in land in the UK, upon which there was a dwelling at some time during the period of relevant ownership (starting with the later of 6 April 2015 or the date of acquisition and ending with the day before the date of disposal). A dwelling is a building (including one that is being constructed or adapted, and can include a caravan or houseboat), which is used as or is suitable for use as such and includes land which is intended to be occupied or enjoyed with the dwelling such as a garden, including also any building or structure on this land (e.g. a detached garage). This will, therefore, include land which is intended to have a dwelling built on it and off-plan buildings.

The NRCGT rules take precedence over the temporary non-residence rules (see **2.2.11**).

Law: TCGA 1992, s. 14B-14H, Sch. B1; FA 2015, s. 37, Sch. 7

Guidance: www.gov.uk/guidance/capital-gains-tax-for-non-residents-uk-residential-property

3.2.2   *Calculating gains and losses*

As mentioned above, from 6 April 2015 non-residents became liable to UK CGT on the sale of UK residential property.

The default way to calculate the gain is to use the market value of the property sold at 5 April 2015 as the base cost (a process known as rebasing). Even though HMRC state that a valuation does not need to be obtained until the property is disposed of, it is advisable for non-residents to obtain this sooner rather than later, as the longer the period from 5 April 2015 to the date of sale, the more difficult it will be to obtain an accurate valuation. This may then open up the possibility of disputes with HMRC over the valuation, especially if large amounts are involved.

It may end up being the case that the non-resident returns to the UK and becomes resident again without selling the property, in which case the valuation will not be needed, as this rule only applies to non-residents, unless the individual leaves the UK again and once more becomes non-resident. It may, therefore, be worth obtaining the 5 April 2015 valuation as a precaution.

It is advisable to obtain a "red book" valuation for tax purposes from a suitably qualified surveyor, e.g. a member of the Royal Institute of Chartered Surveyors (RICS). Again, HMRC do not stipulate this, but it is advisable so as to minimise any potential disputes with HMRC in the future. The cost of this valuation can vary significantly – in the author's experience the price can vary between £150 and £2,500 plus UK VAT. The average cost appears to be between £200 and £400 plus VAT per property.

If an individual decides not to obtain a valuation as at 5 April 2015 until the date of sale, then HMRC guidance suggests that notes should be taken of the condition of the property at 5 April 2015 and a record kept of any specific issues or aspects at the time that may affect its valuation.

A valuation can be checked with HMRC by using form CG34, although the individual needs to be aware that this can only be done after the disposal and will take at least two months, while the NRCGT return needs to be filed within 30 days of conveyance (see **3.2.12**). It may, therefore, be necessary in this scenario to amend the NRCGT return once HMRC have responded to the CG34 form.

An individual can elect for two other methods of calculating the post April 2015 gain. The first is to elect for the straight-line time apportionment method. This takes the gain overall and then apportions it on a time basis between the pre and post April 2015 gains (on a days basis).

The second method for which an individual can elect is to use the total gain or loss overall, with no apportionment. This method is likely to be beneficial if there is a loss that can be claimed overall and is known as the retrospective basis computation.

Some tax reliefs for which a non-resident individual may be eligible are considered in the following sections.

3.2.3   Private residence relief (PRR) – introduction

If a property has been a person's only or main residence during some part of his or her ownership of it, then the individual may be eligible for PRR with the result that no chargeable gain arises for these periods of occupation. In fact the notes to the CGT return CGN1 state that "You don't need to fill in the 'Capital gains summary' if you only sell or dispose of your main home, if you qualify for Private Residence Relief on the full amount of the gain."

PRR for all taxpayers became more complicated from 6 April 2015, with the introduction of the NRCGT regime. On this date, the concept of "non-qualifying tax years" was introduced under s. 222B of TCGA 1992, stating that a dwelling house (or part of one) is not regarded as being occupied as a residence for the purposes of PRR for a "non-qualifying tax year" and so exemption under s. 222 will not be available for this tax year. Section 222B defines a non-qualifying tax year as being one in which *both* the individual and his or her spouse/civil partner are not resident for tax purposes in the territory where the property is located *and also* the individual does not meet an occupancy test, known as the day count test. The legislation also refers to part years, which is in respect of tax years where the individual's ownership of the property is for part of the year.

With regards to the tax residence test, and being resident in the territory where the property is located, the individual either:

(i)   is liable to tax there as a result of his residence or domicile status for more than half of the UK tax year; or

(ii)   would be if the statutory residence test were applied (substituting all references to the UK with the territory concerned).

Both spouses (or civil partners) need to be not resident for a year to be regarded as a non-qualifying year, so If one spouse or civil partner is resident and the other is not, then the tax year will not be regarded as a non-qualifying tax year.

Example

A husband is working in the Middle East and is not resident, but his wife has remained living in the UK in the family home and so is resident. This will not be a non-qualifying year and so PRR may be available.

Regarding the day count test, this is satisfied if an individual has at least 90 qualifying stays in the property in the tax year. To meet this test, the individual must either be present in one of the properties at midnight, or must be present there at some time during the day itself and also the following day, having stayed overnight in the property.

These 90 days do not need to be consecutive and are pro-rated when the non-residence period is less than a full tax year. The 90-day test can be satisfied by aggregating days spent at other properties that the individual (or his spouse/civil partner) has an interest in (so not in rented property) and that are in the same country (qualifying properties). In addition, the nights the individual's spouse or civil partner spends in the property (or other qualifying properties in the same territory) can also be taken into account, but there can be no double counting in this respect, i.e. if one spouse/civil partner spends a night in the property or another qualifying property in the same country and the other does not, then this can be counted as one night towards the 90 day total, but if both spouses/civil partners spend the same night at the property, this will still just be counted as one night and not two.

If the individual and his or her spouse/civil partner are both not resident, and the individual has not satisfied the day count test, then the non-resident individual will be treated as not occupying the property as his or her only or main residence and so the tax year will be regarded as a non-qualifying tax year, with PRR not being available for that year. Any gain that arises in respect of non-qualifying tax years will be subject to CGT regardless of whether the seller is resident or not at the time of sale. Tax years prior to 2015-16 can be non-qualifying, if the gain is subject to NRCGT, so if the individual is not resident at the time of sale.

This rule in respect of non-qualifying tax years does not affect relief for the final 18 months of ownership, certain periods of absences or periods living in job-related accommodation (see below).

Once a property has been a person's only or main residence during his ownership, this sparks off other reliefs or exemptions.

3.2.4   PRR – final 18 months of ownership

The gain for the last 18 months of ownership is exempt from UK CGT as a result of PRR even if the property was let out during that time. This meant that any non-resident who sold such a property before 6 October 2016 (18 months from 6 April 2015), was not subject to UK CGT as all the gain would have been covered by this final 18-month period. For disposals after 5 October 2016, chargeable gains may arise for the period between 6 April 2015, or if later the date of acquisition, and the beginning of this final 18 month period.

3.2.5   PRR – letting relief

If a property has been a person's only or main residence and then is let out, say while the individual is living overseas, then letting relief may be available. The relief available will be the lowest of:

- PRR available;
- The gain relating to the period of let from 6 April 2015; and
- £40,000

3.2.6   PRR absence relief

For PRR to apply, the individual must occupy the property as a residence. Therefore, if a property is not occupied by an individual, e.g. when it is let out, PRR is not available for that time.

279

However, PRR may be available for certain periods of absence when the absence is deemed to be a period of occupation of a residence and so potentially the individual's only or main residence. The above non-qualifying rule for tax years will not apply in this respect. There are three specific periods of absence:

(i) Three years for any reason. This can be different periods which add up to three years.

(ii) Unlimited time while an individual is working wholly overseas in employment (not self-employment). This also includes the individual's spouse or civil partner with whom the individual is living. An important point to highlight is that for this period of absence to apply, a person must not do any work at all in the UK while they are living and working overseas, including very minor tasks such as reading and responding to emails, texts etc., receiving and making work phone calls and so on.

Any work at all performed in the UK, no matter how minor it is, will result in the individual not being able to claim this period as deemed occupation. The individual can visit the UK, say for holidays, but must not perform any work in the UK while visiting. In today's modern world – with internet, mobile connections, email and the like – this is in practice a requirement that may be hard to satisfy for many. It is particularly harsh in the light of the statutory residence test and the third automatic overseas test, which does allow a certain amount of work to be performed in the UK and where the earnings from incidental work performed in the UK (see **2.3.9**) are not taxed in the UK. The reality is that HMRC do take a firm view on work performed in the UK in this respect.

It is also important that, for the above absence, the individual spends all of it actually in employment or in an office abroad. He can change employers, can be posted to other parts of the world and his employment duties can change, but he must remain in an overseas employment or office to be able to qualify for this period of absence.

(iii)   Up to four years because an individual is prevented from living in his home because of the situation of his place of work or because his employer requires him to reside elsewhere (whether in the UK or overseas). This again also includes an individual's spouse or civil partner who is living with the individual. This period of absence is available to both employees and self-employed individuals.

With regards to spouses/civil partners of individuals whose periods of absence are due to (ii) or (iii) above, the spouse/civil partner can still benefit from these deemed periods of occupation even if he or she owns the property concerned but the working individual does not, providing they are living together.

Under (i) and (iii) above, where there is a maximum number of years, HMRC do not in practice deny relief altogether if these limits are exceeded but will allow the first three years of a period of absence for (i) and four years for (iii) as deemed periods of occupation of a residence, providing all other relevant conditions are satisfied.

For any of these periods of absence to be deemed periods of occupation of a residence, the individual must live in the property as his only or main residence both before and after the period of absence (though he does not need to move back in immediately or to have moved out immediately beforehand). There is, however, a relaxation to the requirement of having to live in the property again as a person's only or main residence; this applies if he is unable to live in the property after his period of absence, because of the location of his work or because his employer requires him to reside elsewhere. This relaxation applies to (ii) and (iii) above.

Example

Ben returned to the UK after being assigned overseas by his UK employer. His home in the UK (which he lived in as his main residence prior to working overseas) is in Surrey, but his employer requires him to work in Aberdeen and so he has to move there for his work. This is clearly not within commuting distance of his Surrey home, meaning that his employment prevents him from moving back into it and living in it as his only or main residence. In this situation, Ben may be able to claim that his period of absence

281

while working overseas should be a deemed period of occupation, even though he has not lived in the property following his return and even though he subsequently sells the property (say because he is permanently located to Aberdeen by his employer).

Different types of the above periods of absence can run back to back, e.g. the unlimited time working overseas, then time working elsewhere for four years, say in the UK, and then the three-year period for any reason. The key point is that the individual must move back into the property after this final period to live in the property as his only or main residence, as it is important that there is a period both before and after, where an individual lives in the property as his only or main residence, unless the above relaxation in respect of his employment preventing him from moving back into his main residence applies. The quality of living in the property and the individual's intentions will be more important than the length of time spent living in the property, but the longer a person lives in the property as his main residence the better, as it will then be easier to argue that it is his only or main residence. The individual needs to make sure that he is genuinely living in it as his only or main residence.

Example

Mita purchased a property in the UK on 1 January 2010 and immediately moved in to live in it as her main residence.

On 1 February 2012 she left the UK to live and work in Hong Kong as a result of her UK employer assigning her there. She returned to the UK on 1 January 2018 after her Hong Kong assignment ended, but moved in with family and did not move back into her property. During her time overseas she visited the UK for holidays, but did not perform any work in the UK. She rented the property out after moving out on 1 February 2012.

On 1 April 2018 she left the UK and travelled around the world for a year and moved back into her property on 1 April 2019 to live in it as her main residence again.

On 31 December 2020 she sold her property.

The period of ownership can be broken down as follows:

1 January 2010 to 31 January 2012 – living in as main residence

1 February 2012 to 31 December 2017 – deemed period of occupation due to working wholly overseas

1 January 2018 to 31 March 2019 – deemed period of occupation due to any three-year period

1 April 2019 to 30 June 2019 – living in as main residence

1 July 2019 to 31 December 2020 – final 18 months' exemption

As can be seen the whole gain will be covered by PRR and so no CGT will arise.

If, however, Mita had had customer meetings on her visits back to the UK while working in Hong Kong, then this would have meant she would not qualify for deemed occupation as a result of working wholly overseas.

In this scenario the ownership in relation to PRR would be:

1 January 2010 to 31 January 2012 – living in as main residence

1 February 2012 to 31 January 2016 – deemed period of occupation due to location of work up to four years

1 February 2016 to 31 January 2019 – deemed period of occupation due to any three-year period

1 February 2019 to 31 March 2019 – no PRR, though letting relief may be available

1 April 2019 to 30 June 2019 – living in as main residence

1 July 2019 to 31 December 2020 – final 18 months' exemption

As can be seen, the mere fact Mita had customer meetings in the UK while she was assigned to Hong Kong, has resulted in part of her gain potentially becoming taxable, although letting relief may be available to reduce any potential chargeable gain.

3.2.7   PRR elections

Generally, for both resident and non-resident individuals, an individual who has two residences which he occupies has the opportunity to make an election under TCGA 1992, s. 222(5) to nominate one of the residences to be his only or main residence for PRR purposes (only one residence at any one time is eligible for PRR). This is often called a second home election.

A residence for PRR purposes does not need to be owned by the individual and can include accommodation in which he lives but which he does not own, such as rental or employer-provided accommodation. For individuals who leave the UK and live overseas, this means that the accommodation they live in while abroad is very likely regarded as a residence for PRR, even though it is rented or has been provided by their employer. In this scenario, therefore, an individual should consider putting in a second home election under s. 222(5), nominating his UK home to remain the main residence for PRR, while he is living overseas. This election needs to be made within two years of his moving into the overseas accommodation and so having two residences. If the individual actually owns property overseas which he lives in, then more consideration is needed as to which property to elect as the main residence.

It is very common for non-residents not to realise that their rented or employer provided accommodation overseas is regarded as a residence for PRR purposes and so not to put in a second home election. In the absence of such an election, the decision as to which property is the main residence will be based on the facts and circumstances of the situation (see HMRC's *Capital Gains Manual* at CG 64545 for a list of factors they consider in this respect). As such, the overseas accommodation is likely to be regarded as the main residence for PRR, meaning that – when the individual comes to sell the UK home – a chargeable gain may arise for this period, resulting in a possible CGT liability.

It may be possible to put in a late election using ESC D21 (see CG 64500). If an individual has two residences, one of which is rented or employer-provided accommodation – and where the individual was unaware that the latter is a residence for CGT purposes, and so did not make the relevant second home election – then under ESC D21 he may be able to make such an election late as long as it is made within a reasonable time of becoming aware of the fact that he should have made it. ESC D21 cannot be used if the non-resident owns the property he is living in overseas. Strictly speaking, a second home election should be made every time the non-resident moves accommodation, as there is then a change in the combination of his residences. However, in the author's experience HMRC have agreed that a new election does not need to be made when moving between rented or employer-provided accommodation, so a request for this agreement from HMRC should be considered when sending in the election.

For all second home elections, if the property is jointly owned between spouses or civil partners who live with each other, they can only have one main residence between them and so each spouse or civil partner has to sign the election.

Very often a non-resident will rent out his or her UK home while living overseas. Normally, renting of a property prevents an individual being able to claim PRR for this period of letting, as it is not then a residence for them for the purposes of PRR. However, when looking at absence relief, it does not matter that the property is let out and PRR may still be available if all the relevant conditions are satisfied. In this respect a second home election should be considered even if it just as a protective measure. In the author's experience HMRC may well come back and state that an election cannot be made because the property is being rented out, in which case they should be directed to their own CGT manual and in particular to CG 64477 and 64485.

From 6 April 2015 another type of second home election was introduced under s. 222A of TCGA 1992, which is in respect of gains subject to NRCGT. This election will be made by individuals who sell their property when not resident and will be made on the NRCGT return they file at the time of disposal.

If an individual has a second home election under s. 222(5) already in place before 6 April 2015, then this does not cease to be effective because of the introduction of the NRCGT regime and can still be varied, except for an election in respect of a past disposal. If there is a non-qualifying tax year, any existing second home election under s. 222(5) will lapse for that tax year.

3.2.8   *PRR and job-related accommodation*

In some instances, an individual may be eligible for PRR on a property they own but do not live in as a result of having to live in job-related accommodation. However, this is relatively rare now, and is largely confined to personnel of the armed forces living in

285

military accommodation, so it is a point to be considered when armed forces personnel are posted overseas. There are, however, other occasions when it may be relevant, which are increasing in frequency, such as employees working in war torn areas like Iraq, Afghanistan etc., or in other less secure countries, where individuals have to live in secure accommodation, provided by their employer, for their own safety. See TCGA 1992 s. 222(8A) to (8D) for situations in which an individual may be regarded as living in job-related accommodation.

Similar to the above periods of absence, when an individual is living in job-related accommodation, the property he owns may be treated for PRR as if the individual is occupying the property as a residence and it is then potentially eligible for PRR. The individual has to have an *intention* to live in the property in due course and it may be the case that due to a change of circumstances, he does not actually end up living in the property. This change does not necessarily mean that PRR is denied, but evidence will be needed to back up and show a person's intentions and the reason for any change in these. Whether a second home election needs to be in place depends on whether the job-related accommodation the individual is staying in is under licence (service occupancy) or a tenancy agreement – if under licence then one is not required, whereas under a tenancy it is.

3.2.9   Annual exemption

A non-resident individual will still be entitled to the full annual exemption for capital gains (see **2.4.3**) under the NRCGT regime.

Law: TCGA 1992, s. 222-223A; FA 2015, s. 39, Sch. 9
Guidance: CG 64200C

3.2.10   NRCGT principles and calculations

When calculating the gain arising from 6 April 2015 under the NRCGT regime, two capital gains computations need to be prepared to establish which method is the most beneficial in minimising any capital gains tax due by a non-resident individual.

Example

Bill is not resident for 2018-19 and sells his property on 5 October 2018, which was rented out until 6 June 2018.

The purchase price was £122,500 on 1 June 2006, with acquisition costs such as stamp duty, solicitors' fees etc. being £1,475.

He sold the property for £215,000 with selling costs in respect of marketing, solicitors' and estate agent fees of £2,000.

The market value at 5 April 2015 was £200,000 and Bill renovated the property just before the sale at a cost of £7,500 (all allowable deductions for CGT purposes).

He lived in the property as his only or main residence from acquisition until 1 January 2010 and commenced renting it out from 10 January 2010.

Bill made no other disposals during 2018-19.

It is assumed for the purposes of this example that the tax rates and the capital gains annual exemption for 2018-19 are the same as for 2017-18.

Bill's periods of ownership, and when he is eligible for PRR, are summarised below:

	Period	Months (approx.)
Ownership:		
Post 5/4/2015	6/4/2015 to 5/10/2018	42
Pre 6/4/2015	01/06/2006 to 5/4/2015	106
Total period of ownership	01/06/2006 to 5/10/2018	148
PRR:		
Occupied as main residence	01/06/2006 to 01/01/2010	43
Last 18 months of ownership	6/4/2017 to 5/10/2018	18
Total PRR		61

	Period	Months (approx.)
Ownership:		
Letting period		
Pre 6/4/2015	10/01/2010 to 5/4/2015	63
Post 5/4/2015	6/4/2015 to 5/6/2018	38
Total period let		101

The gain based on the above and using the rebasing method would be:

	£	£
Sale proceeds		215,000
Less: 5 April 2015 valuation	(200,000)	
Renovation costs	(7,500)	
Selling costs	(2,000)	(209,500)
		5,500
Less:		
(1) PRR (last 18 months 18/42 x £5,500	(2,357)	
(2) Letting relief – lower of:		
– £40,000;		
– PRR = £2,357; and		
– Gain for period of let		
6/4/15 to 5/6/18 = £4,976		
(£5,500 x 38/42 months)	(2,357)	(4,714)
		786
Less: Annual exemption for 2018-19		(11,700)
Chargeable gain		Nil
Tax due		£Nil

As can be seen, the gain is covered by the CGT annual exemption for 2019-19 and so no tax arises.

If an election was made to have the pre and post 6/4/2015 gain apportioned on a straight line time basis, then the gain and tax in the above example would be as follows:

	£	£
Sale proceeds		215,000
Less: Purchase price	(122,500)	
Acquisition costs	(1,475)	
Selling costs	(2,000)	
Renovation costs	(7,500)	(133,475)
Total gain before relief		81,525
Apportionment of gain:		
Pre 6/4/2015 (81,525 x 106/148)		58,390
Post 6/4/2015 (81,525 x 42/148)		23,135
		81,525
Post 6/4/2015 gain		23,135
Less: PRR (18/42 x 23,135)	(9,915)	
Letting relief – lower of:		
– £40,0000;		
– PRR = £9,915		
– Gain during let period = £20,932		
(38/42 x 23,135)	(9,915)	(19,830)
Total chargeable gain		3,305

Again, the taxable gain of £3,305 is covered by the annual exemption of £11,700 and so no capital gains tax arises in the UK.

If tax was due on any gain Bill made, then as this is a residential property the rates of tax are 18% for any part of the gain that falls within the basic rate band (£34,500) and 28% for any of the gain in excess of the basic rate band using 2018-19 rates.

If the property is also subject to tax in the country where Bill is resident, then he may obtain relief against this foreign tax for any UK tax he pays, but this will be dependent on that country's tax rules.

3.2.11 NRCGT losses

If a loss is incurred on a disposal subject to NRCGT, then this can be set off against gains arising on the disposal of any other UK residential properties in the same tax year and then carried forward to set off against future gains from the sale of UK residential properties, if the individual is non-resident. Once the individual becomes resident again, the losses can be set off against any other gains as normal.

3.2.12   NRCGT compliance

Warning!

When a non-resident individual sells UK residential property, he is *required to file a NRCGT return within 30 days of conveyance* (usually the completion date), so there is not much time to file this return, especially as a CGT computation also needs to be filed with the return, potentially with valuations. A return still needs to be filed even if no CGT is due on the sale or the individual is filing self-assessment tax returns. In addition, any tax due needs to be paid by this 30-day deadline, although the non-resident can elect for deferral of the payment of this until the usual self-assessment deadline of 31 January following the relevant tax year, providing he is actively filing self-assessment tax returns. The NRCGT return can only be filed online and is not the easiest of forms as, at the time of writing, it cannot be saved (partially or fully completed) and returned to at a later time to finalise, amend, etc. On submission HMRC will allocate an eight-digit case number which should be retained as evidence that the CGT computation has actually been submitted.

The author's experience to date is that some professionals involved in the selling of UK residential properties. are not aware of this requirement to file a NRCGT return. So a return is often not filed, leaving many non-residents in a position where they owe large amounts in late filing penalties, as very often the requirement to file a return does not come to light until they start preparing their self-assessment tax returns, which can easily be a year later if the individual sold the property early on in the tax year concerned. No doubt there are a number of non-resident individuals who have sold UK residential property after 5 April 2015, and who do not file self-assessment tax returns, and who are therefore still blissfully unaware of the fact that they should have filed a NRCGT return. Originally it was proposed that solicitors/conveyancers being the seller's first point of contact would be responsible for making the return to HMRC, but objections to this proposed requirement meant that it was dropped, and now the individual is responsible for any delay in notification of a gain.

The penalty regime, for filing NRCGT returns late, is the same as that for self-assessment tax returns (see **2.8.2**), so if the return is 12 months late the potential late filing penalty could be at least £1,600, and potentially more if tax is due. At the time of writing HMRC have agreed not to charge daily penalties, but they are still charging the fixed penalties. In fact, HMRC are unlikely to be able to charge daily penalties, as the tax legislation requires them to notify the taxpayer of when they intend to start charging such penalties. The purpose of NRCGT returns is to report a disposal to HMRC; therefore, it is very probable that HMRC are not going to be aware that a disposal has occurred and, hence, there is an outstanding NRCGT return. As such, HMRC will not be in a position to notify the taxpayer of when they will start charging daily penalties.

The author's experience at the time of writing is that HMRC having agreed not to charge daily penalties, are not moving with regards to the fixed penalties and are not agreeing to cancel these. This can still leave significant amounts due in penalties, despite there being no tax due on the disposal.

If the property disposed of is in joint names, typically a husband and wife, then each owner needs to file a NRCGT return. In addition, if more than one property has been disposed of, and not on the same day, a return needs to be filed for each disposal.

Another issue is that HMRC still send out letters in the post notifying any late filing penalties. As this regime covers non-residents they are of course living overseas and often in countries where the postal system is not particularly good, if it exists at all. Even in countries like Australia and the US, that do have a good postal service, it can take time for HMRC's letter to be received and often it is a good month before the individual receives the letter. This means that very often it is physically impossible for the non-resident to appeal against these penalties within the deadline, which is 30 days from the date of HMRC's letter. Previously, HMRC were also sending out emails detailing the penalties incurred, but at the time of writing had stopped sending these emails and just notified non-residents by post. One can but hope they start sending emails again, as this is really the only way that many British expats can respond in a timely way. The non-resident could still put in a late appeal, but will then need to explain why it is late and hope that HMRC accept this late appeal. Similarly, there is a 30-day limit to request an independent Revenue review or to appeal to the Tax Tribunal, which non-residents again may struggle to meet. If they have an agent based in the UK, then this may not be such an issue if the appropriate 64-8 authorisation is in place.

Example

Husband and wife, Fred and Wilma, jointly own three rental properties in the UK, none of which they lived in, which they sold during June 2018, all on different days. They were both not resident for 2018-19 and so covered by the NRCGT regime. The properties were not a good investment and Fred and Wilma ended up making a loss on the sales, so no UK CGT was due and they had losses to carry forward. Their friend Barney assisted with all the compliance aspects of the sales, but unfortunately neither he nor Fred or Wilma knew about the requirement to file a NRCGT return, so none was filed.

During November 2019, Fred and Wilma decided to prepare their self-assessment tax returns for 2018-19 and dutifully started declaring the disposals of their UK properties on these returns. They wondered what the reference to a non-resident capital gains tax return was, so googled this and to their horror found out that they should have filed these when they sold their properties. Being good, honest and compliant taxpayers they immediately rectified the situation by filing the required NRCGT returns during November 2019. They each had to file returns and for each disposal so in total six returns were filed, all of which were more than 12 months late.

During December 2019 they filed their self-assessment tax returns showing the disposals of the above properties, so in plenty of time before the 31 January 2020 filing deadline.

To their even greater horror Fred and Wilma received six letters from HMRC notifying them of the late filing penalties they had been charged, which initially totalled £9,600, but had been reduced to £4,200 because HMRC had agreed they would not charge daily penalties. £4,200 is still an expensive mistake to make, especially when no tax was due on the disposal of the properties and they had all been declared on their self-assessment tax returns which were filed on time. To add insult to injury, Fred and Wilma did not receive HMRC's letters until two months after they were issued, and so were too late to put in any appeals.

There is an exemption from filing NRCGT returns, but this is only where there is a no gain/no loss situation as stipulated by the tax legislation (TCGA 1992, s. 288(3A)), e.g. the transfer of assets between spouses. There is no exemption from filing if there is no gain or loss, because of say PRR.

There was a brief glimmer of hope. During September 2017, in the FTT case of *McGreevy*, on the late filing penalties associated with NRCGT returns, the tribunal judge very much found in favour of the taxpayer, agreeing she had a reasonable excuse for not filing a NRCGT return on time and so no penalties were due.

In the author's experience, the standard response from HMRC, on rejecting appeals against these late filing penalties, is to state that taxpayers should have known and been following the progress of the new NRCGT legislation on the HMRC website. Their view is very much that ignorance of the law is not a reasonable excuse. The tribunal judge rejected this idea:

> "that a non-resident with a UK residential property should have been following the development of the legislation intently from its genesis to its enactment and from then to find and read all the information provided by HMRC on their website"

and went on to describe this contention by HMRC as:

> "a prime example of the concept of 'nerdview': a phrase coined by Professor Geoff Pullman of Edinburgh University".

He stated that:

> "the arguments advanced by HMRC about knowledge of the law are little short of preposterous. To say that information about NRCGT returns is 'well within the public domain', as if the public domain had boundaries where one could tell whether something was just in it or well within it, is also claptrap ... There is a serious deficiency exhibited here in common sense, proportion and an ability to consider the position of what HMRC calls its customers."

The tribunal judge then went on to consider if there were any special circumstances and whether HMRC's decision on this was flawed. He concluded that it was. With regards to uncommon or exceptional circumstances, he asked:

> "How common is it for there to be a situation where a person makes an exempt gain and intends to report it in an on time tax return (though they may not be required to do so) but nevertheless is charged a penalty of £1,600? In my view the situation the appellant found herself in was clearly 'out of the ordinary' and 'uncommon'."

Shortly after the *McGreevy* case came another case from the First-tier Tribunal, *Saunders v HMRC*, where the tribunal judge largely followed the view of the judge in the *McGreevy* case and quashed all the penalties due, on the grounds that Patsy-Anne Saunders had a reasonable excuse for not filing a NRCGT return on time. In this case, though (unlike in *McGreevy*) a loss was made.

Sadly, this glimmer of hope was shortlived. During December 2017, two further cases arose out of the FTT, the *Heskeths* and *Welland* cases. The same tribunal judge sat on both these appeals.

The judge dismissed the appeals in full in the *Heskeths* case (involving a husband and wife), stating that she disagreed with the tribunal judge's view in *McGreevy* that ignorance of the law can be a reasonable excuse, even though the cases were similar. She did not consider that the Heskeths had a reasonable excuse for not filing the NRCGT returns on time, because the grounds put forward in the appeals did not cause the failure to file the returns on time. She also considered that there were no special circumstances which could allow the appeals against the penalties.

In *Welland*, again the tribunal judge held there was no reasonable excuse for not filing the NRCGT returns on time, but in this case she did consider there were special circumstances as follows:

> "Although Mr Welland did not raise this as a ground of appeal, it is obvious that the penalties amount to £1,800 because he sold three properties in one tax year: had he sold two of the properties in a later tax year he would no doubt have learned from bitter experience that an NRCGT return had to be made 30 days after completion. Mr Welland was unable to learn from his mistakes, as he was late filing all three returns before he learned of his filing obligation. Does the fact Mr Welland

sold three properties in one tax year amount to special circumstances? Taking into account the principles explained in *Warren,* I find that the circumstances are unusual but not unique. Can it be said it is significantly unfair for Mr Welland to bear the whole penalty? A taxpayer selling a single valuable property who failed to make the return would be penalised once; Mr Welland, selling three not so valuable properties, was penalised three times. And it is clear he did learn from his mistakes: he filed as soon as he realised his mistake and avoided the 12 months penalty on the last of the three sales. I think that does amount to special circumstances, particularly in circumstances (which is not in dispute) where the taxpayer has previously had a good compliance record. Parliament, while intending to penalise non-compliance, must have intended taxpayers to learn from their non-compliance. Because of the three sales in quick succession, Mr Welland was unable to do so. I consider that the penalties should be reduced so that only the penalty on the first sale in tax year 15-16 should be payable. In other words, I reduce the penalty to £700."

In *Jackson*, the judge cancelled the late filing penalties for being six and 12 months late on the grounds that the taxpayer's tax liability had to be referred to in order to establish the penalty due, and that HMRC had overlooked the provisions of FA 2009, Sch. 55, para. 1(3) and 17(3), stating that where an individual is liable for a penalty under more than one paragraph of Sch. 55 which is determined by reference to a liability to tax, the aggregate of the amounts of those penalties must not exceed 100% of the liability to tax.

In Mr Jackson's case, there was no liability to tax on the disposal of his properties. Therefore, the total penalties due for being six and 12 months late, which refer to the tax liability of nil, must be nil. It followed that HMRC should not have raised these penalties and so the tribunal quashed them. The judge did not consider Mr Jackson had a reasonable excuse for filing late, but did follow the tribunal judge in the *Welland* case above and considered there were special circumstances in respect of the penalties for late filing of the NRCGT return for the second disposal Mr Jackson made. This was on the basis that he had no opportunity to learn from his mistake, as both disposals were in the same tax year and so he reduced these penalties relating to the disposal of the second property to nil.

These five cases show, at the time of writing (March 2018), the inconsistency in treatment by the FTT in appeals against late filing penalties for NRCGT returns, for cases that are very similar in nature. The tribunal judge in the *Heskeths* and *Welland* cases acknowledges this and suggests:

> "It would be advantageous if the Upper Tribunal were to make a binding ruling on the matter of when ignorance of the law can be a reasonable excuse, so that future inconsistent First-tier decisions on this matter are avoided".

In the author's opinion, this is a wholly unsatisfactory situation and potentially suggests that the design of the NRCGT regime is fundamentally flawed. It is understandable that for non-residents who are not filing self-assessment tax returns, there should be a system in place by which the individual is required to report any disposals of residential property that are subject to UK CGT. But when a non-resident has been filing self-assessment tax returns for a number of years, why should he also be expected to file an NRCGT return – and then be penalised heavily for not doing so – even though he has declared any relevant disposal on his self-assessment tax return, which has been filed on time?

The whole issue of late NRCGT reporting within such a small time frame may elicit the view in some quarters that this is just another revenue-gathering exercise targeted at non-residents, who are not expected to complain too loudly! Any sympathy for expats and foreigners is in limited supply. Many of the non-residents hit by these penalties are very compliant taxpayers – model taxpayers, some may argue – and understandably feel unfairly treated by HMRC and hit by disproportionate penalties for making an innocent error, even where they then tried to rectify the position immediately the mistake had been discovered. This surely cannot help with trying to encourage compliant behaviour from taxpayers!

Law: TMA 1970, s. 12ZA-12ZN; FA 2009, Sch. 55

Cases: *McGreevy v HMRC* [2017] UKFTT 690 (TC); *Saunders v HMRC* [2017] UKFTT 765 (TC); *Welland v HMRC* [2017] UKFTT 870 (TC); *Hesketh v HMRC* [2017] UKFTT 871 (TC); *Jackson v HMRC* [2018] UKFTT 64 (TC)

3.3   Furniture and possessions

3.3.1   Introduction

It has been mentioned in the example in **1.3.7** that an individual renting out his UK home whilst on foreign assignment will normally have to put his furniture and possessions in secure storage as tenants invariably wish to rent unfurnished property.

The cost of doing this can be substantial in terms of secure storage charges. Another option is to ship the possessions to the country of assignment, especially if the assignment is long term. This is a matter for careful consideration for a number of reasons. Differences in electrical supply may not be compatible with the UK electrical items. Some countries have very strict rules on importation of certain furniture made of different wood, such as cane and hardwoods. Also some countries consider that certain items of possessions that are "normal" in the UK are totally unacceptable and will be confiscated. See the first example at **3.3.2** below.

3.3.2   Specialist removers

Exporting furniture and possessions should be done by specialists in this area as there is importation paperwork that must be adhered to and, at the point of packing, the specialists should indicate which items are banned or will be confiscated.

The choice between air, sea or road transport will depend on the location of the foreign assignment, e.g. transport to Europe will normally be by road but to Dubai in the example below it will be by sea as road transport is not possible because of different war zones *en route*. Air transport is possible but more expensive than by sea – a sea journey may take one and a half months so at some point the assignee will be without furniture and possessions in the new location.

Cars can be transported but create additional problems if they are second hand or classic cars (see **3.3.3** Motor vehicles below). Also a new car bought in the UK will need an upgraded air conditioning unit if imported to some Middle and Far East countries. There may also be restrictions on exporting the car at the end of the assignment term and in some countries there may be duty to pay if the car is re-exported again within a certain period.

Specialist removers such as the British Association of Removers (BAR) and the Federation of International Furniture Removers should be appointed so that adherence to customs regulations, VAT and GST (see **2.5 VAT and GST**) requirements and banned items in the host country are all correctly dealt with.

Example 1

Jimmy and Jayne have been assigned to Saudi Arabia for a three-year period. Jimmy is a DVD film enthusiast and his wife is an antiquarian art book researcher. Both are bringing DVDs and books amongst their possessions.

In order to save money they have packed their belongings into a shipping container and have not used the services of an internationally experienced removal company. When the container arrives at their compound in Jeddah (4-7 weeks later and at a cost of £2,700-£4,500 for a two bedroomed house) two customs agents officially break the seal on the container and, much to their surprise, start to inspect every box. The DVDs and the antiquarian art books are withheld pending censorship and will be returned in due course. Also, one copy of Woman's Own magazine is confiscated due to a title of an article called "How diet affects sex" – it is merely an article comparing diets for the different sexes.

Five weeks later Jimmy receives most of his DVDs back but five have been kept because there were sections in the DVD which showed women in bikinis. Jayne's antiquarian art books are all returned but pages showing Rubens' portraits of nude women have all been blacked out with a marker pen, totally ruining the value of the books. His Monopoly set is also confiscated!

Jimmy is furious and asks for an explanation and the customs official shows him an importation document and points out the section on prohibited goods:

- All games of chance including chess sets, dice, backgammon and the like;
- Alcoholic beverages, any food products containing alcohol such as vanilla flavouring extract, cooking wines, etc.;

- Books, wine making kits, or any other items used in the preparation or manufacture of alcoholic drinks and beverages;
- Pornographic materials and literature including fashion magazines with people wearing underwear or swimsuits;
- Any books pertaining to religion other than Islam;
- Any foodstuffs containing pork and related pork meat products, etc.

Saudi customs regulations change on a regular basis without notice and clearance of incoming goods and personal effects needs to be carefully monitored as non-compliance is solely for the account of the shipper and/or origin agent.

Example 2

Juan, who speaks Spanish, has been posted to Ecuador on a two year assignment as a senior quality control manager for an international banana exporting company. He and his wife will be importing their furniture and possessions including their pet dog to their new home in Quito.

An inventory of goods shipped must be made in Spanish, notarised on arrival or confirmed by the Ecuadorian Embassy in the UK. A work permit valid for at least one year must be submitted.

The pet dog will require up to date health and vaccination certificates but can arrive with its owners and will be customs cleared with baggage on presentation of the International Health Certificate. If arriving with cargo it will be processed taking a few days.

Banned items are the usual pornography, firearms, live plants, drugs/narcotics as well as, oddly, cleaning products, creams, colognes, perfumes and cosmetics.

Guidance: British Association of Removers (BAR); Federation of International Furniture Removers

3.3.3 *Motor vehicles*

Many assignees on long term contracts will consider taking their UK acquired cars to the foreign destination. In the UK a vehicle export licence should be applied for if the car is intended to be abroad for more than 12 months (leaflet V526). Completion of part 2 on the vehicle registration document should be done and sent to DVLA. Subsequently a Certificate of Export will be issued (form V561).

Importing a used/second hand/classic car is prohibited in many countries and only newly acquired cars are acceptable in the foreign jurisdiction. There may also be problems once in the new country regarding the car's specifications, such as tinted windows, air conditioning units, leather or hide upholstery, etc.

Many countries will allow the tax free importation of a new car but this may come with conditions, e.g. Malaysia will, under the MM2H programme (see **5.1.4**), allow the import of a new car without duty but it may not be sold or exported again without certain timeous conditions. In the examples above Ecuador does not allow the importation of second hand cars and new cars have to be inspected at origin and certified as being new. In Saudi Arabia second hand cars may be imported but must be left hand drive vehicles only.

If buying a new car in the UK to export to a foreign country within two months of purchase, and to be kept outside the UK for at least six months, VAT may not be payable (see **2.5 VAT and GST**). See the form V5C/4 "notification of permanent export" section of the individual's V5C registration certificate (logbook). It is then sent to DVLA, Swansea, SA99 1BD and should include a letter stating the circumstances of moving abroad and requesting a vehicle tax refund. However, if going to another EU country the individual will be liable for VAT in that country on importation there at the appropriate rate; this will involve completion of form VAT411.

4. Pensions, insurances and data protection

4.1 Pensions

4.1.1 Significance

Many of those who are working abroad eventually choose to retire abroad. It follows that pensions from former employments may be paid to them in their retirement jurisdiction. The UK has many double tax treaties that cover such payments, ensuring that pensions can be paid (under an NT coding) without tax being deducted in the UK.

The new state pension (currently £164.35 per week) can be paid abroad and is usually covered by the expat's UK personal allowance and so paid gross. Some other government pensions can be paid gross, but some cannot, and these are categorised in HMRC's *International Manual*. The FA 2017 changes to overseas pensions need to be addressed when advising on QROPS (now also known as ROPS), SIPPs and overseas schemes, see below.

For expats working abroad the question is often raised as to whether they can continue to get UK tax relief on pension contributions – the answer is "possibly in certain circumstances". If an individual does not have "relevant UK earnings" on moving abroad – that is, they are being paid and taxed abroad – then he will only be able to receive additional tax relief on net personal contributions of £2,880 per annum for five full tax years following the tax year in which he moves abroad (see the example below). It is not normally possible for personal or employer contributions to re-start or be increased after the individual has moved abroad. For example, if the individual is paying £200 per month as a personal contribution and then moves abroad, he could continue paying that amount (or a lower amount) for the five full tax years after moving abroad, even though he has no relevant UK earnings. Conversely an expat returning to the UK after a long period abroad will not be able to use the annual allowance of up to £40,000 pension contributions carry forward allowances because the expat did not have relevant UK earnings in the previous years.

Example

Rhiannon makes personal contributions of £6,000 per annum along with a similar amount paid from her employer. In March 2018, she moves to Germany to work; she remains employed by her UK company but is now taxed in Germany. The table below shows the allowable pension contributions if the employee and employer contributions continue:

Tax year	Earnings taxed in the UK	Gross annual personal contributions	Gross annual employer contributions
2017-18	£60,000	£6,000*	£6,000
2018-19	Nil	£3,600*	£6,000
2019-20	Nil	£3,600*	£6,000
2020-21	Nil	£3,600*	£6,000
2021-22	Nil	£3,600*	£6,000
2022-23	Nil	£3,600*	£6,000
2023-24	Nil	Nil*	£6,000

*Net payment is £2,880 with additional tax relief of 20% added. After the five years her payments must stop unless her personal employment circumstances have changed. See also the Leon example at 4.1.2 below regarding the addition to minimum qualifying years for a state pension when working in the EEA.

Law: FA 2004, s. 188, 189, 190, 196
Guidance: INTM 343040; PTM 000001; OECD Model Treaty, art. 18

4.1.2   New state pension

An individual on retirement may get less than the new full UK state pension (currently £164.35 per week) if he or she was in contracted-out employment before 6 April 2016. This figure will be calculated and deducted from the benchmark state pension to give a lower weekly pension figure (advice on form FPC DL 021).

There is now a requirement for a minimum of 10 qualifying years on a person's National Insurance record to get any new state pension. To obtain the full amount of payment, subject to contracting-out deductions, 35 qualifying years are needed. However, an individual may be able to use time spent abroad to make up the 10 qualifying years. This applies if the individual has lived or worked in any of the countries below, and annual increases in the state pension also only apply if the individual is living in the following jurisdictions:

- the European Economic Area (EEA), Gibraltar or Switzerland;
- a country that has a social security agreement with the UK that allows for cost of living increases to the state pension as shown here: Barbados, Bermuda, Bosnia and Herzegovina, Guernsey, the Isle of Man, Israel, Jamaica, Jersey, Kosovo, Macedonia, Mauritius, Montenegro, the Philippines, Serbia, Turkey, US;

Note: The UK has social security agreements with Canada and New Zealand, but no yearly increase in the UK state pension applies if an individual lives in either of those countries.

International Pensions Direct Payment is the Department for Work and Pensions' way of paying an individual's pension direct to an account outside the UK. The pension will be paid into an account for the individual in his or her chosen jurisdiction of retirement. Exchange rate factors should also be considered when choosing this option of payment. Payments will be made the week following each 13 week period, after completion of a form IPC BR1 GOV NSP.

Example

Leon has three qualifying years from the UK on his National Insurance record when he leaves university in London. During his time at university he had a holiday job for each of the three years, earning more than the NICs LEL. He then works in London for seven years and moves to and works in Germany (an EEA country) for 30 years, paying contributions to that country's state pension before retiring early.

When he reaches the UK new state pension age in a few years' time he will just meet the minimum qualifying years to get the new state pension. His new state pension amount will initially only be based on the 10 years of Class 1 National Insurance contributions he made in the UK but as Leon has already worked for 30 years in Germany he qualifies there too. In fact his period of work in the UK would have qualified him in Germany in accordance with European law re totalisation of pension payment periods.

Note that if Leon had not worked in the university holidays under the old P38(S) procedure (now under real time information), paying NICs, he would only have seven years of contributions as university attendance does not qualify for credited NICs. See also reg. 8 of the *Social Security (Credits) Regulations* 1975.

Therefore where a person has worked in Member State (MS) UK for 10 years and MS Germany for 30 years, each country must consider Leon's entitlement to a pension on the basis of a record of 40 years of payments. Each country will calculate a theoretical amount based on the full employment record and then this amount is pro-rated in accordance with the record in that country. So, MS UK would pay one quarter of the UK state pension and MS Germany three quarters of its national pension. See also below regarding Brexit.

On retirement, Leon will move permanently to the Philippines to live. As the Philippines have a double contribution convention with the UK he will get the annual uprate in the UK state pension each year and he can have it paid directly to him in Manila by completing form IPC BR1 GOV NSP. Leon and all other expats have to make regular notification of their continued survival on "life certificate" CF(N)698 within 16 weeks of the form being sent out to the foreign address the Pensions Service holds for the expat.

A lack of required pension contributions can be made up by paying additional Class 2 or Class 3 contributions (application form CF83). Class 2 contributions have historically been lower than Class 3 but from 6 April 2019 it will only be possible to pay Class 3 contributions as Class 2 contributions are to be abolished. Under reg. 147 of the *Social Security Regulations*, Class 2 contributions can be paid if an individual is employed or self-employed abroad and meets the following conditions:

- he has lived in the UK for a continuous three-year period at any time before the period for which those NICs are to be paid;

- before going abroad, he paid a set amount in NICs for three years or more (this will be checked when asking to pay Class 2 NICs); and

- immediately before going abroad he was ordinarily an employed or self-employed earner in the UK.

Recently the government have decided to advance the extended timetable for the new state pension age to 68 between 2037 and 2039. This alteration in the pension age will affect those born between 6 April 1970 and 5 April 1978 (currently aged below 47) for whom state pension age under existing legislation is currently age 67. Fortunately those born on or before 5 April 1970 will see no change to their current proposed new state pension age under the existing rules.

The UK government have stated in a briefing paper that they intend to continue to export and uprate the UK state pension payable to overseas pensioners within the EU. Furthermore, the UK will continue to aggregate periods of relevant insurance, work or residence within the EU accrued before Brexit (see the example above) to help meet the entitlement conditions for UK contributory benefits and the state pension, even where entitlement to these rights may be exercised after exit:

> "In relation to benefits, pensions, healthcare, economic and other rights, in the expectation that these rights will be reciprocated by EU member states, the Government intends that: [...]
>
> - the UK will continue to export and uprate the UK State Pension within the EU;
> - the UK will continue to aggregate periods of relevant insurance, work or residence within the EU accrued before exit to help meet the entitlement conditions for UK contributory benefits and State Pension, even where entitlement to these rights may be exercised after exit."

Law: SI 2001/1004, reg. 147; DCC UK/Philippines, SI 1989/2002; EU coordination regulation, no. 1408/71

Guidance: Forms FPC DL 021 and IPC BR1 GOV NSP; CF83; Leaflet NI38; House of Commons Library Briefing Paper, Number CBP-07894, 18 August 2017, page 3

4.1.3   Recent Finance Act changes

The *Finance Act* 2017 made substantial changes to the taxation of overseas pension schemes (see below). This followed major changes in previous Finance Acts, and the latest changes can be summarised as follows:

- Foreign pensions paid to UK residents historically were assessable on 90% of the pension but this change ensures that 100% is taxable in the UK (but not where the pension formed a remittance on the remittance basis of taxation).

- Lump sums paid from overseas pension schemes are to be subject to taxation in the UK but those with foreign service relief up to 5 April 2017 will retain the beneficial tax treatment on the funds that have accrued to that date, so that there is no "cliff edge" taxation.

- An extension from 5 to 10 full tax years of the "look back" facility imposed on the pension trustees and pensioner in such cases as transfers into QROPS/ROPS. This applies to funds that accrue or are transferred after April 2017, so funds accumulated before that date are ring-fenced. The calculations of the ring-fenced funds are complicated but in essence it is the addition of the sums and market value of the assets transferred as a result of the original transfer or subsequent transfers to the relevant non-UK scheme without those transfers being subject to the unauthorised payments charge before 6 April 2017.

- Section 615 schemes were set up in the past specifically for those working wholly abroad, usually on long term assignments (see example below), and a restriction now applies to funding these schemes. But a continued increase in the fund is allowed at the previous rate or in line with the consumer prices index (CPI). See s. 615 below.

The UK government will no doubt be looking at further areas for legislation changes in the future with regard to perceived pension-related tax avoidance.

Law: ICTA 1988, s. 615; ITEPA 2003; FA 2004, Sch. 34; FA 2017, Sch. 3, 4; *The Pension Schemes (Application of UK Provisions to Relevant Non-UK Schemes) (Amendment) Regulations* 2018

4.1.4   *Lifetime allowance and overseas enhancement*

The lifetime allowance is currently £1.03 million (indexed annually from 6 April 2018 by reference to the CPI) and any amount received above this is normally subject to a sanction tax charge of 55% if taken as cash, or 25% if taken as pension.

If the individual was a relevant overseas individual during one or more periods of overseas service after 5 April 2006 the lifetime allowance may be enhanced by a non-residence factor in certain circumstances. This means the increase in the lifetime allowance to set against the benefits paid from the registered pension scheme that relate to the unrelieved contributions or accrual during that period overseas.

The non-residence factor is intended to prevent those overseas service benefits giving rise to a lifetime allowance charge and the calculation is made at the point the pension is transferred to a recognised overseas pension scheme (ROPS) / qualifying recognised overseas pension scheme (QROPS). This is treated as a benefit crystallisation event (BCE8) and is compared with the lifetime allowance (together with any enhancements) at that point. At this time, the values of transfers overseas from all types of arrangement are tested against the lifetime allowance.

Example

Angela has been working for a major Spanish international bank in London. She then began working overseas (Madrid, Spain) on 6 December 2005 and so for these purposes she became a relevant overseas individual on 6 April 2006. She began to accrue benefits under her defined benefits arrangement on 6 November 2005.

Angela's pension entitlement as at 6 April 2006 was £40,000 p.a. This conveniently happens to be pension 'A' day. She had an option under the rules of the registered pension scheme defined benefits arrangement to commute part of her pension entitlement for a lump sum on retirement. She was not entitled to a separate lump sum.

$$£40,000 \times 20 = £800,000$$

Angela returned to work in the UK on 6 June 2009 and so she ceased to be a relevant overseas individual on 5 April 2009, i.e. looking back to the end of the previous tax year. That was before a benefit crystallisation event and before she ceased to accrue benefits under the defined benefits arrangement. Her pension entitlement as at 5 April 2009 was £56,500 p.a.

£56,500 x 20 = £1.13 million

£1.13 million – £800,000 = £330,000

The defined benefits arrangement non-residence factor is therefore 0.2. That is calculated by dividing £330,000 by £1.65 million (the standard lifetime allowance for the 2008-09 tax year).

£330,000/£1.65 million = 0.2

To claim an enhancement, Angela or her adviser must have submitted a completed claim form APSS202 to HMRC no later than five years after 31 January 2010, i.e. by 31 January 2015. The claim form is now completed online.

Angela decides to retire to Spain in 2020 and transfers her funds to a QROPS/ROPS scheme. This is a benefit crystallisation event (BCE8), at which time her pension fund available is £1.45 million. The lifetime limit in 2020 is, say, £1.1 million with CPI indexing, which is increased by the non-residence factor of 0.20. So, £1.1 million standard lifetime allowance at the time of the BCE8 is then added to the £1.65 million lifetime allowance in 2008-09 multiplied by .20 to give a total of £1.43 million so there will be a lifetime allowance charge of 55% on £20,000 if taken as cash.

So if the amount transferred is more than the member's available lifetime allowance the excess will be liable to the lifetime allowance charge. New subsection FA 2004, s. 244(6) provides that if the amount of lifetime charge is an over deduction for some reason, then it is repaid and transferred to a QROPS/ROPS, that amount should not be tested against the lifetime allowance on the basis of a transfer to a QROPS/ROPS (BCE 8). See qualifying recognised overseas pension scheme (QROPS) at **4.1.6** below.

The scheme administrator must tell the member if any tax is due and the percentage of standard lifetime allowance used up by the BCE 8. There are many different benefit crystallisation events but here, when dealing with a QROPS/ROPS, it is categorised as a BCE8.

Law: FA 2004, s. 216, 221-223(3), 224-226, 277; *FA 2004 (Standard Lifetime Allowance) Regs.* 2018, SI 2018/206
Guidance: PTM 095310ff., 095340, 164400; Form APSS202

4.1.5   Double tax treaty relief

An individual who is resident abroad, and who receives a pension or annuity from the UK, can claim exemption from UK tax on form DT/Individual. The form is country specific and depends on the double tax treaty between the UK and the specific overseas country. The form requires the local tax office to confirm that the individual is resident in that country and a tax reference number is normally required on the form, endorsed by the foreign tax office. The terms of a few double tax treaties require that the individual be subject to tax in the foreign country (see Israel below). The HMRC's leaflet DT Digest indicates the treaties that require the "subject to tax" requirement. Certain jurisdictions – such as Cayman Islands, Qatar and Saudi Arabia – require country specific information.

Certain countries (e.g. the US and France) do not recognise the 25% "tax free lump sum" pension as being such, and seek to tax the payment as income. Also, some countries do not tax certain pensions, one example being New Zealand, which excludes from taxation social security pensions from Finland, France, Germany, Philippines, United States of America, and/or war pensions from France and Germany.

Other countries tax foreign pensions received under the double tax treaty (article 17), such as the United Arab Emirates (UAE), but do not have income taxes.

Israel (article XI) states that "Any pension … derived from sources within the United Kingdom by an individual who is a resident of Israel and subject to Israel tax in respect thereof, shall be exempt from United Kingdom tax." The phrase "subject to Israel tax" must require tax to be deducted to ensure that the pension is paid gross from the UK; if not, tax will be deducted by the UK. In the *Weiser* tax case, it was relevant that UK pension income was excluded from tax in Israel for the first ten years of his residence (see **6.5.1**).

Whilst the articles in many double tax treaties are similar it is important for advisers to check the double tax treaty wording of the UK and intended jurisdiction to ensure that the tax imposition on pension payments is understood by the retiree.

With regard to the UAE/UK double tax treaty mentioned above, which came into force in January 2017, article (17) states the UAE will be the taxing state on pensions for expats living there:

> "Subject to the provisions of paragraph 2 of Article 18, pensions and other similar remuneration paid to a resident of a Contracting State shall be taxable only in that State."

This is the standard treaty article which normally gives the taxing right to the jurisdiction (Contracting State) of residence. However, in the case of the UAE there is no tax deducted so in theory the UK pensions should be paid without tax being deducted by the UK but also no tax is payable in UAE so the pension payment or flexible drawdown is received without any taxation. Some commentators suggest that this loophole may be blocked in the future, as too many people take advantage by relocating to the UAE and drawing down their whole pension completely tax free. It is hard to think that the UK would unilaterally tax pensions paid to UAE residents where there is an OECD style treaty in force which allows a pensions payment anomaly to exist.

Cases: *Bayfine UK v HMRC* [2011] STC 717; *Weiser v HMRC* [2012] UKFTT 501 (TC)

Guidance: DT/Individual and notes on the HMRC website.

4.1.6 *Qualifying recognised overseas pension schemes (QROPS)*

The *Finance Act* 2017 changes to the QROPS/ROPS rules only allow UK pension transfers overseas to be made free of UK tax up to the current lifetime allowance of £1.03 million, unless there have been additional enhancements.

Overseas transfers can still be made free of UK tax if both the individual and the pension savings are in different countries within the EEA, e.g. living in France with a Malta QROPS/ROPS. Also allowed without the tax charge are transfers to a country outside the UK which also has a scheme, e.g. retire to New Zealand and transfer the pension there (see **4.1.12** New Zealand below). Finally, the transfer of a public service scheme, occupational scheme or international scheme to a pension scheme in the country of residence should not have a tax charge attaching, e.g. BP UK pension plan to BP America pension plan on being sent to Houston.

The overseas transfer tax charge of 25% of the transfer does not apply to funds that had already been transferred to a QROPS/ROPS before 9 March 2017 (or to transfers requested before that date but which were still being processed). The new QROPS/ROPS provisions also extend from 5 to 10 years the period in which UK tax charges (e.g. unauthorised payments charge of 25% on form APSS253) can apply to payments out of funds in overseas pension schemes that contain pension funds or rights that have benefitted from UK tax relief. If the 25% tax charge arises on transfer, and the individual later retires to an EEA country or the foreign country where the QROPS/ROPS is located, then the 25% overseas transfer charge can be reclaimed and passed on to the QROPS/ROPS fund using form APSS243.

Where the scheme manager of the QROPS/ROPS (or former QROPS/ROPS) becomes aware that the scheme member has at any time in the relevant period for the transfer acquired a new residential address that is in neither:

- the country or territory in which the QROPS/ROPS or former QROPS/ROPS is established, nor
- an EEA state,

the QROPS/ROPS scheme manager must notify HMRC of that new address within three months from the date on which the scheme manager becomes aware of it. This will prevent the avoidance of the overseas transfer charge by making transfer to an EEA country, thereby avoiding the charge, and subsequently relocating elsewhere in the world which does not have an in-country QROPS/ROPS. The HMRC ROPS list is regularly published on the website showing the different countries' schemes. The fact that a ROPS provider is mentioned on HMRC's periodic list is not an endorsement or approval of the pension provider as the list is for self-certification and approval may, on investigation by HMRC, be withdrawn from the list.

Some of the perceived *advantages* of a transfer to a QROPS/ROPS are:

1. That a transfer means the pension is not under threat of company underfunding or being unable to pay pensions

and then being subject to the upper limit restrictions of the Pension Protection Fund.

2. Cash equivalent transfer values (CETVs) are quite good, due to 10 year gilt yields being depressed, thereby giving greater potential transfer values to be enjoyed by the transferee pensioner.

3. A transfer to a QROPS/ROPS can trigger a benefit crystallisation event (BCE8) prior to exceeding the current lifetime allowance threshold of £1.03 million (with CPI enhancements) which then enables the transferred funds to grow tax free above the threshold limit of £1.03 million.

4. The fund can be converted into another currency in the retirement jurisdiction, e.g. euros, US$, etc.

5. Investment of the fund is controlled by the pensioner or financial adviser.

6. On death, the whole fund is inheritance tax free when passed on before 75, and after 75 the beneficiaries (i.e. dependants, nominees or successors) pay tax at their own marginal tax rate.

7. The whole pension fund is available, whereas a defined benefit scheme pension would in most cases provide only, say, a 50% pension to the surviving spouse or civil partner and lesser amounts for the deceased dependants – and some dependants (e.g. children) will not benefit at all if over a certain age, usually 23 years old.

Note: There is a two year time limit for designating funds for the follow-on beneficiaries in (6) and (7) above following the death of the current beneficiary; otherwise there is the potential for a tax charge.

Some of the perceived *disadvantages* of a QROPS/ROPS are:

- The 25% tax charge on funds transferred into a QROPS/ROPS which is not in either the individual's country of retirement or an EEA country where he or she is living in the EEA.

- The flexible drawdown rules are not available in some QROPS/ROPS jurisdictions.

- Extended reporting requirements by the QROPS/ROPS administration departments to HMRC.

- The loss of the 10% foreign pensions deduction when relocating back to the UK following the revised FA 2017 rules.

- Possible increases in administration charges as providers withdraw from offering QROPS/ROPS and as competition for clients reduces.

- The possibility of yet further onerous changes to the taxation rules of QROPS/ROPS under a perceived "anti-avoidance" umbrella.

- Loss of the security of a final salary scheme such as guaranteed yearly increases in the pension payments in line with, say, the CPI.

Whilst a transfer to a QROPS/ROPS in some circumstances may be appropriate it may be better to transfer to a SIPP (see below) because these now allow flexible drawdown, which puts them on an even keel with QROPS/ROPS. Also, management charges are currently slightly less with SIPPs. The Financial Conduct Authority (FCA) in its consultation paper in June 2017, at paragraph 5.10, acknowledges that there may be good reasons for an individual transferring to a QROPS/ROPS:

> "For example, a transfer to a Qualifying Recognised Pension Scheme [sic] (QROPS) may incur the QROPS transfer charge of 25% or there may be complex tax planning depending on the nature of the tax treaties between the UK and the overseas territory where the client is resident."

Law: FA 2004, s. 244A-244M (inserted by FA 2017, Sch. 4)

Guidance: PTM 102000; forms APSS202 and 263; FCA *Advising on Pension Transfers,* consultation paper CP17/16

4.1.7   Self invested personal pensions

In the UK, self invested personal pensions (SIPPs) are lauded as having numerous advantages over other pension plans, including tax deductibility on pension contributions, and greater investment flexibility (e.g. 100% ownership of a sponsoring company shares).

313

For the individual wishing to retire to a foreign jurisdiction which has a double tax treaty with the UK, SIPP flexible drawdown rules can also be beneficial. Once in flexi-drawdown, the money purchase pension annual allowance reduces to £4,000 pa. A SIPP will generally be suitable for an expat who intends to return to the UK in the future, as ongoing charges are usually less and the advantage of the QROPS 10% foreign pensions exemption no longer applies (see above).

QROPS/ROPS are often linked to offshore insurance bonds whereas with a SIPP this is not necessary as investments can be on a platform. Also, anyone with "safeguarded pension benefits" (such as final salary / defined benefit pensions) with a transfer value over £30,000, who wants to transfer to a QROPS/ROPS, requires advice from a "pension transfer specialist" (normally a G60/AF3 qualified person) to sign off on the transfer, which will also incur costs. Some of this cost may be claimed through the employing company, up to £500. A new Chartered Insurance Institute (CII) Level 6 Advanced Diploma in Retirement Income planning (AF8) and Pensions transfers (AF7) will replace AF3, which is expected to be withdrawn from April 2018, and AF7/AF8 qualifications will provide the "pension transfer specialist" qualification to sign off on transfers.

Example

Rose has been contributing for many years to a UK defined contribution pension scheme and has decided to retire to a sunnier climate than the UK.

She notifies the pension trustees that she wishes to transfer her fund to a SIPP. Duly noted, the trustees eventually transfer the pension of £400,000 to the new SIPP provider. Rose has opted to receive her defined benefit pension payments from a previous employer as the scheme is not underfunded on advice from her financial adviser.

Rose intends to retire to Malaysia under the Malaysia My Second Home (MM2H) scheme and will require the 25% tax free lump sum to pay the fixed deposit MM2H programme funding requirement. Under the double tax treaty between the UK and Malaysia, Rose ensures that she fills in form DT/individual, endorsed by the local tax office, and sends this to the UK tax office. Code NT is issued by

HMRC to both the trustees of the defined benefit scheme and the SIPP provider.

Rose is able to have her defined pension payments paid without UK tax, and also those from the SIPP provider, as she is entitled to flexi-drawdown. Flexi-drawdown allows the pensioner to withdraw from the fund without limitation and these payments will be paid gross under the NT coding.

All such pensions (defined benefit, defined contribution schemes, SIPPs and QROPS/ROPS) now have no tax charge on death under 75. Should the pension holder die after that age then the subsequent beneficiaries are taxed at their marginal rates of tax in the jurisdiction where they reside – this may be a low taxing jurisdiction compared to the UK as many expat children choose to reside in the country they have been brought up in.

Law: ITEPA 2003, s. 308C (added by F(No.2)A 2017, s. 7); FA 2004, s. 227ZA(1)(b) (amended by FA 2017, s. 16); FA 2004, Sch. 28, para. 7, 8, 8A; *The Pension Schemes Act* 2015; *The Pension Schemes Act* 2015 *(Transitional Provisions and Appropriate Independent Advice) (Amendment) Regulations* 2017, SI 2017/717
Guidance: PTM 062730

4.1.8   Section 615 schemes

Historically these are not UK approved pension schemes, although they must have to be established for the sole purpose of providing superannuation benefits. They are established under irrevocable trust for non-resident employees by employers whose business is undertaken wholly or in part outside the UK.

Benefits from the scheme are usually taken at 55 years of age onwards. The benefits can be taken on retirement or leaving service at any age and wholly as a lump sum. These superannuation benefits are not liable to UK tax when paid to non-UK residents and, by concession, lump sums paid to UK residents are not chargeable.

Employers with internationally mobile employees employed wholly abroad could set up these favourably taxed schemes in the past. Unfortunately, following FA 2017, these will no longer apply in respect of benefits built up in a section 615 scheme on or after 6 April 2017 but the changes will allow for limited increases after that date. The limit will be the annual amount of increase in the pension previously allowed under the scheme rules or the rate of the consumer prices index. Payments to a scheme solely to fund a deficit in respect of entitlement built up before 6 April 2017 will not lead to a loss of favourable tax treatment. Nor will they be considered additional benefit build up.

Example

Richard has been living and working abroad for a telephonic cable laying company for many years. A section 615 pension was set up for him long ago in Guernsey, after discussions with his payroll department, and he has been paying in during his many years offshore. As he lives onboard the cable laying vessel his outgoings are minimal and he is therefore able to make substantial savings into the scheme.

Richard has no wish to retire to the UK in a few years' time and most likely will retire to Belize, where he can receive his pension tax free. He is able draw a lump sum to purchase a property in Belize and receive a gross monthly pension on the remainder of the tax free fund.

The FA 2017 changes mean that no new pension schemes can be established by him or his employer, and no further contributions can be made to existing schemes. The funds accrued in his section 615(6) scheme before 6 April 2017 will continue to be paid out using the existing beneficial tax rules.

Law: ICTA 1988, s. 615 (as amended by FA 2017, Sch. 3, para. 3)
Guidance: Digest of Double Taxation Treaties, April 2016.

4.1.9 Australian super

Many internationally mobile employees who are assigned to Australia from the UK decide to stay on there in retirement, making occasional trips to the UK (see Outside Australia Pension Rates below). Individually they may have built up pension funds in the UK which they wish to draw in Australia. It is possible to transfer funds from the UK pension fund to an Australian superannuation scheme ("Aussie super").

There are broadly two types of contribution – "concessional" and "non-concessional". Concessional contributions are those for which a tax deduction is claimed against Australian income. Non-concessional contributions (NCC) are contributions where no tax deduction has been claimed in Australia and are usually funded by overseas income or capital. There are caps on the amount of money that can be rolled over into an Aussie super and the non-concessional cap from 1 July 2017 is AUS$ 100,000, but a 2 year bring forward is allowed, making a total of AUS$300,000 maximum (NCC cap).

An individual wishing to transfer his or her UK pension should be over 55 years, and ideally have been resident in Australia for six months and have an Australian Tax File Number (TFN). A TFN is available to foreign passport holders resident in Australia from the Australian Taxation Office (ATO). Transfers to an Aussie super can be from any foreign pension, such as the UK schemes, 401Ks and Recognised Overseas Pension Schemes approved schemes.

Transfers from foreign superannuation schemes into an Aussie super after the six month residence period may involve taxation of the "applicable fund earnings" at the marginal rate of the individual, but an election can be made for the Aussie super to tax at a set 15%. Due to the high marginal rates (up to a maximum of 47%) in Australia, it is often more beneficial to tax at the 15% rate. Note that conversions are made at the Australian dollar when the conversion is made and the Medicare levy 2% will be added to the marginal tax liability.

4.1.10   Outside Australia pension rates

Another matter that should be borne in mind in Australia has been the international social security agreement with the UK. Normally if there is such an agreement with a country the terms may allow a full age pension.

The agreement with the UK was terminated by Australia in 2001, as the UK refused to change its policy of not indexing UK state pensions in Australia, effectively leaving Australia to subsidise a UK pensioner's income from Australian funds. UK pensioners must now live in Australia for 10 years before being able to claim a local age pension.

Once the pensioner has been overseas for a period of six weeks, he or she will be paid at an "outside Australia rate" as detailed below. The actual pension payment rate will change depending on the number of years the individual has lived in Australia during his or her working life ("Australian working life residence"). To be entitled to a full pension the individual needs to have been resident in the country for 35 years to get a full age pension after 26 weeks overseas.

The Australian dollar (A$) figures are a guide only and are effective from 20 September 2017 and alter regularly each quarter.

How much pension while outside Australia	A$ amount per year single	A$ amount per year couple both eligible	A$ amount per year couple one eligible partner	A$ amount per year couple separated due to ill health
Maximum basic rate	21,164.00	31,907.20	15,953.60	21,164.00
Basic Pension Supplement	600.60	988.00	494.00	600.60
Total	**21,764.60**	**32,895.20**	**16,447.60**	**21,764.60**

Guidance: Australian Taxation Office; Election form NAT 11724; Australian Department of Human Resources; Australian Department of Human Resources – Pension rates payable to people outside Australia; www.humanservices.gov.au/individuals/enablers/pension-rates-payable-people-outside-australia; IVCM Expatriate Superannuation

4.1.11   Hong Kong ORSO/MPF

Mandatory pension fund (MPF) payments in relation to Hong Kong employment must be made to an approved registered MPF scheme which will attract tax relief on the contributions by the employee and employer. In contrast, an Occupational Retirement Scheme Ordinance (ORSO) under Hong Kong law provides a tax-efficient vehicle of an international retirement programme, which is recognised to be a genuine pension by Revenue Authorities worldwide. The UK/Hong Kong double tax treaty states at article 17:

> "Pensions and other similar remuneration (including a lump sum payment) arising in a Contracting Party and paid to a resident of the other Contracting Party in consideration of past employment or self-employment and social security pensions shall be taxable only in the first-mentioned Party."

This ensures that Hong Kong has the taxing right on Hong Kong pension payments. ORSO came into force on 15 October 1993, and is the governing legislation for the regulation of voluntary occupational retirement schemes operating in or from Hong Kong. The ordinance applies to all ORSO schemes operated in and from Hong Kong and covers offshore schemes (i.e. schemes whose domicile is outside Hong Kong, where the scheme or trust is governed by a foreign system of law) which provide retirement benefits to members employed in Hong Kong. All ORSO schemes must be registered, or granted an exemption certificate by the Registrar in accordance with the ORSO. See also **7.2.13** (The Hong Kong Trust non-vested solution).

Example

A UK expat has worked in Hong Kong and worldwide for an international company which has its pension MPF plan registered in Hong Kong. He retires at the age of 55 and returns to the UK, where he later decides to draw his pension from the Hong Kong scheme.

The double tax treaty between Hong Kong and the UK gives the taxing right on the pension payments to Hong Kong and the expat receives the payments after Hong Kong tax deductions. On the foreign pages, the notes to that section state that when claiming that a foreign pension is not taxable in the UK the former expat should provide details in the "any other information" section. This would be a simple statement to the effect of "Under the UK/Hong Kong double tax treaty article 17 my [XYZ] pension is taxable only in Hong Kong and as such is not entered on my current tax return".

The MPF rules stipulate that a Hong Kong resident employed from Hong Kong, who works outside that country for limited periods, is sufficiently connected to (and can therefore be enrolled on) the pension scheme, and is covered by the MPF. So a person employed in Hong Kong but working outside Hong Kong is covered by the MPF scheme. For example, a British expat airline pilot and British aircrews employed from Hong Kong by the Hong Kong representative office there would all be covered. The income tax paid in Hong Kong on the pension payments is graduated but is in any case less than the UK basic rate of 20%.

An ORSO scheme provides that as long as the expat earns income from employment, then that income can provide for a pension. Due to the attractions of the treaty between the UK and Hong Kong, schemes are being promoted whereby an expat individual working offshore is "employed" through a Hong Kong company set up under the Companies Ordinance Part XI, and payments funded by the individual are paid into the Hong Kong pension fund, later to be paid out to the retiree in the UK free of UK tax. These schemes would appear to be pure tax avoidance and should be viewed with suspicion. Hong Kong recently had its listing of QROPS/ROPS suspended from the HMRC listing (see above).

However, the transfer from a UK pension scheme to a Hong Kong Capital Corporation Retirement Plan (CCRP) is possible, which may then be linked to an ORSO non-vested trust. Many internationally known pension trustee services offer ORSO trust schemes. See **7.2.13** (The Hong Kong Trust non-vested solution.)

Law: *Occupational Retirement Scheme Ordinance,* Chapter 426, Laws of Hong Kong; *Mandatory Provident Fund Schemes Ordinance,* Chapter 485, Laws of Hong Kong; Legacy Trust Company Limited, Hong Kong

4.1.12   New Zealand

There is a four-year exemption period that applies to lump sum foreign superannuation withdrawals received during a qualification period. The exemption does not require a person to be a non-tax resident for a minimum period.

The exemption period is available to both new migrants and returning New Zealanders. The exemption starts on the first day a person becomes a New Zealand tax resident. It finishes 48 months after the month in which the individual first meet the requirements for being a New Zealand tax resident, by either having a permanent place of abode or by being in New Zealand for more than 183 days in any 12-month period. The exemption also ends if the individual becomes a non-tax resident.

If an individual qualifies for the four-year exemption period, a foreign superannuation withdrawal received during this period is exempt from New Zealand tax.

This exemption applies if the individual:

- first acquired an interest in a foreign superannuation scheme while a non-resident for New Zealand tax purposes; and
- has not previously had this exemption.

If an individual qualifies for a four-year exemption period, and receives a foreign superannuation withdrawal after the exemption period:

- the "schedule method" ignores the individual's years of residence during the exemption period; or
- the "formula method" does not tax the gains that have accrued to the scheme during the exemption period.

The schedule method

This method uses set percentages that represent the proportion of the foreign superannuation withdrawal which needs to be included as assessable income for the New Zealand income tax return. The schedule year percentages increase with the number of years the individual is a tax resident in New Zealand. The rest of the foreign superannuation withdrawal is not deemed to be assessable income, is exempt from New Zealand tax, and is not included in the income tax return.

The formula method

This method is an alternative to the schedule method and can only be used for foreign defined contribution schemes. The formula method uses a number of formulae which are complex and cannot be detailed here.

All of the following conditions have been met, so the individual must ensure that he or she:

- has the information required to use the formula method;
- has not received a distribution from the scheme before 1 April 2014, other than a pension or an annuity; and
- has not already used the schedule method (above) for the scheme.

Where the pension interest came from a previous spouse or partner after they died, or as part of a relationship agreement following a relationship split, the other individual must not have used the schedule method.

New Zealand has many double tax agreements and reference to these may treat periodic pensions and retirement lump sums differently. The UK/New Zealand double tax agreement enables the Form New Zealand/Individual to be completed and sent to the UK for the issue of an NT code by the pension provider. There may also be the opportunity to make up to four years backdated repayment claims for overpaid tax.

Example

James, a former UK citizen, retired to New Zealand and became a New Zealand tax resident. He took his tax free pension lump sum and now receives a yearly pension income of £18,000 from his former UK employer's pension scheme. The sum of £1,300 tax is deducted in the UK.

Because his UK pension scheme was exempt from the foreign investment fund (FIF) rules, he converts the before-tax amount into New Zealand dollars and declares this income in his individual tax return (IR3) each year. As the pension is only taxable in New Zealand under the tax treaty between New Zealand/UK, he therefore cannot claim the UK tax paid as a foreign tax credit in his IR3 return. Instead, James contacts HMRC to claim a refund and apply for an exemption so that his pension will be paid free of any UK income tax in future. He also claims a refund for the previous three years since he arrived in New Zealand.

Guidance: Form New Zealand/Individual; NZ Leaflet IR257; INTM 358660ff.

4.2   Insurance

4.2.1   Significance

Insurance policies for health, safety, life events and death are vital when assigned or living abroad.

Medical costs in foreign countries can be far higher than the British expat, who is used to free health care, can contemplate! Having said that, in many countries an insurance policy will enable medical treatment to be undertaken the same day or at worst within a matter of days. Doctors and consultants in many countries have had training in the UK, Australia and other western countries and are highly competent.

Locally based insurance providers may only cover resident country medical costs whereas international health care providers will cover regions at a greater premium. An aspect for the expat to remember is the disclosure of prior medical conditions as the investigation by the insurance company on making a claim may invalidate coverage because of the previous non-disclosure. This seems to occur all too frequently. Taking UK travel insurance for, say, a year term and falling ill whilst working abroad may well invalidate a claim.

4.2.2   European health insurance card

The European health insurance card (EHIC) ensures that medical care is given as if the expat were a citizen of that European country. The EHIC will not give the exact same medical privileges as an individual would get from the NHS. Whilst maternity care services are covered the EHIC does not give medical cover for anyone who has travelled to Europe simply for medical treatment.

The coverage of EHIC varies widely between each European country. Some nations charge for treatment and this may be reclaimed when back in the UK. Medical repatriation is not covered so travel insurance is also an option to bridge the shortfall in coverage. The EHIC card is valid per individual so each family member should have his or her own card but one adult family member may apply for the family if the children are under 16 (or 19 should they still be full-time students).

The expat should discuss ongoing medical care (e.g. chemotherapy) with a doctor before travelling. Treatments like chemotherapy or oxygen supply provisions need to be booked prior to travelling. It's always a good idea to plan ahead regarding the management of the condition, but the cost adds another consideration. The key for expats going to Europe with continuing health issues is to plan ahead so as not to restrict them from travelling and receiving treatment in Europe. The EHIC should normally be supplemented by a travel insurance policy.

4.2.3   Health insurance

As stated above, health insurance whilst in a foreign country is one of the first factors that an expat should consider on arrival if not before departure from the UK.

Insurances may cover life events, such as critical illness, etc., but it should be noted that a comprehensive policy will be required or additional cover for such events. For instance, many Far East countries have high incidents of dengue virus which can be debilitating for many months and result in a recommended return to UK. Such early repatriation may cause problems in the immediate or long term as far as continuing job prospects are concerned. The recommendation to take anti-malarial tablets long term is often unfeasible from a cost point of view and because of restricted access in some jurisdictions to regular supplies of pharmaceuticals (see **Example** below and the Overview at **6.9.1**).

Insurance in cases of death should also be considered as payment of company lump sums and pensions to surviving spouses may be insufficient in the long term if indeed the assigning company provides any such cover.

Medical insurance policies vary depending on the provider and the coverage required. Generally expats are too busy to read their policies once they have entered into medical coverage abroad. However, there are a number of policy details to be aware of, such as:

- "Reimbursement of the reasonable and customary charges" could result in the expat paying extra on top of the insurance coverage (see **Example** below).
- Pre-existing illnesses are excluded and non-declaration may invalidate any subsequent claims even if unconnected with the current ailment.
- Change of job/location must be advised to the insurance company immediately.
- Mis-statement of age can result in variation in coverage or disqualification.
- Policies may be cancelled by the insurer if it so wishes.

- Congenital conditions, such as epilepsy and hernias, are precluded unless, in the case of the latter, caused by trauma.

"Reimbursement of the reasonable and customary charges" means not to exceed the general level of medical and hospitalisation charges on a like for like basis being made by other hospitals of the same standing in the area.

Example

Steve has a medical insurance policy and is taken ill in Jakarta with dengue virus.

His wife asks the local doctor for the best hospital to send him to and the doctor assumes she means the most expensive and lets her know the address. On admission his medical card is scanned and he is placed in a suite with luxurious furnishings, a spare bedroom for overnight visitors and a nurse of the hospital on immediate standby.

Steve gets better and is discharged but at that point the hospital states that the insurer has only agreed 50% of the costs. On enquiry Steve is made aware of the clause in the policy contract "We reserve the right to determine whether any particular hospital/medical charge is a reasonable and customary charge with reference to but not limited to the Private Health Care facilities and Services regulations and any subsequent amendments". Steve has to pay the difference immediately from his credit card and then hope for a satisfactory appeal to his insurance company to reimburse the difference.

4.2.4   Kidnap, ransom and extortion (KRE)

British expatriates live and travel to some very geographically exotic places in connection with work or leisure. The locations in the world are split into low/medium/high/highest risk areas and, in the highest risk areas, KRE incidents are on the rise.

The author, in a period of secondment of six years in Malaysia, has come across two incidents of kidnapping. The first was a Dutch school boy who was taken from outside one of the local international schools and the second a business man held for five days until the ransom was paid. The business man's family had to find the equivalent of £500,000 sterling to secure his release. The company did not have specific insurance for such an eventuality and the family had to find the funds from company resources. One report "Protection Insurance" in *International Adviser*, June 2016 stated:

> "... if the owners of offshore investments become public knowledge in the name of transparency, those names also become available to criminals and terrorists."

Whilst the incidence of kidnapping is comparatively rare worldwide, it is a growing threat in some regions for both businessmen and their family members, who are now considered "soft" targets. It is, almost always, the case that information regarding wealth circumstances is being passed on by an informant known to both the kidnapped and the kidnapper (e.g. a maid, driver, fellow employee or service professional).

The assignee should ask his assigning employer posting him or her to a high risk area what protection is in place if such a KRE incident occurs. Does the individual, his family or employer have the 24 hour (such as the London based Red24 plc) contact of a special risks contingency provider, i.e. kidnap/ransom negotiator? Does the assigning company have access to specific funds for payment of ransom by way of insurance or, failing that, speedy liquidation of current personal assets? In the case of the latter how long will it take to assess the value of assets and liquidate those assets to pay the ransom?

Another risk scenario is a person at the assignee's local bank who covertly or inadvertently makes information (e.g. large transfer, name, address and date of birth) available to a colleague/ relative/kidnap associate. Indeed, even in the UK banks are not immune as the Daily Mail, 3 August 2011 comments on bank fraud:

> "... each case is likely to involve hundreds or even thousands of customers. The majority of these details were sold on to organised criminals."

To avoid this problem the expatriate should consider each time a transfer is made of funds from abroad to the local bank:

- Check with the local bank manager who is responsible for handling such transfers and what is their authority. Also obtain a copy of the bank's confidentiality rules.

- Insist that no information should be divulged to third parties unless the assignee is informed and the bank's computer should be appropriately red flagged. There is nothing to stop the bank or institution advising when such an approach has been made (see "Data Protection" below).

- Keep capital sums in the local bank jurisdiction to a minimum, with the feeder account from another "safe" offshore banking jurisdiction in, say, the Isle of Man, Jersey or Guernsey.

- In other cases (e.g. retired expats), does their financial adviser have an up to date valuation profile of their assets and can those funds be liquidated quickly or is there some insurance in place to cover the funds' liquidity delay? Typically travel policies that do include "Ransom payment as a result of kidnapping and hostage" are limited in geographical scope and in the financial amount covered.

In the case of the kidnapped businessman mentioned previously, it took four days to secure company funds for his release; meanwhile he was bound and gagged and moved from house to house! Happily he was released – as are 81% of kidnap victims in such cases.

Guidance: Red24 "Outcomes of foreign kidnaps globally" January 2014 – August 2015; International Adviser magazine; Special Contingency Risks

4.3 Data protection

A new EU General Data Protection Regulation is to apply from 25 May 2018, which the UK is party to notwithstanding Brexit. Its implementation will apply to personal data and will apply to data controllers or processors who

a) operate in the EU; or

b) operate outside the EU but handle EU citizens data.

An individual's rights under these new regulations mean:

- a right to be informed of data usage by an organisation has to be transparent to the individual on how their data is retained;

- privacy notices which must be compliant with the new regulations;

- access rights to the personal data by the individual and details of how it is being processed;
- a right to be "forgotten" such as adherence to requests for deletion and removal of personal data;
- processing restrictions to limit usage of personal data;
- portability of personal data, so that data in a common format can be supplied to the individual for use elsewhere;
- objection to direct marketing usage and other restrictions;
- profiling usage of data.

Companies and organisations need to ensure that the new rules are known and in place by May 2018. This will mean reviewing current practices with an appointed Data Protection Officer or Supervisor. Data breaches should be notified by relevant staff within 72 hours of the breach. Penalties for non-compliance could result in a fine of up to 20 million euros, or 4% of global turnover, for failure to notify and further penalties for the breach. Clearly this will be a major step to providing security of data for individuals but it remains to be seen how well it works in practice when many everyday breaches currently go unreported.

Law: *General Data Protection Regulations;* SI 2016/679; EU GDPR, art. 83, para. 4-6

5. Preparing to leave the UK

5.1 Documentation

5.1.1 Passports

For the internationally mobile employee the advantage of a British passport is favourable or visa-free entry to many countries and this can be up to three months at one time without having to go on a "visa run" out of the country. This is particularly helpful when having to obtain a work permit in a country of intended employment because of governmental delays in processing work permits.

Around fifty former Commonwealth countries – e.g. Canada, South Africa, Malaysia – offer immediate entry to their countries, and the addition of other non-Commonwealth nations takes the total to about 170 worldwide.

Also, many other country passport holders in Asia are subjected to intensive scrutiny and financial demands at immigration whereas the British passport holder is normally given speedy access into the country (unless he or she has abused the system before).

British High Commissions in the world give the British passport holder certain insurance in case anything does go wrong but this relies on registering on arrival (see Consulate registration at **6.3** below).

It is important, when travelling extensively abroad for work, that the expat ensures that the passport has numerous pages (e.g. 48 pages) left blank for visa stamps, and that the expiry date is sufficient for the intended period of stay plus three months. If the UK passport holder has few blank pages left before UK departure it is sensible to renew the passport, upgrading to 48 page version. Unused periods are added to the new passport.

Children under 16 years have passports that are valid only for five years whereas their parents have ten years' validity. Currently the British passport allows free unfettered access within the European Union. Matters in this regard may change after the UK has left the EU by the March 2019 deadline. The problem of non-EU access by

British passport holders may be solved by acquiring an Irish passport if the individual has an Irish grandparent or Italian ancestry for an Italian passport. Other parts of the world offer passports and citizenship for various reasons:

- "marriage of convenience" passports where a passport is issued to the spouse of a citizen of that country on certain conditions;

- investment passports such as Malta, Portugal, Italy, Cyprus which give access to the country long term and often with tax advantages;

- provisional passports can be issued in some South American and central American countries where property is owned there;

- honorary diplomatic/consular passports can be issued by certain countries to people with strong business investment ties to the country;

- refugee status passports for those who can travel to a country under a UN asylum refugee status.

Guidance: HM Passport Office; 1951 convention travel document / Geneva passport

5.1.2   *Visas and work permits*

Free and unrestricted movement of labour within the EC took effect from 1 January 1993 but that is not the case elsewhere and visas and work permits are required for other countries. The non-European work permit requirements in rest of the world countries are changing and being re-categorised regularly (see New Zealand below).

Work permits can take months to secure and are costly when applying through specialist agents. Currently, prior to the UK agreeing free movement of labour post Brexit, EU arrangements for highly skilled worker permits are typically not uniform across the different EU states. The "blue card" (see below) may be an option for British workers to reside and work in the EU after Brexit but this remains to be seen. If reforms go ahead then applicants for the blue card can apply after a six month or longer contract has been offered.

Currently Tier 2 General skilled worker permits apply but see "EU work permits" below.

Example

Guy is an IT expert and works for an international ski chalet company. He has been posted to Southern France from the UK to attend to the Alps and Pyrenees sections of the company. He is fluent in French and Spanish.

Guy's duties will be in France and Spain but his head office is based in Andorra for tax reasons and he will need to report and work from there occasionally. Andorra is not part of the EU. Whilst Guy does not need to have a work permit for France and Spain because they are EU countries, Andorra is not and he needs a work permit there. On enquiry he discovers that the relevant "implementing regulations" require him to provide:

- clearance certificate from his country of origin, from the country from where he emigrates to Andorra and from all other countries where he has lived before;
- original and photocopy of his passport, plus a separate passport photo;
- his birth certificate;
- his marriage certificate (or other proof of marital status);
- copy of the tenancy agreement for his accommodation (and a "habitability certificate" for the accommodation;
- proof of his registration with the Cass (Caixa Andorrana de Seguretat Social);
- his curriculum vitae and proof of his occupational qualification;
- original and photocopy of the certificate of registration of the register of business premises of the government of the employing company;
- as a "highly qualified worker", he will also have to present his employment contract and proof of his academic qualifications.

Guidance: www.andorra-intern.com/check/en_job.htm

As a further example, those skilled workers intending to move to New Zealand for work under the "Skilled Migrant Category" ("SMC") will have two categories:

a) the essential skills visa for those under 55 years; and

b) working holiday visa for skilled professionals under 30 years.

The SMC category has two remuneration thresholds: NZ$48,859 for any jobs that are skilled and NZ$73,299 for jobs that are currently not classed as skilled but are well remunerated in terms of New Zealand salaries.

Classification of jobs skills is made by reference to the Australia and New Zealand Standard Classification of Occupations (ANZSCO) levels 1, 2 and 3 but where this is ascertained using the levels then the NZ$73,299 remuneration and above each year is the threshold criteria.

Other factors are the age of the individual applying, health, character and English language skills.

5.1.3   EU work permits

The EU "blue card" work permit may prove to be a way for British expats to access the European jobs market. It is a work permit that 25 out of the 28 current members recognise, enabling non-EU workers with skills to work in Europe. The only members currently who do not participate are Denmark, Ireland and the UK. This may change with Brexit negotiations effectively meaning that after March 2019 UK workers can apply for the blue card. The UK educated and professionally experienced worker could soon apply as long as he or she adheres to the three conditions:

• be a non-EU citizen;

• be educated or professionally experienced; and

• have a binding work offer or contract

EU Blue Card work permit for non-EU citizens.

Contracts for 1 to 4 years in length. Holders are entitled to bring family members. 20 of the participating states currently allow dependants immediate access.

Holders can settle within a period of between nearly 2 to 5 years. Under proposed new rules, holders who have resided in one Member State for a continuous period of three years would be eligible for long-term EU residence. There is, and would be, no salary threshold for settlement as there is in the UK.

Currently, Blue Card applicants must earn 1.5 times the average national salary. This was £33,600 in 2014 (averaged across participating states). Proposed changes would lower it to a range of 80% the average national salary for recent graduates and those on shortage occupations, and between 1 and 1.2 times the average national salary for others. This would be equivalent to between £18,000 and £27,000 a year.

Proposed reforms would shorten this to six months. The job must be relevant to the applicants' qualifications or experience.

Law: EU Council Directive 2009/50/EC
Guidance: Migration Watch, UK

5.1.4   Golden visas

For retirees, many countries offer "golden visas" which allow residence in a country for UK individuals. Payment is required and the visas can be for 1, 5 or 10 years generally, e.g. Thailand, Malaysia ("Malaysia my second home" or "MM2H") and others.

With the UK expected to leave the EU by the March 2019 deadline one option may also be to apply for investment visas/golden visas. As an example, Portugal is offering a residence permit through an investment option. To secure this type of residence permit for UK individuals requires:

- purchase of real estate for 500,000 euros and above;
- transfer of at least 1 million euros to a Portuguese bank account; or

- setting up of a limited liability company with share capital of at least 1 million euros.

The process takes about one year and after five years the UK individual can apply for what is called the "golden visa". Other countries offering golden visas and investment visas are Malta, Italy, Cyprus and also the UK for inward investment.

Residence permits are issued in many foreign countries after the individual has met one or more of the following requirements:

- not a criminal undesirable;
- has a job guarantee;
- has sufficient funds to live on in the new jurisdiction;
- has accommodation/lease in that country;
- has been accepted by his or her professional body or equivalent professional body in that country;
- is in good health (supported by a health assessment in some cases).

In Europe it is the job offer requirement that is an important factor. In non-EU countries it is different and the main factor would be the contract of employment offered. In the case of a self-employed person other matters would require attention as in the example below.

Example

Taking the case of Guy (from **5.1.2** above), had he been self-employed the process of setting up a business in Andorra would be as follows:

- he would need to present his credentials to the government in order to be able to request the creation of a company in the country (authorisation for foreign investment);
- once the foreign investment is approved, a bank account would need to be opened in the country, in which to deposit the company's capital;

- the company's charter would then need to be signed before a notary;
- once the company is incorporated, Guy would have to find a location for which to obtain his business permit, which authorises him to start issuing invoices.

5.2 Travel and relocation costs

5.2.1 Introduction

Where an employee normally resident in the UK goes to work abroad, the travel costs and those of that individual's spouse and children may be eligible for a deduction. If the expenses qualify for such a deduction they are not eligible expenses for the purposes of the removals legislation. The effect of this is that the employee will be able to get the travelling costs as well as £8,000 of removal expenses tax-free.

In the autumn Budget statement the government stated that it will legislate in the 2018-19 Finance Bill to cement into law from 6 April 2019 the existing concessionary travel and subsistence overseas scale rates. Employers will only be asked to ensure that employees are undertaking qualifying travel. Up until now the rules have been by concession, as detailed below.

HMRC have therefore agreed that employers may continue to use the standard overseas benchmark table rates when paying accommodation and subsistence expenses to employees whose duties require them to travel abroad. There has been no need for these employees to produce expenses receipts.

Law: ITEPA 2003, s. 341, 342, 370, 371
Guidance: EIM 34000ff.

5.2.2 Overseas benchmark rates

For most countries, there are benchmark rates for the larger cities as well as an "elsewhere" rate. These rates can be found on the HMRC website and are occasionally updated. Rates are quoted in the relevant foreign currency, US$ or euros and are intended to reflect the accommodation and subsistence expenses that employees incur during a period spent in a foreign country. The benchmark rates do not cover incidental, allowable expenses that employees may incur en-route – for example, the cost of a taxi to the airport in the UK, or necessary refreshments taken at the airport.

Example 1

Employer Maple Syrup Imports Ltd pays for an employee on a business trip to Canada to stay at a hotel in Toronto for two nights on a room only basis to meet suppliers. The hotel invoices Maple Syrup direct for the room charge. The employee arrives in Canada at 3pm on Monday and leaves on the 9am flight on Wednesday. The employer may reimburse the employee's subsistence expenses as follows.

Period and rates Period and rates	Amount (Canadian dollars)
1 × total residual rate (3pm Monday to 3pm Tuesday)	151.50
10-hour rate (3pm Tuesday to 9am Wednesday)	118.00
Total	269.50

Alternatively, Maple Syrup Imports Ltd may choose to reimburse the employee's subsistence expenses using the individual meal rates in place of the over 10-hour and total residual rates.

Example 2

An employee travels on business to New York where he stays for three days as the guest of a business client in the New York Hyatt Hotel and that host pays all the costs. The employer may reimburse, per day, 10% of the appropriate residual rate:

> 3 × 10% of subsistence only rate for New York (US$102.5) = US$30.75 (say US$31)

> Any meals for which the employee does have to pay may be reimbursed using the appropriate meal rates.

Employers are not obliged to use the published rates.

Guidance: www.gov.uk/government/uploads/system/uploads/ attachment_data/file/359797/2014_Worldwide_subsistence_rates.pdf

5.2.3 Compliance by employers

When paying at or below published rates, employers need not include payments on forms P11D and need not apply for an HMRC approval notice or operate any checking system. If employers decide to pay less than the published rates then the affected employees are not automatically entitled to tax relief for any shortfall.

It is always open to an employer to reimburse their employees' actual, vouched expenses, or to negotiate a separate deal with HMRC under the terms of an approval notice. This would be after the employer has assessed the expenses claims with regard to the foreign jurisdiction and in certain circumstances after liaising with Unions: for example there is a BALPA uniformed commercial pilots flat rate fixed expense allowance (FREA) of £1,022 per annum for all uniformed commercial pilots and other uniformed flight deck crew. This allowance was negotiated with HMRC by BALPA and represents an annual tax saving of £408 for higher rate uniformed flight crew taxpayers.

Negotiations with HMRC may more accurately reflect union members expenses. Employers/unions wishing to negotiate amounts must, of course, be able to provide HMRC with evidence in support of their figures. Employers will also need to operate a checking system to confirm that payments are only made on qualifying occasions where employees were in fact obliged to incur and pay expenses of this nature.

Deductions depend on the employee remaining resident and ordinarily resident in the UK. If the employee becomes non-resident on departure these exemptions do not apply. However, HMRC normally treat the expenses of travelling to take up an overseas appointment as arising from that appointment so that if the employee is non-resident and performs no UK duties the expenses will in any case be outside the charge to UK tax.

The exemption in respect of temporary living accommodation abroad applies where the employee intends to move to permanent accommodation to complete the relocation, e.g. for an employee who lives in a hotel until the old home is sold and a new home purchased, or who moves into a rented house at the new location for the same reason, the hotel or the rented property will represent temporary living accommodation. But where a person is posted to a new location and moves into accommodation that he or she occupies for a considerable period as his or her main residence, the provision of the accommodation will not be eligible for exemption. For example an executive from the USA, who is posted to London and who moves into a rented flat there, is not occupying temporary living accommodation unless it can be seen that he or she intends to acquire somewhere else as permanent accommodation.

Example

Katty moves abroad with her recruitment company and places her UK home on the market for sale. She views her job as a permanent/long term assignment in the foreign jurisdiction and as she considers rent payments "dead money", she will purchase a property in the jurisdiction as soon as funds are released from the sale in UK. Therefore her rented condominium would be considered temporary accommodation until the new house is purchased but only on that proviso. See also **3.2.7** (CGT private residence relief elections).

Law: ITEPA 2003, s. 341, 342, 370, 371; TCGA 1992, s. 222(5)
Guidance: British Airline Pilots' Association (BALPA)

5.3 Miscellaneous matters

5.3.1 Professional subscriptions

Whilst the British expat is abroad it is important to keep subscriptions to professional trade bodies and journals up to date. There are a number of reasons for this:

- updating important changes in technical knowledge;
- separately rated membership subscriptions for those living abroad;
- re-applying for jobs will entail references to society/trade body membership;
- jobs abroad require proof of qualifications and experience;

- notification of society/trade body, overseas branch meetings and conferences;
- e-mailing of monthly society and trade journals to the individual.

See also **5.3.6** below (Qualifications).

5.3.2   UK bank accounts

On an assignment or retirement abroad, UK bank and credit card companies should be advised early on of the intended departure and to which country. If possible it is beneficial to have an address in the new country but see **3.1.6** above (Tenancy agreements).

If the UK bank account is closed, and this is not advisable, inform those companies that have existing standing orders or direct debits well before closure. Keeping an existing UK bank account whilst abroad facilitates easier transfers from the foreign country back to the UK when exchange rates are beneficial (see example in **6.2.2** – Offshore accounts).

An existing UK bank account may be with a worldwide banking group and it may be possible to set up a local bank account prior to the assignment or retirement to the foreign country. One problem that can arise when the expat is trying to find accommodation is the fact that a local bank account sometimes cannot be opened until the bank has a local address and the rental lease will not be possible until the expat has a bank account! Borrowing funds locally is also easier if there is a related bank reference point back in the UK, especially if applying for a mortgage.

Most countries now have ATM (cash machine) networks which allow withdrawals of cash locally from the UK account using debit or credit cards, although there will be a transaction charge for this service and also a limit on withdrawals. Some banks do not charge for ATM withdrawals in the particular foreign country but this should be confirmed prior to departure on assignment.

Maintaining an existing bank account in the UK, particularly if the work assignment is for a fixed amount of time, enables sterling to supplement any drop in the value of the assignment country's currency. However, many companies pay salaries offshore in US$.

For pensioners, payment of the UK state pension into an existing bank account in the UK can be advantageous so that sums can be transferred abroad when the exchange rate is more attractive. Some pension providers pay sterling pensions abroad, but funds may be converted into US$ initially and then the receiving country may translate the US$ into the local currency, all of which incurs additional exchange rate costs.

Those who are renting out their UK property whilst abroad would be best advised to open a letting income/expenses bank account before leaving so that the income received and expenses claimed are easily ascertained when completing the non-resident landlord self-assessment tax return at the end of the tax year.

5.3.3   *Investor protection schemes*

The Financial Services Compensation Scheme (FSCS) is the compensation fund of last resort for individuals who have investments with authorised financial services firms. If a firm is in default, or ceases trading, the FSCS may be able to pay compensation to those who have suffered default. The threshold figures are reviewed every five years by reference to the sterling equivalent of 1,000 euros. From 30 January 2017, the protection limit was increased from £75,000 to £85,000 for each eligible depositor, e.g. husband and wife.

The FSCS was set up under the *Financial Services and Markets Act 2000* (FSMA). The costs of the scheme are covered by the financial services industry contributions. The compensation limits generally applied are for:

- bank deposits – covers deposits up to £85,000 for each eligible claim *per banking group*, payable within 20 working days of bank failure;
- insurance contracts – long-term policies such as life assurance and pension policies – 100% without limit;
- miscellaneous insurance (e.g. car insurance) – 100% without limit;
- investment business (e.g. mutual funds) – covers up to £50,000;
- mortgage advice – covers up to £50,000.

The FSCS only pay compensation on an eligible claim once it has been identified. When an authorised firm appears to be in default – i.e. it is unable, or likely to be unable, to pay claims – an investigation will be carried out to establish whether or not this is the case, and this takes time. The FSCS was set up mainly to assist private individuals, although smaller companies and partnerships are also covered. It is important to understand if investments are held individually or pooled and held by a company as this may affect whether FSCS compensation is available. The FSCS does not cover everyone.

Example

Denis has £110,000 deposited in a failed bank where the administrator could pay depositor creditors 60p in the £1. He will get £85,000 from the FSCS after the bank was declared "in default". His full rights are assigned to the FSCS. The FSCS will eventually get £66,000 from the administrator (60% of £110,000). Denis will then get part of his remaining loss at the recovery rate of 60% of the excess over the protected limit, i.e. 60% of £25,000 = £15,000. So, Denis will receive payments of £100,000 in total from the FSCS.

From 6 April 2017, the long service cap came into effect for members who have 21 or more years' pensions service in their scheme. For these members the cap is increased by three per cent for each full year of pensionable service above 20 years, up to a maximum of double the standard cap. The earlier the retirement, the lower the annual cap is set, to compensate for the longer period of payments. See also **4.1.1** (Pensions).

Example

Regina retires early and had not reached her scheme's normal pension age when her employer went into liquidation. She would normally get 90% compensation based on what her pension was worth at the time. The annual compensation she will receive is capped at a certain level. The cap at age 65 is, from 1 April 2017, £38,505.61 (this equates to £34,655.05 when the 90% level is applied) per year. This is set by Department for Work and Pensions.

5.3.4   *Overseas compensation schemes*

If a deposit account is based offshore then there is no compensation available from the FSCS. Instead, policyholders may need to look at a local scheme to see whether there is any protection available to them.

Ireland

Deposit accounts held with Irish banks and building societies may be covered by the Irish government's guarantee.

Jersey

Jersey has a Depositors Compensation Scheme, which provides protection per person, per Jersey bank.

Guernsey

Guernsey has a Deposit Compensation Scheme which provides protection per person, per licensed bank.

Isle of Man

The Isle of Man has a Depositors' Compensation Scheme which provides protection per person, per licensed deposit taker.

Example

Mark and his wife Sophie have decided to put a majority of their savings, amounting to £150,000, into Jersey Bank 1 to earn more interest while Mark works in Kuwait on a three year contract. This is a joint account. Unfortunately the bank is found to be in default and goes into liquidation. Mark and Sophie are joint eligible depositors and therefore would be entitled to compensation amounting to £100,000.

The previous £50,000 Jersey compensation limit no longer applies on a banking group basis but on an individual bank basis, i.e. if Mark and Sophie had deposited £100,000 with Jersey Bank 1 and £50,000 with Jersey 2 Bank within the same banking group, under the Regulations, they would be entitled to £150,000 cumulatively across the two Banks in that banking group.

If the funds in the compensation scheme were not sufficient to meet liabilities then the Board can use additional amounts recoverable from the failed Bank's liquidation, to satisfy any outstanding depositor obligations under the Scheme, up to the maximum £50,000.

Law: *Banking Business (Jersey) Law* 1991; *Bank Depositors Compensation Law* 201; *EU Bank Recovery and Resolution Directive* 2014/59

5.3.5   Individual savings accounts (ISAs)

The maximum amount that each person living in the UK can invest in an ISA is currently £20,000 per year, so a married couple can invest £40,000 each year.

There are many types of ISA, including cash ISAs, stocks and shares ISAs, innovative finance ISAs, lifetime ISAs and AIM shares ISAs.

The individual investor must be:

- 16 or over for a cash ISA;
- 18 or over for a stocks and shares or innovative finance ISA;
- 18 or over, but under 40, for a lifetime ISA.

The individual must also be resident in the UK or, if resident abroad, a Crown servant or the spouse or civil partner of a Crown servant (e.g. diplomatic or overseas civil service).

When moving abroad the expat ISA holder must tell his ISA provider as soon as he stops being a UK resident. However, existing ISAs can be kept open and still receive UK tax relief on cash and investments held in the ISAs. Further contributions to the ISA cannot be made until the expat is UK resident again. If a spouse or civil partner dies on or after 3 December 2014, the surviving spouse/civil partner can inherit the deceased's ISA allowance. Also, the normal ISA allowance can be added to the value held in the ISA when the individual died.

AIM share ISAs not only offer income tax, IHT and CGT reliefs but will also be exempt on death if the AIM ISA has been held for at least two years and the company or companies are qualifying under the AIM requirements. However, they carry high investment risk.

The question of whether it is a good idea to have an ISA whilst abroad, with no recurring top-ups, should be considered; an efficient alternative might be to put the ISA contribution into a pension fund if the full annual £40,000 limit has not been used. Whilst abroad up to £2,880 net can be paid into a pension scheme which is increased to £3,600 with the added tax relief of £720. This might apply to an individual who is a member of a registered pension scheme and is no longer resident in the UK but who was resident in the UK both at some time during the five tax years before that year and also when the individual became a member of the pension scheme. Non-working spouses and children can benefit from this minimum pensions allowance too if remaining resident in the UK. See **4.1** (Pensions).

Example

Victor is a member of a group personal pension plan and he is going to work in France for an overseas subsidiary of his current employer on a five year contract. For the first two years, Victor will still be paid £35,000 by the UK company but after that he will be paid in euros and taxed under the French tax system.

He usually makes ISA contributions of £3,000 per year but will not now be able to as he will be non-resident. Instead he could consider supplementing his pension payments as below.

The maximum gross employee contributions eligible for tax relief are Victor's earnings of £35,000 each year for first two tax years, then £2,880 net each year for the following three years, after which the five year limit expires. After the five years, eligibility for tax relief will then stop unless Victor becomes a "relevant UK individual" again.

Also, the new death benefit rules for pensions mean that the pension, when passed on, can be tax free whereas the ISA will be part of the estate and potentially taxable. Once more, see **4.1** (Pensions).

5.3.6   Qualifications

When the employee arrives in the foreign country, his or her employer may wish to see qualifications to ascertain experience in the particular area of employment. Normally the employer will require notarised copies of original certificates and these may even include 'A' level pass certificates. Also, membership of professional societies will need to be confirmed as well as any examinations taken. Occasionally prospective foreign employers will even wish to see a copy of the examination paper passed even though this may have been many years ago. Normally most examining bodies keep copies of examination papers for this particular purpose. The author recently required such an exam syllabus from 1979 and the Institute of Taxation was able to provide this by email within a few days of requesting it.

The UK's National Academic Recognition Information Centre (NARIC) has extensive experience in evaluating international qualifications and assists institutions, employers and government agencies in identifying how international qualifications compare with their requirements for admission, recruitment, professional registration or funding. NARIC incorporates recommendations on one or more of the following areas:

- comparability of qualifications from around the world;
- grade comparisons: enabling identification of the top-performing students;
- sector-specific competency: highlighting skills coverage and gaps;
- higher education readiness;
- subject-specific comparability.

NARIC benchmarks a broad range of qualifications such as academic, vocational, occupational and professional awards from across the world. The UK NARIC benchmarking can be applied to evaluate all types and levels of qualifications ranging from entry level to Bachelor level through to Doctoral awards.

The European Certificate of Experience allows individuals who have trained and gained work experience in the UK and wish to pursue their profession in another Member State. It is only issued if the destination Member State stipulates that the profession is regulated under directive 1999/42/EC. In order to ascertain whether a profession is regulated in a particular Member State, it is necessary to contact the national co-ordinator for that country.

On the recognition of professional qualifications it states in article 12 of the directive:

"This Directive concerns the recognition by Member States of professional qualifications acquired in other Member States. It does not, however, concern the recognition by Member States of recognition decisions adopted by other Member States pursuant to this Directive. Consequently, individuals holding professional qualifications which have been recognised pursuant to this Directive may not use such recognition to obtain in their Member State of origin rights different from those conferred by the professional qualification obtained in that Member State, unless they provide evidence that they have obtained additional professional qualifications in the host Member State."

Law: Directive 2005/36/EC, art. 12

5.3.7   *Planning for premature repatriation*

Current political tensions in parts of the world such as Venezuela, Middle East, North and South Korea – and also natural disasters – can force an expat and family to have to leave the foreign country prematurely. As stated in **1.3.1** (Employment contracts), the employer may allow for premature repatriation in cases of emergency/war/national disaster. In paragraph **4.2.4** (Kidnap, ransom and extortion) the point is made that certain insurance policies (which can be corporate or personal) cover these situations. One example is the London-based Red24 offering country extraction insurance as stated below:

"Evacuations are coordinated by our 24/7 Crisis Response Management (CRM) Centre, where crisis support specialists, customer service staff and analysts work together to resolve any evacuation quickly and efficiently. Having the red24 team on hand 24/7 also means that clients have a point of contact for updates and communications on the status of the operation at any time—thereby providing peace of mind to clients in an otherwise tense situation."

The Foreign and Commonwealth Office (FCO) advise against travel to various destinations in the world and in the case of Venezuela have stated (at the time of writing):

"The FCO advises against all but essential travel to the remaining areas of Venezuela, due to ongoing unrest and instability. As of the 1 August, all dependents of British Embassy staff have been withdrawn. You should consider leaving the country by normal commercial means. There's a risk of significant disruption to transport links in and out of the country. If the political situation worsens, the British embassy may be limited in the assistance that it can provide."

The FCO leads in dealing with crises involving British nationals working overseas. The FCO's first priority is to support those British expats affected and their families. The FCO suggests a starting point for employers is to:

1. Recognise the scale of the risk when considering operating in high risk areas;
2. Follow FCO Travel advice and subscribe to FCO travel alerts;
3. Provide professional deployment and security briefing for all employees;
4. Consider providing employees with profession hostile environment awareness training;
5. Collect "personal risk profile" data on all employees and subcontractors. Data could also include audio/video recording of staff to allow for voice recognition and taking and storing DNA swabs;
6. Ensure you have up-to-date maps, plans and photographs of work locations and accommodation. Copies should be readily available at a secure location away from the high-risk location;
7. Consider investing in tracking and remote monitoring technologies.

The FCO provides opportunities for representatives of companies to visit its London crisis centre for preparation awareness courses. It also runs table-top learning exercises a number of times a year, normally around August and January. Interested companies should call the FCO's main switchboard on 0207 008 1500 during office hours and ask for the Crisis Management Department. Where available, the FCO will consider sending staff to observe and participate in companies' crisis exercises. Priority will be given to companies with UK nationals in locations where there is a significant threat from terrorism/kidnapping (see **4.2.4**). The FCO's Terrorism Response Team in Counter Terrorism Department can be reached on 0207 008 2977 or main switchboard 0207 008 1500 during office hours.

6.   Arrival

6.1   Arrival

For British expats arriving in a foreign jurisdiction for work or retirement there will be a huge culture shock if the individual has not been assigned or lived abroad previously. From the moment the expat lands in the new destination everything will seem at odds with how things are organised in the UK. Immigration officers will have a poor grasp of English and any discrepancy in a visa application will immediately start the expat thinking or saying "that's not how we do it in England". With this mindset the expat will face frustration from day one and if this is not overcome his or her time in the foreign country may be limited. To overcome this frustration, a pre-arrival investigation should be conducted by the individual (and, as necessary, by his family members) on various expat internet forums. Even better, the individual should attend a familiarization course, such as those provided by Farnham Castle (see **1.4.2** and **Appendix 1**).

Individuals working locally will be occupied for most of the week but spouses and partners may suddenly be on their own having to cope with a strange country and odd customs. This can lead to problems, especially in countries where the spouse or partner cannot work and for whom spare time is therefore plentiful. Learning the new language helps to occupy the time, while joining clubs and expat groups will help overcome this boredom. Whilst this book is not about the social side this is almost as important as, if not more critical than, any chapter in this book, and regretfully many advisers will have recourse to **8.5.5** (Divorce).

In the following sections of this Chapter 6 we point out the immediate important matters to attend to on arrival, such as setting up the local bank account, registering with the British Embassy, local tax compliance and registering a will in that jurisdiction. Matters such as bribery and corruption will to a lesser degree impose themselves on the expat depending on the jurisdiction in which he is located. A lot of newcomers have the mindset that "it won't happen to me" – this unfortunately is rarely the case!

6.2 Bank accounts offshore

6.2.1 Overview

When moving abroad the internationally mobile will require a bank account in the foreign jurisdiction for rental payments, living expenses, etc. Also, an existing UK bank account should not be closed as often there will be problems with opening the foreign account and limits on the amount of withdrawals per day, as detailed at **5.3.2** (UK bank accounts).

The foreign bank account should be in joint names of husband and wife so that withdrawals can be made by either party in emergency medical situations and on a partner's demise in the foreign jurisdiction. Some offshore banks offer far higher rates of interest than UK banks and also have lower maintenance costs.

6.2.2 Offshore accounts

There are some disadvantages to using an offshore bank. Many are less secure from a financial point of view (as illustrated by the past collapse of banks in Iceland, where many of the people who lost deposits were non-residents of Iceland, including institutional investors). Similarly, certain UK banks have suffered government bail outs.

Many offshore banks offer investor compensation schemes (see **5.3.4** – Overseas compensation schemes) which may only partially cover individual investors in the event of a collapse. It is important for the expat to check that there is compensation in place before using such an institution. Compensation schemes are usually capped at a specific amount so expats should split their investments if the amount exceeds the compensation limit.

There is an ongoing association between offshore banking and the proceeds of illegal activities. Recently a Brazilian bank (FPB Bank Inc) went into liquidation, ordered by the Superintendent of Banking of the Republic of Panama, being one of the financial institutions that allegedly moved the bribe payments for Norberto Odebrecht SA, the Brazilian construction company at the centre of a corruption scandal. These problems also arise with tax evasion and money laundering through banks; although steps are being taken to limit this and monitor banking activity (see below).

The problem of mis-selling of investments by Bank officials in respect of their customers has also to be addressed, particularly abroad. In Hong Kong the 2016 case of Mrs Chang was successful in a claim for damages against the Bank of Singapore for breach of contract, negligent advice, misrepresentation and/or undue influence in relation to their investments made through the bank via her investment vehicle Nextday International Limited. In the years 2004 to 2008, the bank had sold Chang a range of investment products which then suffered losses as a result of the 2008 financial crisis. Mrs Chang's limited investment knowledge and lack of investment experience in high-risk, complicated investments meant she was a medium-risk investor with moderate investment objectives. The Court found the bank had an advisory duty in relation to their non-discretionary accounts but this duty was breached by the bank as it was acting through its relationship manager in charge of the Chang account. As such the recommended products exceeded the customer's risk appetite and the relationship manager failed to explain the risks of such products. In this case the bank's usual industry standard disclaimers and non-reliance clauses in the bank/customer terms were arguably inconsistent with an advisory relationship.

In light of the *Chang* decision it would be hoped that banks/financial advisers, etc. will now look at their typical exclusion clauses with greater customer care and oversight in the future.

Expats are sometimes in locations not easily serviced by international banks and so all transactions are carried out at a distance. It is convenient not to have to visit the bank to open an account and then effect transactions online, say, from a Western Australian ocean oilrig. Also, in terms of movements in worldwide exchange rates, offshore banks can offer accounts in different currencies which can help expats to spread the risk in their sterling salaried accounts when working abroad.

Example

Kim works in Hong Kong in a high powered job. She has substantial funds in a UK building society account which regularly tops up her UK bank account when the balance reduces below £1,000.

She is paid part of her salary in Malaysian Ringgits and the balance is paid into her Isle of Man sterling account. Whilst the Brexit 23

June 2016 referendum results were coming through on the Thursday night and Friday morning it became clear that the value of her sterling account was to be reduced substantially. The impact of this was that it would cost substantially more to remit funds to Hong Kong if needed and the value of sterling against all other currencies would be less.

Her UK bank and building society was shut due to the time difference. Her Isle of Man bank 24 hour enquiry centre said that she only had a sterling account with them but if she had opened a US$ account as well the transfer could be made from Sterling to US$.

Sterling dropped from 1.4716 on 22 June to 1.32 on 27 June, at which time Kim had begun to arrange a US$ account with her Isle of Man bank into which she transferred her sterling. By 28 October sterling had dropped to 1.2185. So whilst Kim had initially been unable to act quickly to the fast changing exchange rate she did eventually "stop the rot".

It is therefore, in such circumstances, often wise to have a foreign bank account denominated in US dollars, euros, Australian dollars or Japanese yen.

Case: *Chang Pui Yin v Bank of Singapore Limited* [2016] HKEC 1721

6.2.3   Keeping UK accounts

As discussed at **5.3.2** above, the UK bank account should be retained as it may be needed for payment of school fees, subscriptions, credit card payments, council tax, etc., that still arise in the UK. Transferring money from abroad is expensive and some non-UK currency is not recognised and requires conversion into US$ and then sterling and vice versa, thereby incurring double charges.

The UK bank should be advised of the individual's offshore jurisdiction of residence and intended period of UK absence so that contact is limited to the correct time zone and debit/credit card withdrawals are not blocked. Unfortunately most of the main clearing banks have shortcomings in the area of dealing with British expatriates abroad and often it is simpler to open an offshore account in Jersey, Guernsey or the Isle of Man where the banks are more used to dealing with expats and have a 24-hour telephone enquiry service. All banks now have tax information exchange and FATCA administration requirements.

6.2.4   *Income disregard calculation*

When the British expat is abroad, self-assessment returns may have to be made to report income such as state pension, bank/building society interest, UK dividend income, NSI, purchased life annuities and unit trust income. Where it is more beneficial to them taxwise the annual personal allowance normally attributed against total UK income is excluded and the items of income mentioned are disregarded. In some cases this may prove to be beneficial from the taxpayer's point of view but HMRC should make two calculations:

1. include all sources of UK income, deduct the personal allowance due for that year, and charge at the normal tax rates applicable; and

2. exclude the items of income mentioned above.

HMRC should then issue an assessment for the more beneficial option.

This calculation, however, is not made in the year of departure from and arrival in the UK. HMRC would normally issue a "section 125 indicator" to show that the calculation should be done and reconciled. Sometimes this is overlooked and it is up to the tax adviser to point out the benefit to the taxpayer. HMRC provide a calculation worksheet HS300 to assist in the calculation to prove a non-UK resident individual is limited to the tax deducted at source such as that on UK property income, income from UK employment or self employment.

Example

Richard and Judy are non-UK resident in 2018-19 as Richard works full-time in Oman. They both have rental income from a buy to let amounting to net £10,000 but as a Form 17 has been submitted (having signed the declaration of deed on the property) the net rents are shared ¼ and ¾ respectively. Richard has a state pension, of £7,700, bank interest received gross of £10,500, dividends of £4,500. Judy has no other income other than rents.

Under the normal calculation the 2018-19 assessment would be:

	Richard	Judy
	£	£
State pension	7,700	
Net rents after expenses	5,000	15,000
Bank interest (gross)	10,500	
Dividends	4,500	
Less personal allowance	(11,850)	(11,850)
Taxable UK income	15,850	3,150
Tax payable	1,427	630

However, under "income disregard" the calculation to compare is:

	£	£
Net rents after expenses	5,000	15,000
Tax at basic rate 20%	1,000	3,000

Richard's income tax is lower under income disregard but Judy's income tax is higher. Therefore Judy's assessment is not reduced to the income disregard but Richard's assessment is amended to show the lower figure.

Note: In the first calculation above, the personal allowance of £11,850 is set against pension and rental income first and then any balance is set against the most tax beneficial source of income. This might be bank/building society interest or dividend income because an adviser would want to use the balance of allowance in the most beneficial way to take advantage of the savings rate band of £5,000 @ nil%, the personal savings allowance of £1,000 for basic rate taxpayers and the dividend allowance of £2,000 (£5,000 before 6 April 2017).

HMRC software does not always allocate the personal allowance in the most beneficial way so the figures should be reconciled as this could show the incorrect tax payable. As stated above, HMRC should be on the lookout for the income disregard calculation option as their manual states "Review and required update the reasons for the over/underpayment automatically selected by the system." HMRC acknowledged this in August 2017:

> "We have decided to make changes to the 2016-17 calculator in-year across our systems and interfaces. These changes

address the errors in the current calculator and will enable affected customers to be able to file online and receive the correct calculation. What will happen next? We are planning to implement this change in October 2017 and the exact date will be confirmed as soon as it is known. We are asking commercial software developers to deliver in-year updates to align with HMRC's systems, to avoid filing error submissions."

If the past consultation document "Restricting non-resident entitlement to UK personal allowances" ever becomes law then in the above case *both* Richard and Judy might be better off under the income disregard option. Currently personal allowance entitlement is available for an individual who is UK resident, or where the individual, at any time in the tax year:

- is a national of a European Economic Area state;
- is resident in the Isle of Man or Channel Islands;
- has previously resided in the UK but lives abroad for the sake of their own health or that of a member of their family who is resident with them;
- is a person who is or has been employed in the service of the Crown;
- is employed in the service of any territory under Her Majesty's protection;
- is employed in the service of a missionary society; or
- is a person whose late spouse/civil partner was employed in the service of the Crown.

The effect of the loss of personal allowance for non-residents and the option for the income disregard was not considered in the consultation.

Law: ITA 2007, s. 25(2), 56, 810, 811

Guidance: Form 17; Consultation document *Restricting non-resident entitlement to UK personal allowances*

6.3 Embassy registration

6.3.1 Introduction

When travelling or living abroad it is recommended that the British expat registers with the embassy, High Commission or consulate.

355

Most countries will have an embassy but in some smaller countries the British government's representation is through a High Commission or consulate. Registration is recommended because in cases of crisis (see below) the representation of British expats requiring assistance is usually provided by this extension of the British government overseas.

In certain countries where there is no embassy, consulate or High Commission the British expat can seek assistance from other nations represented (e.g. another EU member in that country) and there are also some informal agreements with Australia and New Zealand to assist British expats where there is no representation but where those two countries have representation.

All British expats going abroad should have a copy of "Support for British Nationals abroad: A guide" which is issued by the Foreign and Commonwealth Office.

Guidance: www.gov.uk/fco

6.3.2   The support

Coverage and support is provided in over 180 countries throughout the world but the guide is full of phrases such as "... there is no legal right to consular assistance. All assistance provided is at our discretion." The support that is offered is limited and there are many exclusions and provisos that limit that support, some of which are detailed further below.

The embassy in the foreign country will also give support for UK businesses that are looking to trade with the country in which the British expat is located. This can be helpful in getting a business off the ground but again the support only goes so far.

Worryingly, in a world that seems beset by natural disasters, the guide states:

> "Equally there may be some occasions – for example, natural catastrophe – where we cannot provide the usual kinds of help, or where we provide extra help when the Foreign Secretary has agreed to our doing so."

It is clear that expats should not be reliant on the embassy to bail them out of trouble and it is sensible to have insurances in place to cover these crisis events. Below are detailed the three main areas of crisis that may happen to a British expat abroad.

6.3.3   Kidnap/hostage situations

In such situations the local British embassy will work with the foreign government to secure release of the British expat. A team of advisers / civil servants in London act as caseworkers for the family and in some cases the British police will appoint a family liaison officer in the UK.

It is pertinent that the guide states that the British government "will not make substantive concessions to hostage takers" and these "concessions" are itemised as paying ransom, changing policy or releasing prisoners.

Help does extend to putting the family in touch with a charitable specialist agency called *Hostage UK*. The help offered is mainly as support for those family members who are not the kidnap victims. Direct support/intervention is mainly through such organisations as *Red24* who will directly assist policyholders in the country. See **4.2.4** (Kidnap, ransom and extortion).

Guidance: Hostage UK

6.3.4   Murder

Unfortunately the incidents of British expats being murdered abroad each year is on the rise and since 2010 over 400 have been registered. The first port of call for help is usually the British Embassy or consulate in whichever foreign country the incident has happened. Help is limited and it is suggested that "you get professional legal advice" and "we can put you in touch with ...".

Several incidents of murder of UK nationals in Spain seem to highlight deficiencies in what is perceived to be standard assistance from the UK government representatives abroad.

Example

Gary was attacked by 12 local men in Benalmadena, Spain, and was killed. Delays arose, with the result that eventually the Prime Minister at the time had to intervene. Stephen Twigg MP stated in Westminster on 11 December 2013:

"Our British consular staff deal with thousands of deaths of British nationals around the world, often in difficult, traumatic and complicated situations. They deserve praise for their work. More often than not the support from consular staff is of the highest standard. In this case, however, the Dunne family were left vulnerable; they felt alone and received little help."

6.3.5   National crises

Situations of crisis in a foreign country – e.g. civil unrest, terrorism or conflict – will elicit the following response:

> the FCO sending extra staff to the country to reinforce current Embassy staff numbers;

> work with the local authorities to support those British nationals affected;

> the setting up of an information hotline.

However, there are three types of crisis event where a large number of British nationals may have been killed or injured, e.g.:

- tsunami or hurricane;
- civil or political unrest; or
- other events causing hardship or disruption to large numbers of British nationals, such as volcanic eruption (e.g. Montserrat), collapse of a travel company (e.g. Monarch airlines), and airport shut downs (e.g. Venezuela – see below).

Support will only be provided for British Nationals, European Union nationals and certain Commonwealth nationals but not other countries' nationals (e.g. foreign wife or husband, even if they have been living lawfully in the UK).

A terrorist attack requires that the British Embassy put in place "exceptional assistance measures" but financial assistance is restricted and may not be provided if the expat has travelled to the country against FCO advice. In a pandemic the embassy will not be able to repatriate the expat. In cases of political or civil unrest the embassy may assist in providing additional transport out of the country but the expat will have to sign an "Undertaking to Repay" form. This will be extremely difficult if the country is beset by such problems as in the example below.

Example

At the time of writing, Venezuela is suffering from civil unrest and economic turmoil. The Venezuela situation is a "worst case scenario" for British expats because of a number of situations that have arisen as follows:

1. The border with Colombia is intermittently closed.

2. Airlines are refusing to fly in and out of Venezuela.

3. The risk of kidnapping of foreigners has been heightened beyond the normal high level.

4. There is a shortage of fuel.

5. Bribes are being solicited by authorities at Maiquetia (Caracas) International Airport.

6. UK health authorities have classified Venezuela as having a risk of Zika virus transmission.

Taking each point in order, the implications for a British expat in that country or a country with similar problems would be as follows:

1. Driving to Colombia is not possible as the border is closed to road traffic and only pedestrians are allowed to cross, which would mean leaving an abandoned car and having to carry possessions.

2. Many airlines have pulled out of Venezuela, so air travel to other countries is restricted and difficult to obtain. Further airlines are expected to pull out soon.

3. Drug running and disparate armed groups are active along the border with Colombia, and kidnappings are common as is violent crime. (Venezuela has one of the highest murder rates in the world.)

4. Fuel is in short supply because of the economic situation and also intermittent petrol shortages throughout Venezuela which makes transport unreliable and most fuel when available is low-grade (91-octane) petrol.

5. Having to bribe an immigration official to leave the country is sometimes necessary, otherwise the expat will not be able to leave the country on one of the few airlines still operating. However, embassy official policy on bribing is that it is illegal and the expat could become liable to prosecution in the UK even though in Venezuela it may be the only way of securing an exit from the country. See **6.8.1** (Bribery and corruption).

6. If a pandemic exists it will be virtually impossible to get out of the country by normal means.

Finally, if the expat was considering leaving Venezuela by boat the advice is that there have been incidents of piracy and armed robbery directed at boats in and around Venezuela's waters, especially east of Puerto La Cruz and in waters between Venezuela and Trinidad!

6.4   Remittances home

6.4.1   General considerations

One of the questions most frequently asked by British expats is whether they will end up with a tax liability in the UK if they remit funds back to the UK. This is an issue particularly for those expats whose family who have remained in the UK and who need to be supported, and for those with UK mortgages or other liabilities that need to be paid.

For an individual who is non-resident, the answer is "no" – the amounts he transfers back into the UK will not attract UK tax. If he is non-resident the remittance basis of taxing overseas income and gains (see **8.7**) does not apply – it only applies to resident individuals who are not UK domiciled (see **2.1**). Hence, any overseas income received while the individual is non-resident – interest on foreign bank accounts, dividends from foreign companies, rental income from rental property located overseas, and so on – will not attract UK tax if the money is later remitted into the UK, even if the person is resident at the time.

Whether earnings are taxable in the UK depends on the individual's circumstances at the time the earnings are earned, and on what they are "for". This means that if the individual was not resident at the time the work was performed, and if it was performed overseas and not in the UK, then none of the earnings will be taxed in the UK. Such earnings will therefore not attract UK tax if remitted back to the UK, even if the individual is once more resident in the UK at the time of the remittance. This would apply, for example, to a bonus that related to an individual's time working overseas, but that was received after he had returned to live in the UK and so was resident again (assuming it was a straightforward bonus with no conditions attached).

Even for earnings that are for work performed in the UK when the individual was non-resident, or all the individual's earnings when he was resident in the UK (e.g. in the year of departure or arrival that does not qualify for split-year treatment and where exemption is not available under a double tax treaty), remitting these earnings into the UK will not cause an additional UK tax liability to arise. This is because these earnings will already have been taxed in the UK, regardless of whether or not they are brought into the country. If earnings are exempt from UK tax under a double tax treaty, bringing them into the UK will not cause the loss of this exemption.

The only time the remittance basis of taxing overseas income and gains will be relevant is for an individual who is domiciled overseas but resident in the UK. This will not be the case for most British expats living overseas (see **8.7**).

6.4.2   *Exchange/currency controls*

UK expats are generally used to free movement and transfer of capital sums anywhere they choose. The UK does not impose capital transfer restrictions (although this has not always been the case). Other countries do impose exchange control restrictions and non-adherence could result in the expat being in serious trouble.

Exchange control was introduced into the UK shortly before the outbreak of the 1939/45 war but was abolished on 24 October 1979. Since then, an individual has been able to transfer money in and out of the UK without restriction, subject to adhering to money laundering regulations. Some other countries still need official government authorisation to import and export currency.

When going abroad to work, an individual may be paid:

1. wholly in the local currency; or
2. partly in the local currency with the rest in US dollars or in sterling.

In the case of (1) above, there may be some compensation if there is an alteration in the exchange rate such that the currency falls below a benchmark, but this would be determined according to the contract terms (see **1.3.2** – Employment contracts). Countries can devalue their currency on an economic whim, e.g. Switzerland which devalued its currency in 2011 because it was massively overvalued. These sorts of unilateral actions by a country can, of course, cause financial difficulties for the expat resident in that country on a local salary.

British expats should become adept at familiarising themselves with the exchange rates on a monthly or even daily basis when considering transfers of currency to and from the UK. Retaining a UK bank account is beneficial for keeping credit facilities open and ensuring the credit on return to the UK. Currency exchange rate fluctuations can cause financial difficulties whilst abroad, and a slump in a foreign currency's value can last for several years (see the example below). Fluctuations in exchange rates can make a big difference to an expatriate's income, especially where substantial outgoings are involved such as rents, medical bills and schooling costs.

Example

The 1997 Asian financial crisis resulted from a series of currency devaluations, together with the Thai currency market failing because of the Thai government's decision not to peg the local currency (baht) to the US$. This had a contagious effect and spread throughout South Asia, resulting in stock markets dropping and in escalating economic problems. Currencies dropped by as much as 38%, and some stock markets fell 60%. The effect also spread to Western countries, but not to such a large extent.

Consider, therefore, the internationally mobile employee (IME) having been offered a job in Singapore in the early part of 1997. Suppose that he arrived just at the time of the float of the Thai baht, to see the Singapore dollar depreciate against the US dollar from US$1.43 to US$1.75 in January 1998, i.e. a decline of 18.3% (which was less than other regional currencies: 70% in the case of Indonesian rupiah and 35% for the Philippine peso). This would have an impact on the individual's standard of living and throw into question his or her ethos of going to work abroad. One saving grace would be that assets in a UK bank account could help supplement the shortfall in the host country in such circumstances (see **6.2.3** – Keeping UK accounts).

Also, whilst the UK cannot introduce exchange control restrictions without Parliamentary approval, other less developed nations can do so on a whim, which would affect the ability of expats to move capital in and out of the country.

About 20% of the world's countries impose exchange control restrictions. The list of countries with such restrictions will most likely grow and, as happened in Cyprus, currency withdrawal restrictions can be implemented through the banks overnight or over a weekend, so that all accounts are frozen by the government.

Certain articles of agreement in the International Monetary Fund allow countries classed as "transitional economies" to use exchange control restrictions, such as article 14, section 2 below:

> "A member that has notified the Fund that it intends to avail itself of transitional arrangements under this provision may, notwithstanding the provisions of any other articles of this Agreement, maintain and adapt to changing circumstances the restrictions on payments and transfers for current international transactions that were in effect on the date on which it became a member."

6.4.3   Currency gain taxation

Currency other than sterling is a chargeable asset and its disposal can give rise to a chargeable gain or an allowable loss. Foreign currency bank accounts can also give rise to chargeable gains or allowable losses for periods up to 5 April 2012, but now exemption is available to individuals in respect of currency acquired for personal expenditure outside the UK.

Often currency will be acquired and/or disposed of in the course of a transaction involving other chargeable assets, for example, on the sale of shares or a house abroad for foreign currency. It is important to recognise the currency as a chargeable asset in its own right and to deal with it accordingly.

The *Knight* UK tax case (see below) highlighted the importance of correctly accounting for capital disposals in foreign currency. The two taxpayers, under the Lichtenstein Disclosure Facility, stated that they had purchased a Swiss property in August 1998 and disposed of the property in January 2010, and this included a number of expenses incurred in relation to the property. This was all done in Swiss francs.

The taxpayers calculated the gain in Swiss francs, then multiplied the gain by the exchange rate applicable at disposal to produce the chargeable gain in sterling. HMRC contended that the correct method was to convert each item into sterling at the appropriate exchange rate in force when the item was earned/incurred, then to calculate the gain in sterling. It had already been decided previously that the HMRC method was the correct method and the case was lost. In practice this would have the effect in the example below.

Example

Lewis lives and works in London. He purchases a house in Provo in the Turks and Caicos Islands for US$1million (the local currency used is the US$) when the exchange rate is £1 to US$1.5. He then sells the property a few years later, just after Brexit, for US$1.5 million when the exchange rate is £1 to US$1.2.

He appears to have made a gain of half a million US$, exchanged at US$1.2 to £1 = £416,666. He also incurred legal expenses, estate agents' fees and advertising costs, as well as an airfare from London, travelling to Provo to sign over the title deeds on exchange of contracts. Stamp duty was paid by Lewis at 10% on the original purchase price.

When the house was acquired, its sterling equivalent after allowable deductions was US$1 million @ 1.5 = £666,666. When sold, the figure after deductions was equivalent to US$1.5 million @ 1.2 =

£1.25 million. So the gain is actually £583,334 (i.e. £1.25 million – £666,666) not £416,666!

The exchange rate used would be the spot rates on the days of purchase and disposal. HMRC's periodically published average rate of exchange should not be used in this instance.

The Turks and Caicos Islands do not impose capital gains tax but Lewis has to report the chargeable gain on his self-assessment return and pay the tax by 31 January following the tax year of sale.

Taxpayers should ensure they account for non-sterling items correctly when calculating CGT. Also, allowable expenses and disbursements would include professional fees (solicitors, estate agents), stamp duty and advertising, but the airfare would not necessarily be allowed.

Law: TCGA 1992, s. 38(1)
Cases: *Bentley v Pike* [1981] STC 360; *Knight v HMRC* [2016] UKFTT 819 (TC)
Guidance: CG 78310-78314, 78315

6.5 Foreign tax compliance

6.5.1 Introduction

Foreign tax compliance in the country of residence for the retiree working expat is important as can be seen from **8.1** (Tax departure certificates/sailing permits). On arrival the expat should explore the requirements to register with the local tax office. See **6.5.2** (Local accountants) below.

For instance, it was mentioned at **4.1.5** (Double tax treaty relief) that Israel's tax laws to a new immigrant allow pension income (i.e. any non-Israeli income) to be excluded from tax in Israel for the first ten years of residence. This is similar in other countries provided that the expat follows the correct procedures. See, for example, **4.1.12** (New Zealand).

In the case of Israel there are seven conditions necessary to benefit from the 10-year exemption. These are that the taxpayer:

- must be resident in Israel at least 142 days each year;
- must spend no more total days in another country;

365

- must be permanently resident;
- must not originally have elected for an initial acclimatisation year;
- must provide a letter of non-UK residence from HMRC; and
- these conditions must be met for four full years.

It is also a requirement that the spouse should be resident.

Whilst tax treaties have been modelled on the original OECD template, each one the UK has with other countries may be different on specific matters (see **6.5.3** below).

6.5.2   Local accountants

On arrival in the foreign jurisdiction, expats should ensure that they appoint a local accountant/tax adviser almost immediately.

In many countries there is local representation by the world's major accountants such as KPMG, EY, PwC, etc., who will also have international tax advisers on the payroll.

Local accountants will in many cases only be familiar with local tax compliance and as such will not be wise to the broader international tax implications of what an expat may do in terms of investment, house purchase, etc. For instance, for an expat investing in an offshore personal portfolio bond and returning to the UK there may be an annual cumulative 15% charge (see **8.4.1** Offshore bonds) and this will not necessarily be known to an accountant in the foreign jurisdiction. Fees will vary between accountants in the foreign jurisdiction and a simply prepared tax return may be one third of the price the expat would pay in the UK for such a service.

Certain financial advisers have tax qualifications under the Chartered Insurance Institute (CII) and have the appropriate competence under examination by passing the CII Advanced Financial Planning paper AF1 Personal Tax and Trust Planning. Others will be both Chartered Institute of Taxation and Society of Trust and Estate Practitioners qualified. Jurisdictions such as Dubai, Abu Dhabi, Hong Kong and Singapore have financial advisory firms and may have such specialists as part of their service of financial advice. Taxation advice charges will depend on whether commissions are derived from the expat's investment profile with the company.

The expat may want to ensure that he has representation of accountancy and tax advice in the UK whilst he or she is abroad. This is a good idea but if his affairs are complex it is necessary to appoint a firm with expat handling experience as this is a highly specialist area. The adviser will have to be well versed in the latest rules on NRCGT (see **3.2** – Capital gains on selling UK property), residence (at **2.2** – Residence), etc.

6.5.3   Double tax treaties

The UK has many double tax treaties with other countries based on the OECD model treaty. However, as has been detailed in **4.1** (Pensions), many of the double tax treaties treat different sources of income in different ways so an understanding of the double tax treaty and its implications is important.

For instance the treaty with Colombia was signed in 2016 but has yet to come into force and whilst the treaty with Mexico has been in force for many years it does not give personal allowances in the non-discrimination article 25, as follows:

> "(5) Nothing contained in this Article shall be construed as obliging either Contracting State to grant to individuals not resident in that State any of the personal allowances, reliefs and reductions for tax purposes which are granted to individuals so resident or to its nationals."

The treaties with Hong Kong and Mexico are the same, whereas other treaties allow the claim for personal allowances, so advisers should look at the treaty provisions to check this for their clients. Some double tax treaties have been in place for many years whereas others, such as the United Arab Emirates (UAE) one, are new (1 January 2017). Article 17 states:

> "(1) Subject to the provisions of paragraph 2 of Article 18, pensions and other similar remuneration paid to a resident of a Contracting State shall be taxable only in that State."

Therefore, under the terms of the double tax treaty, an expat drawing a pension from the UK at the age of 55 onwards can apply for an NT code and receive the pension gross but as they are a resident of the UAE which has no income tax they will not pay tax on the pension. It could be said that this is tantamount to tax avoidance but the simple truth is that this is what the double tax treaty allows.

In addition, there are also different inheritance / estate duty taxes double tax treaties with some countries of the world (see **2.1.7** Historical treaties). These, too, all have different implications for deemed domiciles from April 2017.

There are also tax information agreements in force with many jurisdictions. And some countries have no agreements in place with the UK and therefore there could be "double taxing".

Following Brexit there may be amendments to certain treaties that then facilitate inward investment to the UK but this remains to be explored.

Law: ITA 2007, s. 56(3); Tax treaty non-discrimination art. 22 (5); Italy (SI 1968/304), Pakistan (SI 1957/1522), Ireland (SI 1978/1107), USA (SI 1979/998) and France (SI 1963/1319)

6.5.4   *Common reporting standard (CRS)*

A "requirement to correct" (RTC) in terms of tax was included in the F(No.2)A 2017 which requires taxpayers having outstanding offshore tax non-compliance as at 5 April 2017 to correct the position on or before 30 September 2018, which is prior to the wholesale adoption of the CRS and higher penalties from 1 October 2018. More details are expected imminently as regards procedure. It applies RTC to income tax, capital gains tax and inheritance tax. A taxpayer who does not comply will have a "failure to correct" (FTC) penalty imposed, being a penal set of sanctions for offshore tax evasion in respect of outstanding years that have not been corrected. Note that if declared ahead of the 30 September deadline then the taxpayer will pay the tax, interest and penalties under the current rules. The "asset moves penalty" (FA 2015, Sch. 21) and the "asset based penalty" (FA 2016, Sch. 22) will also both apply to any FTC.

The new penalties that will be applied look at:

- the "behaviour category" – i.e. whether the omission was careless, deliberate, or deliberate with concealment; and
- the "territory category" – i.e. the jurisdiction where the assets are held.

Ideally the tax adviser has a client who has been careless but who, on realising such, makes an unprompted disclosure thereby possibly having no penalties imposed; but having said this, HMRC have the power to impose a careless error penalty of up to 30 per cent of the undisclosed tax. Taxpayers committing deliberate evasion with *concealment* could pay the standard FTC penalty of 200% of the tax, which can be reduced down to 100% upon review of the quality of the disclosure, the level of disclosure and the seriousness of the offence.

The time limits for reporting a "failure to correct" matter have been extended so that HMRC can assess tax up until 5 April 2021. So in the cases of:

1. FTC despite reasonable care being taken – all years 2013-14 onwards, i.e. seven years up to 2020-21;
2. FTC is careless – all years 2011-12 onwards, i.e. nine years up to 2020-21; and
3. FTC is deliberate – all years 1997-98 onwards, i.e. 23 years up to 2020-21.

Reasonable excuse defence

The F(No.2)A 2017, Sch. 18, para. 23 (1) states:

"Liability to a penalty under paragraph 1 does not arise in relation to a particular failure to correct any relevant offshore tax non-compliance within the RTC period if the person concerned satisfies HMRC or the relevant tribunal (as the case may be) that there is a reasonable excuse for the failure."

Example 1

Anthony was domiciled in the UK at the time of his death in 2012, although resident in the Bahamas. Anthony's son Henry was his sole heir and was executor of Anthony's estate. The estate inherited by Henry included £250,000 relating to a beach front plot of land on the island of Andros.

As part of his inheritance, Henry took control of the assets following Anthony's death. Henry did not disclose the land on Andros in the Bahamas as part of Anthony's estate when it was declared to HMRC. However, now he has come to sell it the purchaser has hired an attorney to determine the validity of the title and check encumbrances to the title.

The attorney searches for any unpaid real estate taxes or claims resulting from a civil action against the vendor, such as unpaid real estate taxes and judgments in a civil action connected with the real estate of the creditor, which would expose the buyer to liability for the amount of the unfulfilled claim. Henry's attorney therefore recommends that he declare the inheritance of the Andros land in the UK to determine validity of title in the UK. Henry's failure, as executor, to disclose the land as part of Anthony's estate is an offshore matter as the property was held in a territory outside the UK, i.e. Andros in the Bahamas.

The failure to declare the property as part of Anthony's estate must be corrected under the RTC. It is also deliberate evasion with concealment unless Henry or his advisers can persuade HMRC otherwise! This may be by way of the worldwide disclosure facility (WDF) or the RTC.

Example 2

Taxpayers in the UK are approached to invest in a scheme that has set up a research and development laboratory in the Borneo jungle to find a vaccine to combat dengue virus by studying the immunity of the indigenous population. Investors in the partnership share offer, mostly HNWIs, pay 20% direct cash and there is an 80% loan organised by the partnership. The partnership claimed a first year trading loss of £193 million and this was shared amongst the partners who claimed tax relief in total of £77 million. In the accompanying documents on the partnership offer was a letter from one of the major accountants stating the tax advantages of the investment and giving details of how to claim the relief against other income on personal tax returns.

Edwin, who is an investor, learns of the failure in the film investment scheme in a court case won by HMRC and notices the scheme is very similar to the one he is in through the partnership. He becomes worried and contacts a tax adviser who confirms that the scheme is an "avoidance arrangement", i.e. an arrangement where it is reasonable to conclude that the main purpose, or one of the main purposes, is the obtaining of a tax advantage. The new advice given by the tax adviser after the avoidance arrangement has taken place cannot be related to the facilitation of the initial avoidance arrangement.

If Edwin had relied solely on the original advice, he would not have a reasonable excuse; this is because the advice would have been disqualified as it was given by an interested person, as the accountancy firm involved in facilitating the avoidance arrangements was paid a fee for that work. Therefore there will be no disqualification on the grounds of it being from an interested person who gave the original advice.

HMRC are likely to accept that Edwin had obtained, and followed, independent advice about the avoidance arrangements from someone with the appropriate expertise: HMRC will accept that anyone who is a member of a UK-recognised legal, accountancy or tax advisory body will have the appropriate expertise to give advice on UK tax matters. As the advice took account of all of his relevant individual circumstances he would then have had a reasonable excuse for not making the correction and no FTC penalty would be applied.

It is also perfectly acceptable for an adviser to offer a second opinion on a potential avoidance arrangement. This will not be included as disqualified advice, in which case the transaction may properly be categorised as innocent error. It is important to note that a taxpayer will not be able to rely on the automatic defence of having taken professional advice because the advice may be disqualified for various reasons under para. 23 (3).

The view on tax relief from the original accountants would probably be classed as arrangements which accord with established practice, and would be on the basis that HMRC had, at the time the arrangements were entered into, indicated their acceptance of that practice.

HMRC state if a taxpayer is unsure, or is unable to obtain a second opinion on advice that he has previously taken, then HMRC will discuss the technicalities in conjunction with their specialist team. In these circumstances the penalty could be reduced.

Law: *Finance (No. 2) Act* 2017, s. 67, and Sch. 18

Guidance: HMRC's *Requirement to Correct tax due on offshore assets*

6.6   Buying or leasing property

6.6.1   General considerations

When the expat leaves the UK to work or live abroad he or she will have the option of buying a property or leasing. Many countries (e.g. Philippines and Bali, Indonesia) will not allow foreigners to own land although they will be allowed to lease condominiums.

Some countries such as Malaysia and Australia will impose capital gains tax liabilities on the sale of property assets and this should be factored into an expat's calculation if he or she is on a short to medium term contract. In Malaysia the purchase of a property is subject to real property gains tax (RPGT) for locals as well as expats but after five years locals do not pay RPGT. An expat will initially have a 30% charge tapering down to a minimum 5% liability indefinitely after five years. Also, surprisingly if a spouse inherits a property from his or her deceased spouse that transfer will be exempt but if the property is sold within five years the same RPGT charges will apply. This makes it difficult for grieving spouses to sell up and leave the country without incurring a 30% RPGT charge.

It is clear, therefore, that when purchasing foreign property the long term tax liabilities and restrictions should be considered before entering into the contract.

In Australia new rules have been introduced for foreign residential capital gains withholding tax (FRCGW) for contracts entered into from 1 July 2017. These rules apply a withholding tax on property disposals where the contract price exceeds AU$750,000 so that a withholding tax of 12.5% is retained. The foreign resident seller must submit a tax return in Australia at the end of the financial year showing any gain from the disposal and credit will be given for the 12.5% withholding tax. The foreign resident seller of the property can apply for a variation of the withholding rate in certain circumstances. Only an Australian resident entity (solicitors, tax agents and others) can obtain a clearance certificate.

As far as leasing property is concerned, in many parts of the world the lease agreement "is not worth the paper it is written on". As in the UK, a foreign landlord will draw up a lease agreement which may seem to cover all matters pertaining to deposits, repairs, replacements, early surrender, maintenance, etc., but on making a claim the landlord may prevaricate and imply that the problem is not covered by the lease agreement or that the fault is that of the lessee to be paid for by the lessee. Subsequent termination of the lease, either prematurely or otherwise, often results in a retention of the deposit to "make good" spurious faults left by the tenant expat. As the expat has little time to argue the case before his next posting, the deposit is usually foregone.

6.6.2   Expat clauses

The insertion of an "expat clause" is often included in the lease agreement so that should the assignee's overseas employment be terminated prematurely the lease agreement will end within two months. Foreign landlords find the concept of an expat clause alien but it is important to ensure this is part of the agreement as a protective measure:

a)   Produces to the Landlord satisfactory written evidence of such transfer posting or termination or rejection of work permit;

b)   Gives the Landlord at least TWO (2) months notice in writing of such termination or rejection or gives the Landlord TWO (2) months rental in lieu of such notice;

c)   PROVIDED ALWAYS that the right to exercise the clause may only be invoked after a period of TWELVE MONTHS (12) from the commencement of this tenancy.

6.7   Foreign wills

6.7.1   Significance

It is vital that a will in the foreign jurisdiction covering assets there is made as quickly as possible after arrival. The process of re-sealing a foreign will in the UK can be time consuming and expensive and if the individual has assets in many different countries the cost and delay can be exacerbated. (Many years ago, when the British Empire covered one third of the world and was administered by British civil servants and entrepreneurs who were located in the "Colonies", it was important that their wills drafted there would be acceptable in the UK on their death. The re-sealing process allows reciprocal re-sealing in many countries that were colonies, protectorates or territories, so the *Colonial Probates Act* 1892 was introduced).

In England a similar situation arises where a valid will has been made and registered under the *Wills Act* 1837; provided the will has been executed properly (e.g. witnesses should not benefit) the named beneficiaries will benefit after debts, losses and funeral/administrative expenses. It should be noted that *The Administration of Estates (Small Payments) Act* 1965 ensures that assets not exceeding £5,000 are distributed without the need for grant. It was expected that this figure would be increased to £50,000 but this has been deferred following criticism of the proposed probate fee increases.

On intestacy a surviving spouse is entitled to the grant of letters of administration in priority to all others and will receive all personal chattels, £250,000 absolutely and a life interest in one half of the residue. Any issue will receive one half of the residue plus the other half of residue on the death of the parent. In these cases, if the surviving spouse benefits by reason of will or intestacy he or she will be exempt from tax under the inter-spousal exemption, whereas the children and others inheritance will be chargeable to tax at 40% after deduction of any available nil rate band. Any lack of will or valid marriage certificate could result in a heavy tax bill.

A US domiciled citizen has a potential maximum estate tax of 40% but a US citizen's US spouse may receive unlimited marital transfers free of estate tax after debts, losses and funeral/administrative expenses which in this case could be substantial. However, under the Uniform Probate Code adopted by many states where there is no valid will and the individual dies intestate then the rules become complicated commonly with the spouse obtaining one half of the community property. If the surviving spouse is the father of the child(ren) he receives the entire intestate estate but if there was no recognised marriage certificate then the estate would go to the deceased's descendants by reason of legal claim. As a consequence, a potentially large US estate tax bill could arise.

Law: *Administration of Estates Act* 1925, s. 47(1); *Inheritance Tax Act* 1984, s. 18

6.7.2   Re-sealing a foreign will

The *Colonial Probates Act* 1892 allows for application for grant of representation in certain territories and countries of the world where someone has died and has UK assets. The reciprocal territories/countries must be within those mandated by the UK's *Colonial Probates Act* 1892 and *Colonial Probates (Protected States and Mandated Territories) Act* 1927, which lists the territories/countries that are signatories (see below). These are mostly commonwealth and former commonwealth countries such as Zimbabwe (formerly Rhodesia), etc.

If the deceased died in a non-recognised re-sealing country, the probate process is different when applied, e.g. the United States, Switzerland, Germany, Ireland, Spain, France, but see also EU Succession below.

The requirements for re-sealing will be Court sealed documents issued in the deceased's country, together with a translation if not in English. Once these documents have been obtained the probate registry may well request an affidavit of foreign law which is the sworn statement from a lawyer in the deceased's country which addresses in detail the legal process that has been followed in the deceased's country. It must be signed by a lawyer conversant with the laws of the country in which the deceased died.

A list of countries/territories whose probate documents can be re-sealed in England may be found on the Worldwide Lawyers website.

Example

John leaves the UK to work in Malaysia and joins the Kuala Lumpur chapter of the Hash House Harriers (a jungle running club). He is lost in the jungle on a weekend hash and is never found after an extensive search.

John never had a will drawn up in Malaysia but had a UK will leaving his assets to his parents. John had assets in the UK and Malaysia. His parents applied for an order in the UK under section 1 of the *Presumption of Death Act* 2013, and this was granted.

Whilst the process of re-sealing a UK will in Malaysia is easier than applying for a brand new grant of probate there is another problem in a situation of a missing body in Malaysia; the National Registration Department will not issue a death certificate because s. 18 of the *Births and Deaths Registration Act* 1957 requires a dead body to be found before registration, a similar position to the UK prior to the enactment of the *Presumption of Death Act* 2013. See the Malaysian *Evidence Act* 1950, s. 108.

375

Therefore there is a period of seven years before application to the High Court can be made. In Italy the period of waiting on presumption of death is 20 years and France 10 years.

Example

Alec has been living and working in the US for a number of years and dies there with a US will but does not have a UK will. He does, however, have a share portfolio with a London stockbroker with assets amounting to £100,000.

Unfortunately, as US probate cannot be re-sealed in the UK, this means that to release assets in the UK a new application will need to be made in the UK.

Typically, when making the application for probate in the UK, an affidavit of law signed by a US attorney will be required which sets out the legal process that has been followed in the US State Court. As a result of this, to obtain probate in the UK, lawyers would require the sealed and certified court papers issued in the US (the letters of testamentary and will), death certificate and details of the UK assets to be collected.

Application to re-seal a foreign will in the UK may be made by an individual, through a solicitor or a probate practitioner, i.e. notary public or barrister. Normally an individual must apply to the Registry or sub-Registry and will have to attend at least one appointment for oath before the grant is administered to him or her. In the case of foreign wills in acceptable jurisdictions covered by the *Colonial Probates Act* 1892 attendance is not required to swear an oath but the following needs to be supplied:

- the original grant or an official duplicate, or exemplification together with an official copy of the will;
- two copies of the above;
- the form PA1;
- an official copy of the death certificate;
- a written request from each of the grantees for the grant to be re-sealed and confirming that the deceased was domiciled in the country in which the grant was issued. This request can be addressed to the court or it can

authorise a named individual or firm of solicitors to apply on their behalf;

- a form IHT207 *unless*:
  - the assets in the UK exceed £150,000;
  - the deceased died before 6th April 2002; or
  - if any one of the boxes on page one of the form IHT 207 has been ticked then IHT421 (this is part of form IHT400) should be submitted.
- an application fee of £155.00 plus £0.50 for each copy of the grant required. Payment by cheque should be made payable to Her Majesty's Courts Service (HMCTS is an acceptable abbreviation). Where the net estate does not exceed £50,000 the application fee is not payable, but copies must be paid for.

The questions to be answered may need a substantial amount of research into the deceased's past if this is not immediately known to the executor(s) or those entitled to a grant.

For instance, PA1 at question D8 asks whether the deceased's domicile was England and Wales at the date of death and, if not, where was the domicile? Clearly this may not be easily ascertained and the importance of this is substantial in calculating the IHT liability that may arise as a result of completion of another form required at the same time, i.e. IHT 400. A person may have altered his or her domicile of *origin* to a domicile of *choice* for many reasons including mitigation of tax, i.e. by choosing a foreign country, or a foreign spouse choosing the UK to benefit from the inter-spousal IHT exemption. It is sometimes very difficult to prove that domicile of choice supersedes that of origin. A person may go to extraordinary lengths to alter his or her domicile of origin and to all intents and purposes have done so to relatives and friends but in the eyes of HMRC he or she may still be deemed to be UK domiciled. See **2.1.1** (Domicile). An incorrect assessment of the deceased's domicile may have severe consequences at a later date.

See *Gulliver* where HMRC at paragraph 12 required the provision of substantial supportive documentation as evidence of domicile of choice of Hong Kong:

"Having opened their enquiry into Mr Gulliver's tax return, HMRC have sent him requests for a large amount of information and a large number of documents. On 11 October 2016, they sent a formal notice under the provisions of Schedule 36 of the Finance Act 2008 requesting answers to 123 questions and the provision of 33 categories of document. These requests were not limited to matters arising after 4 March 2003 (the date of the Letter) and involved a searching examination of a number of aspects of his personal and professional life dating back to 1981."

For a comprehensive list of documents required by HMRC see the *Residence, Domicile and Remittance Basis Manual* at RDRM 23080.

Law: *The Non-Contentious Probate Fees Order* 2017; 1990 Uniform Probate Code (US)
Case: *Gulliver v HMRC* [2017] UKFTT 222 (TC)
Guidance: http://worldwidelawyers.co.uk/2015/12/23/resealing-grants-of-probate-and-releasing-inheritance-in-the-uk/

6.7.3   Brussels IV

The European Union succession rules ("Brussels IV") apply within the agreeing EU member states from 17 August 2015. However, the UK along with Ireland and Denmark agreed an opt out and so there is the option when drawing up a will related to EU assets that the UK rules will apply but this must be stipulated in the will drafted by the notary. At paragraph 38 it states:

"This Regulation should enable citizens to organise their succession in advance by choosing the law applicable to their succession. That choice should be limited to the law of a State of their nationality in order to ensure a connection between the deceased and the law chosen and to avoid a law being chosen with the intention of frustrating the legitimate expectations of persons entitled to a reserved share."

Example

David is a UK born and bred domiciliary living in France and owns property in both those jurisdictions. He dies without having made a will.

In this case, France will apply the rules in the EU Regulation. As David died habitually resident in France, France will apply forced heirship law (*réserve héréditaire*), to both the English and French property. However, the English courts are unlikely to accept this and will apply English intestacy law to the English property because it is immoveable property located in England.

This will lead to uncertainty and potential dispute if David had wanted to override French forced heirship rules for his English property. To avoid such issues, David could have elected via his British nationality for English law to apply in a French will, so that France would have applied English law to his estate as a whole.

Law: EU regulation no. 650/2012

6.7.4   Forced heirship

Many offshore jurisdictions have forced heirship rules which have a set devolvement. In some civil law countries, such as France, there is a set distribution requirement or, similarly, in Islamic countries the devolvement follows Sharia law. These will not necessarily be what the deceased would have wanted.

Example

Sam has not made a will. He lives in Dubai, has purchased a condominium and has a car there which he bought when he arrived.

In the UAE a non-Muslim can register a will locally within Dubai International Financial Centre (DIFC guidelines), Wills and Probate Registry. Assets are normally frozen immediately on death so his car, condominium and bank account will be inaccessible. Normally, with no DIFC will, Sharia law applies and that provides under forced heirship rules that a surviving wife who has children (see also "Guardianship of minors" at **6.7.5** below) qualifies for one eighth of the estate and the balance goes to family members. This may take many months or even years to resolve.

So, his girlfriend will not benefit from his estate and even if they held assets jointly the UAE does not have the right of survivorship whereby assets pass directly to the joint owner. Sam should have executed a will in accordance with DIFC requirements immediately on arrival. (Law number 15 of 2017.)

The following principles apply for DIFC arrangements for an expat who is residing there:

- the testator must be over 20 years old and not be Muslim;
- it deals with assets in Dubai only;
- it must be written, and signed in front by the Registrar or his authorised officer;
- executors must be over 20 years old;
- the testator must intend DIFC law to apply; and
- executors and guardians mentioned in the will must agree to comply with DIFC probate rules by attending in person or by way of witness statement.

6.7.5   *Guardianship of minors*

In the case of the married couple dying together (or within a short period of one another) the question of who acts as guardian for the surviving children can cause problems if there is no provision in the will or if there is no will.

The Emirates States also have certain strict rules regarding the guardianship of minors in cases of divorce and these apply to British expats in these situations. See **8.5.5** (Divorce).

In Dubai, if minor children are residing there with their parents, guardianship in a case of both parents becoming deceased will pass automatically to the husband's family unless there is a valid DIFC will registered that states otherwise.

See also the section in the wills questionnaire at **Appendix 2**.

6.8   Bribery Act 2010

6.8.1   *Bribery and corruption*

The UK's *Bribery Act* 2010 came into force on 1 July 2011 and whilst it mainly covers acts committed in the UK it also applies to similar actions of bribery committed abroad. The act covers individuals and business as follows:

- Sections 1 and 2: Bribing (Cases 1-2) by way of offering or promising to give a financial or other advantage for the purpose of bringing about an improper performance of a function or activity. Being bribed (Cases 3-6) by requesting, agreeing or receiving a financial (or other) advantage for bringing about the improper performance of a function or activity. It also covers requesting, agreeing to or receiving an advantage either directly or through a third party.

- Section 6: Bribing foreign public officials by offering, promising or giving financial (or other) advantage to a foreign public official where such an inducement is not allowed under the laws applying to that foreign official. The inducement must be intended to obtain business or a business advantage (see Example below).

- Sections 7 and 8: Failure of commercial organisations to prevent bribery if an individual associated with the organisation bribes another individual with intent to obtain, retain business (or an advantage) for their organisation. The meaning of "associated with" refers to an individual who performs services for the organisation e.g. employee, agent or subsidiary (see Example below).

- Section 12: Territorial application applies to British nationals or someone who is ordinarily resident in the UK, to an incorporated body in the UK and to Scottish partnerships.

- Section 13: Defences for certain bribery offences are limited to the proper exercise of any function of an intelligence service, or the proper exercise of any function of the armed forces when engaged on active service.

In many parts of the world businesses function on both low level and high level bribery. In Indonesia "coffee money" is the expected norm and "rasuah" in Malaysia is commonplace, without which business applications and formalities are rejected or delayed. Clearly Western business practices are at a disadvantage when they, rightly, refuse to entertain such practices. It is therefore important to have procedures in place to protect the employee and business from such practices in order that the penalties are not applied, i.e. the maximum for individuals is 10 years' imprisonment and an unlimited fine, and companies similarly face an unlimited fine. The publicity can also be damaging, as illustrated by the recent report in the US by the National Association of State Boards of Accountancy (NASBA):

> "KPMG's discovery that it had received advance information of which engagements would be inspected by the Public Company Accounting Oversight Board led to its firing of five partners, plus another staff member, and contacting both the Securities and Exchange Commission and the Public Company Accounting Oversight Board. One of KPMG's employees who had previously worked for the PCAOB had received the leaked advance warnings from a PCAOB staff member."

Law: *Bribery Act* 2010
Guidance: NASBA State Board Report, May 2017

6.8.2   *Company policy*

Company policy for its staff regarding these offences should be clear in the company handbook. In addition, international assignees are likely to come into contact with such "opportunities" when transacting business abroad, especially in parts of the world where bribery and corruption are endemic. For those with a low corruption risk a simple requirement in the employee contract is necessary, such as:

> "The employee will not participate in any way whatsoever in any corrupt acts, including bribery [*Bribery Act* 2010] extortion, fraud, embezzlement, money laundering, tax evasion (*The Criminal Finances Act* 2017) or similar acts. Any such incident or approaches by other parties to enter into such arrangements should be reported to [Department] immediately in writing. In the event of a breach of the preceding requirement the Company will have the right to terminate this contract of employment with immediate effect by giving notice in writing. The employee will indemnify the Company for any liability or loss suffered by the Company due to a breach by the employee of this clause."

For those with a high corruption risk a more complex employee contract is necessary that incorporates the following points:

- clauses re preventing corruption, covering gifts, hospitality, entertainment, facilitation payments, fraud, bribes, tax evasion, etc., and compliance with anti corruption laws and regulations;

- confirmation of no previous convictions for fraud, bribery, money laundering, etc.;
- affirmation of regular attendance on money laundering, bribery and corruption awareness courses;
- provide any assistance as is necessary in an investigation;
- submit documentation (work sheets, receipts, bank statements, accounts) in order that a full audit can be undertaken should there be a requirement to investigate;
- a clause re termination of contract in the event that it is found that any impropriety has taken place.

The first case under the *Bribery Act* 2010 has come before the courts where the defendant company was found guilty of not having strict enough internal controls to ensure staff did not make an illegal bribery payment of £10,000 to a contact. The guilty verdict was given as the jury was not convinced that there were sufficient internal controls.

Example

Reginald works for a big construction company and is charged with tendering on behalf of his company for a dam project in West Africa. There are a number of other international construction companies tendering for the same project from France and China. The tender offer he knows is likely to be below the others because of the company's patented building design that uses a particular self-cooling cement design that saves both time and money.

Reginald receives a call from the official at the government's Public Works department to meet to discuss the tender application. The meeting appears to be informal with no one taking notes and after some niceties the official states that his tender is very attractive but there are a number of other departments involved in the application process and in order to prevent delays in building approvals he should make a further additional off-the-record payment to facilitate speedy approval. The official would be in charge of seeing this through and distribution of the additional payment to the other departments.

Reginald knows that this is a common ploy abroad where a tender is low compared to others, which may have already secretly received bribery assurances, to tarnish the lower tender by accusations of bribery to disbar that lower tender. He states that it is not company policy to make additional undocumented payments. The official then has the problem that he cannot legitimately disbar the tender and if a higher tender is accepted he will have to account for the decision.

Example

Phil has worked in Asia for many years as a purchaser for an international supermarket chain. One of his wealthy business contacts, who owns an Asian drinks company, wants the UK stores Phil represents to import the business contact's energy drinks for sale there. The wealthy businessman states separately that he would like to be Phil's son Ginger's godfather and as such, and in keeping with such an honour, he would like to make prepayment for the education fees at an English private school for his godson. The contact would, as Ginger's Asian godfather (or "Phor boon thahm"), undertake prepayment of the fees at the school. The school, as a charity, has fewer requirements in terms of checks than other institutions and organisations.

This is clearly a bribe, notwithstanding the "personal family connection" supplemented by the role of Asian godfather, and in fact Phil may indirectly be agreeing to be a conduit for money laundering and/or tax evasion. See also the *Criminal Finances Act 2017* below.

6.8.3   Court costs

The costs of criminal and civil sanctions against staff and the company are not normally allowable as a deduction for tax purposes. Therefore penalties and court costs are similarly disallowed. There are some historical cases involving companies and individuals claiming such expenses.

In *Warnes & Co Ltd*, the company claimed a deduction for a penalty and legal costs against its trading profits. The High Court expressed the view that a penal payment for infringement of the law could not be a loss from the trade.

In *Alexander von Glehn & Co Ltd*, the company had been sued for penalties in respect of alleged infringements in the course of its trade. The case was settled by the company paying a compromise penalty of £3,000 (without costs) and it also incurred legal costs amounting to £1,074 in respect of the proceedings. The Judge (at page 244 in the summary) explained that the expenditure was not deductible as it related to unfortunate incidents after the profits had been earned.

In *McKnight v Sheppard*, a stockbroker was found guilty by the Stock Exchange council's disciplinary committee on four charges of gross misconduct and was suspended for six months on each charge. Mr Sheppard incurred legal fees of over £200,000 in connection with the disciplinary proceedings and appeal. The Inspector of Taxes declined to accept that the fines and fees were deductible. Mr Sheppard appealed against this decision on expenses (not pursuing the question of the fines) arguing that these could be allowed. However, where a member of a company's staff is alleged to have undertaken illegal activities (e.g. bribery), and where the individual is defended by the company and found to be not guilty, the costs of defending the company's reputation and that of its staff would be allowable.

Also, a company may have benefited from illegal activity and paid bonuses to staff for successful illegal tenders on which PAYE to discredited employees and corporation tax has been paid and subsequently fined – such taxes and costs cannot be deducted and should be added back even though it has been fined for illegal activity.

Law: ITTOIA 2005, s. 34; CTA 2009, s. 54

Cases: *CIR v EC Warnes & Co Ltd* [1919] 12 TC 227; *CIR v Alexander von Glehn & Co Ltd* [1920] 12 TC 232; *McKnight v Sheppard* [1999] 71 TC 419; *James H Donald (Darvel) Ltd* [2017] UKFTT 446 (TC)

Guidance: BIM 37965, 38515, 38520

6.8.4   Theft Act 1968

It should also be noted that the *Theft Act* 1968 has numerous penalties for theft, robbery, fraud, blackmail, etc. one of which is false accounting:

"(1)   Where a person dishonestly, with a view to gain for himself or another or with intent to cause loss to another,—

a)   destroys, defaces, conceals or falsifies any account or any record or document made or required for any accounting purpose; or

b)   in furnishing information for any purpose produces or makes use of any account, or any such record or document as aforesaid, which to his knowledge is or may be misleading, false or deceptive in a material particular;

he shall, on conviction on indictment, be liable to imprisonment for a term not exceeding seven years."

Law: *Theft Act* 1968, s. 17(1), (2)

6.8.5   *Money laundering*

The fourth EU Money Laundering directive came into force on 26 June 2017 and applies to a "relevant person" and its subsidiaries, whether in the UK, EU or elsewhere. Under regulation 18(1):

"A relevant person must take appropriate steps to identify and assess the risks of money laundering and terrorist financing to which its business is subject."

A relevant person must establish and maintain policies, controls and procedures to mitigate and manage effectively the risks of money laundering and terrorist financing identified in any risk assessment undertaken by the relevant person under regulation 18(1).

A relevant person must, where relevant, communicate the policies, controls and procedures which it establishes and maintains in accordance with this regulation to its branches and subsidiary undertakings which are located outside the UK. If any of the subsidiary undertakings or branches of a relevant parent are established in a third country which does not impose requirements to counter money laundering and terrorist financing as strict as those of the UK then the relevant parent must ensure that those subsidiaries or branches apply measures equivalent to those required by the fourth money laundering directive, as far as allowed under the law of that third country.

A senior individual (board level or equivalent management body) must be responsible for the relevant person's compliance with the fourth money laundering directive. This individual must be a member of the board of directors or, if there is no such board member, the equivalent management body. A nominated officer must also be appointed and an independent audit function must be established.

Customer due diligence is necessary to combat money laundering (and terrorist financing). Different due diligence measures will be required for different customers. A particular type of customer to receive enhanced customer due diligence, in the form of "unexplained wealth orders", is a "Politically Exposed Person" (PEP). So in these cases a relevant person who proposes to have, or to continue, a business relationship with a PEP, or a family member or a known close associate of a PEP, must:

1. have approval from senior management for establishing or continuing the business relationship with that person;
2. take adequate measures to establish the source of wealth and source of funds which are involved in the proposed business relationship or transactions with that person; and
3. where the business relationship is entered into, conduct enhanced ongoing monitoring of the business relationship with that person.

On the other hand, simplified customer due diligence is applied in low risk cases. For these purposes, "risk" refers to the risk that the firm will be subject to money laundering or terrorist financing.

Law: *The Money Laundering, Terrorist Financing and Transfer of Funds (Information on the Payer) Regulations* 2017, SI 2017/692

Guidance: Financial Conduct Authority, FG 17/6 – *The treatment of politically exposed persons for anti-money laundering purposes; UK national risk assessment of money laundering and terrorist financing*

6.8.6   *Civil/regulatory breaches*

A designated supervisory authority will have the power to impose a financial penalty on and/or censure a person for contravening a relevant requirement applying to him or her. Also, an officer of the relevant person may be subject to a financial penalty or be publicly censured. However, a designated supervisory authority must not impose a penalty on an individual under this regulation for contravention of a relevant requirement if the authority is satisfied that all reasonable steps had been taken and that the individual had exercised all due diligence in the matter.

6.8.7 Criminal offences

Anyone who recklessly makes a statement which is false or misleading with regard to a money laundering investigation commits an offence. This attracts a penalty of a fine or up to two years in prison. This is an addition to the previous money laundering regulations where a person in contravention could be exposed to a fine or up to two years in prison.

6.8.8 Criminal Finances Act 2017

The *Criminal Finances Act* 2017 has received Royal Assent in the UK Parliament and came into effect on 30 September 2017. As in the *Bribery Act* 2010, s. 7 (see **6.8.1** above), guidance will be issued to assist companies and organisations to set up appropriate procedures to prevent tax evasion facilitation offences by their employees and agents. Similar to the *Bribery Act*, monitoring of tax facilitation offences is likely to include the following:

- risk assessment;
- prevention procedures;
- due diligence;
- staff training; and
- monitoring/reviews.

Previously, companies and organisations were only liable to prosecution if the heads of the organisation were engaged in such criminal conduct but there is now a new offence of failing to prevent the facilitation of tax offences. The new offence may be committed by a limited company or a partnership but not by an individual.

The main tenet of the legislation of the offence is that where an individual has committed an offence which has facilitated a tax offence by another, then the organisation with which he is connected may be prosecuted for its failure to prevent the employee or agent committing the evasion offence. Suppose, for example, that an employee of (say) a bank, estate agent or a firm of accountants facilitates a tax offence by a customer or client (see Example of Phil at **6.8.2** above). Not only will that employee, Phil, be liable to prosecution, as he is currently liable for criminal conduct, but the international supermarket chain will be liable to prosecution for this new offence within s. 46(2) below:

> **"46 Failure to prevent facilitation of foreign tax evasion offences**
>
> (1)   A relevant body (B) is guilty of an offence if at any time—
>
> > (a)   a person commits a foreign tax evasion facilitation offence when acting in the capacity of a person associated with B, and
> >
> > (b)   any of the conditions in subsection (2) is satisfied.
>
> (2)   The conditions are—
>
> > (a)   that B is a body incorporated, or a partnership formed, under the law of any part of the United Kingdom;
> >
> > (b)   that B carries on business or part of a business in the United Kingdom;
> >
> > (c)   that any conduct constituting part of the foreign tax evasion facilitation offence takes place in the United Kingdom;
>
> and in paragraph (b) 'business' includes an undertaking."

Similar to the *Bribery Act* a defence is available if the employer has in place "reasonable" prevention measures. A reasonable prevention procedure is one that "identifies and mitigates its tax evasion facilitation risks" which may assist in reducing the prosecution risk.

Law: *Criminal Finances Act* 2017

Guidance: Anti Money Laundering Supervision: Estate Agency Businesses

6.9   Emergency and repatriation costs

6.9.1   *Overview*

It was mentioned at **1.3.2** (Contracts overview) that British expats should ensure they are fully conversant with the contract terms regarding the company rules on sickness leave, sick pay, holidays, etc. From the point of view of holidays there may be issues regarding residence in the UK, and as far as sickness is concerned there may be ongoing issues that require repatriation to the UK.

At **4.2.3** (Health insurance), the example is given of Steve, who is suffering from dengue virus in Jakarta. If it steadily gets worse, will his company repatriate him and his wife to UK in an air ambulance (bearing in mind that air ambulance providers have varying exclusions, e.g. no accompanying spouse)? If not, is it covered by the health insurance policy (see also **6.9.3** below) held by the couple? Failing that, will they have personal funds available to pay for the international air ambulance?

This is where the adviser who is involved at the outset of contract negotiations should have raised these issues with Steve to flag up any deficiency in the terms of the contract that was to be signed with the company. Also, if the contract does contain provisions for emergency repatriation, will the company be able to claim the expenses against its tax liability in the accounts?

Example

Steve (continuing that earlier example) steadily gets worse with dengue virus and his doctor states that, because of the different strains of the virus, if Steve recovers he will be susceptible to an even more hazardous situation if he contracts another strain in the future. The doctor's advice is to repatriate back to the UK where he is unlikely to contract dengue again. This means that Steve's job abroad should be concluded as soon as he is well enough to be transported by air ambulance or on a medically assisted commercial flight out of the country. This, of course, comes at a heavy cost!

At this point his wife contacts the HR/personnel department in the UK and requests medical evacuation. The company contacts the company group insurers who come back within the day and state that they have been informed by the insured employee's doctor that the patient had contracted a strain of dengue virus previously.

The group insurers advise the company that from their understanding anyone who has suffered from dengue virus once would have been advised by his or her doctor that a further contraction of the disease could be fatal and to avoid such countries that are prone to contraction. The company refers to its cover documents that state cover will be disallowed where the insured has gone abroad knowing they "may require medical treatment OR against medical advice".

The company contacts its consultant medical lawyer to see if the company could have a potential liability. The lawyer says that not to repatriate Steve, who had made HR/personnel aware of his previous dengue on another job, would be viewed badly in a subsequent court case/publicity and he states that under the *Reporting of Injuries, Diseases and Dangerous Occurrences Regulations* 2013 (SI 2013/1471), there is a health and safety reporting requirement by the employer as below:

"Diseases offshore

10. Where, in relation to a person at an offshore workplace, the responsible person receives a diagnosis of any of the diseases listed in Schedule 3, the responsible person must follow the reporting procedure, subject to regulations 14 and 15."

Following a review by the lawyer of all the relevant circumstances, the company hires an air ambulance to repatriate Steve from Indonesia hospital to a UK hospital, at a cost of £45,000. The company will claim the cost as an expense.

Medical treatment outside the UK is exempt (i.e. not taxed as a benefit in kind) if the employee is working for the company overseas and requires treatment. The company must have committed in advance to pay, unless it arranges and pays the provider directly for the employee's treatment or insurance. If a taxable benefit does arise, the value to use is the cost to the company of providing the treatment or insurance or (if the company reimburses the money to the employee) the amount it reimburses. Payments for medical treatment and insurance in connection with the cost of medical treatment required while the employee is working abroad are not liable for Class 1 NICs, regardless of how the treatment or insurance is arranged. The company will exclude from Class 1 NICs any payment the employer makes:

1. to a third party (for example a doctor or hospital) for medical treatment;

2. to reimburse an employee for the cost of treatment;

3. to an insurance provider to cover the cost of premiums for insuring against such treatment costs; or

4. to reimburse an employee for the cost of premiums for insuring against such treatment.

No Class 1A NICs liability will arise in connection with the provision of medical treatment or insurance for an employee carrying out the duties of an employment outside the UK.

There may also be no chargeable benefit if the treatment is intended to return the employee to the state of health enjoyed before the injury or illness where the employee's injury or illness:

- can be shown to be a risk of the employee's occupation;

- is due to a cause which is reasonably attributable to the nature of the employee's office or employment; and

- is not a risk common to everybody. (See Steve above – dengue virus would not be a risk common to everyone particularly as Steve has had a strain of the virus before and the second contraction may be one of the four types which when contracted makes the individual even more sick. This would not be a risk common to everybody.)

In the case of holidays, reference should be made to **2.2** (Residence).

6.9.2   HMRC leaflets RDR1 and RDR3

For the purposes of the statutory residence test (SRT), "exceptional circumstances" will be, by their nature, out of the ordinary. HMRC suggest, as examples of circumstances that are likely to be exceptional, local or national emergencies, such as civil unrest, natural disasters, the outbreak of war or a sudden serious or even life-threatening illness or injury to an individual.

There may also be limited situations where an individual who needs to stay in the UK, or to come back to the UK – to deal with a sudden or life-threatening illness or injury to a spouse, person with whom he or she is living as spouse, civil partner or dependent child – can have those days spent in the UK ignored under the SRT, subject to the 60-day limit. See further at **2.2.5** (Exceptional circumstances).

6.9.3   *Insurance*

If an employer takes out a medical insurance policy purely to cover an employee against work-related injury (and/or illness), and the policy does not provide cover for any family or household members of the employee, the premium paid by the employer is intended to provide insurance against its own liabilities as an employer, so in these circumstances there will be no charge as a benefit to the employee. If the insurance covers injury incurred both at work and outside work, a benefit will result.

If a company employs an individual, and pays for special treatment to speed recovery and return to work, the costs incurred by the employer will not give rise to a chargeable benefit because the employee has not been provided with any benefit. The treatment merely returns the employee to the level of health and fitness he enjoyed before whilst performing the duties of his employment. However, if the individual suffers injury at home, and the employer pays for his treatment, this will give rise to a chargeable benefit.

7. Overseas tax and investment planning

7.1 Investment bonds

7.1.1 Significance

There are disparities worldwide in the terms of life insurance and life insurance bonds. In the US life insurance bonds are often referred to as private placement life insurance (PPLI) and elsewhere as a life insurance wrapper. Financial advisers in the UK and overseas advising expats tend to refer to the terms "investment bonds", "personal portfolio bonds" and "offshore insurance policies" as detailed below. Other European countries also use investment type life insurance policies for tax planning purposes, e.g. Spain.

For British expats going abroad the use of these types of bonds can provide tax deferral, tax savings and easy assignment options. However, there are also certain aspect of both offshore and UK onshore bonds that can result in latent tax liabilities if not handled correctly by the policyholders or their advisers.

7.1.2 Life insurance/assurance

Firstly, it is important to distinguish between life "insurance" and life "assurance". Assurance is insuring against an event that is definitely going to occur, such as death. Insurance is insuring against something that might occur. The distinction is sometimes not evident in some countries such as the US where policies are generally termed as life insurance.

Life insurance/assurance policies can also attract tax benefits that the policyholder can use to mitigate tax, such as writing the policy in trust for specific beneficiaries and thereby ensuring the proceeds do not form part of the deceased's estate on death and so avoiding the requirement for probate, etc.

The types of policy are "term" and "whole life". Term policies ensure that a capital sum is paid in the event of death within a specified period or before a certain age. Whole life policies ensure a capital sum is paid on the eventual death of the insured. Both types of policy can be written in trust so that the proceeds are paid into a flexible power of appointment trust, so the trustees can pay out the proceeds to the beneficiary or beneficiaries.

Usually all life offices have the required approved wording in their standard forms of trust documents. The term policy is often useful for a donor who makes a lifetime gift to a donee where the gift itself is a PET. If the donor dies within three years of the gift it may become chargeable to IHT and no tapering tax relief is due but if the donor dies after more than three years, but within seven, reduced tapering applies. The decreasing term policy covers this variable position. As liability for IHT is that of the donee for lifetime gifts it would normally be the donee who takes out the policy on the life of the donor to protect his or her potential IHT liability for the seven years. The proceeds resulting from the donor's death would be paid directly to the donee to settle the IHT demand in respect of the PET that has now become chargeable.

7.1.3   *Investment bonds*

Investment bonds are usually single premium, unit linked, whole of life plans in which the money is collectively invested by professional fund managers with other investors' funds. These investment bonds for the expat can be issued by onshore UK companies but usually they are issued by offshore companies situated in Dublin, the Isle of Man, Guernsey, etc. This money is invested in a range of investment mediums according to the risk/fund profile, enabling investment to be spread over a wider range of funds and markets than would otherwise be possible for an individual. It should be noted (but the point is not covered here) that companies may also hold these types of bonds although the taxing treatment will then come under the corporation tax rules.

As with unit trusts, the value of the underlying assets is divided into units of equal value, with each client owning units in proportion to the amount of money he or she has invested. Investment bonds can be designed to provide:

- income;
- capital growth; or
- a mixture of income and capital growth.

A person may currently withdraw up to 5% per annum of the original investment for up to 20 years free of any liabilities to tax as the withdrawals are treated as a return of capital originally invested, so investment bonds are suitable as a tax-efficient income replacement. Money is allocated to units at what is called the offer price, from which an initial charge of between 5% and 7% is deducted, the "bid-offer" spread (which is also a feature of buying shares). However, some companies allocate 100% of money into the investment bond rather than 93%-95%, a significant attraction, even though there may be early surrender charges within a defined number of years.

Law: CTA 2009, s. 560-562

Guidance: *Insurance Policyholder Taxation Manual* IPTM 3900.

7.1.4   Onshore life insurance policies

These are often marketed to those in the UK for protection and tax planning purposes. For tax purposes, the most important distinction is between "qualifying" and "non-qualifying" life insurance policies.

Qualifying policies do not usually give rise to a chargeable event gain unlike non-qualifying policies which often give rise to chargeable gains. However, a qualifying policy does give rise to a chargeable event gain if the policy has been surrendered or premiums have ceased within the first 10 years of the policy, if the allowable gross £3,600 premium limit has been exceeded, or if the policy has been purchased from a third party. The insurer can advise whether the policy was a qualifying policy.

Non-qualifying policies are all policies that are not qualifying policies and often these will be single premium life insurance policies, although additional premiums may be allowed. Tax is normally deducted and shown on the chargeable event certificate whereas offshore policies do not have any tax credit attaching. See HMRC Helpsheet HS320.

A policy is commonly a "restricted relief qualifying policy" (RRQP) if it was issued before 21 March 2012 and varied after that date so as to increase premiums payable so they exceed the standard £3,600 annual premium limit. A qualifying policy may become an RRQP in other circumstances, for example following certain assignments which then result in the assignee exceeding the standard £3,600 annual premium limit. The policy will attract full relief for the period up to the date that it becomes an RRQP or, if later, to 5 April 2013. From that date relief is restricted to the standard £3,600 annual premium limit when calculating any gain. It is unlikely that these sorts of policies will be encountered very often now.

A reduction to a chargeable gain is available if the life insurance policy is an RRQP. The gain may be top sliced (because the policyholder's apportioned gain results in being thrown into a higher tax bracket) or a time-apportioned reduction can be claimed, in which case the calculation is done in the following order:

1. RRQP calculation;
2. time apportioned reduction (see also the example at **8.4.1** – Offshore bonds);
3. Top-slicing relief (see also the example at **8.4.2** – Bonds and returning expats).

7.1.5   *Personal portfolio bonds (PPB)*

If there is any doubt as to what sort of policy/bond is held, and whether there has been a chargeable event which is taxable, the insurer should be contacted for clarification. Not all payments from the insurer are taxable. For tax purposes, the most important distinction is between "non-qualifying" and "qualifying" policies, although most foreign policies are non-qualifying policies. Non-qualifying policies will normally give rise to a gain, but a number of things can affect whether tax is paid or not.

A personal portfolio bond (PPB) is a life insurance policy, life annuity contract or capital redemption policy under whose terms some or all of the benefits are determined by reference to:

1. fluctuations in, or in an index of, the value of property of any description; or
2. the value of, or the income of, property of any description,

and where the terms of the policy or contract permit the selection of the index, or some or all of the property, by the holder of the policy or contract or a person connected with the holder. The *Finance (No. 2) Act* 2017 has ensured that changes to the property categories can be made quickly to move into line with the ever-changing investment landscape, so that the anti-avoidance rules within ITTOIA 2005, s. 516-526 will continue to apply.

Personal portfolio bonds are life insurance policies where the benefits payable are determined by the value of certain property chosen directly or indirectly by the policyholder, rather than investment funds generally available to other policyholders. The charge will arise if the policy is a PPB at the end of the insurance year. Individuals are treated as having made a gain of an amount equal to 15% of premiums paid, with the premiums paid being treated as increased annually by 15%, on a compound basis until the penultimate year. However, there is no annual charge in the year the policy ends. See **8.4.1** (Offshore bonds) for an example of the calculation.

Most policies will not be PPBs but it is important for the expat to check this before departure with his or her financial adviser and, if it is, to change the policy to become "collective". Most providers (but not all) will automatically advise the client if they know the individual is returning to the UK (but can obviously only do so if aware of the location change).

The individual will not usually be entitled to tax credit relief for tax treated as paid on gains on offshore policies as the income accumulates tax free offshore. If the policy is from the UK branch of a foreign insurer, then basic rate tax is treated as paid. It may also be possible that the gain should be treated as if basic rate tax has been paid on it for some policies from insurers resident in other European States, if the insurer has been taxed on the investments underlying the policy, but normally no tax is treated as having been paid.

Law: ITTOIA 2005, s. 507, 516-526; F (no 2) A 2017, s. 10

7.1.6 *Managing offshore investment funds*

The individual has a wide choice of investment funds as an expat investor in respect of the offshore funds industry. These offshore funds are similar to the UK unit trust schemes, but are normally established in countries that have no tax or reduced rates compared to the UK. The advantage is that the high rates of income offered by many of these funds is not taxable in the UK while the individual is resident abroad, sometimes termed as "offshore roll-up". A wide spread of investment and the mix of currencies together give a degree of security not afforded when the investment is solely in sterling. This can be supplemented by A, AA, AAA gradings of investments, which reflect the security/risk loading of the investment. See **Appendix 2** (Adviser fact find and wills questionnaire). However, a return to the UK by the policyholder may result in a UK tax liability from the date of return, including accrued income which is paid after arrival back in the UK.

Ideally the individual should review his fund up to six months before returning to the UK so that, if necessary, he can switch into low yield high growth funds which are acceptable or purely collective funds; by doing this the expat will then minimise tax exposure back in the UK (see also the example at **8.4.1** – Offshore bonds). In addition, a switch prior to return to the UK will create a higher base cost for UK tax purposes. Whilst some switching of funds can be made free of charge, if moving funds between different investment funds the individual may incur further charges on redemption. Also, further penalties are administered indirectly through the bid/offer spread when reinvesting the proceeds in low yield/high growth funds.

7.1.7   *Offshore bond marketing*

Offshore life insurance bonds and personal portfolio bonds are marketed for individuals who believe that they may be non-UK resident by the time the bond is surrendered or matures. However, even if this is not the case an expat with such policies will benefit from both foreign time apportionment relief and top-slicing tax relief once the expat is back in the UK when the policy is surrendered or matures.

These bonds can be held in joint names with others, usually the spouse. Individuals can arrange to hold the investment in different proportions to reduce or even eliminate a tax liability when calculating the tax on the final profit when the bond is encashed when back in the UK. An individual can make withdrawals of up to 5% of the initial investment in each policy year (ending on the anniversary of the policy). This avoids any UK tax liability or reporting requirement if the expat is in the UK. The 5% withdrawals are treated as partial surrenders which are only taken into account in calculating the final profit on the bond when it is surrendered or on death of the policyholder (see also the example at **8.4.2** – Bonds and returning expats). This would effectively allow the 5% withdrawals to be taken each year but never taxed as the total gain would (under current legislation) only be liable to income tax if UK resident during the year in which the gain is cashed in or on death.

These types of onshore and offshore bonds can be very tax efficient in terms of utilising the 5% withdrawal facility as no report of the figure needs to be inserted on the UK self-assessment return. This type of policy pays out a lump sum on its maturity or if the policyholder (or another life assured) should die. Sums may be withdrawn or loans, allowed by certain providers, taken from the insurer or by arrangement while the policy is in force. The type of offshore policy can never be a qualifying policy and is most likely to give rise to a taxable chargeable event gain in the future.

One area that has come before the courts in the UK on a number of occasions has been the part encashment of investment bonds. When an investment bond is taken out it is usually divided into 100 sub-policies which can then be assigned or encashed in whole, leaving the balance of policies in the bond to accumulate. Usually an individual will liaise with his or her financial adviser when contemplating a part encashment and (usually) the adviser will recommend encashment of a number of sub-policies for tax planning reasons. The encashment form from the bond provider has three options:

1. encash whole sub-policies up to the desired amount;
2. partly encash across all policies up to the desired amount but choosing specific funds; or
3. partly encash across all policies up to the desired amount but choosing from all funds.

In the *Lobler* case, the taxpayer (not his adviser) picked option 2 rather than option 1, which had the effect of creating a withdrawal of the amount desired against which only a 5% tax free withdrawal facility could be set, so the balance was a chargeable event as the policy was not terminated. This usually occurs in early years of a policy where 5% accruals have not built up and a large withdrawal is made across all segments, i.e. options 2 and 3.

Since the Judge's criticism of the taxation of excessive bond withdrawals in the *Lobler* case, and previous cases of similar "unfairness", HMRC have been focused on new tax relieving provisions for encashment of these types of bonds. HMRC proposed new rules in 2016 for consultation as:

1. taxing the economic gain;
2. the 100% allowance; or
3. deferral of excessive gains.

Option 1. This option would retain the current 5% tax deferred allowance but would bring into charge a proportionate fraction of any underlying economic gain whenever an amount in excess of 5% was withdrawn. Unlike the current rules, if the policy was not in profit, no gain could arise from an excess event (the *Lobler* problem).

Option 2. Under this option, no gain would arise until all of the premiums paid have been withdrawn. It would change the current cumulative annual 5% tax deferred allowance to a lifetime 100% tax deferred allowance and ensure that only economic gains, i.e. profits, are taxed.

Option 3. This option would maintain the current method for calculating gains but if the gain (not the 5% withdrawal) exceeds a pre-determined amount of the premium (e.g. a cumulative 3% for each year since the policy commenced), the excess would not be immediately charged to tax. Instead it would be deferred until the next part surrender or part assignment.

However, the *Finance (No. 2) Act* 2017 put some rules in place that allow the individual to ask for a review of the gain by HMRC on a "just and reasonable basis" as long as they submit a letter in writing within four tax years following the year in which the gain arose. The HMRC officer allocated to the case will consider whether the gain is disproportionate, taking into account anything HMRC consider appropriate, including:

- the economic gain on the rights surrendered/assigned as in (1) above;
- the amount of premiums paid as in (2) above; and
- the amount of tax payable if no recalculation is made.

HMRC state that:

> "An interested person may apply to an officer of Revenue and Customs for a review of a calculation under section 507 on the ground that the gain arising from it is wholly disproportionate."

There is no appeal process, but it was suggested that there are already safeguards through the complaints procedures to be independently assessed by a small team at HMRC. Any further right of appeal would be to the Adjudicator.

One option to mitigate the tax charge, other than applying to HMRC for their "review", is to make a large pension contribution payment in the relevant tax year, or to surrender the whole bond in the same year. If the problem comes to light later, as it sometimes does, then "deficiency relief" may judiciously be used to effect a full surrender loss against the previous part surrender gain. See IPTM 3880.

Personal portfolio bonds

Where a policy is regarded as a personal portfolio bond (PPB), the UK regulations impose a tax charge, depending on the assets held in the bond, on UK resident individual policyholders. Normally the UK resident policyholder's annual tax charge is based on the yearly "deemed" gain, which is calculated at the end of each policy year (see also the example at **8.4.1** – Offshore bonds) on a 15% yearly cumulative basis whilst the policy is in force after the year of UK residence arrival (again, see the example at **8.4.1** – Offshore bonds). So, this only becomes relevant when a non-UK resident policyholder establishes UK residence, not when making visits to the UK for short periods within the allowable SRT limits (see **2.2** – Residence).

It is possible to endorse the bond to restrict the assets within the bond to those that are permitted within the PPB acceptable investment regulations (i.e. collective funds) before the end of the policy year in which the individual becomes UK resident, in which case no income tax for the PPB tax charge will be payable. The individual should, however, check the position with the PPB provider as this is a particularly complex area and has been targeted by UK anti avoidance and time limiting provisions.

Law: ITTOIA 2005, s. 507, 507A, 509(1), 528; F (No 2) A 2017, s. 9

Cases: *Shanthiratnam v HMRC* [2011] UKFTT 360 (TC); *Anderson v HMRC* [2013] UKFTT 126 (TC); *Joost Lobler v HMRC* [2013] UKFTT 141 (TC), [2015] UKUT 152 (TCC); *Tailor v HMRC* [2017] UKFTT 845

Guidance: HMRC Helpsheet HS321, *Gains on Foreign Life Insurance Policies;* IHTM 3555; IPTM 9000

7.1.8   *Managing policy switches*

It is sometimes possible to switch policies from a non-qualifying offshore bond to an approved scheme similar to UK schemes which are acceptable. This can enable the individual expat to ensure the offshore bond is a collective investment policy within 12 months of return to the UK.

The legislation does allow another collective investment scheme resident outside the UK to be selected if it is a unit trust scheme or an arrangement ensuring rights of co-ownership under the law of the territory outside the UK, so units in an authorised unit trust are permitted property that may be selected without making the policy a PPB.

For this purpose, the PPB legislation follows the standard definition of collective investment scheme given in s. 235 and subsequent related legislation. For these purposes a unit trust is authorised if the Financial Services Authority (FSA, now termed the Financial Conduct Authority) has made an order of authorisation under s. 243 of the *Financial Services and Markets Act* 2000 (FSMA).

However, it is possible for an authorised unit trust to lose its authorisation so that the link between the value of the units and the policy benefits must be broken to keep the policy outside the definition of a PPB. This should be done "as soon as reasonably possible" after the unit trust has lost its authorisation.

Law: FSMA 2000, s. 234, 235; *The Financial Services and Markets Act 2000 (FSMA 2000) (Collective Investment Schemes) Order* 2001 (SI 2001/1062)

7.2   Offshore trust options

7.2.1   *Trust options*

From the standpoint of UK resident and domiciled settlors and beneficiaries, offshore trusts have had few tax advantages for many years following the *Lord Vestey* case when the whole taxing structure was changed.

Offshore trusts with UK beneficiaries, at the current time or in the future, should be aware of the offshore income gains (OIG) requirements and completion of HMRC form 50(FS). The legislation is so widely drafted that even potential indirect benefit is caught, as seen in the *Botnar* "power to enjoy" case. From this point of view, the use of trusts is well rehearsed in the Claritax Books publication *Financial Planning with Trusts* and reference can be made to that publication.

Having said this, certain offshore trusts are still effective for inheritance, asset protection and tax planning. In this section the potentials of some common (and some not so common) trusts are explored as follows:

Type	Key details
Bare trust	• Absolute transfer into trust which is a PET. • Settlor's right to payments is not advised.
Discretionary trust	• Chargeable lifetime transfer. • Settlor(s) should not normally benefit.
Loan trust	• Initial small gift is chargeable but normally covered by IHT exemption. Balance of fund is on loan. • Settlor can obtain loan repayable on demand or regular payments. Exempt.

Type	Key details
Discount trust	• Gift into trust by settlor who receives pre-determined payments as agreed at outset. • Age/health "discount" agreed at outset and is treated as a PET or CLT (but subject to review on death).
Excluded property trust	• Offshore assets held by a non-UK domicile placed in trust for settlor/beneficiaries. • Trustees have ultimate discretion on trust distributions. IHT excluded property.
APT trusts	• Asset protection trusts are intended to protect assets of the settlor. • Creditor protection is secured by protection against unreasonable, unjustified or other spurious claims.
QDOT	• US citizen married to a non-US citizen defers US estate duty through a temporary QDOT trust. • Surviving non-US citizen has time to undertake US citizenship, receive hardship payments, etc.
QTIP	• Gives a life interest to the surviving US spouse but acts as an asset protection trust. • Ideal for second marriage situations where assets left ultimately to the predeceased's family.
ORSO	• Hong Kong trust that provides asset protection and tax-free rollup for beneficiaries. • Linking pension fund assets to a non-vested trust vehicle gives asset and tax protection.

Law: TCGA 1992, s. 86, 87; ITA 2007, s. 714-715; SI 2009/3001, reg. 20, 21
Cases: *Vestey v CIR* [1980] STC 10; *CIR v Botnar* (CA) [1999] STC 711

7.2.2   Using offshore trusts

In the sections below the use is reviewed of specific bespoke offshore trusts which are commonly available to expats. The expat living and/or working abroad, with particular personal circumstances and requirements, has a number of varying options to choose from in terms of bespoke trusts. These will depend on the individual's domicile, residence, jurisdictional location, future intentions and spousal inheritance requirements.

With the tax benefits of being non-resident under the SRT, the provision by financial institutions abroad to service expats with tax-efficient trusts, some linked to offshore investment bonds and life insurance policies, is common. Returning to the UK means that settlors and beneficiaries come within the UK tax rules and this should be borne in mind when suggestions are made on specific trust vehicles. It is, of course, relevant that the tax rules and asset protections of the trust vehicles below can be used by individuals in their own or their beneficiaries' interests.

Formerly, determination of domicile could be sought from HMRC on DOM1 but this is no longer the case. One alternative is to ensure there is a chargeable transfer for IHT purposes so that the domicile issue is addressed by way of the discretionary trust route (see *Gulliver*, where the question of domicile arose between locations of UK and Hong Kong). In that case, the subsequent circumstances did not support the non-domicile ruling but that is not to say it is not now an appropriate way of securing a ruling. Similarly, a non-resident with a child at university may wish to provide funds under bare trust for the child to purchase a property in the vicinity of the university, which would not attract the higher rate of SDLT and which would obtain capital gains tax advantages as can be seen in the example below in **7.2.4** (Bare trust).

Case: *Gulliver v HMRC* [2017] UKFTT 222 (TC)
Guidance: IHTM 44111

7.2.3   Trust reporting

The reporting of a trust used to be in paper form by completing form 41G and sending it to HMRC. Since 10 July 2017 the report should be made through HMRC's online trust registration service (TRS), so 41G is now redundant. The money laundering regulations (MLR 2017) issued on 22 June 2017 require the trustees of UK and offshore trustees to report details of "beneficial owners" of all "relevant trusts".

Beneficial owners are the settlor, trustees and beneficiaries, including those who are discretionary, protectors, etc. "Potential beneficiaries" are also included in reporting and this would relate to someone who is mentioned in a letter of wishes by the settlor when he lodges the letter with the trustees.

"Relevant trusts" are:

- UK express trusts; or
- non express trusts which have UK income or assets,

on which the trust should pay one or more of income tax, CGT, IHT, SDLT, etc.

Non-UK trustees will be outside reporting until such time as they are required to report becoming subject to taxation in the UK. If the TRS was accessed for the first time in the 2016-17 tax year, the time limit for registration via the TRS was extended to 8 January 2018 and then no later than 5 March 2018. All other trusts were required to report to the TRS by 31 January 2018. Teething problems existed but HMRC say that those who have an agent code should now be able to access the agent services account and register their client's trust or complex estate. Penalties for late submission of returns have been declared as being £100 for the first three months after the due date, then £200 for the period 3-6 months late and 5% of the tax liability or £300, whichever is the greater, after the six months.

The information required is detailed. For instance, if the trust purchased a UK property and rented it out then there will be many questions such as:

- name of the trust, its assets, and their respective values (e.g. London property £1.65 million, UK equities £655,700, etc.);
- names, National Insurance numbers, unique tax reference numbers of beneficiary or potential beneficiary if relevant, but just passport or identification number if not in the UK;
- unnamed beneficiaries / potential beneficiaries such as unborn children need only be reported as such.

This will mean a lot of extra work involved with the administration of offshore trusts where they hold UK assets that are now subject to tax reporting requirements. The reporting deadline was 31 January 2018 but if the, say, BVI trust has not yet become subject to tax (e.g. income tax, CGT, IHT, SDLT, etc.) then the deadline for reporting will be the 31 January after the year in which the first charge to UK tax is applied. For example, if an offshore BVI trust buys a London property on 17 June 2018, and starts to earn rental income, the date of reporting would be 31 January 2020. However, if UK tax is incurred by a company within the trust structure then the trust will not yet be liable to the reporting requirements. The company should be making returns of rental income under the NRL2 form and SA700 tax return by 31 January following the end of the tax year of assessment.

Law: IHTA 1984, s. 44(2); *Money Laundering, Terrorist Financing and Transfer of Funds (Information on Payer) Regulations* 2017, SI 2017/692, reg. 44, 45; EU Fourth Money Laundering Directive (EU) 2015/849

7.2.4   Bare/absolute trusts

A gift to a bare/absolute trust is a potentially exempt transfer for the donor/settlor and will not be chargeable after seven years from the date of gift. The beneficiary obtains an absolute entitlement to the asset, which becomes part of his estate for IHT purposes. The donee should be aged at least 18 years (if a minor the parent usually acts as legal guardian), mentally capable and not an undischarged bankrupt. The gift should be notated (see pro-forma below), so that it is clear that the assets or funds are given without strings attached. It should also be dated for the reason of timeous reference. If the donor dies within three years of the gift then tapering IHT relief may apply. For stamp duty purposes, the transfer into trust would be an exempt transfer.

Whilst an asset may be the subject of the donor's gift, cash will not incur a capital gains tax problem and that may be included in an onshore or offshore investment bond to provide 5% tax free withdrawals yearly. If the 5% is exceeded in one year, or subsequent years, the excess will give rise to a chargeable event gain and a certificate will be issued. This event will be reportable on the UK return of income for a UK resident (see **7.1.9**) but not if the individual is resident overseas. Many of the offshore life insurance institutions provide specific bare trust forms for those wishing to benefit others by this method of gifting. A form of bare trust gift deed might be documented as follows:

This Memorandum of Gift made on [DATE]

The undersigned Donor [FULL NAME] of [ADDRESS]

Gifts out of true love and affection for the Donee [e.g. MY DAUGHTER [NAME]] of [ADDRESS] gives a [e.g. A PROPERTY] in [ADDRESS] for the use and benefit of the Donee absolutely and at the same time delivered thereof to the Donee releasing all control thereon as evidenced by the attached Schedule.

The said Donee at the same time accepted the said gift of [e.g. PROPERTY] evidenced by the attached schedule and took possession of the same and exercised his/her full power, control and domain thereon.

This memorandum is executed to confirm the above gift having been made by the Donor voluntarily and of own free will so that no one in whatever capacity may hereafter claim the said gift from said Donee or his/her legal representatives or assignees.

Signatures:

Donor...

Donee...

Witnesses:

Name ....

Address...

Name...

Address...

SCHEDULE TO MEMORANDUM OF GIFT

Example

Mi Ling from Hong Kong, aged 18 years, is in her first year of a five year course at Cambridge University and her father decides, rather than buy a property there himself, to provide the funds by gift into bare trust for his daughter to acquire a three bedroomed property. The advantages of this are that Mi Ling will:

- have accommodation available rent free;
- pay the nil or reduced SDLT rate because the purchase is her first and only property (see SDLT at **9.5.2**);
- obtain tax free income up to £7,500 per annum from rent-a-room relief;
- obtain CGT main residence relief on sale.

(See also the sections on lettings relief, capital gains and stamp duty land tax.)

Law: FA 2003, Sch. 4ZA
Guidance: IHTM 16030

7.2.5   *Discretionary trusts*

Income tax

The first £1,000 of income is taxed at the standard rate (currently 20%). Any further income generated on assets whilst they are held within the trust is taxed at the trust rate, which is currently 45% for investment income and 38.1% for dividend income.

Any income which is distributed to beneficiaries may enable some of the tax paid to be partly reclaimable by that beneficiary, depending on his or her personal income tax position. That is, if the UK tax allowances of the beneficiary due each year have not been utilised then these allowances may cover the rental/investment income so paid out and taxed in the trust, leading to a refund position. Clearly if income is accumulated within the trust, tax at the full rate will be suffered.

Inheritance tax

Inheritance tax on discretionary trusts is assessed at every 10-year anniversary. If the value of the assets in the trust on the relevant anniversary exceeds the inheritance tax nil rate band threshold in place at the time then the excess is subject to IHT at a rate which is currently a maximum of 6%. However, no IHT is payable if the total value of the trust on the relevant anniversary is within the nil rate band, and this is often expected to be the case when the property is put into the trust.

IHT is also charged on the same basis if the assets leave the trust between the anniversaries.

IHT is not charged on the death of a trust beneficiary, because the trust does not form part of the beneficiary's estate. The trustees will need to take the value into account when reviewing the trust asset(s) (which they will need to do regularly once there are any real appreciating funds within the trust) and also when considering whether any payments should be made to the beneficiaries.

Capital gains tax

Capital gains tax on residential property placed into the trust, on which any gain arises following disposal by the trustees, would be taxed at the trust rate, currently 28%. The trustees do, however, have one half of the annual allowance (i.e. they currently have £5,850) but this is capped at a minimum exempt amount of £1,170 per trust if there are five or more trusts (10 or more, if for the benefit of a disabled person). Also, where the value of the disposals of trust assets exceeds the CGT annual exemption amount by four times, i.e. £11,700 x 4 = £46,800 for the 2018-19 tax year, the disposals should be reported to HMRC on the trust return.

Note that if assets are to be transferred out of the trust, rather than sold within the trust, in most cases any capital gain could be held over, i.e. deferring the gain until later (but see **2.4.4** (CGT non-residence) re clawback). This means that no CGT would be payable at that point of transfer. Rather, the CGT would be "held over" and paid by the beneficiary who received the trust asset, on his or her subsequent sale/disposal of that asset. This hold over relief may or may not prove advantageous, depending on whether the assets in question increase or decrease in value and on the CGT rate (and indeed rules) at the time of disposal.

Example

Wong, living in Asia, invested £1 million in a London property for capital appreciation and rental income. The London property gives capital appreciation of about 6% p.a. but incurs an SDLT charge (inclusive of the 3% additional property charge) of £73,750.

411

Rent on the property is £2,500 per month net. The net rents received on the London property will be taxable at 20%, after allowances under double tax treaty, and the annual tax is £3,630.

Wong gifts the property, now valued at £1.2 million, to a discretionary trust for the benefit of his son who is at an English private boarding school. No SDLT is payable where property is gifted into discretionary trust. The CGT on the £200,000 increase can be held over and the inheritance tax of £175,000 (£1.2 million – £325,000 x 20%) can be paid by ten equal annual instalments of £17,500, together with interest.

The trustees are subject to the discretionary trust income tax rate on £30,000 rents but if the rents are distributed to Wong's son for school fees then a reclaim of tax may be made on his behalf and the marginal rate on the excess will be just 20% and not the trust rate of 45%.

Subsequently, the trustees can either sell the property and pay the tax at 28% or hold over the gain by passing it absolutely to Wong's son. If Wong's son occupies the property as his main residence as a trust beneficiary, or if the trustees pass it to him absolutely and he subsequently sells it as his main residence, then there will be reduced gains tax under the main residence legislation.

Law: IHTA 1984, s. 227; TCGA 1992, s. 222, 225, 260, 281; SI 1987/516 (*Stamp Duty (Exempt Instruments) Regs*), Category L

7.2.6   Loan trusts

Many of the offshore life insurance companies provide versions of the gift and loan back schemes. These schemes are approved by HMRC as being acceptable planning vehicles and not within DOTAS, i.e. "non-abusive arrangements involving 'loan trusts' are excepted from being prescribed by regulation 3(4) of the published draft."

The procedure is relatively simple in that the individual wishing to save inheritance tax in the long run makes a gift into trust of, say, £10, which is covered by IHT exemption, and then loans the trust a larger amount. The loan is interest free and repayable on demand but the trustees are free to invest the loan. This is usually done through a single premium bond which allows monthly, quarterly or yearly withdrawals of the principal loan. The payments are usually restricted in essence to 5% of the original capital loaned to the trust, mainly when it is linked to the single premium bond.

So, the principal is repaid over 20 years but whilst held in the trust the principal has been accumulating in value outside the estate of the individual within the trust. Over 20 years this could amount to a substantial amount accrued outside the individual's estate for IHT saving.

Expats have the benefit of investment income accruals rolling up offshore with no tax deduction. Also, as the loan is still part of the individual's estate for tax purposes, it is not a chargeable transfer or potentially exempt transfer. On death, the balance of the loan is part of the individual's estate for IHT purposes, but subject to the past 5% withdrawals which should have been utilised/gifted/spent.

This type of loan trust is ideal for those who still want access to their funds but are willing to forgo the investment accrual to a beneficiary via the trust.

Example

Roberta has accumulated funds, whilst abroad, in an offshore bond but she is now returning to the UK permanently to retire at 65 on a very handsome occupational pension. She decides to terminate the bond which has been a good investment, especially as she invested in US$ stocks.

Notwithstanding that in the UK she will get foreign residence relief and top-slicing, she wants tax free access now to benefit her grandchildren. She encashes the bond and with the £200,000 places it in an onshore gift and loan discretionary bond. Her grandchildren are the beneficiaries. Her actuarial life expectancy is 86 years old in 20 years' time.

She sets up the trust with a gift of £3,000 (covered by her annual allowance) and loans the £200,000 to the trustees, who invest in a single premium bond allowing 5% withdrawals per year. Her 5% withdrawals each year should not be used to supplement her pension income which has been gifted. This is because such withdrawals are treated as capital in Roberta's hands and if it is clear to HMRC that these have been used to supplement the gifts out of income those payments will not be categorised as exempt.

413

On form IHT403, which the executors complete, there is a space to include investment income but to include the 5% withdrawals there would be incorrect as these constitute a capital payment. Notwithstanding this, she is able to give her children regular gifts out of "income" which are exempt for IHT purposes.

Law: IHTA 1984, s. 21
Guidance: Form IHT 403, p. 6

7.2.7   *Discounted gift trusts*

The discounted gift trust works differently from the loan trust but is also excepted from DOTAS. It is available for onshore or offshore policies provided by life companies. It can be an associated bare trust as above, an interest in possession trust or a discretionary trust as in the example below.

In straightforward cases, the settlor has retained a right to an annual income and that right is not property as the trustees hold it on bare trust for the settlor. As stated above, a bare trust is not a settlement for inheritance tax purposes. The settlor is excluded from other benefits under the policy and so the POA charge does not apply. So the gift will constitute a potentially exempt transfer, or an immediately chargeable lifetime gift potentially subject to a 20% IHT charge after allowances.

The settlor retains a right to payments for life, which is valued, and the balance is gifted and held by trustees for the benefit of the beneficiaries and is outside the IHT net after a seven-year period has expired as it is a chargeable lifetime transfer. Because of the discount, the amount taken into account for IHT purposes is smaller if the individual dies within the seven years.

There can be issues regarding the discount, as was seen in the *Bower* case, but in normal circumstances a discount by the life insurance company is fairly accurate, taking age and health matters into account. If the discount certificate is unreasonable then HMRC can dispute the life company's findings and protracted negotiation may entail, sometimes with an unsatisfactory outcome as in *Bower*. The certificate is provided by the bond insurance company after a medical review and is held in a sealed envelope to be opened at the appropriate event, i.e. on the death of the bond holder. HMRC have stated in the past that the open market value of the retained rights will depend on, inter alia, the settlor's sex, age, health and thereby insurability as at the gift date. If the settlor were to be uninsurable, for any reason, then the open market value of the retained rights as at the gift date would be nominal and the gift would be close to the whole amount invested by the settlor.

In such a case the reliance on the discount could backfire and from an IHT point of view the position would be problematic.

Example

Joan (aged 62) and James (65) are married and wish to get an immediate IHT benefit from excess funds they hold amounting to £400,000. They take out a discounted gift trust written under discretionary terms, not a bare/absolute trust.

Both Joan and James have used up their nil rate bands two years ago and their annual exemptions of £3,000 for each of the years. They contribute half the intended investment each and decide on an annual 5% withdrawal facility. Joan and James undertake medicals at the request of the life company and it is supplied with the examination details so that the life company can get an actuarial statement for their underwriter to calculate the discount. The underwriter states that Joan's right to 5% each year is valued at £153,000 but James' right is £140,000 which means the residual amount is £47,000 and £60,000 respectively.

These residual amounts of £47,000 and £60,000 are chargeable lifetime transfers as there is no nil rate band available to either as these have been used up. As the gifts are into discretionary trust the IHT lifetime tax due will be at 20% x £47,000 and £60,000, i.e. £9,400 and £12,000 respectively. Should Joan and James die within seven years then the discounted amounts calculated become taxable but with IHT tapering relief after the three-year period from the date of gift into the discount gift trust. The executors will, on death, make negotiations with HMRC to confirm the discount agreed by the underwriters.

Should they both survive the seven years then there will be no further additional IHT payable by their estates. See also Discretionary Trust above. The growth in their investments has also been outside their estates for the beneficiaries. Therefore if Joan and James survive the full seven years the only tax they will have paid will be IHT at lifetime rate of 20%, jointly amounting to £21,400 rather than £160,000 (i.e. £400,000 @ 40% = £160,000).

Law: IHTA 1984, s. 3(1); FA 2004, Sch. 15, para. 8; *The Inheritance Tax Avoidance Schemes (Prescribed Descriptions of Arrangements) Regulations 2017*, SI 2017/1172, reg. 5

Case: *HMRC v The Executors of the Estate of Marjorie Edna Bower & Others* [2008] EWHC 3105 (Ch)

Guidance: R&C Brief 22 (2013): Discounted Gift Schemes; IHTM 44111

7.2.8   Excluded property trusts

Any property that is situated abroad, and within a settlement where the settlor is non-UK domiciled, is treated as excluded property. The settlor should not be a reversionary beneficiary for these purposes. In the case of property settled by will or intestacy, it will be the date of the testator's or intestate's death that is relevant in terms of the settlement date. The domicile of the trustees and beneficiaries is not relevant.

If a UK domiciled individual is married to a non-UK domiciled spouse, and the spouse has overseas *situs* assets, these will be exempt from UK IHT as long as the spouse is a non-UK domicile. If the spouse were to move to the UK, and thereby to become deemed domiciled in the UK, then ideally, prior to that event, the overseas assets owned by the spouse should be placed into an offshore trust for his or her (and the children's) benefit so as to take advantage of the excluded property exemption applying to a non-UK domiciliary.

Deemed domicile can now, since 6 April 2017, be applied by HMRC after 15 tax years of arrival in the UK depending on the date of arrival. For those who are born and bred in the UK, but have since made a domicile of choice elsewhere, a return to the UK could jeopardise their foreign domicile of choice by reason of being resident in the year following UK re-arrival; such individuals are now termed "formerly domiciled residents" (FDRs). However, depending on the *situs* of the foreign assets an excluded property trust could save IHT of 40% on the value of those offshore assets placed in trust and paid out of the trust assets to the children and the original settlor.

Example

Edward was born in Hong Kong whilst his British father was an army officer stationed there in 1968 until the territory was handed back to the Chinese. Edward then relocated to Germany with his family but left there in 1986 to attend university in England for three years.

He moved to Singapore in 1992, after a spell with a London stockbroker. His wife Jill is a UK born and bred domiciliary but has made a domicile of choice of Singapore too. After 20 years in Singapore, Edward and Jill have obtained their permanent residence cards, and have decided not to go back to England.

Unfortunately his plans have to change and in 2018 he considers going back to the UK to look after his ailing mother. He decides to set up an excluded property trust for his two children who live and work in Singapore. As Edward was not born in the UK, although he was born of British parents, he does not meet conditions (i), (iii) and (iv) of IHTA 1984, s. 267(aa) although he meets (ii). He can therefore set up an excluded property trust for his non-UK assets solely for the benefit of his children, who remain permanent residents of Singapore, before he returns to the UK. Provided he does not receive any benefit from the trust he will not be subject to any income tax, capital gains tax or inheritance tax and neither will the children.

Edward's mother dies two years later and bequeaths him her total assets (including her residence). Edward signs a deed of variation (see **1.7.1** above) in favour of his children which utilises his mother's and her late husband's residence nil rate bands and nil rate band totalling £500,000 each.

Sadly, his wife dies whilst they are in the UK and her will leaves her assets totalling £950,000 to Edward. She is treated as a "formerly domiciled resident" from the tax year after her return to the UK. She had previously made inter-spouse lifetime allowable gifts to Edward of £325,000, which were covered by the non-dom inter-spouse exemption, and therefore the IHT due is £250,000 (£950,000 - £325,000 @ 40%). Edward decides to elect to be treated as UK domiciled within two years of her death so as to attract the UK domiciled inter-spouse exemption.

On his subsequent departure to live permanently in Singapore, Edward will be treated as UK trailing domiciliary for a period of four years of non-residence, ensuring his domicile of choice will revert thereafter. If Edward were to add assets to the excluded property trust he set up for the children then, as he is deemed to be UK domiciled, those assets would not be treated as being within the excluded property provisions. See also **2.1.3**.

Law: IHTA 1984, s. 6, 18(2), 48, 81, 82, 84(3), 267, 272; F(No2)A 2017, s. 30

Case: *Barclays Wealth Trustees (Jersey) and Dreelan v HMRC*, 2017 EWCA (Civ 1512)

Guidance: IHTM 04251, 04281, 04030, 16000

7.2.9   Asset protection trusts

An asset protection trust (APT) is a trust intended to protect assets of the settlor against unreasonable, unjustified or greedy creditors or other persons. The trust and its assets are invariably offshore so that the trustees and the laws governing the trust are different to those in which the settlor resides. The jurisdiction of the APT is often a tax haven or low tax jurisdiction. Often the accusations of a "sham trust" vehicle (see below) are levelled at the settlement set up by the potential creditors.

Those potential creditors who are likely to make claims include:

- creditors of the settlor;
- members of the settlor's family (ex-spouses, etc.);
- the trustee in bankruptcy;
- public authorities (e.g. claiming assets disposed of as proceeds of crime); and
- criminal prosecution authorities, see below.

It is perhaps worth noting that a survey in the *Economist* magazine a number of years ago reported that a US law practice had 400 APT clients and had to defend only 24 cases and all cases were settled out of court for about 15% on average of the original claim. However, in a recent case in the UK High Court a Russian "oligarch" named Pugachev had set up five trusts in New Zealand to defeat his creditors back in Russia (the liquidators of his banking business). Mr Pugachev had made himself a protector of the trusts (see also

7.2.14 below), was able to nominate new trustees in place of the old ones, had a reservation of power over the trust and was a discretionary beneficiary. He did in fact use his power to replace the original trustees with new corporate trustees, no doubt to facilitate his control. The High Court in its judgement declared it a sham, as follows:

> "The whole scheme was set up to facilitate a pretence about ownership (or rather its absence) should the need arise. When Mr Pugachev is Protector (and to the extent Mr Pugachev is under a disability, when [his son] is Protector) the true effect of all the trust deeds in this case, properly construed, is to leave Mr Pugachev in control of the trust assets. Mr Pugachev is the beneficial owner. They amount to a bare trust for Mr Pugachev."

A recent criminal case at Southwark Crown Court concerned a charge of conspiracy to cheat the public revenue of £107.9 million relating to a massive tax fraud, where much of the structure was intentionally incorporated in offshore jurisdictions, such as the British Virgin Islands and the Island of Nevis via the offices of a Panama-based trust company to ensure secrecy so as facilitate the fraud. This put HMRC at risk of losing a large amount in tax while the perpetrators extracted large sums of money through these offshore trusts to purchase expensive properties in the UK, Dubai and Australia. It is noticeable from that case that HMRC pursued the taxpayers initially for the repayment of tax relief they received from investing in these tax fraud schemes. See the Edwin example at **6.5.4** (common reporting standard).

See also ORSO schemes at **4.1.11** above.

Case: *JSC Mezhdunarodniy Promyshlenniy Bank v Pugachev* 2017 EWHC 2426 (Ch)

Guidance: http://www.mynewsdesk.com/uk/hm-revenue-customs-hmrc /pressreleases/six-jailed-for-total-of-45-years-as-hmrc-smashes-ps100m-fraud-2266689 (HMRC press release 10 November 2017)

7.2.10   Sham trusts

The basis for family claims would be that the transaction was a "sham", and that the assets comprising that sham should form part of the estate. However, the burden of proving that the trustees are complicit is high, i.e. a common intention of the settlor and trustee(s) that the trust is a sham. In the *Charman* divorce case, the Judge's comment on the refusal of the request for compliance was:

> "... all this forensic activity was to no avail because the Judge in Bermuda, Mr Justice Bell, somewhat churlishly in my view, declined to assist the English Court in the face of opposition from the trustees."

In *Shalson*, his Lordship Rimer explained the principle:

> "When a settlor creates a settlement he purports to divest himself of assets in favour of the trustee, and the trustee accepts them on the basis of the trusts of the settlement. The settlor may have an unspoken_intention that the assets are in fact to be treated as his own and that the trustee will accede to his every request on demand. But unless that intention is from the outset shared by the trustee (or later becomes so shared), I fail to see how a settlement can be regarded as a sham. Once the assets are vested in the trustee, they will be held on the declared trusts, and he is entitled to regard them as so held and to ignore any demands from the settlor as to how to deal with them. I cannot understand on what basis a third party could claim, merely by reference to the unilateral intentions of the settlor, that the settlement was a sham and that the assets in fact remained the settlor's property. One might as well say that an apparently outright gift made by a donor can subsequently be held to be a sham on the basis of some unspoken intention by the donor not to part with the property in it. But if the donee accepted the gift on the footing that it was a genuine gift, the donor's undeclared intentions cannot turn an ostensibly valid disposition of his property into no disposition at all. To set that sort of case up the donee must also be shown to be a party to the alleged sham. In my judgment, in the case of a settlement executed by a settlor and a trustee, it is insufficient in considering whether or not it is a sham to look merely at the intentions of the settlor. It is essential also to look at those of the trustee."

Separately, and more recently, in *ND v SD*, concerning powers to set aside the trust under the *Matrimonial Causes Act* 1973, the Judge stated:

"I decline to make any order in the exercise of my discretion under s 37(2)(a) of the *Matrimonial Causes Act* 1973. As I have already pointed out earlier in my judgment, this is essentially a 'fall back' position adopted by the wife as a 'hedge' to her primary case that The ABC Trust is a sham entity."

Law: *Matrimonial Causes Act* 1973, s. 37(2)(a)

Cases: *Shalson v Russo* [2005] Ch 281; *Charman v Charman* [2007] EWCA (Civ) 503; *ND v SD* [2017] EWHC 1507 Fam

7.2.11   US qualified domestic trusts

Married US citizens can transfer assets between each other in lifetime (or on death) as they are treated as a single economic unit, much as in the UK. But a US citizen married to a UK domiciled spouse creates problems on transfer of assets.

US citizens are subject to federal and state taxes on assets wherever situated in the world, in a similar way to UK IHT. A previous exclusion amounted to US$5.49 million (inflation adjusted each year) applies but non-US citizens not domiciled (NCNDs) who own property situated in the US are subject to estate tax after a small exemption of US$60,000. Amounts above this are subject to tax at 40%. The US Senate's approval of an estate exemption increase to US$11.2 million per individual, under the *Tax Cuts and Jobs Act* 2017, ensures that a couple will be exempt to the tune of over US$22 million. This amount is expected to be reduced from 2026 if no further changes are made subsequently by the US Congress.

Gifts to a US citizen spouse benefit from an unlimited exemption similar to the inter-spouse IHT exemption from a non-UK domiciled spouse to a UK domiciled spouse in the UK. Transfers from a US domiciled spouse to his or her non-domiciled UK spouse are not exempt, similar to the UK's IHT position on gifts to non-domiciled spouses (see **9.2** – Non domicile IHT planning). Also, jointly owned property held by a non-US domiciled spouse results in the whole amount being included as an asset of the non-domiciled spouse unless it can be shown that the survivor contributed to the asset.

In cases such as the example below, spouses with a non-US domicile living in the US can be subject to double taxation in both the US and the UK. The US/UK Estate and Gift tax Treaty ensures that where a UK domiciled individual is subject to US estate duty on that property, the tax will not be greater than the tax that would have been paid on his worldwide assets had the individual been US domiciled. Note that the US can impose domicile: "a person acquires a domicile in a place by living there, for even a brief period of time."

Tax deferred is tax saved: the marital deduction exemption made to a qualified domestic trust (QDOT) allows a temporary deferral of the estate duty tax of the surviving non-US spouse. The tax charge will then apply on the death of the non-US domiciled spouse or if he or she should receive a distribution in the meantime. Although this action defers the tax liability, income distributions from the QDOT are not subject to QDOT tax. Similarly, hardship distributions are not subject to the tax, e.g. for reasons of maintenance, health, education and other care support. According to the IRS:

> "A distribution of principal is treated as made *on account of hardship* if it is made to the spouse from the QDOT in response to an immediate and substantial financial need relating to the spouse's health, maintenance, education, or support, or the health, maintenance, education, or support of any person that the surviving spouse is legally obligated to support."

The QDOT tax is computed at the time of the US spouse's death using the rates at that date. If, in the intervening time, the non-US spouse has become a US citizen then the distribution from the QDOT will not be taxable if:

- the surviving non-US spouse had either been a US resident from the date of death of the US spouse OR no taxable distributions were made from the QDOT prior to the surviving non-US spouse getting US citizenship; and
- the US trustees notify the Internal Revenue Service (IRS) that the surviving non-US spouse has become a US citizen.

Example

Michael, a US citizen, is married to Lulu, who is not a US citizen. He has an estate of US$7 million. His accountant has told him that having joint property with a non-domicile spouse is not recommended (see above) and all assets are in Michael's name. They have two children who are US citizens.

Michael dies on 1 December 2017. In his will he leaves US$5.49 million (the exemption which is now increased to US$11 million after 31 December 2017 by the *Tax Cuts and Jobs Act* 2017), to his two children, including the house, and the remaining amount to Lulu. The US$1.51 million is potentially taxable as Lulu does not obtain any inter-spouse exemption.

The family CPA suggests a QDOT is created before filing the return to the IRS. The return must be filed nine months after the death. Lulu is then allowed to live in the family home, but pays a market rent to the children, and US$1.51 million in stocks is invested to return 5% per annum. US$75,500 is received by the trustees and used to pay trust expenses and to provide for Lulu's "hardship" payments. Further distributions can be made if Lulu does not have other reasonably available liquid assets. The estate duty to the children is exempted and the duty regarding the QDOT is deferred.

Lulu has the opportunity to acquire US citizenship so that there is no deferred estate tax payable (2056A-5(c)(1)). However, the QDOT terms should be flexible so that if Lulu does become a US citizen then the trust can be adjusted for such a situation.

Law: *United States-United Kingdom Estate and Gift Tax Convention* 1980, art. 4, 8, 9; UK SI 1979/1454; Internal Revenue Code, s. 2010, 2056, 2056(a), 2102(b); IRS Form 706-NA; *Tax Cuts and Jobs Act* 2017, amending Internal Revenue Code of 1986

7.2.12 *Qualified terminable interest property trusts*

A US qualified terminable interest property (QTIP) trust is a type of trust, similar to an immediate post death interest in the UK, which enables one spouse to provide for a surviving spouse, and also to maintain control of how the trust's assets are ultimately distributed once that surviving spouse dies. Normally QTIPs are used in cases of second marriage where the deceased wishes to benefit children of a previous marriage. Income and sometimes capital from the trust is made available to the surviving spouse for life.

The administrators of the trust provide the beneficiary spouse with appropriate living expenses and exert control over how the funds are handled should the surviving spouse die. The surviving spouse never has a power of appointment over the original capital. This prevents assets being dissipated through ill judged decisions and redirection to other individuals, e.g. new spouses in cases of remarriage.

A surviving spouse named within a QTIP receives payments from the trust based on the income the trust investment is producing annually. No borrowings or liens against QTIP property can be made by the surviving spouse so the assets are protected for the ultimate beneficiaries. Payments are normally made to the surviving spouse for life. When the surviving spouse dies, the assets in the trust become the property of the listed beneficiaries as they are not transferable to another person.

The QTIP should have at least one trustee appointed to manage the trust, but multiple individuals or organisations may also be appointed. The trustee (or trustees) will responsible for running the QTIP and for the management of the asset investments.

Example

Grant's marriage to Georgina, both US citizens, is his second and he wants his children to benefit from the estate ultimately. He ensures that a QTIP trust benefits Georgina on his death for her lifetime, and on her death the assets are to be distributed to Grant's two children who are US citizens.

The initial gift into trust is exempt from gift and estate tax as a spousal transfer at that stage. On Georgina's death the assets in the trust are then passed on to Grant's children and at that stage the estate taxes are due appropriate to her estate, and not by reference to Grant. The estate tax charge is subject to the exclusion amount of US$5.60 million in 2018 but now increased by the US senate to circa US$11 million.

The executors of Grant's will need to make a QTIP election, or partial election, on the estate tax form, detailing the assets that form the trust. A long time friend of Grant and his attorney will act as trustees as per his wishes. Once the election has been lodged with the return, which must be within nine months of Grant's death, it cannot be rescinded.

7.2.13   The Hong Kong trust non-vested solution

Hong Kong adopted the English common law on trusts into their legal system many years ago when it was bound to the UK. It has an expansive number of double tax treaties with other countries (32 countries with 27 giving taxing rights to Hong Kong) and it has lower tax rates where tax is payable.

Historically, Hong Kong was not necessarily the ideal place to have a trust set up but recent modernisation of the trust law there does improve things markedly for settlors and beneficiaries. In 2014, changes were made to the common law rules, and matters relating to trusts were put on a statutory footing. A few of the modern changes making Hong Kong an attractive jurisdiction for trusts include the abolition of the rule against perpetuity, improvement of beneficiary protections, restricting trustees' exemption from liability (e.g. fraud, misconduct, etc.) and obtaining insurance for trust asset protection.

In the *Man* case, prior to the modernisation of the trust rules in Hong Kong, the common law standard-of-care requirement by trustees was looked at in detail. Land owned in Hong Kong's New Territories by a "village clan" was sold by layperson trustees for HK$342 million but just over two weeks later was sold on by the purchaser company for HK$446 million! Naturally the "village clan" questioned the increased sell-on figure and suggested that the trustees managing the sale had been negligent in disposing of the land for such a low figure compared to the market price. The Court said there was a duty of care to sell the land at an appropriate price and not to do so was a breach of duty and the trustees, who were inexperienced village lay persons, should have sought professional assistance.

The new trust reforms in Hong Kong have therefore cemented the duty of care into statutory legislation, along with other modern aspects of trust law, to make Hong Kong one of the trustee legally constrained jurisdictions for protection of beneficiaries but also one of the most flexible of offshore jurisdictions.

Foreign settlors and beneficiaries only attract tax exemptions when they are non-residents of Hong Kong. The non-vested solution arises when the settlor arranges for trustees in Hong Kong to be vested of the assets subject to the trust deed which gives them, the trustees, power to appoint experts in management of assets, to have unrestricted rights to investment decisions, etc. However, the trustees are bound by legal constraints on the use of their powers in

Hong Kong so that they can be subject to criminal sanctions in any case of impropriety.

Following on from this, the perception of handing all power to the trustees when setting up a Hong Kong non-vested trust fills most settlors with trepidation. In most cases, in other jurisdictions, this would possibly be justified but Hong Kong has ensured that any trustee exemption clause will be invalid if there is a case of trustee fraud, wilful misconduct and/or gross negligence. These statutory controls are mandatory in Hong Kong and apply to new trusts created on or after 1 December 2013, and to pre-existing trusts with effect from 1 December 2014. See also *Armitage v Nurse.*

Any trustee exemption clause will be invalid to the extent that it seeks to relieve a trustee from liability for a breach of trust arising from the trustee's own fraud, wilful misconduct or gross negligence, or to grant the trustee any indemnity against trust property for such liability.

Law: *Trustee Ordinance,* (Cap. 29) and the *Perpetuities and Accumulations Ordinance* (Cap. 257); *Occupational Retirement Scheme Ordinance,* Chapter 426, Laws of Hong Kong

Cases: *Armitage v Nurse and Others* [1997] EWCA 1279 (Civ); *Man v Man* [2006] 4 HKLRD 484 and [2009] 9 HKCFAR 674

7.2.14 Protector of trust

In certain circumstances, where a settlor is providing funds on trust for the benefit of named beneficiaries, the settlor will be placing control in the hands of the trustees and only a letter of wishes is in place. The trustees are not necessarily bound to follow the letter of wishes and can, if they see fit, ignore the instructions in the letter of wishes from the settlor.

One option is to name a "protector" in the trust deed. The protector will have oversight and can ensure that the settlor's wishes are followed. This, linked with a "flee clause" (see **7.2.15** below), may go some way to calm a nervous settlor who has an independent trust company in some far off jurisdiction which he or she is never likely to visit. The protector, say a trusted family friend, would oversee the trustees' actions and either halt the proposed trustee action or suggest another course of action. If the protector is the settlor then this may have adverse tax implications at a later date with regard to the trust's residence status.

It is interesting that one of the TRS reporting requirements (see **7.2.3** – Trust reporting) is to name the "protector" and to provide details. This is stated to be to provide new data for HMRC to gauge how many trusts have protectors but in light of the *Charman* case below it may be significant in determining whether the trust is onshore or offshore.

The protector's powers could be such that the clause allows for him or her to:

- make investment policy decisions;
- instigate the flee clause (see below);
- discharge one or more trustees;
- have an oversight of fees payable to the trustee company;
- transfer powers to a replacement successor protector.

The protector's powers may be detailed in the trust document as follows:

> "The 'Protector', shall mean the Person named in the Schedule [...] attached hereto to act as a Protector or such other person as may be appointed or become the Protector in accordance with this settlement."

Where a settlor acts as protector then he has a reserved power over the settlement and a court may instruct him in cases of marital breakdown, bankruptcy or criminal proceedings to use those powers. A protector independent of the settlor, albeit a family friend or acquaintance, would not necessarily be swayed by such an instruction. In one of the biggest divorce cases heard before the UK courts the settlor acting as protector was addressed and succinctly put as follows:

> "I put to [the solicitors in Jersey] the question of making certain of the powers exercisable only with your consent and of giving you the power to appoint new trustees. Their response was to suggest your appointment as 'protector' of the settlement who would in effect have to bless all the trustees' decisions before they could be implemented. Neither I nor [your accountants] really like this as it could be argued

that the protector was in effect a trustee and prejudice the off-shore status of the trusts. [Your accountants] are confident that the letter of wishes will not be ignored and, correctly drafted, would afford adequate protection. As a letter of wishes is morally binding only and [the proposed corporate trustee] an unknown entity, I would suggest that, at the very least, you should have power to appoint and remove the trustees and will so provide."

Case: *Charman v Charman* [2007] EWCA (Civ) 503

7.2.15   Flee clauses

The insertion of a "flee clause" in an offshore trust document is a protective measure that gives the settlor or protector the option to move the location of the trust at a moment's notice, for example in cases of jurisdictional insecurity. So if, say, a *coup d'état* occurs (or more likely, the sudden imposition of tax as in Cyprus) there is an undelayed smooth transition to a default jurisdiction. If the trust asset is company shares the transfer forms could already be signed and held in escrow to be received by the default jurisdiction. The transfer clause may state "... of some other state or territory in any part of the world...". Further sub-clauses may be inserted to link the governing law to another specific offshore jurisdiction so that, in the case of an "emergency" event, the trust can be moved by the protector instantly.

This failsafe option should already be in place, rather than having to search for a new location for the trust assets when the emergency event happens. This is because the slowness of migrating a trust tends to delay matters, by which time anti-migration factors may be in place. The trustees, on retirement (or removal), would wish to secure contractual indemnities and maybe vet the incoming trustees and other administrative matters. Quick moving events make speed of jurisdictional change vital, and if a flee clause is already in place it effects an immediate exit strategy for the trust. Obviously this "belt and braces" approach comes with additional administration and costs and it may be considered unwarranted in view of the stability of the particular offshore jurisdiction.

8. Returning home

8.1 Capital gains

8.1.1 Capital gains tax planning

Please refer to **2.4** and **3.2** for guidance on the capital gains tax rules in respect of non-residents and for reference to legislation and HMRC guidance.

An individual returning to live in the UK needs to consider the tax implications – both in the UK and in the country where he is resident – of selling assets (including investments), and to determine whether he should sell any of them before or after becoming resident again in the UK.

The UK has specific rates of tax for capital gains (unlike some countries, like Australia, where taxable gains are treated like any other income and taxed at an individual's marginal rate of tax), and these are quite low: the highest rate is 28% for 2018-19 for higher and additional rate taxpayers, the lowest being 10% for basic rate taxpayers – see **2.4.2**). For this reason, a lower tax liability overall may arise by waiting until the individual is a UK tax resident again and selling when living back in the UK. In addition, the UK has an annual capital gains exemption of £11,700 per person for 2018-19, whereas many other countries have no equivalent exemption. If an asset is jointly held, e.g. by a husband and wife, then each owner will have this exemption and so potentially £23,400 of a taxable gain on the disposal of a jointly-owned asset may be covered by this exemption (see **2.4**). An individual, even if he is not considering selling any assets in the foreseeable future, should consider whether any assets in his sole name should be in joint names with his spouse/civil partner. Non-tax issues should also be considered, however, if an individual is thinking of this change in ownership.

The individual will also need to be aware of any unused losses he may have from previous tax years in the UK, as this too may have a bearing on his decision as to when to sell.

The first step, therefore, is for the individual to prepare CGT calculations for both the UK and the country he is resident in, to see if there is a loss or gain on the potential sale of the asset(s) and what the potential tax liability is in each country. If a loss then it may be advisable for the individual to wait until he is resident again in the UK, so that he can claim the loss and use it against taxable gains that may arise either during the tax year concerned or in future tax years, assuming he does not need the loss in his host country.

If a gain arises, then if the asset is not UK residential property or an asset used in a trade via a branch or agency in the UK, it will be outside the scope of UK CGT if it is sold while the individual is not resident in the UK, so no tax will arise in the UK. The individual will need to check the tax implications in the country where he is living and resident. If he is living in a country that does not tax capital gains, then it will normally be advisable to sell while he is still resident and living there, i.e. before becoming resident once more in the UK.

With regards to the sale of residential property in the UK see section **3.2** for a more detailed explanation. If there is potentially a gain, then if the property is sold while the individual is non-resident, the taxable gain will be under the NRCGT regime (see **3.2**). If he waits to sell it when he is resident again in the UK, then the gain will be from acquisition and so may be larger, depending on the individual's circumstances.

In this respect, the individual needs to decide whether or not he will return to live in the property as his main residence. If it was his only or main residence before living overseas, and if he were to move back into the property again and to live in it as his only or main residence, then the period during which he was absent from the property and working overseas may be regarded as a deemed period of "residence" for private residence relief (PRR) purposes (as opposed to residence for SRT purposes). In that case, no taxable gain would arise for this period, subject to the important point below.

One important condition is that the individual did not perform any work whatsoever in the UK while working overseas. If he did, then the period will not be a deemed period of residence as a result of working overseas (which has no time limit as to the length of the period of absence), but he may still be able to have a deemed period of residence for three years with there being no specific reason for the absence.

If a second home election has not been made within two years of having two residences, thereby nominating the property to remain the individual's main residence while living and working overseas, then depending on the individual's circumstances, it may be possible to put in a late election under ESC D21. If the individual's spouse jointly owns the property then the above will also apply to him or her, although if the individual's period of absence is deemed to be a period of residence as a result of working overseas, then this may also apply to the spouse whether or not he or she had been working overseas (see **3.2**).

If an individual does not intend to move back into a property that was once his main residence, he may need to re-consider this if his period of absence, or part of it, could be regarded as a deemed period of residence for PRR purposes, if he were to live in the property again as his only or main residence after his period of absence.

If a loss has been made overall on the sale of UK residential property, then (as with the sale of any other asset) it may be advisable to wait until the individual is resident again in the UK and sell the property at that stage. Once more, this assumes that he does not require the loss in the country he has been living in, and that the property has not been his main residence at any time. If it has been, then this loss will be restricted with regards to the period for which it was his main residence and eligible for PRR.

Alternatively, if the individual is non-resident when selling the loss-making property, he will have the option of electing to use the acquisition cost as the base cost under the NRCGT regime, allowing him to claim the full loss. While non-resident, he will not be able to set off this loss against gains other than other non-resident capital gains, but once he becomes resident again the loss can be utilised as normal against any other gains from any type of asset.

Example

David and Victoria have been living overseas in Dubai for many years and have decided to return to the UK to retire during 2018-19. Over the years they have built up an investment property portfolio of six rental properties in the UK, one of which, Chestnut Cottage, was their only or main residence prior to leaving the UK for Dubai.

While living in Dubai they have always lived in rented accommodation and they do not intend to move back into Chestnut Cottage to live there again upon their return to the UK. Rather, they plan to purchase a new property to live in and they will continue to rent out Chestnut Cottage.

To help finance their retirement they intend to sell two of the rental properties, but not Chestnut Cottage, and to also sell their shareholding in Don and Vlad Limited, which unfortunately was not a very good investment and will make a loss of £50,000, with potentially higher losses the longer they hold onto the shares – the company is in a bit of bother, so David and Victoria have decided to "cut their losses and run".

Similarly, one of the investment properties they intend to sell, Riverine Lodge, will make a loss overall of £75,000, with £25,000 arising since 6 April 2015, as it was built on a flood plain and it floods regularly. The other rental property, Duck House, will make a healthy gain of £200,000 since acquisition, with £100,000 arising since 6 April 2015. All their assets are in their joint names.

David is an employee and has not performed any work in the UK while working overseas. Their taxable income in the UK for 2018-19 is £40,000 each after their personal allowances.

A second home election nominating Chestnut Cottage to remain their main residence for PRR purposes while they are overseas has not been made. Indeed, David and Victoria are blissfully ignorant of the fact that one was required; after all, they do not own the accommodation they have lived in while in Dubai so why would one be needed?

They are aware that Dubai will not tax them on the disposal of their assets, so they intend to sell their two rental properties and shareholding while still resident in Dubai and before they become resident in the UK, believing they will not end up with a tax bill.

If they were to do this, the gain and allowable loss on the two rental properties from 6 April 2015 under the NRCGT regime will be as follows:

	£ 100%	£ 50% share
Duck House gain	100,000	50,000
Less: Riverine Lodge loss	(25,000)	(12,500)
	75,000	37,500
Less: annual capital gains exemption		(11,700)
Taxable gain		£25,800
Capital gains tax liability in the UK:		
Tax at 28% (all their basic rate band has been used up with other taxable income)		£7,224

Both David and Victoria will have a tax liability on the sale of their rental properties of £7,224 each i.e. a total of £14,448.

Neither of them was aware that they could have elected to use the original cost figure as the base cost for Riverine Lodge under the NRCGT regime. Had they done so then their CGT liability would have been as follows:

As can be seen, by electing for the acquisition cost to be used when calculating the loss on the sale of Riverine Lodge, their overall tax liability under the NRCGT regime is £448, a reduction of £14,000.

David and Victoria will need to make sure they each file NRCGT returns within 30 days of completion of the above properties, to avoid hefty penalties arising (see **3.2**).

The sale of their shares in Don and Vlad Limited is outside the scope of UK CGT, as they were non-resident at the time of sale and the disposal is not covered by the NRCGT regime. Had they delayed selling their shareholding until they were resident in the UK again, they could have claimed the loss from the sale of these shares, which they can then carry forward to use against future gains from the disposal of any other assets.

With regards to Chestnut Cottage, David and Victoria should consider moving back into it and living in it as their only or main residence for a time, so that they can claim the period they were living and working overseas as a period of residence. In this way, it will not attract CGT. A second home election should have been made within two years of moving into accommodation in Dubai that was

433

their main residence. A residence for PRR does not need to be owned and can include rented or employer-provided accommodation. Luckily for David and Victoria, they should be able to put in a late election under ESC D21, nominating Chestnut Cottage to remain their main residence while they were living in Dubai. The election needs to be made by both of them.

If the individual is a temporary non-resident, and so has become resident again in the UK during the five-year period discussed at **2.2.11**, then any gains made during this period of temporary non-residence will be assessed to UK tax when the individual returns to the UK (see **2.2.12(iv)** and **2.4**). If he is near the end of this five-year period, then he may wish to delay his return to the UK until after the period has ended if he has made potential taxable gains during this period. If he were to return after that period, then the gains will escape UK tax. Conversely, if he has made a loss during this period, then he may want to think of returning to the UK and becoming resident again during this five-year period so he can claim the loss.

Some countries may have an exit type charge, which individuals need to be aware of when leaving a country. For example, assets owned at the time an individual ceases to be resident in Australia may be deemed to have been disposed of at that time at market value, so an Australian tax liability may arise even though the asset has not actually been sold. The individual can elect to defer this tax charge until the asset is actually sold. In addition, if the individual is returning to live in the UK then under the UK and Australia double tax treaty, there will be no tax liability in Australia if the individual is resident in the UK at the time of actual sale and has made the above deferment election. If the individual intends to move on to other countries after living in the UK, he needs to be mindful of the fact that this clause is not in all of Australia's double tax treaties, so if he still owns the asset, a tax liability could still arise in Australia when the asset is eventually sold.

8.2 Share options

8.2.1 Introduction

Many companies incentivise their internationally mobile employees by offering them share options in connection with their overseas postings, which vest and then are exercised on completion of those postings. The share option may have restrictions or conditions relating to performance and may be issued either by the UK company prior to departure or by an overseas subsidiary on completion of a term abroad.

The Office for Tax Simplification published its findings on "unapproved" employee share schemes and subsequently the *Finance Act* 2014 simplified the taxing structure for such existing and future share options with effect from 6 April 2015. This means that existing share options still in hibernation are affected by the new taxation rules, as well as new options since 6 April 2015.

Example

An internationally mobile employee (IME) working in Singapore is granted an option by his employer on 1 January 2017 whilst not resident in the UK. On 31 December 2017 he leaves his job in Singapore and relocates to the head office in London to work. On 31 December 2019 the option vests and he exercises his share option.

Under previous share option rules no income tax charge arose in the UK. However, under the new rules, the share option agreement has a relevant period between 1 January 2017 and 31 December 2019. One year of this period was spent in Singapore and two subsequent years were spent working in London. Therefore the IME will be subject to UK income tax on two thirds of the profit realised by the exercise. Class 1 primary contributions will also be due and the company will be subject to secondary contributions. The total maximum cost is therefore 45% tax plus 2% Class 1 NICs plus 13.8% employer's NICs.

Law: SSCBA 1992, s. 4(4)(a); ITEPA 2003, Pt. 7, Ch. 5; FA 2014

8.2.2 Income tax charge

Incentivising internationally mobile employees by way of approved UK share incentive schemes (e.g. SAYE, EMIs and SIPs) can still offer limited tax benefits. Such schemes encompass stock options, stock purchase plans, restricted stock/share plans, share awards and stock appreciation rights, all of which come within the new taxing rules.

A tax charge under PAYE will invariably arise on vesting or exercise of the options. This is because these share benefit outcomes arise within the ambit of readily convertible assets (RCAs). Tax deduction under PAYE will be required but, under real time information, reporting the disparity between the tax and NICs deductions needs to be handled carefully.

Tax deductions after allowances will depend on the individual's marginal rate of tax and could be 20%, 40% or 45%, so a higher rate taxpayer could be paying an effective rate of tax and NICs of 47% (45% + 2%). If the employer's 13.8% NICs liability is transferred to the employee, or is reimbursed by the employee, this effective rate would be much higher i.e. 50.28% for a 40% taxpayer and 54.59% for a 45% taxpayer (i.e. 45% tax plus 2% Class 1 NICs plus 13.8% employer's NICs, less the 45% tax relief on those reimbursed contributions).

Whilst the tax and NICs charges for options in the UK will be high, the tax treatment for options exercised whilst the employee is abroad will vary.

As can be seen in the examples below, the tax treatment can vary depending on whether there is a double tax treaty in force and, if there is, whether it relieves share options. In many cases, options will be exercised in a jurisdiction that does not have a treaty with the UK and this reduces the potential tax liability. HMRC give an example of a person posted to Dubai (non treaty country and no local income tax) and comment that "In this example, the fact that there is no tax treaty between the UK and Dubai, means that there is no treaty time apportionment. However, the rules of Chapter 5B mean that the UK charge is on income relating to UK duties only."

Guidance: ERSM 163190

8.2.3   *National Insurance Contributions*

A number of National Insurance matters need to be considered, such as the application of Class 1 NIC, the location of the posting (e.g. EEA or rest of the world (ROW)), whether there is a double tax treaty in place and, if not, what the treatment would be.

From a UK perspective, the calculation of tax will depend on the UK days of residence as a proportion of the total period including the overseas work period. See the example at **8.2.1** above.

On top of the potential income tax liability, an NICs charge may also be imposed but the charge will depend on the internationally mobile employee being UK insured for the 52-week period after leaving the UK, or having a "certificate of coverage" (A1) – see below. So, whilst transfers with option agreements between European or social security jurisdictions will not result in a charge in both countries, other non-agreement countries may result in a potential double charge.

In cases where there is a bilateral treaty in place, and the assignment is to the UK, the employer can apply for a certificate of coverage to ensure that the employee on assignment to the UK is kept within the home country social security system. Where this is granted, the assigned employee will continue to pay home country social security and will not be subject to the UK's NICs treatment. In the third example (Sally) at **8.2.4** below, the US/UK bilateral treaty – regarding a US citizen coming to the UK for a period of less than five years – can apply for the certificate so that FICA and medicare continue to be paid in the US and no Class 1 primary or secondary contributions are paid in the UK. Conversely, a UK employee seconded to one of these countries should obtain a certificate of coverage A1 and continue to pay Class 1 contributions in the UK rather than the country of assignment. However, a self-employed person working in the US/UK from the other state will normally be covered and taxed in the country where the duties are carried out.

See **Appendix 3** for a list of the countries with which the UK currently has social security agreements in place.

8.2.4   Host country treatment

Another matter to review is whether the offshore jurisdiction treats the share option as taxable and will give relief for tax paid in the UK. Or, if there is no taxation of the share option in the jurisdiction and the option is exercised abroad, there may be no tax liabilities at all.

Example 1

Keith applies for a job in Australia with a construction company as financial officer. He is offered membership of the company's employee share scheme (ESS) as part of the employment package and the shares can be redeemed after a three year holding period. Due to company expansion in SE Asia he is transferred after three

437

months in Australia to Malaysia under the three year contract and is treated as having been a temporary resident in Australia, i.e. a temporary visa under the *Migration Act* 1958.

After three years, when he is tax resident in Malaysia, the shares held on capital account are redeemed for a cash amount of 1 million Australian dollars on exercise (gain is AUS $750,000 x 3/36ths = 62,500 @ 10%). Keith had been a temporary resident when the CGT event happened, and he will only be taxed on the gain or loss from ESS interests that relate to his employment in Australia. His company will show on the ESS annual report to the Australian Tax Office (ATO):

- the actual assessable amount of the discount, after taking into account the foreign service element discount; or

- the gross amount.

In the case of the first point the company should also provide to the ATO, as an addendum, the dates relevant to the foreign service. The remaining gain or loss will be disregarded.

In Malaysia, a tax-resident employee benefiting from an employee share option scheme (ESOS) is liable to income tax at a maximum 28% on the difference between the price paid and the market value at the date of exercise. In Malaysia, if an employee has a share option scheme (ESOS), as a tax resident under the Malaysian *Income Tax Act* 1967 he is normally taxable to income tax on the price paid and the market value at the date of exercise of the ESOS at up to a maximum of 28%. However, under the same Act it is only income of any person that accrues or is derived from Malaysia, or received in Malaysia from outside, that is taxable. For capital gains tax purposes there is no tax liability on the gain in Malaysia when he sells the shares as the share issuing company is not a real property company. Any small amount of tax on the gain on time apportionment in Australia will not be allowed as a credit in Malaysia as no taxation arises there.

On Keith's return to the UK, no income tax or NICs will be imposed as the exercise was abroad.

In summary, the SSE was made when he was temporarily resident in Australia, the large Malaysian ESOS gain is not taxable there, and for UK tax purposes the whole period over which the gain accrued was overseas.

Example 2

Andrew works for an international online betting company and has received employee share options on 5 April 2016 with a three year vesting period. The company opens up a branch office in the Turks & Caicos Islands in the West Indies and transfers Andrew there to set up and run the branch from 5 April 2017. He is contracted to be there for three years.

The share option is exercised on 5 April 2019 whilst he still works in the Turks & Caicos Islands. As there is no double tax treaty between the Islands and the UK there is no treaty apportionment between the two countries. Instead, the UK charge to tax and NICs on the gain will be apportioned. The foreign service deduction will be 730 days over the total period of 1095 days, so two thirds of the gain is not chargeable to tax under PAYE. The NICs Class 1 contributions will be applicable for a two-year period as Andrew has moved to a "non-agreement" country and is therefore subject to NICs until 5 April 2018. This will be at 2%/12%, depending on the apportioned chargeable amount. See ITEPA 2003, s. 41F(3).

Example 3

Sally works for Fargo Bank and is assigned from the US to the new head office in London. As part of the remuneration package she was granted a share option after a six-month settling in period.

The UK assignment is for a period of four years. After three years the share options are exercised by Sally within the rules of the scheme. She is charged to tax on the whole of the gain and, as she is a 45% tax rate payer, she is subject to tax at that rate. The company pays secondary contributions of 13.8% (over £45,000 earnings). However, whilst the whole of the gain is subject to income tax at her marginal rate of 45%, she does not have to pay any employee Class 1 contributions as she was covered for US social security purposes (certificate of coverage) for the period.

8.2.5   *Termination payments*

At the Budget 2016, the UK government announced that it would align the employer NICs treatment of termination payments with income tax and that it would tighten the scope of the £30,000 exemption to prevent manipulation.

The existing £30,000 income tax exemption will be retained and employees will continue to benefit from an unlimited employee NICs exemption for payments associated with the termination of employment, but the employer will be subject to Class 1A NI contributions from 6 April 2019. Currently, Class 1A NICs at 13.8% are a burden of the employer not the employee.

The exclusion of the foreign service relief (FSR) from 6 April 2018 (as detailed in the table below) will have an ongoing effect on termination payments with regard to periods worked overseas. This new restrictive legislation will not apply to seafarers or to those who are non-resident for the tax year in which their employment is terminated and who have been within the FSR rules.

These FSR changes to the taxation of termination payments made to internationally mobile employees apply from 6 April 2018 (ITEPA 2003, s. 414(2), introduced by F(No.2)A 2017, s. 5)). Previously, termination payments could be excluded from UK tax where an internationally mobile employee:

1. had spent 75% or more of his or her employment in respect of overseas duties/employment;
2. had worked for the company for more than ten years, of which the last ten years were spent working overseas; or
3. had worked for the company for more than 20 years and not less than half of the time had been spent working abroad, including ten of the last 20 years.

If the employee had not qualified for any of the above he could claim relief for part of the employment period spent abroad after deducting the statutory £30,000 (see the example below).

Example 1 – rules before April 2018

Amanda has spent 22 years working for her employer with work abroad and receives a £100,000 when her employment is terminated, perhaps comprised of both pay in lieu of notice and statutory and contractual redundancy pay, which would be treated as follows:

Spends 17 years out of 22 years employed working abroad.	• Point 1 above • Exempt from tax
Spends 10 of the last 12 years working abroad.	• Point 2 above. • Exempt from tax.
Spends last 8 years and 5 of the first years working abroad.	• Point 3 above. • Exempt from tax.
Spends first 4 years working in the UK then abroad for 7 years then IN the UK until termination.	• See below.

In the last case above, Amanda had spent seven years abroad but did not qualify under points 1-3 above. However, she would have been entitled to deduct the £30,000 statutory exemption and would then be taxed on 15/22 of the remaining £70,000 (= £47,727) at her marginal rate of tax.

From 6 April 2018, Amanda would no longer be able to benefit, as previously, from the FSR exemptions above unless she is resident abroad when the payment is made. (Seafarers are not affected by this rule change.)

Instead, from 6 April 2018, Amanda would now be charged to tax on any payment over the £30,000. This termination payment, if made from a foreign source, relating to previous periods of employment in the UK which were not merely incidental duties, may escape UK taxation under a foreign source rule. The *National Insurance Contributions Bill* 2018 should introduce a Class 1A charge on amounts over the £30,000 when it is expected to apply from 6 April 2019.

Example 2 – rules from April 2018

From 6 April 2018 Amanda receives basic annual pay of £120,000, but after six months she is made redundant with immediate effect due to the loss of an important contract with an overseas customer which she has been generating for the last 12 months. Due to this immediate termination she is offered a compromise payment of £100,000, made up of:

1.   £60,000 contractual PILON;
2.   £30,000 compensation; and
3.   £10,000 vested share options.

Amanda cedes £70,000 of the compensation after discussions with the HR department for the company, agreeing to pay that amount into her company pension fund. Note: tax relief is due on the pension contributions because of unused carry forward annual allowances being available and the subsequent option for 25% tax free lump sum withdrawal facility when the pension is in drawdown.

In applying the (F(No.2)A 2017, s. 5) rules from 6 April 2018 regarding taxation of termination awards, HMRC state that the "post employment notice pay" (PENP) figure needs to be calculated to see if it exceeds or is below the termination payment. Certain payments do not form part of the termination payment, such as bonus and, in this case, share options. If the PENP is less than the termination payment the PENP figure is treated as general earnings and subject to tax and Class 1 NICs. If PENP is equal to or greater than the termination payment, the first £30,000 will be exempt and the balance subject to Class 1A contributions from 6 April 2019, following enactment of the *National Insurance Contributions Bill*.

The formula concocted by HMRC is:

$$\text{PENP} = \left(\text{BP} \times \frac{D}{P} \right) - T$$

where:

BP = Basic pay in the period, i.e. £120,000pa (but paid at monthly or weekly pay periods);

D = Days in the post employment notice period, i.e. 182 days or six months;

P = Days in the whole period, i.e. 365 days or 12 months (NB strictly the reference is to days);

> **T** = Total amounts of payment/benefits etc. in connection with the termination, e.g. payments regarding the termination, salary, fees, gratuity and cash benefits. In Amanda's case this will be nil (the vesting share options being taxed separately).

In Amanda's case this will create a PENP as follows: £120,000 x 6 months/12 months minus nil = £60,000.

This £60,000 PENP is compared with the "relevant termination award" (RTA) which is not redundancy payment, i.e. £90,000 (ignoring the share option which is taxed separately) less ceded pension sacrifice £70,000 gives an RTA of £20,000. This figure is less than the PENP figure of £60,000 and so the RTA figure is treated as earnings and is also subject to Class 1 NICs. The share options are taxable and Class 1 primary and secondary NICs are payable (see **8.2.2** above).

Note that in many cases where PENP is less than the RTA a tranche up to £30,000 is covered by the exemption and the balance over that amount is subject to tax and NICs. The permutations can be complex, depending on the termination offer, and expert advice should be sought (both by the employee and the employer) prior to agreement.

It may now make sense for those working abroad to opt for a "host based" contract of employment and a separate home based contract for UK non-incidental duties. This may then have the effect of classing a foreign service termination payment as subject to potential double taxation and/or as exempt from UK taxation if the individual is non-resident.

Alternatively, a termination payment may be classed as bonus and thereby apportioned over the foreign service period, or part of the termination payment may be waived to enhance company pension entitlement, thereby attracting tax relief – both of which may suit the company and employee better. Worldwide payroll providers offer a multi-country payroll facility to enable flexibility in payroll options.

Law: *Employment Rights Act* 1996, s. 111A; *ITEPA* 2003, s. 62, 401, 402A-E, 403, 412A, 413-414A-C; *Finance (No 2) Act* 2017, s. 5; *National Insurance Contributions Bill 2018; The Social Security (Contributions)(Amendment No. 2) Regs* 2018, SI 2018/257

Guidance: ACAS code of practice 4, Settlement Agreements; ACAS *Settlement Agreements – A Guide*

8.3   End of posting review

8.3.1   Introduction and overview of tax considerations

When the expat is planning to return to the UK, either permanently or following a long period of overseas employment, and will then be regarded as UK resident under the statutory residence rules (SRT) from the date of his arrival (but see **2.2.6** – Split-year tax treatment variables), there are a number of things that should be checked before return.

Split-year tax treatment applies to overseas earnings, as well as overseas investment income, where the source has ceased prior to the expat establishing residence status. However, the expat is still liable to UK tax on his or her UK investment income for the whole of the tax year, after deducting the personal tax allowance.

Other tax considerations are as follows:

- Gains on assets acquired whilst the individual is resident overseas for five years or more, that are actually made in the years between the tax year of departure from the UK and the tax year of return (i.e. in full years of non-residence), are exempt.

- Capital gains tax is charged in the tax year of return only on gains arising from disposals made after the date of arrival in the UK.

- If assets are showing a loss, and it is the expat's intention to dispose of these assets, then the disposal should be deferred until after he has become UK resident again so that the loss can be claimed later. (The tax loss will be wasted if the asset is sold whilst the individual is non-resident.)

- The expat should ensure that all overseas interest-bearing accounts of large amounts are closed in the tax year prior to his arrival in the UK, so that interest accrued up to the date immediately before foreign departure is credited to the account prior to then establishing UK residence status. This may help to avoid a charge to UK tax.

Quick checklist	
1 – before UK return	Consider disposing of existing UK and foreign assets prior to return after more than five years abroad if these are showing gains. This will help the individual to obtain a CGT exemption and then an uplift on subsequent reacquisition. By contrast, retain any assets showing a loss.
2 – in UK	Reoccupy the UK residence before moving to another property so as to obtain certain CGT exemptions. See **3.2** CGT on sale.
3 – in UK	Consider opening NISA accounts, tax free for investments up to £20,000 each for spouses, and consider repeating every year.
4 – in UK	Register with HMRC to receive the annual tax return SA100, so as to obtain tax reliefs, e.g. on pension contributions, and the annual personal allowance of (for 2018-19) £11,850 per individual, ensuring that assets are equalised between spouses.
5 – in UK	Register with the local surgery in the UK again immediately on return.

8.3.2   *National Insurance contributions*

When returning to the UK after a long period abroad, some benefits – e.g. state pension, bereavement allowance, etc. – will depend on the expat's contribution record in the past. Class 2 or Class 3 voluntary contributions may have continued to be paid to secure benefits on return to the UK.

Expats retiring after 5 April 2016 now have to have at least 35 qualifying years of contribution to get the full state pension under the new single tier pension rules. In these circumstances, catch-up payments can be made but these are limited to 10 years. Many expats living abroad do not make payments on a regular basis into the fund and then have a reduced or nil pension on retirement. However, expats will be able to obtain a summary by completing NI38 and will learn whether they will receive the full state pension on retirement and what they have to do to top up.

8.3.3   Tax enforcement abroad

It is often the case that UK tax will be due on UK assets owned by a foreign domiciliary which will require attendance by UK or foreign executors, especially if the foreign will has to be re-sealed in the UK under the *Colonial Probates Act* 1892 (see **6.7.2** – Re-sealing a foreign will).

The question arises whether tax demanded by HMRC of foreign executors should be paid as it may be unenforceable in a foreign jurisdiction and as the executors have a duty of care to the beneficiaries not to pay unenforceable debts. The option HMRC may have on an estate of the deceased who has become deemed domiciled in the UK and taxable on worldwide assets, which the foreign executor refuses to acknowledge (for whatever reason), is to apply to the court and realise the UK assets in whole or part payment of the UK liability. The EC Mutual Assistance Recovery Directive ("MARD") applies in respect of recovery of taxes within Europe (i.e. the EU) and there are some agreements with other countries, but these are limited in number.

In the Hong Kong case of *Laufer deceased*, UK IHT was due in the region of between £2.65 million and a lower figure of £2.395 million due to certain beneficiaries being charities. Hong Kong had abolished estate duty with effect from 11 February 2006. HMRC acknowledged the difficulty in the collection of the tax in a foreign jurisdiction, especially as the UK assets were valued only at £1.050 million, and accepted £1.615 million in tax with additional interest added at the appropriate rate. The executor was under a duty not to pay an unenforceable debt as to do so would result in the beneficiaries being financially worse off. There were US, Hong Kong and Irish beneficiaries as well as charities and HMRC stated that they would enforce the claim against the Irish beneficiaries who were of course situated in the EU under MARD. In the end the Hong Kong recorder Wong directed the executor to pay the IHT of £1.615 million.

The *Laufer* case, along with others concerning the enforcement of taxes in non-MARD jurisdictions, gives will writers and executors potential problems in discharging tax liabilities in a foreign jurisdiction. Consideration should be given, when drawing up a will with substantial assets and some beneficiaries situated abroad, as to how the tax burden may be allocated if non-MARD jurisdictional assets are included. The executors may wish to consider insurance to protect their position or obtain indemnities from beneficiaries. This is a difficult area for anyone concerned with dealing with a will, foreign or UK, which has assets situated abroad other than in Europe.

Law: *Revenue (Abolition of Estate Duty) Ordinance* 2005; Council Directive 2008/55/EC; MARD 2010, OECD Model Tax Treaty, article 27

Cases: *Scottish National Orchestra Society Ltd v Thomson's Executor,* 1969 SLT325; *McGowan v Hamblett* [2007] NZLR 120; *In the matter of Edgar Martin Laufer deceased and pursuant to Order 85 of the Rules of the High Court (Cap 4A),* HCMP2967/2015

8.4   Offshore bonds

8.4.1   Significance

As was stated in **7.1** (Overseas tax and investment planning), an expat returning to the UK should contact the insurer or adviser for clarification if the expat is in any doubt as to what sort of policy/bond is held (personal portfolio bond (PPB) or investment bond).

Not all bonds are taxable but a PPB could be subject to UK tax almost immediately on return (see the example below). For tax purposes, the most important distinction is between "non-qualifying" and "qualifying" policies, although most foreign policies are non-qualifying policies. Policies are also referred to as investment bonds, single premium life policies and personal portfolio bonds but to all intents and purposes they are lump sum investments, held either onshore or offshore. Non-qualifying policies will normally give rise to a gain, but a number of things can affect whether tax is paid or not. However, the 5% withdrawal each year is not taxable and accumulates until the 20th year.

The advantages for expats of having offshore personal portfolio bonds (PPBs) were considered at **7.1**. If the insurer has complete

447

discretion over the selection of the property or index determining the benefits then the policy would not be a PPB. Yet in circumstances where the policyholder has influence or can have influence over the selection of the assets then that "ability to select" is that of the policyholder and the policy is treated as a PPB.

Where a policy or contract is a PPB at the end of the "insurance year" there is a PPB gain if the sum of premiums paid and the total amount of PPB excesses exceeds the total amount of part surrender gains. The charge will arise if the policy is a PPB at the end of the insurance year. Individuals are treated as having made a gain of an amount equal to 15% of premiums paid, with the premiums paid being treated as increased annually by 15%, on a compound basis until the penultimate year. However, there is no annual charge in the year the policy ends.

If, on arrival in the UK, the PPB holder did not then intend to become UK resident, or to remain in the UK for at least two years, the holder is given until the end of the "insurance year" in which UK residence was established to vary the bond as described. The date of arrival in the UK is substituted as the reference date for determining the "insurance year" if the holder intended to establish UK residence on arrival. No annual PPB charge is made in these circumstances for any "insurance year" before that in which the variation was made.

Example

Ralf returned permanently to the UK on 1 September 2007 when he lost his job abroad and was treated as being UK resident for tax purposes. Ralf had taken out a PPB overseas on 27 May 2007 shortly before he lost his job and was advised (incorrectly) that the PPB was just as tax efficient in the UK. The first insurance year to begin after 6 April 2007 ends on 26 May 2008 so this is the ordinary time limit for varying the terms of the policy to limit the property and indices that were selected.

Ralf did not advise his PPB provider or financial adviser of his change of address back in the UK but on the surrender of his bond HMRC became aware of the PPB status as the provider sent a corrective statement and chargeable event certificate. Ralf will be subject to an annual charge of 15%, on a compound basis until the penultimate year, as follows:

- Ralf had started the policy at the start of "insurance year" 1 with a premium of £5,000.
- During year 4 he made a withdrawal of £3,500 and during year 7 a further withdrawal of £2,750.
- A further premium of £2,000 was paid in year 9.
- The policy was surrendered in year 11 for £5,500.

Ralf therefore has annual gains as in column 3 below.

Gains arise on "excess events" at the ends of "insurance years" 4 and 7 as follows:

Year 4: £2,500 on the withdrawal of £3,500
(that is, £3,500 – 4 x 0.05 x £5,000)
Year 7: £2,000 on the withdrawal of £2,750
(that is, £2,750 – 3 x 0.05 x £5,000)

Year	Accumulation x 15% = Col 3.	Invested (withdrawn) during the year.	PPB gain & carry forward to next year Col 1.
			£
Year 1	£5,000	£5,000	750
Year 2	£5,750	Nil	862
Year 3	£6,612	Nil	991
Year 4	£7,603	(£3,500 – 4yrs x 5% x £5,000 = £2,500)	1,140
Year 5	£6,243	Nil	936
Year 6	£7,179	Nil	1,076
Year 7	£8,252	(£2,750 – 3yrs x 5% x £5,000 = £2,000)	1,238
Year 8	£7,490	Nil	1,123
Year 9	£8,613	+ £2,000	1,592
Year 10	£12,205	Nil	1,831
Year 11 surrender	**Nil**	**£5,500**	**£11,539**

Ralf, or his adviser, now has to calculate his final position with regard to the investment:

Proceeds on surrender in year 11	5,500
Previous capital withdrawals (in years 4 and 7)	6,250
Less premium paid initially and in year 9	(7,000)
Less gains on previous part surrenders	(4,500)
Gain in year 11	250

The gain of £250 when deducted from the PPB gains of £11,539 makes a total deficiency of £11,289 available for deficiency relief. So whilst it looks like Ralf will benefit from deficiency relief of £11,289 the PPB annual gains charge above is not counted for deficiency relief. Normally deficiency relief will be restricted to the smaller of:

- the loss on the final chargeable event calculation excluding PPB annual gains, i.e. taken as £0 above; or
- the total of gains on previous "excess events" which were £4,500 in years 4 and 7.

This is probably not the outcome Ralf was expecting!

As previously stated, PPBs are life insurance policies where the benefits payable are determined by the value of certain property chosen directly or indirectly by the policyholder, rather than investment funds generally available to other policyholders which would constitute a standard single premium investment bond. Incidentally, the *Finance (No. 2) Act* 2017 has included a new facility to extend the property categories, thereby alleviating the potential anti-avoidance rules being instigated.

Law: ITTOIA 2005, s. 516-526, 539 (including s. 520(5)-(7) as inserted by F(No.2)A 2017, s. 10)
Guidance: IPTM 3650, 3660, 3860

8.4.2 Foreign time apportionment

If these bonds are held when the expat is non-resident, a discount is allowed for this period when calculating the gain. This is done by applying the number of days spent abroad from inception of the bond to the date it is cashed in (see the examples below).

This discount for non-residence can also apply with top-slicing relief afterwards where the bond is encashed for a gain that results in an increased marginal tax rate because of the encashment. However, the number of years to be used for top-slicing purposes must exclude the non-residence period, so reducing the years available for top-slicing. Also, if there has been an "excess event" the years for top-slicing will be limited depending on when the excess event was.

Example

Nick takes out a life policy on 17 March 2010 from an insurer based in the Isle of Man whilst working in Dubai. He returns to the UK on 20 April 2014 and is UK resident from that date. He fully surrenders the policy on 5 October 2018, giving rise to a chargeable event gain of £100,750.

The policy is a "foreign policy" (see IPTM 3330), so an apportionment of the gain applies. There must also be a restriction in the number of years for top-slicing relief (see IPTM 3830).

The policy ran for a total of 3,125 days, including the days on which it was taken out and surrendered. Nick was not resident in the UK for 1,495 days of this period, so he is due a reduction in the gain of £100,750 x (1,495/3,125) = £48,199. As such, he is liable on a gain of £52,551, which is the figure that should be entered on his self-assessment tax return for the 2018-19 on SA106 (2019) at boxes 43 and 44, being the amount of the gain and number of years.

The gain is £52,551 and the policy ran for eight complete years but Nick was non-resident for four complete years so the number of years for top-slicing relief to be entered in box 44 must be reduced to the four during which he was UK resident.

8.4.3   Excess events

Another point to bear in mind for those who have taken out an offshore bond after 6 April 2013 is the often overlooked restriction made to top-slicing relief given in cases where a chargeable "excess event" occurs back in the UK. If more than the permitted 5% allowance is withdrawn then a chargeable event arises on the excess above the 5%.

This "excess event" can cause a problem if the individual is resident in the UK and exceeds the 5% threshold per annum because, since 6 April 2013, withdrawals in excess of that amount will not attract top-slicing relief as the number of years for top-slicing is treated as only one. However, this restricted top-slicing does not apply in the final insurance year the bond is surrendered.

Example

Anita takes out a life policy with an insurer based in the UK on 1 May 2013, with an initial premium of £10,000.

She moves to Germany to live and work on 6 April 2015 for a full year. She returns to the UK on 6 April 2016 and immediately thereafter withdraws £2,500 from the bond so she exceeds the 5% accumulated withdrawal facility by a small amount of £500.

She fully surrenders the policy on 30 April 2018, giving rise to a chargeable event gain of £15,000. However, Anita is a higher rate taxpayer back in the UK throughout at 40% and in that year the chargeable event pushes her income into the 45% tax bracket.

Year 4 (1 May 2016 to 30 April 2017)

On the chargeable event gain on 30 April 2017 the total allowable element is (4 years x 5% x £10,000) = £2,000. So the £2,500 exceeds net total allowable payments by £500, so an excess event arises in year 4.

The total value of parts surrendered is £2,500 during the life of the policy and no other part surrenders were made but if they had then they too would be taken into account. This gain is reported on her tax return in the same way as Nick in the previous example.

On the full surrender on 30 April 2018 she will need to report the gain on her return to the UK in the tax year 2018-19 but she will be entitled to relief for her period of non-UK residence.

The policy ran from 1 May 2013 to 30 April 2018 (1,826 days). There were 365 foreign residence days spent in Germany.

Anita is due a time apportioned reduction of:

£15,000 x 365/1,826 = £2,998.

The chargeable event gain is therefore £15,000 – £2,998 = £12,002. This has thrown her into the higher rate 45% tax bracket. But Anita has taken in excess of the 5% cumulative withdrawals in the fourth year. This is an excess chargeable event and therefore the figure for top-slicing would be one year and not the four UK resident years due to the chargeable "excess event" mentioned in year 4 above.

Excess event withdrawals are to be avoided in these circumstances as they affect top-slicing relief adversely. Advisers should make those clients aware, who might be entitled to top-slicing relief, that exceeding the accumulated 5% is to be avoided unless it is in the final year of closure of the bond.

In calculating the number of days in the material interest period, both the start date and the end date of the policy are included in the calculation. In the above example, this includes 1 May 2013 and 30 April 2018 as whole days. Likewise, 5 April 2015 and 6 April 2016 are included as whole days within the UK resident element of the period, and 6 April 2015 and 5 April 2016 are included as whole days in the calculation of foreign days.

Law: ITTOIA 2005, Pt. 4, Ch. 9
Guidance: HMRC Helpsheet 320 *Gains on UK Life Insurance Policies*

8.4.4   *Bonds and returning expats*

In **section 7.1** (Overseas tax and investment planning), the advantages for expats of having offshore investment bonds were considered. Those expats returning to the UK who have taken out investment bonds offshore will sometimes want to know whether they should encash the bond prior to return and invest the proceeds in another type of investment. Also, a question that sometimes arises is whether the individual can compare the income tax and IHT implications of holding a bond and alternatively investing in an income-paying investment that grows at, say, the same capital accrual rate. This is difficult, in that the two different types of investment have varying tax liabilities and reliefs, as illustrated in the following example:

Example

Ginger, who is single, has taken out an offshore bond for £1 million whilst in the Philippines but, after two years there, he plans to return to the UK.

Ginger is concerned that his offshore bond will not be such a good, tax-efficient investment in the UK and maybe he should encash it with a penalty for early surrender, say, 1% for the remaining eight years of a ten year early surrender penalty period.

453

After speaking to his London stockbroker he is considering investing the net amount, topped up to £1 million, in equities. His London stockbroker considers that Ginger will receive a high gross annual dividend return of 5%. Ginger asks his financial adviser to look at the comparison in terms of capital growth of 100% in 18 years for the equities and 100% capital growth on the bond in terms of:

1. net income available per annum;
2. total income tax payable;
3. inheritance tax liability; and
4. total taxes payable.

Assuming Ginger dies, say, in the 21st year since taking out the bond, and plans to leave the equity shares or his remaining bond capital to his nephews and nieces, what is his total tax exposure? His financial adviser *estimates* tax rates and personal allowances for each year to be:

Dividend allowance	=	£2,000
Personal allowance	=	£12,500*
Basic rate @ 20 %	=	£50,000*
Higher rate @ 40%	=	£100,000
Over £150,000 @ 45%		

*The personal allowance and basic rate band detailed are the figures indicated by the former Chancellor of the Exchequer, George Osborne, as a commitment target to increase both. Note, however, that the personal allowance is not allowed in the last year of encashment of the bond as the chargeable event is well over the limit for personal allowance restriction (i.e. nil). Calculations below assume that the savings nil rate band of £5,000 and the personal savings allowance of £1,000 have been dispensed with, as interest rates are high, but the dividend allowance is still £2,000 to encourage investment.

Scenario A – equities

£1 million is invested in UK equities in year 1 earning 5% gross dividends every year. No other taxable income is received in the UK and therefore Ginger is living off £50,000 dividends each year, charged to varying rates of dividend tax after allowances and the £2,000 dividend exemption from 6 April 2018.

After 18 years, having received 5% each year in dividends, the share values have, say, increased by £1 million over the 18-year period. Assume for these purposes that each year there will be a tax liability as follows:

Taxation is £50,000 – £14,500 (£2,000 dividend allowance + £12,500 personal allowance) @ 7.5% = £2,662.

1. Net income in the year would be £47,338.
2. A total income tax burden over 18 years of £47,916.
3. Inheritance tax liability would be on £2 million. £2 million – £325,000 @ 40% = £670,000.
4. Total taxes payable £717,916.

Scenario B – holding the bond

£1 million is invested in the offshore investment bond in year 1, taking 5% withdrawals every year. After two years abroad, policyholder Ginger goes back to the UK but keeps the offshore bond, continuing to withdraw the 5% each year on the bond's collective investment funds.

No other taxable income arises in the UK. Therefore he is living off £50,000 net each year, tax deferred at that stage. After 20 years Ginger dies having taken 1 million in withdrawals but the policy has grown by £1 million over the 20 years.

Policy proceeds	£1 million
Add withdrawals taken	£1 million
Total	£2 million
Less cost	£1 million
Chargeable gain subject to income tax	£1 million

Time apportionment for overseas days = 365 days x 2 years = 730 days.

Total days 365 days x 20 years = 7,300.

The gain taxable is fraction 6,570/7,300 days x £1 million = £900,000 taxable in the 20th year, which charged at the tax rates in that year amounts to £387,000. However, top-slicing relief applies because the amount takes the majority of the gain into the higher rates in one year. Therefore £900,000 is divided by 18 years = £50,000 taxed at 20% basic rate = £10,000. This figure is then multiplied by 18 years = £180,000 tax payable. Note that as this is an offshore policy no basic rate credit is given, whereas an onshore bond would attract a 20% tax credit.

This figure is then deducted from the £387,500 charged at the higher and basic rates to give a total top-slicing relief of £207,500.

1. Net income would be £50,000 x 18 years giving a total over 18 years of £900,000.
2. Total income tax paid is £180,000 (i.e. £10,000 x 18 years).
3. Inheritance tax liability would be on £1 million – £325,000 @ 40% = £270,000.
4. Total taxes payable are therefore £450,000.

Ginger has therefore had annual "income" of around £50,000 under both methods but has paid more total taxes the dividend route by an amount of £267,916. His net assets left to nephews and nieces after IHT in Scenario A is £1.33 million but is only £730,000 in Scenario B.

Expats generally come into two categories: those who do not mind how much the government takes after they have passed on, and those who will do as much as legally possible to prevent the government extracting their life savings in tax. This is usually an emotive issue and few expats fall in between these two stances.

When completing the Tax and Financial Planning Questionnaire (**Appendix 2**) it will become evident which stance the expat will take. Of course the investment risk element has to be taken into account as well and both scenarios have differing risk profiles; the share portfolio may not produce 5% dividend return each year, and the capital appreciation may be more or markedly less, so affecting income and the subsequent IHT bill. The investment bond funds may also not perform to expectation but, as has been stated above, bonds offer more ongoing tax planning opportunity with assignments of individual policies, etc. However, as previously stated, the choice may rest entirely on whether the individual wants to leave more or less to the government and also estate beneficiaries.

8.5   Foreign spouse tax implications

8.5.1   Introduction

Many people, including expats, marry someone who is not the same nationality as they are and this can give rise to visa problems as well as inheritance problems. See **9.2** (Non Domicile IHT planning).

In many cases civil partnerships or same sex marriages will have been entered into abroad. Some such agreements may not be acceptable in the UK and also, in some foreign countries, gay or lesbian relationships may (on religious grounds) not be acknowledged/recognised, or may even be declared illegal. Whilst there is a general trend by countries towards acceptance of same sex marriages there are 76 countries worldwide (mainly situated in Africa, the Middle East and SE Asia) that do not acknowledge civil partnerships or gay marriage.

Expat same sex couples who marry in another country may encounter problems when returning to the UK. Schedule 20 of the *Civil Partnership Act* 2004 (CPA 2004) lists the relationships which are "specified relationships" for the purposes of overseas relationships. Relationships falling within the descriptions in Schedule 20 can be treated as civil partnerships only if the other requirements are met. There is also the problem that some countries will not recognise civil partnership/marriage unions between same sex couples performed in another country (see the example below) and this can cause difficulties concerning inheritances.

Example

Celia and Sue were both English professors working in British Columbia, Canada, where they formed a marriage between them both. On their return to the UK their marriage in Canada was not recognised under British law.

Subsequently, when the *Civil Partnership Act* 2004 was introduced, their marriage was instead converted into a civil partnership, but the couple wanted recognition of their marriage in Canada, arguing that it was legal in the country in which it was executed. It also met the requirements for recognition of overseas marriages and

457

consequently should be treated in the same way as one between opposite-sex couples.

Taking a strong stance, the couple rejected the conversion of their marriage into a civil partnership, believing it to be both practically and symbolically a lesser substitute than a marriage. They argued that their marriage in Canada fulfilled all requirements even though it was performed abroad. The UK Court at the time did not side with the couple and refused to recognise their overseas marriage. Subsequently, the *Marriage (Same Sex Couples) Act 2013 (Commencement No. 2 and Transitional Provision) Order* 2014 brought into force provisions which allowed same-sex couples to marry from 13 March 2014. Also same-sex couples who married abroad under foreign law, and who were previously treated as civil partners, were recognised as married as of 13 March 2014.

Note: The law now requires couples to wait at least 16 days after giving notice to the local register office before a marriage ceremony can take place. The first marriages took place on 29 March 2014. An exception is where the Registrar General has waived the notice period because one member of the couple was seriously ill and not expected to recover.

Law: *Civil Partnership* Act *2004,* s. 2, 212, 215-218, Sch. 20; *The Marriage (Same Sex Couples) Act* 2013, Sch. 6; SI 2014/93, reg. 4

Case: *Wilkinson v Kitzinger* [2006] EWHC 2022 (Fam)

8.5.2 Civil partnership / marriage Acts

On the accidental death in London of Gaydar founder Gary Frisch, a South African computer graduate who had set up the Gaydar website in 1999, his will left the bulk of his estate worth an estimated £6.5 million to his business partner and former lover.

IHT of around £2.5 million would have been payable because there was no civil partnership or marriage in place at the date of his death.

The IHT on Frisch's estate could have easily been avoided nowadays by him and his partner if there had been a formal marriage in place. In these circumstances, the adviser would also be looking at the domicile position of the deceased and if this proves to be somewhere other than the UK further investigation should be made to determine the tax position.

The Acts mentioned above create a legal status of civil partner / marriage partner and once these are in place they will be treated for the purposes of all taxes in the same way as a married couple, with the advantages of exempt transfers for CGT and IHT together with the income tax advantages of equalising estates.

Law: *Civil Partnership Act* 2004, s. 2; *The Marriage (Same Sex Couples) Act* 2013, s. 1

8.5.3 Tax advantages/disadvantages

Where a number of properties are owned, whether jointly or solely by one partner or both, then only one will be treated as the main residence for principal private residence exemption purposes and any other properties will be treated as a taxable investment property. However, if the partners do not elect then HMRC will decide on the facts of the case at the relevant time; an election would be made within two years of the certificate being issued – see also **3.2.7** (PRR elections).

For tax purposes, same sex couples who are married will be treated the same way as other married couples, e.g. inheriting pension benefits on the partner's death, and tax benefits. Also anti-avoidance rules apply in equal measure, such as for IHT advantages where transfers between the two partners will be exempt from tax during lifetime and on death (but see the *Burden* case).

One effect of a marriage / civil partnership union is that where one partner has been living in another's property, and/or is being supported, then he or she can make application for reasonable financial provision under the *Inheritance (Provision for Family and Dependants) Act* 1975.

Law: TCGA 1992, s. 222(5), (6); *Inheritance (Provision for Family and Dependants) Act* 1975

Case: *Burden and Burden v United Kingdom,* ECHR 13378/05, [2008] ECHR 357

8.5.4 Co-habiting couples

It is estimated that there are over two million co-habiting couples in Britain, but co-habitation has no legal security in front of the courts as there is no statutory "common law marriage". A co-habitation agreement can be set up between the couple, which is normally drafted by solicitors or lawyers for the parties. Currently there is a private member's bill before the UK Parliament regarding co-habitees' rights, termed the *Cohabitation Rights Bill*, which aims to give some protection for co-habiting couples if it becomes law.

In a small victory for co-habitees, in the recent case of *Lewis v Warner* the sole executor and heir, Mrs Lewis, had sought a court order to evict Mr Warner (co-habitee of her mother, Mrs Blackwell) from the house arguing that his claim to live in the family home should be rejected because Warner was well off and was in no need of support. The judge in the appeal court stated:

> "It is clear that the [county court] undertook the appropriate balancing exercise under the 1975 Act...the Recorder was fully entitled to reach the conclusion, on the evidence, that the deceased's will did not make reasonable financial provision for Mr Warner's maintenance."

This enabled Warner to be granted first option to purchase the house from Mrs Blackwell's estate, for the estimated value of £385,000.

Also, the UK Privy Council (ostensibly advisers to the Queen) has recently confirmed that cash held in a joint bank account invariably passes by survivorship to the other account holders on the death of one account holder, without forming part of the deceased's estate – this would therefore give some security to a co-habitee in such cases. For IHT purposes, though, the deceased's share of the account is still reportable on IHT400.

The intestacy rules (see **Appendix 4**) create severe problems for those in a co-habiting relationship, so the couple should be advised to consider drawing up mutual wills or severing their property so that it is held as joint tenants or as tenants in common, which provides some protection on a death of the other co-habitee. Long term co-habitees may wish to make a declaration of trust in respect of property that belongs to them both and which they both share.

From a capital gains tax (CGT) point of view, any house that is shared by co-habitees will be treated as if it were their principal private residence. However, other CGT reliefs applicable to married couples and formalised civil partnership relationships will not apply, e.g. "nil gain/nil loss" when gifting assets between the couple.

Law: TCGA 1992, s. 222; *Inheritance (Provision for Family and Dependants) Act* 1975, s. 1(2)(b).

Cases: *Lewis v Warner* 2017 EWCA Civ 2182; *Whitlock v Moree* 2017 UKPC 44

8.5.5 *Divorce*

It is unfortunate that expats often find that one partner is happy with being overseas and the other is not – this will sometimes result in a split and eventual divorce. For the adviser faced with this unhappy state of affairs there is the knowledge that foreign divorce law is not similar to the UK court's guidelines and, in particular, countries practising Sharia law (e.g. the Emirate States) follow other rules for those divorcing in those jurisdictions. However, there is certainty as to the tax implications, and pre-divorce tax planning can avoid unnecessary impositions of tax at this time.

The CGT inter-spouse exemption only applies to assets transferred whilst a married couple are living together, so if one spouse returns to the UK then that will not be the case. Therefore it is important to ensure that assets transferred are made during the year a couple are living together, otherwise CGT will be an important issue (other than where there are exempt assets, such as a business transfer). Also, it is worth remembering, for expats who have been abroad for five years, that no CGT will be due on assets transferred whilst non-resident but this excludes property such as a UK residence that is rented out. See **3.2.5** – PPR absence relief.

As far as IHT is concerned, the inter-spousal exemption continues to apply until divorce. After that date, gifts may come within the exemption for family maintenance or non-gratuitous benefit or by reason of a Court order. Where gifts do not come within these exemptions then gifts will be potentially exempt transfers which may become chargeable within the following seven years if the donor dies. It should be borne in mind if the donor, but not the donor's spouse or civil partner, is domiciled in the UK the lifetime gifts exemption is limited to a cumulative total of £325,000, without grossing-up for tax – see **9.2** (Non domicile IHT planning). This places restrictions on transfers that can be made to the foreign spouse or civil partner without the balance becoming a PET, which is then possibly subject to charge within seven years of the gift as a "failed PET".

461

If the couple were married up to 31 December 1973, a woman automatically acquired the domicile of her husband on marriage and if this is a UK domicile then the £325,000 restriction would not apply. If her husband was not UK domiciled she would have become non-UK domiciled on marriage and also the restriction would not have applied or apply today if she has not changed her husband's inherited domicile. This is a point to watch out for in long term marriages which break down as there will potentially be a large distribution of assets from one party to the other; a latent IHT charge may well be avoided or revealed by the adviser asking a simple question "were you married before 1 January 1974?".

Pre-nuptial and post-nuptial agreements are becoming more common in the UK and this may prove a good thing as it gives immediate certainty regarding the assets that are not in dispute to be transferred from one party to the other, so that both the CGT and IHT implications are beneficial. In the UK's *Granatino* Supreme Court decision the Judge said:

> "The principle, however, to be applied is that a court should give effect to a nuptial agreement that is freely entered into by each party with a full appreciation of its implications unless, in the circumstances prevailing, it would not be fair to hold the parties to their agreement. A nuptial agreement cannot be allowed to prejudice the reasonable requirements of any children of the family, but respect should be given to individual autonomy and to the reasonable desire to make provision for existing property."

Law: TCGA 1992, s. 10A, 165, 222; IHTA 1984, s. 10, 11, 18
Cases: *G v G* [2002] EWHC 1339 (fam); *K v K* [2003] 1 FLR 120; *Radmacher (formerly Granatino) v Granatino* [2010] UKSC 427
Guidance: RDRM 22240, 22250

8.6   Tax departure certificates

8.6.1   Overview

Tax departure certificates, or "sailing permits", are common in many foreign countries and take different forms; these certificates or permits are usually issued to departing expats who can show that they have settled all tax liabilities prior to the intended date of departure.

In countries where there is no income tax, such as Saudi Arabia, the exit permit takes the form of a departure tax. Non-compliance can result in restriction in exiting the country. This can in turn result in additional expenses (e.g. hotel accommodation, etc.) until the certificate/permit has been issued. However, in certain cases delays not instigated by the expat leaving can be unforeseen – see the discussion of Saudi Arabia below.

Before leaving the United States for an extended amount of time, all US resident aliens and non-resident aliens (with certain exceptions, such as students, tourists, certain government officials, etc.) must prove they have met all federal tax requirements. This is done by obtaining a tax clearance document called a "sailing permit" or "departure permit" from the IRS. Without this, the documentation is extensive and can lead to delays if not correctly completed on submission. See below.

In Malaysia, a "stoppage order" is issued by the Inland Revenue Board of Malaysia to the Director of Immigration to prevent someone leaving if his or her taxes are not fully settled before departure. See below.

In Canada, a departure tax system applies on leaving that country which subjects assets to a CGT charge with a few exceptions. See below.

It is therefore vital for expat individuals and companies to follow the exiting requirements of each different country, failing which the consequences can be dire!

8.6.2 *Specific country examples*

USA

The sailing permit requirements in the United States involve obtaining a permit, and filing form 1040-C or form 2063 (whichever applies) with the local IRS office before leaving the United States.

The expat must pay all the tax shown on form 1040-C and any taxes due for past years. It is advisable for expats who have been working in the US to get the permit from an IRS office in the area of their employment, but it also can be obtained from an IRS office in the area of their departure. The sailing or departure permit should be obtained at least two weeks before the planned departure date, but the expat cannot apply earlier than 30 days before that date.

The administration requirements of getting a sailing or departure are numerous:

- passport and alien registration card or visa;
- copies of US income tax returns filed for the past two years (or, if less than two years, the returns filed for that period);
- receipts for income taxes paid on the returns;
- receipts, bank records, cancelled cheques and other documents that prove deductions, business expenses, and dependents claimed on those annual returns;
- a statement from each employer showing wages paid and tax withheld from January 1 of the current year to the date of departure if an employee. If self-employed, a statement of income and expenses up to the date of intended departure;
- proof of estimated tax payments for the past year and current year;
- documents showing any gain or loss from the sale of personal property, including capital assets and merchandise;
- documents relating to scholarship or fellowship grants including verification of the grantor, source, and purpose of the grant;
- documents indicating qualification for any special tax treaty benefits claimed;
- document verifying proposed date of departure from the US (e.g. airline ticket);
- document verifying the US taxpayer identification number (e.g. a social security card or an IRS-issued CP 565 showing the individual taxpayer identification number (ITIN)); and, in some cases,
- if married and residing in a community property state, the same documents listed above for a spouse. This applies whether or not the spouse requires a certificate.

Saudi Arabia

The Saudi Arabian visa system ("iqama") requires that expats leaving the country must pay an exit fee and then a re-entry fee on return. This will include family members if applicable.

This new departure and re-entry tax was first announced in the Saudi government's fiscal balance programme in 2016 to raise tax to supplement the loss in oil revenues for the Kingdom. The online payment service ran into a few teething problems and there were cases of expats stranded at the airport unable to depart the country.

Malaysia

The Malaysian Inland Revenue Board can issue a "stoppage order" if an expat working there has not paid his or her taxes. A taxpayer will be allowed to leave the country if the amount of tax or debts due on the certificate has been settled in full. Documentary evidence or receipt must be submitted to show that the payment has been made.

For immediate cancellation, the payment receipt is to be submitted to the Inland Revenue Board of Malaysia (IRBM) branch office that handles the individual's income tax file. For payment by cheque a taxpayer is allowed to leave the country after the cheque has been cleared by the bank. A revocation letter will then be issued to the taxpayer.

Example

Harry, a foreigner working in Malaysia, was issued a certificate under s. 104 of the ITA 1967 as he had tax arrears of 45,900 Malaysian Ringgits (RM), equivalent to £8,345. He is soon to return to his home country after the expiry of his contract of employment in Malaysia. He will be allowed to leave the country if he settles all the tax arrears and submits documents to prove that payment has been made.

If Harry attempts to leave Malaysia without making payment for all tax due, he will be liable if convicted to:

- a fine of not less than two hundred Malaysian ringgit (RM 200) and not more than 20,000 ringgit (RM 20,000); or

- imprisonment for a period not exceeding six months; or
- both.

A police officer or an immigration officer may arrest, without warrant, any person whom he reasonably suspects of committing or of being about to commit an offence by not complying with a certificate issued under s. 104 of the ITA 1967.

Canada

On cessation of residence in Canada, the individual is deemed to have disposed of certain types of property at their fair market value (FMV) when departing Canada and to have immediately reacquired the assets for the same value, i.e. there is a deemed disposition, resulting in a potential capital gains tax charge. This CGT charge applies to most properties. Some exceptions are:

- Canadian real or immovable property, Canadian resource property, and timber resource property;
- Canadian business property (including inventory) if the business is carried on through a permanent establishment in Canada;
- Pension plans, annuities, registered retirement savings plans, pooled registered pension plans, registered retirement income funds, registered education savings plans, registered disability savings plans, tax-free savings accounts, deferred profit-sharing plans, employee profit-sharing plans, employee benefit plans, salary deferral arrangements, retirement compensation arrangements, employee life and health trusts, rights or interests in certain other trusts, employee security options (exercised) subject to Canadian tax, interests in certain personal trusts resident in Canada, and interests in life insurance policies in Canada (other than segregated fund policies); and
- property owned on becoming a resident of Canada, or property inherited after becoming a resident of Canada, if a resident of Canada for 60 months or less during the 10-year period before emigration.

Canada offers the option to provide an asset or a lien over property as security for the future tax.

8.7 Remittance basis

8.7.1 Overview

This is largely outside the scope of this publication, as most British expats living overseas are going to be UK domiciles and so the remittance basis will not apply. Even for those UK domiciles who have lived for many years overseas, who have no intention of returning to live in the UK again and so can perhaps argue that a domicile of choice with another country has been acquired, the remittance basis will not apply as they will be non-resident. In addition, under the relatively new deemed domicile rules (see **2.1.3**), which came into effect from 6 April 2017, an individual with a UK domicile of origin will be a deemed domicile if he becomes resident again in the UK, despite having adopted a domicile of choice (see **2.1**). What follows, therefore, is a brief overview, and the reader should be aware this is a very complex area and should seek further advice.

The remittance basis is of relevance to individuals who:

- are foreign domiciles;
- are tax resident in the UK; and
- pay taxes on their overseas income and gains on the basis of what they remit to the UK (as opposed to the arising basis, which taxes the individual on his worldwide income as and when it arises and regardless of whether or not it is remitted to the UK. The arising basis is how most people living in the UK are taxed.)

In respect of British expats, the remittance basis may apply in the situation where a spouse or partner has a foreign domicile of origin, not having lived in the UK previously, or if he has only lived in the UK for a limited time, and so is not caught by the deemed domicile rules (see **2.1.3**) by virtue of having been resident in any 15 of the previous 20 tax years (including split years and years when he was under 18). This deemed domicile status can only be lost by being non-resident for five consecutive tax years.

An individual who is eligible to claim the remittance basis can make a choice between being taxed in the UK on:

- only his overseas income and gains that he remits to the UK; or
- his worldwide income on the arising basis.

At first glance, this would seem a simple and obvious choice – the remittance basis. However, this is not necessarily so. If an individual decides to elect for the remittance basis, then there are downsides – he will lose his entitlement to certain allowances, such as the personal allowance (see **2.3.2**) and also to his annual capital gains exemption (see **2.4.3**). A comparison therefore needs to be made each tax year to see if it is beneficial or not for an individual to claim the remittance basis for a tax year. (An individual can swap between being taxed on the remittance or the arising basis each tax year, so if he elects to be taxed on the remittance basis for (say) 2018-19, he does not need to continue being taxed on the remittance basis after this and can be taxed on the arising basis for 2019-20 if more beneficial).

If the individual's taxable income in the UK is at such a level that he has already lost the personal allowance, and he has not made any taxable gains during a tax year, then it may be beneficial for him to claim the remittance basis of taxing his overseas income or gains depending on his circumstances and bearing in mind the remittance basis charge (RBC) below. However, if the individual's taxable income is below £100,000 (for 2018-19) and, hence he is entitled to the full personal allowance, then it is necessary to establish whether or not it is beneficial for him to claim the remittance basis. Very often the individual will have a lower tax liability in the UK by being taxed on the arising basis rather than on the remittance basis, especially if foreign tax has been paid and so a foreign tax credit may be available against the UK tax on the overseas income.

If an individual's unremitted overseas income and gains are below £2,000 for a tax year, then the remittance basis applies automatically, with no loss of the personal allowance or the annual capital gains exemption, and he will not be subject to the RBC below if he has been resident in the UK for a number of years. The individual needs to give notice if he does not wish for the remittance basis to apply in this situation, which may be the case if the foreign domiciled person has remitted foreign dividends that will be taxed at the lower dividend rates (see **2.3.1**) if on the arising basis.

If the foreign domiciled individual is working overseas, as well as in the UK, then there may be the opportunity to take advantage of overseas work days relief (OWR) whereby the earnings from work days performed outside the UK may not be taxed in the UK if they are not remitted to the UK (see HMRC's RDR4).

Remittance basis charge

Another downside of claiming the remittance basis arises if the individual has been resident in the UK for a number of years, in which case he will incur a remittance basis charge (RBC) in addition to the UK tax that is due on any income or gains remitted to the UK.

There are a number of levels of the RBC. If an individual has been resident for seven of the nine previous tax years (including split years) then he will incur an RBC of £30,000. If he has been resident for 12 of the previous 14 tax years, the RBC will increase to £60,000 and for 2015-16 and 2016-17 only it increased to £90,000 for those individuals who were resident for 17 out of the previous 20 tax years. This latter RBC was abolished from 2017-18 onwards with the introduction of the deemed domicile rules on 6 April 2017.

For many foreign domiciles who have been resident in the UK for a number of years, the RBC makes claiming the remittance basis unfeasible and it is generally only very wealthy individuals who may still have a lower UK tax liability by claiming the remittance basis and incurring the RBC. It may also be beneficial for an individual with a significant transaction during a tax year, such as the sale of an overseas property.

Remittances to the UK are not just the simple transfer of funds into the UK, but can also include more indirect methods such as the use of overseas credit cards in the UK, paying for a UK product, service or any other liability with overseas money, gifting overseas funds to a spouse who then remits the funds into the UK, bringing assets into the UK, bringing the finance from overseas loans into the UK, paying off UK loans with overseas funds and so on. See RDRM 33050 for HMRC examples of remittances.

469

It is common for individuals to just have one or two overseas bank accounts into which all their different sources of overseas income and gains are paid. This results in what is known as a mixed account. HMRC's view is that it is not possible to distinguish what type of income or gains is remitted first from such an account, so the legislation sets out an order in which income and gains are deemed to be remitted, with capital (such as funds that the individual had before becoming resident in the UK) which is tax free when remitted, being deemed to be remitted last from the account.

If an individual wishes to claim the remittance basis he must do so on the "residence, remittance basis etc." pages of his self-assessment tax return (including making a claim when it applies automatically). In addition, if the individual wishes to be able to use losses on foreign assets in the future, he must make an election for this when he first claims the remittance basis. This is the only time the election can be made and it cannot be reversed at a later date. Care is needed when deciding whether or not to make this loss election, as it is not always beneficial to do so, for example if the individual also has UK capital losses, due to the deemed order in which foreign and UK losses are set off against gains. This is a difficult election to make as the individual is looking into the future for many years and trying to anticipate what his situation may then be.

Law: ITA 2007, s. 809A-809Z10
Guidance: RDRM 30000

8.7.2 *Potential planning*

The main area of planning with regards to the remittance basis is the setting up of various offshore bank accounts prior to the individual becoming resident in the UK, so that his various sources of income and gains can be separated into different accounts, thereby allowing the individual to remit different types of income and gains in the most tax-efficient order, for example remitting capital (which is tax free) first.

If British expats have a foreign domiciled spouse or partner, they may be able to take advantage of the remittance basis, so if they are potentially returning to live in the UK, consideration should be given to the question of which overseas sources of income and assets are in the foreign domicile's name. Overseas funds may be required in the UK when an individual first arrives there, and before he starts receiving a UK source of income such as earnings. If he is a foreign domicile who is eligible to claim the remittance basis, he needs to consider transferring overseas income to the UK prior to becoming resident (or in the overseas part of the tax year of arrival) to avoid overseas income or gains potentially becoming taxable in the UK if the income arose and is remitted to the UK after the individual becomes a tax resident. However, the setting up of a UK bank account before arriving in the UK may prove to be difficult if the individual is non-resident and does not already have a bank account in the UK. This is another good reason for individuals to keep UK bank accounts open.

As mentioned above, the remittance basis is only available to foreign domiciles who are tax resident in the UK. Therefore, for most expats with a UK domicile of origin, the remittance basis will not be relevant.

9. Back home

9.1 Non domicile IHT planning

9.1.1 Introduction

The deemed domicile rules (see **2.1** – Domicile) ensure that those foreigners who have been resident in the UK for 15 out of the last 20 tax years are subject to IHT on their worldwide assets, similar to UK born and bred domiciled individuals also known as formerly domiciled residents (FDRs).

Many expats whilst working or living abroad marry foreign spouses. For marriages since 1 January 1994, those foreign spouses retain their original home country domicile status until they choose/elect for a UK domicile or are resident in the UK long enough to attract the deemed domicile status. Some foreign spouses are extremely wealthy and, should they choose to become UK domiciled or should they acquire a deemed domicile, their assets could be subject to large amounts of IHT. There are advantages and disadvantages in a foreign spouse becoming a UK domicile by choice.

9.1.2 Non domiciled spouses

The UK IHT inter-spouse gift exemption during lifetime is limited to a relatively modest cumulative total of £325,000 where the donee spouse is a non-UK domicile.

Any transfers above the figure of £325,000 are then treated as potentially exempt transfers with the usual seven year trailing period, and tapering relief after three years from the gift. This places restrictions on lifetime transfers that can be made to the non-domicile spouse by the UK domiciled spouse without there being a potential delayed charge to IHT under the seven-year rule. Note that transfers from a non-domiciled spouse to a UK domiciled spouse are unrestricted, as also are gifts between two non-domiciled spouses.

Where the non-UK domiciled spouse has been UK resident for 15 out of the last 20 tax years then UK domicile is "deemed" to apply, with the consequent taxing implications on his or her own worldwide assets unless the assets had been placed into a foreign excluded property settlement (see **7.2.8** – Excluded property trust).

In certain situations (e.g. where the non-domiciled spouse has few assets abroad) an election by the non-domiciled spouse to be treated as UK domiciled is an appropriate course of action. An election may also be made on death by the personal representatives, if appropriate (see below). These circumstances will vary but in cases where a wealthy older UK domiciled spouse is married to a younger non-domiciled spouse, and it is intended that the younger spouse should benefit, then the election will ensure that no IHT is payable initially. Subsequently, the younger spouse's estate can be reviewed from a tax planning point of view and if the non-domiciled spouse leaves the UK permanently, for more than four successive tax years, his or her previous foreign domicile of origin can then be reinstated (see **2.1** – Domicile).

Law: IHTA 1984, s. 4, 6(1), 11, 18(2), 19, 20, 21, 267(1)(b)

Case: *Barlow Clowes International Ltd (in liquidation) and Others v Henwood* [2008] EWCA 577 (Civ)

Guidance: IHTM 11033, 13043, 13044

9.1.3   Advantages of electing for UK domicile

An election for a non-domiciled spouse to be treated as UK domiciled, and to benefit from the inter-spouse exemption, can be made in writing to HMRC at any time (see below). Some of the advantages of an election will be:

- The benefit of the inter-spouse exemption, so no IHT is payable. This then gives time for planning on the use and distribution of the assets, such as investment in AIM shares, businesses, agriculture, forestry, etc., which attract exemptions either fully or partially.

- The inheritor spouse can make use of PETs to divest the estate to beneficiaries in an orderly manner.

- Prior to the election, the non-domiciled spouse can make use of excluded property trusts to divest his or her foreign assets to family, etc.

- The election avoids the restrictions of the non-domiciled spouse gifts limit of £325,000: a lifetime limit where a UK domiciled spouse gifts to his non-domiciled spouse.

- It also removes the treatment whereby any balance of gifts over the £325,000 to the non-domiciled spouse mentioned above becomes a PET, with tax implications for the non-domiciled spouse should the UK domiciled spouse die within seven years of the PET gift.

- An election to be treated as domiciled in the UK does not mean that the individual is treated as "deemed domiciled" under the 15/20 year rules, which can have income tax and CGT advantages too.

The election is irrevocable and must be made in writing by the non-domiciled spouse and must include:

- the full name and address of the individual making the election, or of the personal representatives if appropriate where the person has died;
- the individual's date of birth (or, if relevant, his or her date of death);
- the full name of the UK domiciled spouse.

Elections could first be made from 6 April 2013. Such elections can be for seven years going back from a lifetime election date, or on a death an election can go back seven years from the date of death. Obviously it is necessary that the person making the election was married to the UK domiciled individual to benefit.

Example

David, who is domiciled in the UK, transfers assets worth £1m in 2021 to his spouse Cherry, who is domiciled in Singapore. Subsequently, in 2022, Cherry transfers some Singapore quoted F&N shares to the trustees of an offshore Singapore trust. David dies in 2023 and three years have not elapsed since the PET to his wife so the gift is fully chargeable with no tapering relief.

At the time of David's transfer, the value transferred was exempt to the extent of £325,000 (foreign spouse gift exemption) and was a PET to the extent of the balance of £675,000. Following his death, the failed PET is chargeable, subject to deducting the £325,000 of the lifetime nil-rate band, so £350,000 is subject to tax at 40%.

Cherry's transfer of F&N shares into trust was that of excluded property (per IHTA 1984, s 4, 6(1), and see Trusts at **7.2**). Following David's death, Cherry has the choice of electing to be treated as domiciled in the UK. If she does so, the gift from David in 2021 will become fully spousal exempt, as will any other inheritance she receives from him.

However, Cherry will then be treated as domiciled in the UK for all IHT purposes. This means that her transfer to the trustees of the excluded property trust is no longer one of excluded property and will potentially be subject to IHT on her death. If she leaves the UK on 31 December 2024 the first year when trailing IHT expires is four consecutive tax years of non-residence, i.e. from 6 April 2029.

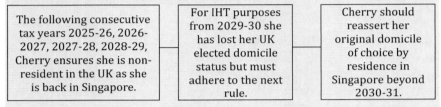

The following consecutive tax years 2025-26, 2026-2027, 2027-28, 2028-29, Cherry ensures she is non-resident in the UK as she is back in Singapore. — For IHT purposes from 2029-30 she has lost her UK elected domicile status but must adhere to the next rule. — Cherry should reassert her original domicile of choice by residence in Singapore beyond 2030-31.

Cherry will need to consider all the consequences of making an election. Should she decide to go ahead with the election, the requirements to deliver an account in respect of the transfer to the excluded property trust must be met.

NOTE: Use can also be made of the small gifts exemption, annual allowance, gifts for family maintenance and gifts out of normal income between spouses who are UK and non-UK domiciled.

9.1.4   Disadvantages of electing

A disadvantage of an election for a non-domiciled spouse to be treated as UK domiciled is that worldwide assets will come within the IHT net on the person's demise. Other matters to take into account will be:

- The trailing tax cut-off date of four tax years after departing the UK permanently and reinstating the original domicile abroad or elsewhere.

- PETs, including those made to foreign non-domiciled relatives, could become subject to tax by HMRC if made within seven years prior to death (or 14 years where there has been a discretionary trust).

- A non-domiciled spouse, whilst lacking in assets initially, may be subject to tax on inheritances in the future which would come within the UK IHT net for these purposes.

- Care should be taken where there are historical treaties (see **2.1.6**), as an election could jeopardise the advantages of such treaties which refer to "deemed domicile" not choice of domicile.
- Excluded property trusts may become an asset once the election has been made, as seen in the example above.

9.2   Relocation

9.2.1   Introduction

Once an individual has returned to the UK to live, he will first need to establish what his residence status is for the tax year of return under the statutory residence test (see **2.2.1**). If resident, which is likely to be the case, this will be from the beginning of the tax year, so from the previous 6 April.

In this situation, the individual will then need to see if split-year treatment applies (see **2.2.6**) and, if so, at what point the year of return is split between a UK and an overseas part. This will be crucial in determining how he will be taxed in the UK, and on what income and gains, and consequently what needs to be declared in the UK.

If split-year treatment does not apply, the individual will need to look at any double tax treaty (see **2.3.3**) in place to see where he is regarded as treaty resident (probably the UK after returning) and what relief is available under the treaty on any double taxed income. This is likely to be income in the period from 6 April to the date of the individual's return to the UK, although it may be a longer period, depending on when the individual breaks tax residence in the country he has just left. A claim will need to be made (usually via the individual's self-assessment tax return) for any treaty relief available.

If the individual has returned from a country where he has not been taxed, such as a Middle Eastern country, then he may not be in a double tax situation, but some of his earnings prior to returning from the previous 6 April may become taxable in the UK unless exemption under a double tax treaty can be claimed.

With regards to an employee's relocation costs, there is no tax relief for costs in respect of the removal of personal belongings etc. back to the UK if borne by the employee.

If the employer has paid for some or all of these costs, the question of whether or not these are taxable in the UK will depend on the exact nature of the costs and on the amounts involved. The general rule is that if an employer bears the cost of any of the employee's own personal liabilities, then this is taxable. There is tax relief available up to £8,000 for certain relocation expenses, which includes the shipment of personal belongings and travel and subsistence expenses in respect of the relocation back to the UK for both the individual and his family, including the cost of having to stay in short term accommodation in between residences (see ITEPA 2003, s. 272(1) and s. 284 for qualifying expenses). However, £8,000 in respect of an international move is unlikely to cover all the costs of relocating if the employer is paying for all the costs involved with the move back to the UK, so some of the individual's relocation costs and benefits may be taxed in the UK, because they exceed this £8,000. There will also be a liability if the expenses or benefits provided by the employer do not qualify for relief.

Travel and subsistence costs may be eligible for relief under ITEPA 2003 sections 341, 342, 370, 371, 373 or 375. If so, they are not eligible for relief under s. 271 above.

The above relief is available if an employee is changing his main residence (i.e. the place he lives in, as opposed to tax residence under the SRT) as a result of starting a new employment or being relocated by his employer because of a change in the place or duties of his employment. HMRC state in their *Employment Income Manual* that where an employee comes to the UK from abroad, HMRC will usually accept that the main residence has changed if the employee has become resident in the UK for tax purposes. The employee does not need to have disposed of his previous residence to be able to claim this relief; there just needs to be a change in main residences.

The new main residence must be within reasonable travelling distance of the new place of work, while the previous main residence must not be. Reasonable travelling distance is not defined in the legislation, but HMRC's view on this is as follows:

"You should apply common sense and take account of local conditions. The usual time taken to travel a given distance is an indication of whether that distance is reasonable. Employees in the London area, for example, commonly travel much greater distances, or take longer to travel the same distance, to work than those in other parts of the UK. You should bear in mind that employers will not normally pay for employees to move to places that are not convenient for the place of work."

There is a time limit to the relief. The removal expenses must be incurred, and any removal benefits provided, by the end of the tax year following the tax year in which the relocation occurred. In limited cases, such as children's schooling and exams and difficulties disposing of the previous residence which delay the relocation, HMRC may extend this time limit by an extra year if they regard it reasonable to do so. In this respect, it does not matter when the employee actually moves into the new residence.

The above relief will also be relevant if the employee is subsequently relocated by his employer, within the UK or overseas again.

An individual may be assigned to the UK for less than two years (e.g. a British national who has become an Australian citizen and lives permanently in Australia, but whose Australian employer has assigned him to the UK for less than two years, with him intending to return to live in Australia after the assignment). Such an individual is potentially eligible for detached duty relief (relief for travel and subsistence expenses while in the UK, including his accommodation and food costs, while still employed by his overseas employer). In such cases, HMRC no longer allow claims for both detached duty relief and the above relocation relief to be made at the same time. In this scenario, a detached duty relief claim is usually made rather than a claim for relocation relief.

Law: ITEPA 2003, s. 271-289
Guidance: EIM 03100

9.2.2 Registering with HMRC

When an individual returns to live in the UK, he should contact HMRC to inform them of his return so that HMRC can update their records. Previously this was done on a P86 tax form, but this form is no longer available, so the individual needs to write a letter to HMRC informing them of his or her return.

The individual's UK tax situation while living overseas may have been very simple and so may not have been required to file tax returns while abroad. For example, he may not have performed any work in the UK, and he may not have been receiving any UK sourced income, or if he did, it was perhaps covered by his personal allowance and so no UK tax was due. If tax returns were required, they may have been reasonably simple. The individual will need to re-assess his UK tax situation once a tax resident again in the UK, as he will then be taxable in the UK on his worldwide income and gains and may also remain taxable in the country he has just left, and so potentially in a double tax situation for a time. His tax affairs in the UK are likely to be more complex than they were while he was non-resident, depending on his circumstances.

The individual will need to see if he is required to file a self-assessment tax return (see **2.8.1**). If so, he will need to complete an SA1 form. HMRC will then issue a UTR (unique taxpayer reference) and set the individual up for self-assessment. This will change in the future, once self-assessment tax returns have been phased out and everything is done via digital tax accounts.

If the individual is to be an employee in the UK, HMRC will become aware of this via his employer (if a UK employer) who will register the employee with HMRC via their payroll and RTI (real time information – part of the PAYE system).

If the individual commences self-employment in the UK, he needs to register for this (see **9.5**) so that HMRC will become aware of the circumstances.

9.2.3   *Capital gains tax reporting*

An individual may dispose of a residential property in the UK while non-resident (including the overseas part of the arrival tax year). This will be covered by the NRCGT regime (see **3.2**) and an NRCGT return will need to be filed within 30 days of completion, as well as the capital gains summary pages of the individual's self-assessment tax return, if he is required to file tax returns while non-resident.

The disposal of any other asset is outside the scope of UK CGT and so does not need to be declared.

If the disposal of an asset occurs when the individual is resident again (including the UK part of the year of arrival), then the disposal is within the scope of UK CGT and may need to be declared on the capital gains summary pages of the self-assessment tax return. HMRC's guidance on when a disposal should be declared on these pages is as follows:

- the individual sold or disposed of chargeable assets which were worth more than £46,800 (for 2018-19);
- the chargeable gains before taking off any losses were more than £11,700 (the annual exempt amount for 2018-19);
- there are gains in an earlier year taxable in the current tax year. This will be relevant for an individual who was a temporary non-resident (see **2.2.11** and **2.2.12 (iv)**) and so liable to UK CGT upon his return to the UK;
- a claim for an allowable capital loss or a capital gains claim or election needs to be made for the year;
- an individual was not domiciled in the UK and is claiming to pay tax on his foreign gains on the remittance basis;
- an individual is chargeable on the remittance basis and has remitted foreign chargeable gains of an earlier year; or
- an individual disposed of the whole or part of an interest in a UK residential property (when either non-resident or UK resident) and the disposal was in the overseas part of a split year.

HMRC go on to state that the capital gains pages are not required to be filed when the individual only sells or disposes of:

- private cars;
- personal possessions (chattels) worth up to £6,000 each, such as jewellery, paintings or antiques;
- stocks and shares held in tax-free investment savings accounts, such as ISAs and PEPs;

- UK government or "gilt-edged" securities, for example, National Savings Certificates, premium bonds, and loan stock issued by the Treasury; or
- the individual's main home, if he qualifies for private residence relief on the full amount of the gain.

HMRC also confirm the following do not need to be included on the capital gains summary pages:

- betting, lottery or pools winnings;
- compensation for personal injury or mis-sold payment protection insurance (PPI); and
- any foreign currency bought for the individual's own personal use (or the personal use of his family) outside the UK.

As mentioned above, if an individual returns within the five-year period such that he becomes a temporary non-resident, then any gains he made during this period of non-residence will become taxable upon his return, taking into account any gain that has been taxed under the NRCGT regime.

Guidance: HMRC capital gains summary notes (SA108); https://www.gov.uk/government/publications/self-assessment-capital-gains-summary-sa108

9.2.4 Income tax reporting

Once an individual becomes resident again in the UK, he will be taxable in the UK on his worldwide income. This means that he will need to declare all his income, wherever it arises, on his self-assessment tax return, except for overseas income arising in the overseas part of the year of return if a split year or income not remitted to the UK if the individual is claiming the remittance basis (see **8.7**).

As with capital gains, if an individual is a temporary non-resident (see **2.2.11**) and receives any of the income under **2.2.12** during this period of temporary non-residence, then this will become taxable when the individual returns to the UK and becomes resident again and will need to be declared on the person's self-assessment tax return.

9.2.5   *Reporting of foreign income*

While living overseas, a non-resident may well have made overseas investments, the income of which did not previously need to be declared in the UK, as the individual was non-resident and so the income was not taxable in the UK. This overseas income may include interest from bank accounts and investments, dividends from foreign registered companies, rental properties located overseas, etc.

Once an individual has returned to the UK and has become resident in the UK for tax purposes, he needs to start declaring this income to HMRC. He will become taxable on his worldwide income from the time he became resident (but not for the overseas part of the year of return if split-year treatment applies).

The declaration of this income is made on the foreign pages (SA106) of the self-assessment tax return, except for the following:

- foreign employment income, which is shown on the employment pages (SA102);
- foreign income from a business or partnership, which is shown on the self-employment pages (SA103S or SA103F);
- taxable gains from the disposal of foreign assets, which are shown on the capital gains pages (SA108); and
- income from furnished holiday lets in the EEA which are declared on the UK rental pages (SA105). This presumably will change following Brexit.

It is also in these pages that an individual will make a claim for double tax relief (usually foreign tax credit relief), if his or her foreign income is being taxed both in the UK and overseas, including the above income declared on other supplementary pages. See HMRC's helpsheet 263 for calculating foreign tax credit relief: https://www.gov.uk/government/publications/calculating-foreign-tax-credit-relief-on-income-hs263-self-assessment-helpsheet.

The taxable income from foreign sources is calculated in the same way as for UK sourced income and is assessed on the arising basis – i.e. as and when it arises, and not when it is remitted to the UK – unless the remittance basis is being claimed by a foreign domicile. It is necessary to declare the gross amount before any foreign tax that was withheld. The amount must be shown in sterling, using the exchange rate in place at the date the income arose, though HMRC accept the use of average exchange rates which they publish on their website at https://www.gov.uk/government/publications/exchange-rates-for-customs-and-vat-yearly.

If the individual has only a small amount of either foreign interest or dividends, then he is not required to file the foreign income pages and can just declare this on page TR 3 alongside his UK interest and/or dividends. This relaxation occurs if the individual has:

- untaxed foreign interest of up to £2,000; or
- taxed foreign dividends up to £300.

It is important to understand that this is an "either or" option, so in order to take advantage of this relaxation, the individual must have only foreign bank interest up to £2,000 or only foreign dividends up to £300 and not a mixture of the two, even if the amounts involved are less than the above limits.

Example

Emma returned to the UK during 2018-19, following an assignment in Spain. She still has a deposit account in Spain from which she received interest of £100 during 2018-19. No Spanish tax was withheld from this. She also has some shares in a Spanish registered company and received dividends from this company during 2018-19 of £150, with Spanish tax withheld at source. As Emma received a mixture of foreign bank and dividend income, she is unable to take advantage of the above relaxation and so will be required to complete and file the foreign income pages.

If she had just received interest from her Spanish account of £1,950 and no foreign dividends, then there would be no requirement for her to file the foreign pages and she could just declare this on page TR 3 of the core tax return.

The country where the foreign bank interest arose needs to be shown on the tax return in the "Any other information" box on page TR 7.

With regards to rental income from overseas properties, the taxable profit or allowable loss is calculated on the same basis as for a UK rental property business. However, overseas rental properties are treated as a separate overseas rental business to a UK rental business, meaning any loss arising on an overseas rental property can only be set off against a profit arising on another overseas rental property and cannot be set off against profits arising from UK rental properties. If the loss is not utilised against other overseas properties, then it is carried forward to set off against future profits arising from the rental of overseas properties. This may be relevant for returning expats, as an individual may have purchased a property to live in while living overseas and may have decided to keep it on his return to the UK and rent it out. Or he may simply have acquired an overseas property to rent out as an investment.

As well as claiming a foreign tax credit, an individual may also be able to claim a special withholding tax (SWT) credit on the foreign pages. The EU savings directive allows for the automatic exchange of information between member states on cross-border savings and investment income. Rather than exchanging information, some states (and certain related territories outside the EU such as Gibraltar, Jersey, Luxembourg, Lichtenstein and Switzerland) impose a special withholding tax (SWT) instead. For UK residents this is treated as a payment on account of UK tax and so can be claimed against the UK tax due, with any SWT exceeding the individual's UK tax liability being repaid to him. It is treated in the same way as any other tax deducted at source. This may be another area that will change following Brexit.

Sometimes, overseas income cannot be remitted to the UK because of exchange controls or a shortage of foreign currency in the country where the income arises. In these circumstances, the individual can claim that the income is unremittable and should not be taxed in the UK until these restrictions are lifted, at which point it is then taxed in the UK (using the exchange rates at the time the restrictions are lifted) regardless of whether or not the income is actually remitted to the UK.

Guidance: HMRC foreign pages notes (SA106): https://www.gov.uk/government/publications/ self-assessment-foreign-sa106; HMRC HS263 – Calculating Foreign Tax credit Relief on Income https://www.gov.uk/government/publications/calculating-foreign-tax-credit-relief-on-income-hs263-self-assessment-helpsheet

9.2.6   Property purchase

When an individual returns to the UK, and does not already own property in the UK, he may decide to purchase a UK property to live in as his main residence. Alternatively, he may already have a property in the UK, but this may be rented out and he may wish to continue renting it out. This could be, for example, because he has got married overseas and started a family, so his original home is no longer large enough.

SDLT

When purchasing a property in the UK the individual will potentially be liable to stamp duty land tax (SDLT – see **9.3**) depending on the cost of the property. The rate of this may increase if he already owns property in the UK or elsewhere in the world.

Private residence relief

If the property will be the individual's main residence, then while he lives in it as his only or main residence, under current rules any gain arising on the eventual sale of the property will not be subject to UK CGT. This private residence relief (PRR) applies for the period he lives in it as his only or main residence and also for the last 18 months of ownership regardless of what it is used for during this final period (see **3.2.3** and **3.2.4**). If he has another residence, say a flat in London which he lives in during the week while working there, then he needs to consider putting in a second home election nominating one of the properties to be his main residence for the purposes of claiming this relief (see **3.2.7**).

Sometimes, there is a delay in the individual moving into the property, perhaps because it needs renovating or altering. As long as this period is no more than 12 months (24 months if HMRC agree there is a good reason) PRR will apply for this period before he moved into it. This also applies if land has been purchased and a property is built on it and the individual intends to move into it as his main residence. If, however, the individual does not move into the property until after this 12-month period (or 24 month period, if agreed by HMRC), then none of the period prior to him moving into it as his main residence will qualify for PRR (see ESC D49).

485

ESC D49 may also allow this period of deemed residence where the delay in taking up residence is due to the individual continuing to occupy his previous residence while arrangements are made to sell it but where delays in those arrangements are causing a delay in moving into the new property. This may apply if the individual owns property overseas which he lives in and he purchases a property in the UK with the intention of moving into upon his return to the UK, but before he is able to sell his overseas home.

Guidance: CG 65003-65009; ESC D49 Private Residence Relief: Short Delay by owner-occupier in taking up residence

9.2.7 Reoccupation of UK property

Very often an individual will keep his UK home, either for his own use when he visits the UK or to rent it out while he is living and working overseas. He will then move back into the property to live in it again once he returns to the UK. In this situation, assuming it was his main residence prior to moving overseas and he did not own any other properties, he needs to see if his period abroad can be deemed to be a period of occupation of a residence for PRR purposes. This will be the case if he has worked full-time overseas with no work done at all in the UK, and/or for any three-year period for no specific reason, in which case he needs to make sure he spends some time living in the property as his main residence after the period of absence. He also needs to make sure that a second home election is made, declaring that his UK property remains his main residence while living overseas.

In this respect he may need to rely on ESC D21 (see **3.2.6** and **3.2.7**). If he owned property that he lived in while overseas, he will not be able to make this late election.

If the individual upon his return cannot return to live in his UK home again because his employer requires him to work in a different location that is not within commuting distance, the period may still be regarded as a period of occupation of a residence for him (aside from the period of absence of three years for any reason) and so potentially attract PRR. A condition of this is that the requirement for him to work elsewhere by his employer was reasonably imposed to secure the effective performance of his employment duties.

Law: TCGA 1992, s. 223

9.3 Stamp duty land tax

9.3.1 Introduction

Stamp duty land tax (SDLT) is payable if a property or land is purchased for more than a certain price in England, Wales and Northern Ireland. In Scotland there are different rules. The current SDLT threshold is £125,000 for residential properties and £150,000 for non-residential land and properties. SDLT relief for first-time buyers was introduced from 22 November 2017 – see below. For a more detailed analysis, see *Stamp Duty Land Tax* from Claritax Books.

If there is a loan/mortgage on a property gifted into (say) a trust then there can be a charge to SDLT on that element of the gift as it will be treated *per se* as consideration as effectively the donee is taking over the liability. Also, a 3% additional charge arises on top of the normal rates if buying another residential property where more than one is owned, whether in the UK or elsewhere. The extra 3% will not apply if the new property replaces an existing main residence. Any delay in selling the old main residence may result in the extra 3% SDLT being paid but it can be claimed back if the property is sold within 36 months.

SDLT is also charged at 15% on residential properties costing more than £500,000 bought by certain corporate bodies or "non-natural persons" such as an offshore trust. This charge, together with various exceptions, is considered at **9.3.2** below.

SDLT is payable within 30 days of completion, though this is set to reduce to 14 days at a time to be announced in 2018-19. Also, returns by agents will have to be filed online from 1 March 2019, and any SDLT payments will have to be made electronically at the same time.

Certain buildings used for the following purposes are treated as non-residential property:

487

- residential homes or other institutions for children;
- halls of residence for students in further or higher education;
- homes or other institutions for persons in need of personal care due to old age, disability, past or present dependence on alcohol or drugs or past or present mental disorder;
- hospitals or hospices;
- prisons or similar establishments; or
- hotels, inns or similar establishments.

9.3.2   UK property rates

Property or lease premium or transfer value	SDLT rate
Up to £125,000	Zero
The next £125,000 (the portion from £125,001 to £250,000)	2%
The next £675,000 (the portion from £250,001 to £925,000)	5%
The next £575,000 (the portion from £925,001 to £1.5 million)	10%
The remaining amount (the portion above £1.5 million)	12%

First time buyer stamp duty on purchase value from 22 November 2017	SDLT rate
Up to £300,000	Zero
The next £200,000 (the portion from £300,001 to £500,000)	5%
Above £500,000 (go to rates above)	N/A

See the example of Mr Wong at **9.3.4** below. Note: a first time buyer is defined as an individual (or individuals) who have never owned an interest in a residential property in the United Kingdom *or* *anywhere else in the world* and who intends to occupy the property as his or her main residence. This first time buyer relief applies for transactions with an effective date (usually the date of completion) on or after 22 November 2017. On the SDLT return a special stamp duty code (code 32) will need to be entered on the return made by the individual or solicitor.

Payment of an extra 3% on top of the normal SDLT rates applies if purchasing an additional property, whether the first property is in the UK or elsewhere in the world. See the examples at **7.2.4** (Bare trust) and **7.2.5** (Discretionary trust). The rates applying in these cases are therefore as follows:

Dwellings	**SDLT rate**
up to £125,000	3%
over £125,000 to £250,000	5%
over £250,000 to £925,000	8%
over £925,000 to £1.5 million	13%
over £1.5 million	15%

Non-residential and mixed use property

The rates applying in this case are as below:

Non-residential or mixed use land or property.	**SDLT rate**
Up to £150,000	Zero
The next £100,000 (the portion from £150,001 to £250,000)	2%
The remaining amount (the portion above £250,000)	5%

A "mixed use" property is one that has both residential and non-residential elements, e.g. a flat connected to a shop, doctor's surgery or office.

The more common non-residential properties are:

- commercial property, e.g. shops or offices;
- agricultural land;
- forests;
- any other land or property which is not used as a residence;
- six or more residential properties bought in a single transaction (see the example of Alan at **9.3.3** below).

15% charge

SDLT is charged at 15% on residential properties costing more than £500,000 bought by certain corporate bodies or "non-natural persons". See the example of Jerome below. These include:

1. companies;
2. partnerships including companies; and
3. collective investment schemes.

The 15% rate does not apply to property bought by a company that is acting as a trustee of a settlement or bought by a company to be used:

- for a property rental business;
- by property developers and traders;
- as property made available to the public;
- by financial institutions acquiring property in the course of lending;
- as property occupied by employees; or
- as farmhouses

9.3.3   Multiple dwellings purchases

Multiple dwellings relief can be claimed where several properties are purchased together: see the example of Alan below. Where the relief is claimed, the rate of SDLT which applies to the consideration attributable to interests in the dwellings is determined by reference to the amount of this consideration, divided by the number of dwellings (i.e. the mean consideration attributable to the dwellings). This is subject to a minimum rate of 1%.

Example

Alan has retired after many years in the oil and gas sector abroad and has built up savings of £2.6 million which he wants to invest in a south coast block of flats for annual income. His commercial letting agents find a new block of 20 unoccupied and untenanted flats with a purchase price of £2.5 million. There is no headlease and none of the flats is subject to a long lease.

The purchase is of multiple dwellings and as such attracts relief as it involves the acquisition of six or more dwellings – i.e. in this case the 20 flats. The freehold is treated as if it were interests in the individual dwellings. The chargeable consideration divided by the number of dwellings is £125,000. This is below the normal 3% SDLT threshold but the minimum rate of tax under the multiple dwellings relief is 1%. The SDLT tax due is therefore 1% of £2.5 million = £25,000. The relief must be claimed in a land transaction return or an amendment to a return, using relief code 33 at question 9 of the SDLT1 form.

9.3.4   Foreign purchasers

HMRC (Individual and Small Business Compliance department) make compliance checks regarding property purchases in respect of stamp duty payments. An enquiry will ask 11 detailed questions regarding the property purchase, the last of which states "In all cases, please provide appropriate evidence and full explanation to support any declaration that justifies SDLT being due at a rate below the prevailing rate of 15%." See the following example.

Example 1

Jerome, who is resident in Bahrain, purchases a London flat in Mayfair for £1.1 million through a BVI company. The solicitors deduct the SDLT and account for it as follows after entering code 35 (relief from 15% rate of SDLT) at question 9 of the SDLT1 form:

£925,001 – £1,100,000	= 175,000 @ 13% =	22,750
£250,001 – £925,000	= 675,000 @ 8% =	54,000
£125,001 – £250,000	= 125,000 @ 5% =	6,250
£0 – £125,000	= 125,000 @ 3% =	3,750
TOTAL	=	£86,750

Subsequently the BVI company receives a letter from the stamp duty office stating that the 15% rate exemption is being investigated and a compliance check is to be instituted under FA 2003, Sch. 10 para. 12 (see HMRC factsheet CC/FS1a). The stamp duty officer's letter states:

> "Thank you for your Stamp Duty Tax return for the above acquisition.
>
> Every year we check a number of returns to make sure they are correct and that our customers are paying the correct amount of tax. I would like to check this return."

A failure to meet the compliance requirements would mean that the actual SDLT would be £165,000. The SDLT officer wants documents to be supplied by the company such as copies of latest accounts, names of directors and shareholders, current letting lease for the property, etc. The property has been rented out after a relatively short period to an unconnected individual and documents of the lease agreement are supplied. This is the relief that is being claimed from the higher charge because the property is a commercial letting.

The memorandum and articles of association of the BVI company usefully state:

> "To furnish, fit and equip all houses and buildings for the time being belonging, leased or hired to the Company, and to make the same fit for use and occupation and to enter into agreements for letting and selling houses, buildings, furniture and fittings to any company, corporation, authority or individuals either for cash or an instalment basis and to collect rents and other moneys in connection with such property. To borrow and raise money for the Company's business in such manner as the Company thinks fit in furtherance of its business objectives."

HMRC conclude the review by writing to the BVI company, the officer stating "I am satisfied that the Stamp Duty Tax position on the acquisition of the Mayfair flat is correct" on SDLT108.

Example 2

Mr Wong, living in Asia, gives his son Chang the funds to purchase a Cambridge flat for £325,000, close to the university where he is going to study in one year's time. In the meantime it will be let out pending Chang's arrival and occupation when he goes to the university. The stamp duty payable will be £1,250, calculated as follows:

SDLT band	%	Taxable sum	Tax
less than £300k	0	£0	£0
£300k to £325k	5	£25,000	£1,250

Had Chang's father himself purchased the property for his son the SDLT would have been under the additional residential property stamp duty rules, resulting in a charge of £16,000.

Note: It is not necessary that Chang as a first time buyer must occupy the property immediately following purchase. At the effective date of the transaction, there must be a clear intention to occupy the dwelling as Chang's only or main residence and the fact that circumstances make it either impossible or impractical to occupy the dwelling immediately do not prevent relief being due. In this case, Chang has an intention to occupy the property when he gets his place at Cambridge University.

In order to obtain the lower rate of SDLT a person must intend to occupy the property as his or her only or main residence. There is no requirement to occupy the property immediately, and relief will not be denied if the property is let pending occupation, but there must be a clear intention to occupy. The purchaser must not, either alone or with others, have previously acquired a legal or beneficial interest in freehold or leasehold land which is, or includes, residential property, or an equivalent interest in land situated anywhere in the world.

Law: FA 2003, s. 55A, 116, and Sch. 4A, 4ZA, 7

Guidance: SDLT calculator; SDLTM 20000ff.

493

9.4 Annual tax on enveloped dwellings (ATED)

9.4.1 Overview

It could be said that the recent taxation imposed on offshore investors holding UK property has been a way of extracting tax revenues from perceived abuses of the beneficial non-resident rules, or just a revenue raising exercise!

One of the areas was UK property and, in particular, expensive London property held by offshore companies such as in the BVI, also often linked to trust structures offshore. In the past, this offshore company/trust structure offered substantial tax advantages in terms of income tax, inheritance tax, SDLT (see **9.3**) and capital gains tax. The historical tax treatment was that no IHT liability arose on residential property owned through offshore companies because the shares were wrapped inside an offshore trust, and if the individual acquired UK deemed domicile the property/shares/trust asset was excluded property and not subject to tax.

The UK government saw this "tax avoidance" area as one that was ripe for taxing and that would give rise to little objection from UK voters. A raft of changes was introduced to put this disparity on an even keel. The first, in 2012, was the introduction of the ATED charge which collected substantial amounts of tax. Subsequently, the threshold limit was reduced from £2 million to £1 million and then (from 1 April 2016) to the current level of £500,000, thereby increasing the tax take substantially.

Law: IHTA 1984, s. 6

9.4.2 Annual tax on enveloped dwellings

ATED is an annual tax payable mainly by companies that own UK residential property where the "dwelling" is valued at more than £500,000. The charge applies if the dwelling is owned completely or partly by:

- a company;
- a partnership where one of the partners is a company; or
- a collective investment scheme (e.g. a unit trust or an open ended investment vehicle).

Property valuation returns must only be submitted on or after 1 April in any chargeable five-year period or multiples of five years, e.g. property valued at 1 April 2017 is then re-valued at 1 April 2022. Also existing ATED properties at 2012 should have been re-valued at 1 April 2017 for the purposes of the annual ATED return. This ATED property valuation filing date is set in advance so that the return for the chargeable period 1 April 2017 to 31 March 2018 was required by 30 April 2017.

Some properties are not treated as dwellings. These include:

- hotels;
- guest houses;
- boarding school accommodation;
- hospitals;
- student halls of residence;
- military accommodation;
- care homes; and
- prisons.

Chargeable amounts for 1 April 2018 to 31 March 2019

Property value	Annual charge
More than £500,000 but not more than £1 million	£3,600
More than £1 million but not more than £2 million	£7,250
More than £2 million but not more than £5 million	£24,250
More than £5 million but not more than £10 million	£56,550
More than £10 million but not more than £20 million	£113,400
More than £20 million	£226,950

Relief from ATED is available for property if it is in any of the categories below:

1. let to a third party on a commercial basis and occupied (or available for occupation), where the third party is not connected with the owner (see Example 1 below);
2. open to the public for at least 28 days a year;
3. being developed for resale by a property developer;
4. owned by a property trader as the stock of the business for the sole purpose of resale;
5. repossessed by a financial institution as a result of its business of lending money;
6. acquired under a regulated home reversion plan;
7. being used by a trading business to provide living accommodation to certain qualifying employees;
8. a farmhouse occupied by a farm worker or a former long-serving farm worker (see Example 2 below); or
9. owned by a registered provider of social housing.

Example 1

A foreign company set up in the BVI purchases London property for over £500,000 which is let out without any undue delay. The memorandum and articles of association include the wording below:

> "To furnish, fit and equip all houses and buildings for the time being belonging, leased or hired to the Company, and to make the same fit for use and occupation and to enter into agreements for letting and selling houses, buildings, furniture and fittings to any company, corporation, authority or individuals either for cash or an instalment basis and to collect rents and other moneys in connection with such property. To borrow and raise money for the Company's business in such manner as the Company thinks fit in furtherance of its business objectives."

The property is rented out to an unconnected third party and comes within the first of the reliefs above, so there is no ATED to pay. However, NRL2 should be completed and submitted to HMRC to receive rentals gross. A form SA700 will be submitted detailing the income and expenditure and any net profit will be chargeable to *income tax* (and not corporation tax) unless the company is within (3) or (4) above, or carries on a trade in the UK through a permanent establishment (PE). The trading profits and certain gains attributable to that PE will be chargeable to UK corporation tax. See also **2.3.8** (Property letting).

Example 2

Gerrard currently works in Melbourne and has bought a 500 acre dairy farm in the Cotswolds with a farmhouse costing £1.75 million through his BVI company. The four bedroom farmhouse is valued at £750,000 at purchase (the fixed valuation date).

Gerrard is not expecting to retire for a few years and he views the farm income as a supplement to his pension investments. He employs Jack, the previous owner's farm manager, to tend to the farm in his absence and Jack occupies the farmhouse. His duties include tasks that are necessary for the operation of the trade such as ploughing, spraying, harvesting, milking, birthing, etc.

The farmhouse is large and Jack only occupies a few rooms for his comfort and the other rooms are left untouched for Gerrard. The occupation of part of the dwelling is regarded as occupying the whole of the dwelling for establishing the relief. That is to say that where only part of a single-dwelling interest is occupied for purposes that would qualify for farmhouse relief then the whole will be treated as qualifying for relief. Relief from ATED would seem to be applicable in these circumstances.

Gerrard will also be entitled to agricultural property relief (APR) on gift, or on his demise, as the farm is in the UK, thereby reducing the IHT charge. However, it must be remembered that buildings must be of a nature and size appropriate to the farming activity that is taking place. This can be a contentious area with HMRC – the property must also be valued as if it could only be used for agricultural purposes. Any value over and above this "agricultural value", such as the market price of a country residence, does not qualify for APR.

Note that it is proposed that from 2021 a beneficial ownership register will apply. A foreign company planning a UK property investment will then be required to submit ownership information in a form that is easily accessible to law enforcement organisations.

The company, say in the BVI, would then be allocated a special identification number, which it would have to provide to the Land Registry office when registering a purchase of land or real property in England and Wales. UK companies are already required to do this.

Law: IHTA 1984, s. 115-120, Sch. A1 (inserted by F (No 2) A 2017); FA 2013, s. 148, 149; CTA 2009, s. 5(2), (3), 19; CTA 2010, s. 1125

Cases: *Lloyds TSB plc (Antrobus' Personal Representative) v Twiddy* [2004] DET/47/2004; *Executors of Lady McKenna v HMRC* [2006] STC (SCD) 800

Guidance: Draft legislation to be published in summer 2018 by the Department for Business, Energy & Industrial Strategy (BEIS)

9.4.3 ATED gains tax

The sale of an ATED related property will give rise to a gain or a loss. This should be reported to HMRC online.

The total of all ATED-related chargeable gains and allowable losses for a tax year are aggregated. If there are net chargeable gains for the year, the net amount is chargeable to capital gains tax for that tax year at the rate of CGT for ATED-related gains, which is 28%.

If the ATED-related allowable losses in the tax year exceed the chargeable gains, any excess is carried forward to future years when it may only be offset against further ATED-related chargeable gains, not other capital gains. Also, any overall ATED loss in a tax year cannot be carried back and set off against chargeable gains in any tax year before the one in which the loss arises.

An overall gain prior to April 2013 will be subject to corporation tax, or will be outside the scope of tax if it is a non-resident company such as a BVI company. Gains after April 2013 will be subject to tax at 28% relative to the time the "non-natural company" (e.g. BVI company) was subject to the new ATED rules. At this stage the gain calculated is restricted to the lower of:

- the full ATED-related gain; and
- 5/3 times the difference between the consideration for the disposal and the threshold (currently £500,000) amount for that disposal.

However, where only a proportion of the gain is an ATED-related gain, the amount excluded from charge is reduced by the same proportion. Also, the fraction is reduced when there are groups of disposals of ATED residential properties.

Law: TCGA 1992, s. 2D, 2F, 4(3A); FA 2013, Sch. 25
Guidance: CG 73650

9.4.4   *Further new rules*

Since 6 April 2017, all UK *residential* properties owned by an individual through an offshore corporate structure have been subject to IHT. So, any non-UK domicile owning shares in an offshore company that owns UK property, or an individual who created an offshore trust to hold the shares of the offshore company, will be subject to IHT on that individual's death in relation to the value of the UK property. The ten yearly trust periodic tax charge may also arise. Further, any debt financing used to purchase will not be treated as excluded property and so will itself also be subjected to IHT in the lender's hands.

Individuals with such arrangements in place will need to consider "de-enveloping" the structure if they do not wish to suffer the tax consequences. This may be simpler said than done as winding up such schemes is difficult. One possible answer may be to take out life insurance written in trust, subject to age and health, to pay the IHT liability when it eventually arises.

As stated, UK residential property which is let commercially is not subject to the ATED tax, but it is now subject to IHT. If the UK property is sold by the offshore company the proceeds of such sale will continue to be regarded in the same way as UK residential property for two years following the disposal. For the purposes of what is residential property, the definition of a "UK dwelling" will follow the non-resident CGT definition rather than that which applies for the ATED.

In the autumn Budget statement of 22 November 2017, detailed changes were announced to the taxing rules from April 2020 of non-resident companies' income from UK property. From then net profits will be chargeable to *corporation tax* rather than income tax at 20% as detailed in the example previously. In addition, capital gains arising to such non-resident companies on the disposal of UK property will be charged to corporation tax (currently 19% but reducing to 17% in 2020-21) rather than CGT. Therefore, in the future, once all the legislation is in place, non-UK companies will be subject to corporation tax and not income tax. This will create costly corporate compliance requirements, as well as restrictions on losses and interest reliefs. (The government had consulted on this option generally and a summary of responses was issued in December 2017 (see https://tinyurl.com/y8o2ony5). The government plans to publish an Explanatory Note and draft legislation in summer 2018.)

9.4.5   *Excluded property trusts*

As briefly mentioned above, the excluded property trust was, in the past, an effective way of holding the shares of the offshore company which owned the UK property. So even if the foreign domiciled settlor became deemed UK domicile (see Domicile at **2.1**), the IHT position would still have been tax beneficial. From 6 April 2017, if an offshore trust owns shares in an offshore company, the asset of which is UK residential property, that trust property is no longer to be treated as excluded property. This is so whether the value of those shares is derived directly or indirectly from residential property in the UK. One of the consequences of this is that the trustees will pay IHT on the value of the property at every ten year anniversary. If the property comes out of the trust, say by gift, there may well be an IHT exit charge.

To add to these new taxing impositions, the IHT "gift with reservation of benefit" (GROB) rules may apply to ensure that the whole value of the property comes within the individual's estate for IHT purposes. This often happens in cases where the settlor also makes himself/herself a beneficiary of the trust or lives in the property.

Example

Lim from Singapore set up a BVI company ten years ago to purchase a London property which cost £1.1 million at the time. His accountant adviser in Singapore suggested the shares of the company be placed into a trust offshore in Singapore, to hold the company shares in the event of Lim going to live in the UK. (See also **7.2.3** – Trust reporting.) This would have avoided a charge to IHT under the excluded property legislation at that time (see also **Offshore trusts**).

With the advent of ATED he rented out the property commercially for £4,200 per calendar month, thereby avoiding the annual charge. Subsequently, with the change to the non-resident CGT rules from 6 April 2015, and the IHT changes to offshore trusts holding UK property brought in on 6 April 2017, he is considering his options. He knows that if he keeps the property he will be subject to IHT on an increasing value and if he sells he will be subject to non-resident CGT. He is faced with one of the possible options (1) to (5) below.

His property was refurbished in 2016 at a cost of £120,000, of which half has been allowed as a revenue expense, and he has an *income tax* loss to carry forward to the 2017-18 tax year. The remaining £60,000 was for a new double garage which is claimed as a capital expense. Taking various options open to him his adviser suggests:

(1) *Gift the offshore company shares.* This may trigger an IHT charge, either immediately or if the individual fails to survive the seven year PET period for gifts. The redistribution of the share capital of an overseas company which owns UK residential property may also trigger an IHT charge. SDLT will also be in point – see (4) below.

(2) *De-envelope.* Taking the property out of this corporate structure may also be subject to tax charges and, in terms of winding up the vehicle, an NRCGT. If there has been added finance borrowing this "de-enveloping" may prove time-consuming and expensive. It was expected that the UK Government would give relief to wind down these enveloped structures but this has not been forthcoming. De-enveloping might incur an NRCGT charge and/or an ATED CGT charge but could use the "default" method of charge as above. Lim could wait until the income tax loss has been utilised and then sell, incurring an NRCGT charge on the gain since the April 2015 value under the "default method" (also deducting the £60,000 capital enhancement of the new garages).

(3)   *Do nothing.* IHT will be charged on the value of the residential property at the time of the chargeable event (e.g. death, lifetime gift or at the trust's ten year anniversary) taking into account any debts relating exclusively to the property (e.g. amounts outstanding on a mortgage which was taken out to purchase the property).

(4)   *Transfer offshore company shares to a UK company.* Having a permanent establishment in the UK holding the shares might then become subject to corporation tax on the rents at currently 19% (17% in 2020-21) which is lower than the current income tax rate of 20% for non-UK resident companies. Transferring to a UK company will probably incur stamp duty, capital gains and UK company set up costs/audit costs. Under the transfers between connected persons rules an SDLT charge may apply based on market value.

(5)   *Sell.* Wait until the income tax loss has been utilised and then sell, incurring an NRCGT charge on the gain since the April 2015 value under the "default method" plus the £60,000 capital enhancement of the new garages. The fact that the property is wrapped up in an offshore company may prove problematic for prospective purchasers.

HMRC might have difficulties in identifying whether a chargeable event has taken place and hence whether a liability to tax has arisen and can be enforced offshore. In view of this potential problem the government may yet introduce "de-enveloping" options to the current structures. In *Jimenez*, a recent information notice issued by HMRC to a Dubai-resident UK national has been quashed by the England and Wales High Court, because it did not allow HMRC powers to act extra-territorially. In that case reference was made to territorial limits of income tax claims:

> "But, of course, the Income Tax Acts impose their own territorial limits. Parliament recognises the almost universally accepted principle that fiscal legislation is not enforceable outside the limits of the territorial sovereignty of the kingdom. Fiscal legislation is, no doubt, drafted in the knowledge that it is the practice of nations not to enforce the fiscal legislation of other nations."

Law: TCGA 1992, s. 17, 162; FA 2003, s. 53; CTA 2010, s. 1122

Cases: *Mrs EM Ramsey v HMRC* [2013] STC 1764; *Jimenez v First-Tier Tribunal and HMRC,* 2017 EWHC 2585 (Admin)

9.5 Self-employment in the UK

For a more detailed explanation see **2.3.16**.

When an individual returns to the UK, he may decide to set up in business as a self-employed consultant, rather than finding a new employment. If so, he needs to make sure he registers with HMRC in this respect.

If he decides to operate through a limited company rather than as a sole trader (often he may not have the choice in this respect, as some organisations insist that their consultants operate through a limited company, particularly in the IT profession), then he needs to make sure he complies with all Companies Act requirements and obligations, which may make operating through a limited company more expensive. (See https://www.gov.uk/topic/company-registration-filing/starting-company and https://www.gov.uk/topic/company-registration-filing/running-company.)

One area the individual needs to be wary of, particularly if he is just performing work for one entity, is his status as to whether he is either employed or self-employed. Often HMRC will try to argue that an individual is employed rather than self-employed and there is much case law in this area. HMRC have a tool on their website that enables an individual to check his or her employment status (https://www.gov.uk/guidance/check-employment-status-for-tax), though this has been quite widely criticised as failing to address some of the complexities. For a more detailed analysis, see Employment Status from Claritax Books. The provisions of IR35 will also be relevant for individuals who set up through a limited company.

Other areas that need to be considered are corporation tax (if operating through a limited company), VAT, NIC and PAYE obligations. It may well be the case that the individual has to register for VAT and will have to set up and operate a PAYE scheme.

This is a very large and complex area which is outside the scope of this publication, so further advice on this should always be sought.

Guidance: https://www.gov.uk/topic/business-tax/self-employed; https://www.gov.uk/working-for-yourself; https://www.gov.uk/topic/business-tax/ir35; https://www.gov.uk/government/organisations/companies-house; HMRC's manuals on business Income, employment status, and company taxation

Appendix 1 – Intercultural training

The content of this appendix has kindly been provided by Farnham Castle Intercultural Training (FCIT). It gives an overview of the services that might be provided by FCIT for British expats preparing for an overseas posting.

"A seemingly insignificant or trivial mistake can often jeopardise working relationships and immediately affect business success. An awareness of cultural differences and sensitivities will minimise and mitigate costly misunderstandings and promote better communication ... "

Our global business cultural training consultancy helps clients:

- develop a global mindset and cultural awareness;
- move successfully into new markets;
- develop and improve international competencies;
- strengthen global presence and performance; and
- turn workforces into effective global teams.

Our programmes for assignees and partners cover:

- cultural awareness and adapting to life in the host country;
- culture in context – understanding key cultural concepts in attitudes, values and communication;
- the country today – a brief look at topical issues in the host country and how they may affect the assignee;
- working in the host country – customs, etiquette and ethics;
- communicating effectively – building relationships and developing trust; and
- everyday living – all that is needed to know to make the most of an assignment.

Farnham Castle Intercultural Training understands cultural diversity and responds to clients' requirements by preparing bespoke learning solutions, professionally delivered with the relevant levels of area expertise, business knowledge, practical skills, content delivery and follow up support.

They design course content specifically for client companies' needs, taking into account each delegate's cultural and business experiences, personal circumstances and requirements, to ensure that delivery is relevant and adds value.

They offer face to face and remote training, one to one and group sessions, interactive workshops, one to one coaching, podcasts and webinars.

Main areas of expertise:

- cultural skills for business;
- global mobility;
- global HR;
- leadership and management; and
- language solutions.

For further details, visit www.farnhamcastletraining.com.

© *Farnham Castle Intercultural Training, but reproduced with permission.*

Appendix 2 – Tax Fact Finder

FINANCIAL AND TAX PLANNING ANALYSIS

For   _____

Home Address   _____

_____

_____

Correspondence Address (if different from above)

_____

_____

Office Phone	_____	Fax	_____	Email	_____
Home Phone	_____	Fax	_____	Email	_____
Mobile	_____				

	Name	Date of Birth	Nationality / Place of Birth
Self	_____	_____	_____
Spouse / Partner	_____	_____	_____
Child / Dependant	_____	_____	_____
Child / Dependant	_____	_____	_____
Child / Dependant	_____	_____	_____
Child / Dependant	_____	_____	_____

Employment Details

Self		Spouse / Partner	
Job Title	_____	Job Title	_____
Employed / Self Employed	_____	Employed / Self Employed	_____
Contract Since	_____	Contract Since	_____
Renewal Date	_____	Renewal Date	_____
Expatriate Since	_____	Expatriate Since	_____
Basic Salary p.a.	_____	Basic Salary p.a.	_____
Bonuses / Other Income	_____	Bonuses / Other Income	_____
Estimated Monthly Disposable Income After Bills	_____	Estimated Monthly Disposable Income After Bills	_____
Expected Retirement Age	_____	Expected Retirement Age	_____
Percentage of Current Income Required on Retirement	_____	Percentage of Current Income Require on Retirement	_____

Children's Education

Name	School Fees	University Fees

Assets / Property Owned

Location	Value	Outstanding Mortgage	Monthly Repayment	Net Rental Income (if any)

Liabilities (Car Loans etc.)

Type / Location	Amount	Monthly Repayment	Final Repayment Date

Liquid Cash Assets

	Bank / Building Society	Location	Account Type	Approx. Balance (Currency)
Offshore				
Onshore				
Local				

Lump Sum Investments (Unit Trusts / Mutual Funds / Shares

Company	Location	Approx. Value (Currency)

Regular Savings Plans

Company	Contributions (Amount & Currency)	Commenced	Maturity Date

Pension Funding

Desired Retirement Location _____ Desired Retirement Activities _____

1) Present Employment
2) Past Employment
3) State Pension
4) Personal Arrangements

Insurance

Type	Sum Assured	Premium	Term & End Date / WOL
Life			
Critical Illness			
Income Replacement			
Medical			
Are you a smoker?	Yes ☐		No ☐

Expected Capital Expenditure

Short Term	Medium Term	Long Term
_____	_____	_____

Attitude to Risk / Reward

1	2	3	4	5

$\longleftarrow \qquad\qquad\qquad\qquad\qquad\qquad \longrightarrow$

Low Risk   Medium Risk   High Risk

(Cash)

Financial Priorities

Please number your priorities in order of importance:

Wealth Preservation / Protection   ☐   Retirement Planning   ☐

Portfolio Management   ☐   School Fees Planning   ☐

Savings   ☐   Insurance Cover   ☐

Property Purchase / Mortgage Repayments   ☐   Other (Please State)

_____

Additional Information

1. Cash buffer required? _____ Amount? _____

2. How much of your disposal income are you willing to save

   i) On a regular basis? _____

   ii) On a lump sum basis? _____

3. Is there any other information that you feel will help us to help you?

_____

_____

510

Declaration

This information has been provided by myself (and Spouse/Partner if applicable) in strictest confidence. I understand that recommendations and advice provided will be based on this information only, which should be updated in the future as my circumstances change. I understand that completion of this form places me under no obligation to take up any recommendations. I have read the 'general data protection regulations (GDPR)' on the company website pertaining to my data and understand my rights afforded by such regulations.

Signature (Self)   Date

Signature (Spouse / Partner, if applicable)   Date

Consultant _____ Signature

Will review questions

If you have children under 18 have you appointed guardians in case of joint deaths?

Who will be your Executors (ideally two) and their full names and addresses?

Do you have any preference from burial, cremation, woodland burial, etc. on your death?

Do you wish your spouse/partner to receive everything you own should they outlive you?

Do you wish to give any specific amounts to any individuals or charities?

Do you wish to gift any specific assets e.g. watches, rings, pieces of art to anyone?

Who will benefit from your other assets other than those items already mentioned above?

If none of your beneficiaries survive you who would you want to benefit on your death?

Where do you consider yourself to be domiciled i.e. UK or elsewhere?

Both dying at the same time means the younger spouse is deemed to inherit from the older spouse.

Such a situation would normally exclude the insertion of a survivorship clause: Explain and note below.

Do you wish to draft mirror or mutual wills? Explain implications and note below.

Additional Notes

_____

_____

_____

_____

_____

_____

_____

Inheritance Tax Summary

Are there Wills held in each jurisdiction where assets are held? If so, where are they located?

Have you set up any Trusts in the last 14 years? If so, please give details in Additional Notes section.

Did you make any gifts in excess of £250 to any one individual during the tax year? If so, please advise.

Detail personal assets e.g. household contents, jewellery, cars yachts, etc.

Detail main property, holiday homes in UK and abroad.

Are assets owned jointly with partner/spouse or solely/tenants in common?

What investments are owned such as gilts, equities, funds (e.g. Investment funds/unit trusts)?

Bank and building society deposits totals currently and whether the accounts are joint or in sole names?

Business assets. Have you been in business or inherited a business for the last two years?

If so please state the nature of the business and the value of the assets/shares.

Do you own any AIM shares or a controlling interest in a quoted company?

Do you own a farm or agricultural property for the last 2 years and have a right to vacant possession?

Do you expect to make any gifts to individuals in the future other than those stipulated in your will?

Are you expecting any inheritances/gifts in the future from individuals other than your spouse/partner?

Please detail any debts, credit card balances and loans e.g. car, holiday, home improvements?

Do you have any life insurance policies that will pay out on death? Are these written in trust for beneficiaries?

Do you have any pension death benefits payable on death and have you advised the trustees of the beneficiaries?

Are you considering making any gifts to charities or political parties in your will?

Referrals

1.

2.

3.

4.

5.

Appendix 3 – Social security agreements

Countries with which the UK has social security reciprocal agreements

Austria*	Jersey
Barbados	Korea
Belgium*	Kosovo
Bermuda	Luxembourg*
Bosnia-Herzegovina	Macedonia
Canada	Malta*
Chile	Mauritius
Croatia*	Montenegro
Cyprus*	Netherlands*
Denmark*	New Zealand (benefits-only treaty)
Finland*	Norway*
France*	Philippines
Germany*	Portugal*
Gibraltar (EEA via UK)	Serbia
Guernsey	Slovakia*
Iceland*	Slovenia*
Ireland *	Spain*
Isle of Man	Sweden*
Israel	Switzerland (EC regulations apply from 1 June 2002)
Italy*	Turkey
Jamaica	United States of America
Japan	

* EEA country

Appendix 4 – Intestacy distribution rules from 1 October 2014

Under the *Administration of Estates Act* 1925 (AEA 1925), and subsequently the *Inheritance and Trustees' Powers Act* 2014, intestacy rules apply (in England and Wales) when a person dies without making a valid will. The rules below show how the deceased's estate will be divided up.

Married couple or civil partners without children	• All assets after liabilities to the surviving spouse or civil partner provided he or she survives the deceased by 28 days. • If the surviving spouse or civil partner dies within 28 days the estate is distributed as if the spouse or civil partner had not survived the intestate.
Married couple or civil partners with children	• Jointly held assets and personal possessions are left to the survivor. • First £250,000 and chattels to the surviving parent. • 50% of residue to the survivor. • 50% of residue to children (legally entitled to assets when 18). • Note that joint assets do not form part of the £250,000.
Simultaneous deaths of husband and wife	• In such circumstances of not knowing who died first the older spouse's assets are passed under intestacy directly to descendants as below. No inter-spouse transfer exemption will apply. • The younger spouse's assets do not include the older spouse's assets and are passed directly on in accordance with the boxes below.
Single with children	• All the estate will be equally divided between the children.
Single without children	• Parents. • Siblings. • Nephews and nieces. • Siblings of the half blood or descendants.

	- Grandparents. - Uncles and aunts. - Cousins or their descendants. - If there are no descendants of the parents or grandparents the estate will pass to the Crown.
No descendants	- If there are no descendants of the individual's parents or grandparents the estate will pass to the Crown = *bona vacantia*.

Note: A person can still make a claim under the *Inheritance (Provision for Family and Dependants) Act* 1975 if the deceased was supporting him:

> "A person is to be treated as being maintained by the deceased (either wholly or partly, as the case may be) only if the deceased was making a substantial contribution in money or money's worth towards the reasonable needs of that person, other than a contribution made for full valuable consideration pursuant to an arrangement of a commercial nature."

Law: The *Inheritance and Trustees' Powers Act* 2014, Sch. 2, para. 3 amending the *Inheritance (Provision for Family and Dependants) Act* 1975, s. 1(3)

Appendix 5 – Sufficient hours worked

These rules are based on legislation at FA 2013, Sch. 45, para. 9(2), 14(3) and 28.

1. Calculating whether worked full-time (sufficient hours) overseas for statutory residence test (SRT) purposes

For each tax year or relevant period if a split year:

1. Identify *disregarded days* = Days worked[1] in the UK (including days worked both in the UK and overseas).

2. Calculate *net overseas hours* = Total number of hours worked overseas (for all employments and self-employments) excluding overseas hours worked on disregarded days.

3. Calculate "sufficient hours overseas" by starting with the total number of days in the reference period and deducting:

   - disregarded days;

   - employment gap days up to a max. of 15 days;

   - work days on annual, parental and sick leave; and

   - non-working days whilst on leave ("embedded days"),

where:

Total number of days in reference period	366 if leap year or total number of days in relevant period if a split year.
Disregarded days	UK work days.

517

Employment gap days[2] up to a max. of 15 days	If over end of tax year, deduct gap days in relevant tax year.
	If more than one change in employment in the tax year can subtract up to 15 days per gap up to a max. of 30 days per tax year (these day limits modified for split years by reference to an HMRC table).
	N/A for self-employed.
Work days on annual, parental and sick leave[3]	Annual and parental days as long as reasonable.
	No disregarded days can be included i.e. days when worked in the UK even if also worked overseas or took, say, a half day of annual leave. This type of day included in disregarded days deduction and not annual leave.
Non-working days whilst on leave – embedded days	Only for non-working days (days when not expected to work and do not actually work, e.g. weekends, bank/public holidays) which are preceded and followed by three consecutive days of annual, sick or parental leave.

4. Divide total days in reference period in (3) above and divide by 7 (round down to nearest whole number or if less than one round up to one).

5. Divide net overseas hours calculated in (2) above by the number calculated in (4) above. Satisfied full-time work overseas test if 35 or more hours for the tax year concerned (or relevant period if a split year).

2. Calculating whether worked full-time (sufficient hours) in the UK for SRT purposes

For any 365-day period:

1. Identify *disregarded days* = Days worked[1] overseas including days worked both in the UK and overseas.

2. Calculate *net UK hours* = Total number of hours worked in the UK (for all employments and self-employments) excluding UK hours worked on disregarded days.

3. Calculate "sufficient hours in the UK" by starting with the total number of days in the reference period and deducting:

- disregarded days;
- employment gap days up to a max. of 15 days;
- work days on annual, parental or sick leave; and
- non-working days whilst on leave ("embedded days"),

where:

Total number of days in reference period	Note this is for any 365-day period and not the tax year.
Disregarded days	Overseas work days.
Employment gap days[2] up to a max. of 15 days	If more than one change in employment can subtract up to 15 days per gap up to a max. of 30 days per year (by reference to HMRC table). N/A for self-employed.
Work days on annual, parental and sick leave[3]	Annual and parental days as long as reasonable. No disregarded days can be included i.e. days when worked overseas even if also worked in the UK or took, say, a half day of annual leave. This type of day included in disregarded days deduction and not annual leave.
Non-working days whilst on leave – embedded days	Only for non-working days (days when not expected to work and do not actually work on e.g. weekends, bank/public holidays) which are preceded and followed by three consecutive days of annual, sick or parental leave.

4. Divide total days in reference period in (3) above and divide by 7 (round down to nearest whole number or if less than one round up to one).

5. Divide net UK hours calculated in (2) above by the number calculated in (4) above. Satisfied full-time work in the UK test if 35 or more hours for a particular 365-day period.

Notes:

1. Days worked = worked more than three hours on a given day.

2. Change in employments during a tax year (or relevant period if a split year) for full-time work overseas or during a 365-day period for full-time work in the UK and there is a gap between these employments and no work is performed during this gap.

3. Weekends and public holidays excluded, as are days on compassionate leave and potentially days off if working on a rota basis and these are not part of annual leave as stated in employment contract.

Table of primary UK legislation

521

Taxes Management Act 1970

Theft Act 1968

Table of UK statutory instruments

Index of cases

Index of countries and regions

General index

Deferred earnings
Definitions and terminology

556

Taxation (UK)
(*see also main headings for* Capital gains tax; Domicile; Inheritance tax, Main residence, Pensions, Self-assessment compliance; Share options; Tax and investment planning, *etc.*)

Printed and bound in Great Britain by
Marston Book Services Limited, Oxfordshire